Time, Tense, and Reference

Time, Tense, and Reference

edited by Aleksandar Jokić and Quentin Smith

A Bradford Book
The MIT Press
Cambridge, Massachusetts
London, England

© 2003 Massachusetts Institute of Technology

This book was set in Sabon on 3B2 by Asco Typesetters, Hong Kong.
Printed and bound in the United States of America.

Library of Congress Cataloging-in-Publication Data

Time, tense, and reference / edited by Aleksandar Jokić and Quentin Smith.
    p.   cm.
Based on a conference held Apr. 11–13, 1997 at Santa Barbara City College.
"A Bradford book."
Includes bibliographical references and index.
ISBN 0-262-10098-3 (hc. : alk. paper)—ISBN 0-262-60050-1 (pbk. : alk. paper)
1. Time—Congresses. 2. Language and languages—Philosophy—Congresses. 3. Tense (Logic)—Congresses. I. Jokić, Aleksandar. II. Smith, Quentin, 1952–
BD638.T567   2003
115—dc21   2002045521

10 9 8 7 6 5 4 3 2 1

Contents

Contributors

Miloš Arsenijević Department of Philosophy, University of Belgrade

Anthony Brueckner Department of Philosophy, University of California, Santa Barbara

William Lane Craig Research Professor of Philosophy at Talbot School of Theology, La Mirada, California

Arthur Falk Department of Philosophy, Western Michigan University

Jan Faye Department of Education, Philosophy and Rhetoric, University of Copenhagen

James Higginbotham School of Philosophy, University of Southern California

Aleksandar Jokić Department of Philosophy, Portland State University

Robin Le Poidevin School of Philosophy, University of Leeds

Ernest Lepore Rutgers Center for Cognitive Science, Rutgers University

Kirk Ludwig Department of Philosophy, University of Florida, Gainesville

L. Nathan Oaklander Department of Philosophy, University of Michigan, Flint

Mark Richard Philosophy Department, Tufts University

Nathan Salmon Department of Philosophy, University of California, Santa Barbara

Quentin Smith Department of Philosophy, Western Michigan University

James E. Tomberlin Department of Philosophy, California State University, Northridge

Michael Tooley Department of Philosophy, University of Colorado, Boulder

Preface

Bringing together leading philosophers of time and leading philosophers of language was a mere dream one of us (Aleksandar Jokić) had back in 1996. Having personally known philosophers of time Hugh Mellor and William Newton-Smith and the philosopher of language Nathan Salmon—having been privileged to learn about their respective work from those philosophers themselves—Jokić knew that bringing these two groups of philosophers together would amount to an enormously educational experience for everyone involved.

This vision became a reality on April 11–13, 1997, when the conference "Time, Tense, and Reference" became the inaugural event at the newly created Center for Philosophical Education (CPE) housed in the Philosophy Department at Santa Barbara City College. Hugh Mellor, as a representative of philosophers of time, opened the conference, and David Kaplan, as a representative of philosophers of language, was the closing speaker. It turned out to be everything it was expected to be. In the words of David Kaplan as he began his talk: "I've learned a lot from this conference." (The entire conference was professionally videotaped; this quotation is from one of the tapes, available from CPE.)

This book is the result of a longer project that only began with the conference. Seven of the contributors to this book also took part in the conference: Miloš Arsenijević, Anthony Brueckner, William Lane Craig, L. Nathan Oaklander, Mark Richard, Nathan Salmon, and one of us (Quentin Smith). The other contributors wrote chapters especially for the book. The general impression arising from the conference, that philosophers of language and philosophers of time have much to gain by working together and that their respective fields are significantly enriched as a result, convinced us to pursue this joint venture further. We therefore enlarged the group of philosophers involved with the project, while original members revised (some significantly) their original contributions or else wrote new papers entirely. Much of the work on expanding the project was done by Quentin Smith; and slowly, through many revisions, the current two-part, four-section structure of the book emerged.

Working on this book has been a rewarding experience for us. We are thankful to Dr. Steven Humphrey, president of CPE's executive board, for his support of this project from the start. Thanks are also due to Joseph White and James Chesher, CPE's other directors.

Introduction

Quentin Smith and Aleksandar Jokić

Semantics and Metaphysics

Among the many fields of philosophy, there are two that are more intimately interconnected than most but whose practitioners have too long pursued relatively independent paths. On the one hand, there are philosophers of language, who have devoted much attention to indexicals ('now', etc.), temporal operators ('it was the case that', etc.), and tensed sentences. On the other hand, there are the philosophers of tensed or tenseless time (also called A-time or B-time, dynamic time or static time, etc.). The philosophers of language have developed theories with important implications for the tensed/tenseless time debate, though they have rarely explored the implications their theories have for the philosophy of time. Likewise, the philosophers of tensed or tenseless time often make new or substantial contributions to the philosophy of language in the course of developing their arguments, though they rarely write essays that aim to establish theses in the philosophy of language as an end in itself or that aim to bring their results to the attention of philosophers of language.

One goal of this collection of original essays is to present work by both groups of philosophers so that the reader may see the many relevant similarities and implications between these two fields of philosophy. We include essays by philosophers of language (Ernest Lepore and Kirk Ludwig, Nathan Salmon, Mark Richard, James Higginbotham, Anthony Brueckner, and Arthur Falk) and ontologists and philosophers of time (L. Nathan Oaklander, Robin Le Poidevin, Miloš Arsenijević, Quentin Smith, William Lane Cralg, Michael Tooley, and James E. Tomberlin).

Sometimes the philosophers of language discuss the implications of their proposals for the philosophy of time. For example, Lepore and Ludwig's truth-theoretic semantics include quantifying over "times" in the sense of the tenseless or B-theory of time; Salmon shows that his philosophy of language is consistent with the tensed theory of time; and Richard, by rejecting temporary transients, develops a philosophy of language that is aligned with the tenseless tradition. Conversely, sometimes the philosophers of time discuss how their arguments contribute to current debates in the philosophy of language, such as the nature of the truth conditions of tensed sentences (Le Poidevin, Oaklander, Tooley, and others), the nature of circumstances of evaluation and contexts of use (Craig, Smith, and others), whether temporal indexicals have sense or are directly referential (Brueckner and others), the cognitive significance of tensed language (Higginbotham, Richard, Falk, and others), and the analogies between temporal and modal operators (Arsenijević, Craig, Tomberlin, and others). Some of these threads are brought together in new ways by Mark Richard and Jan Faye in their substantial introductions to parts I and II.

A collection that brings together these two traditions is especially pertinent now. Since the late 1980s, there has been a veritable explosion of articles and books on the tensed/tenseless theories of time, while, correspondingly, philosophers of language have increasingly focused on temporal indexicals, temporal operators, and tenses, following in large part either David Kaplan's (e.g., Salmon) or Donald Davidson's (e.g., Lepore and Ludwig) pioneering work in these fields. A sampling of these recent publications shows that these intersecting domains are among the most-studied areas in recent philosophy, comparable perhaps to the enormous attention paid to normative ethics following the 1971 publication of John Rawls's *A Theory of Justice*. Books on the philosophy of time include William Lane Craig's *The Tensed Theory of Time*, *The Tenseless Theory of Time*; and *Relativity and the Metaphysics of Time*; Peter Ludlow's *Semantics, Tense, and Time*; Jan Faye's *The Reality of the Future*; Natasa Rakic's *Common Sense Time and Special Relativity*; Mauro Dorato's *Time and Reality*; Robin Le Poidevin's *Change, Cause and Contradiction*; F. M. Christensen's *Space-Like Time*; Roger Teichman's *The Concept of Time*; Quentin Smith's *Language and Time*; Peter

McInery's *Time and Experience*; Storrs McCall's *A Model of the Universe*; L. Nathan Oaklander and Quentin Smith's *Time, Change and Freedom*; George Schlesinger's *Timely Topics*; Michael Tooley's *Time, Tense, and Causation*; and D. H. Mellor's *Real Time II*. The wide attention received by the collections of papers on this topic—*The Philosophy of Time*, edited by Robin Le Poidevin and Murray MacBeath; *The New Theory of Time*, edited by L. Nathan Oaklander and Quentin Smith; and *Questions of Time and Tense*, edited by Robin Le Poidevin—have led some to think that familiarity with this field is becoming a sine qua non of being a contemporary philosopher. The overflow of work on this topic led to the creation of the Philosophy of Time Society, featuring regular talks at philosophy conferences and a separate journal, *Journal for the Philosophy of Time Society*. (For further references, see www.QSmithWMU.com.)

A few of the many books on philosophy of language are Mark Richard's *Propositional Attitudes: An Essay on Thoughts and How We Ascribe Them*; Nathan Salmon's *Frege's Puzzle*; Howard Wettstein's *Has Semantics Rested on a Mistake and Other Essays*; Joseph Almog, John Perry, and Howard Wettstein's well-known collection *Themes from Kaplan*; Toshiyuki Ogihara's *Tense, Attitudes, and Scope*; Robert Goldblatt's *Logics of Time and Computation*; C. Anthony Anderson and Joseph Owens's collection *Propositional Attitudes: The Role of Content in Logic, Language, and Mind*; John McDowell's *Mind and World*; Terence Parsons's *Events in the Semantics of English*; Hans Kamp and Uwe Reyle's *From Discourse to Logic*; Jack Copeland's collection *Logic and Reality*; Norbert Hornstein's *As Time Goes By: Tense and Universal Grammar*; John Perry's *The Case of the Essential Indexical and Other Essays*; and Peter Øhrstrøm's *Temporal Logic: From Ancient Ideas to Artificial Intelligence*.

Analyses like those of Lepore and Ludwig, Richard, and Salmon make it increasingly difficult to maintain that one can do philosophy of language without any metaphysical commitments as to the nature of time, and it is equally difficult to maintain that the metaphysical issue of whether time is tensed or tenseless can be resolved independently of the philosophy of language. The line between philosophy of language and metaphysics is blurred, and one is tempted to view them instead as a continuum. The sophistication of the analyses in this book shows that one can connect philosophy of language and metaphysics without returning to the relatively simplistic view of the ordinary-language philosophers of the 1940s and 1950s, who often gave the impression that the "nature of reality" was directly read off from "how people ordinarily talk." Since the demise of the ordinary-language movement, many philosophical investigations are pursued largely separate from analyses of natural language. But the philosophy of A-time or B-time, perhaps more than any other area, has shown the continuing relevance of the idea that natural language is, in some carefully qualified sense, a guide to the nature of reality. Even the sharpest critics of the thesis that the metaphysics of time depends on the philosophy of language acknowledge that defense of certain theses in the philosophy of language is necessary to adequately or completely establish a theory of time; see, for example, the chapters by Oaklander and Tooley.

Why do philosophers of time venture into other branches of philosophy, in this case philosophy of language, and more specifically theory of reference, semantic content, and cognitive significance? To put the question another way: Why do philosophers of time adopt issues that properly belong to another branch of philosophy? What do they hope to gain by doing this, and what justifies their hope that this sort of adventure will illuminate their proper subject matter: time itself?

The most basic issue in philosophy of time is ontological (whether there are tensed facts or only tenseless facts, or whether the future, present, and past are or are not equally real), which leads to competing ontological positions. The chapters in this book indicate that conflict on the ontological level cannot (always) be resolved by doing, as it were, just ontology. They make clear the many ways in which thinkers have to look at issues in other areas of philosophy (here, philosophy of language), hoping that the best solutions in these fields will point to the most adequate ontological thesis.

Of course, this relationship is not one-way. It is not the case that the ontology of time is dependent on the philosophy of language, but not vice versa; rather, philosophies of language can be justified or evaluated in terms of their ontological commitments. If, for instance, a proposed linguistic problem solution to a posits entities that an adequately justified ontology forbids, then that solution is in doubt. For example, if Lepore and Ludwig's truth-theoretic semantics or Richard's theory of cognitive significance is taken to imply a B-ontology and there are reasons to reject this ontology, then one may have reason to question these philosophies of language. Likewise, if the A-theory is ontologically unacceptable (perhaps on scientific grounds, or because of McTaggart's paradox), then the varying philosophies of tensed language articulated by Craig, Smith, and others will be called into question. This suggests a certain primacy of ontology—that is, the notion that we approach problems in the philosophy of language with an adequate ontology already at our disposal (even if only implicitly). This notion is extensively explored in some of the chapters in this book, such as Oaklander's and Tomberlin's. Philosophers of language must presuppose or decide certain ontological issues in order to develop their semantic theses (semantics may be loosely regarded as "the relation of linguistic constructions to reality").

This may be an oversimplification, since the language-ontology interconnection is itself a matter of intense debate: philosophers of language may well deny that their philosophies imply a certain ontology attributed to them by others. A typical case in point is an interchange between Salmon and Smith; in response to an argument offered in Smith's *Language of Time* that Salmon's theory in *Frege's Puzzle* implied a false tenseless theory of time, Salmon replies (in his chapter in this book) that there is no such implication and that his theory in fact is consistent with a tensed theory of time.

Assuming there is agreement on which ontology a certain philosophy of language implies or which philosophy of language a certain ontology implies, the question of primacy becomes especially acute. Whether the ontology of time should rest on philosophy of language or whether a philosophy of language should be based on an adequate ontology need not have a universal answer; it is perhaps best decided on a case-by-case basis. (And, though it is often the most natural place to start searching for an answer, philosophy of language is not the only place to look for help in trying to decide conflicts between opposing ontological claims. For example, in "Ethics and Ontology: Present Rights of Future Individuals and Property Instantiation," Jokić has argued in favor of a thesis in the metaphysics of time—that future items can presently have properties—on the basis of the best solution to a problem in moral philosophy that establishes the claim that future individuals are possible possessors of moral rights.)

More importantly, as the chapters in this book will reveal, the real situation is one of relative degree of primacy or even an inextricable interdependency. Given this, the real question is which theses have an evidentially more secure footing. We can judge the acceptability of a proposed solution to a matter in the philosophy of time on the basis of the acceptability of its ontological commitments, but a certain ontological thesis can also be strengthened or weakened on the basis of some—that is, the best—solution to a problem in the philosophy of language (e.g., the problem of the truth conditions of tensed sentences). Depending on which one we consider to rest on the more solid footing (to have the stronger case for being indefeasibly justified), we will be inclined toward the philosophy of language because of its ontological commitments or vice versa.

To display these various and complicated interconnections is one goal of this book. Another goal, equally important, is to put forward new theories and significantly advance the state of knowledge in philosophy of language and philosophy of time. These goals are intended to take a second step toward exhibiting an interrelationship between the semantics and metaphysics of tense, following upon Peter Ludlow's example of a synthesis of these two fields in *Semantics, Tense, and Time*. There, Ludlow took the first major step toward solving the problem of the lack of a sufficient interconnection between workers in the philosophy of language and the philosophy of time, by combining a comprehensive philosophy of language (including even substantial results in linguistics, such as those developed in Noam Chomsky's *The Minimalist Program*— in particular, its notion of an internal or I-language) with details of the most recent debates among defenders of the tensed and tenseless theories of time, such as Craig and Smith.

Ludlow's book may be regarded as an example of the sort of synthesis whose completeness (or detailed attempt at completeness) is what we are advocating in this introduction. It is not as if metaphysicians of time have not previously discussed philosophies of language, or as if philosophers of language have not discussed the philosophy of time. They have—but not in the systematic and comprehensive way that Ludlow exhibits in his book. The difference between Ludlow's book and this one may be viewed as the difference between a book that synthesizes in a novel way the conclusions achieved in the two relevant fields (what we will call a *Ludlow-type synthesis*), and a book that presents separate arguments in the two fields that serve as material for future philosophers to synthesize into integrated theories of language and metaphysics of the type exemplified in Ludlow's book.

Viewing a Ludlow-type synthesis as an ideal way to formulate both a metaphysics of tense (one that is informed by the semantics of tense) and a semantics of tense (one that is informed by the metaphysics of tense), we intend the new offerings in this book as raw material for various possible Ludlow-type syntheses. Ludlow, contemplating the diverse and often incompatible theories in semantics and metaphysics, argued that certain of these theories are preferable to others in achieving the most plausible synthesis. As Ludlow emphasized, other philosophers, contemplating the same material, may reach different conclusions about what is the most plausible synthesis. And this is precisely the point of presenting such a diversity of theories here. Clearly, for example, a philosopher who aims to use the material in this book for a new Ludlow-type synthesis cannot consistently use both Lepore and Ludwig's semantics of tense and Salmon's semantics of tense. Lepore and Ludwig's semantics of tense falls within the (broadly construed) Tarskian-Davidsonian semantic tradition, whereas Salmon's falls within the (broadly construed) Marcusian-Kaplanian tradition. But one need not simply accept one theory and ignore the other. Ludlow's practice is to find a way to integrate plausible and mutually consistent ideas from different traditions in the philosophy of language. Work that uses just one theory or one tradition falls short of a Ludlow-type synthesis; for example, because it uses only Davidson's semantics, J. J. C. Smart's philosophy of time lacks the comprehensiveness that is essential to a Ludlow-type synthesis. The effort and ingenuity needed for a Ludlow-type synthesis would require, for example, that a philosopher determine which ideas in Lepore and Ludwig's theory, and which ideas in Salmon's, are most plausibly defended, and then work out a way to integrate these ideas in a consistent manner. The same holds for the theories of the cognitive significance of tense advanced by Richard,

Higginbotham, and Falk, and for the theories of metaphysics of time advanced by Oaklander, Tooley, Le Poidevin, Arsenijević, Smith, Craig, and Tomberlin.

As noted, this book aims to offer, not a Ludlow-type synthesis itself, but the material for various Ludlow-type syntheses. That is, in the course of this book one comes to see exactly what sort of ideas need to be integrated in order to achieve such a synthesis, and the broad range of theories that need to be evaluated in terms of plausibility and mutual consistency in order to make the best use of these theories.

Like Ludlow's *Semantics, Tense, and Time*, this book is based on the recognition that advancing knowledge in a particular field requires sophisticated technical expertise in that filed. This book is therefore intended as material for technical experts: philosophers who recognize that technical expertise in both the philosophy of language and the metaphysics of time is required to adequately advance knowledge in either field.

The book is divided into two parts, "The Philosophy of Tensed Language" and "The Metaphysics of Time," each of which is further divided into two sections. Some chapters consist of a straightforward and independent presentation of the author's theory; others consist partly or entirely of debates between authors, allowing critical interaction.

The issues discussed in the book are manifested in questions associated with each of its four sections. Section A of part I, "The Semantic Content of Tensed Sentences," takes up these questions: What are the truth conditions of tensed sentence tokens? What is the nature of the propositions expressed by sentence tokens? These questions are addressed in Ernest Lepore and Kirk Ludwig's "Outline for a Truth-Conditional Semantics for Tense" and Nathan Salmon's "Tense and Intension."

Section B of part I, "The Cognitive Significance of Tensed Sentences," takes up second set of questions pertinent to the philosophy of language: What is the cognitive significance of tensed sentences? What thoughts or senses are grasped and what are "tensed beliefs"? In recent years, it has become explicitly clear that the word 'tense' is used in several technical philosophical senses, applying to syntactic constructions, the semantic content of these constructions, propositions, properties, beliefs, and language-independent facts or states of affairs that make up the universe.) These questions are addressed in Mark Richard's "Objects of Relief," James Higginbotham's "Tensed Second Thoughts," Anthony Brueckner's "Tensed Sentences, Tenseless Truth Conditions, and Tensed Beliefs," Mark Richard's "Need We Posit A-Properties?" and Arthur Falk's "Time Plus the Whoosh and Whiz."

Section A of part II, "Tenseless Theories of Time," addresses metaphysical questions. Are all times equally real, and are the only temporal determinations relations of earlier than, later than, and simultaneity? Or is only the present real—that is, do so-called future and past events not "exist," or is their ontological status inferior to that of the present? Are there some tensed facts, but only mind-dependent tensed facts? These issues are discussed in L. Nathan Oaklander's "Two Versions of the New B-Theory of Language," Robin Le Poidevin's "Why Tenses Need Real Times," and Miloš Arsenijević's "Real Tenses."

Section B of part II, "Tensed Theories of Time," explores metaphysical theories of tensed time in more detail. What does it mean to say that all times are not equally real? Does a tensed theory of time require us to deny the reality of the past or future? Does it mean that some events have the property of being future, others the property of being present, and still others the property of being past? Or does it mean that only the present "exists" in any sense, such that there are no events that exemplify futurity or pastness? Or are the present and past real, the future being unreal? And if the future is unreal, can it nonetheless be the case that the only states of affairs that are real are tenseless states of affairs? These issues are addressed in Quentin Smith's "Reference to the Past and Future," William Lane Craig's "In Defense of Presentism," Michael Tooley's "Basic Tensed Sentences and Their Analysis," and James E. Tomberlin's "Actualism and Presentism."

As the authors make clear, answers to the questions posed in chapters on the philosophy of language imply certain answers to the ontological questions posed in chapters on metaphysics. Conversely, the ontological questions clearly have answers that involve commitments to certain answers to the questions about language. At the same time, the reader will realize that many of the theories are incompatible and that the task of achieving a Ludlow-type synthesis requires evaluating the incompatible theories to determine which can be most plausibly integrated into a language-and-metaphysical theory of tense and time.

The chapters in this book are designed to do more than display these interconnections between the semantics and metaphysics of tense. The chapters themselves offer significant new advances or theories in the philosophy of language and the philosophy of time, superseding or further developing available theories. For example, Lepore and Ludwig's chapter offers the first systematic truth-theoretic semantics of tense, and Tooley's develops the first version of the tensed theory of time that holds that reality is made up only of tenseless facts. Salmon's theory introduces a new account of propositions that develops further the broadly Kaplanian tradition in the philosophy of language and makes us view operators differently. The debate between Richard and Higginbotham on cognitive significance surpasses in sophistication most previous discussions of this topic.

This book also includes the currently most extensive discussion and debate about presentism (Craig, Smith, Tomberlin) in the literature (for singly authored books, see Craig's *The Tensed Theory of Time* and Ludlow's *Semantics, Tense, and Time*).

Oaklander, Le Poidevin, and Arsenijević offer new analyses of the tenseless truth conditions of tensed sentences that respond to the most recent criticisms of the extant accounts developed by defenders of the tensed theory of time. The failure of defenders of the tenseless theory to deal with the myriad criticisms of their truth condition analyses developed in the late 1980s and early 1990s prompted Craig to say in a 1996 article in *Synthese* that the tenseless theory is in demise; but the new analyses by Oaklander and Le Poidevin show that the tenseless theory may be able to make a "comeback" against these criticisms. However, Arsenijević ultimately uses his novel way of looking at the tenseless truth conditions of tensed sentences to argue for the reality of tenses.

Continuing in the Grünbaum tradition of arguing that there is temporal becoming, but that it is mind-dependent, Falk offers the first explanation of the psychological mechanism or function served by a mind-dependent temporal becoming. Thus, contra some authors in Oaklander and Smith's *The New Theory of Time*, Falk argues that the succession of perceptions to memories requires (not merely B-relations) but properties of presentness and pastness that are mind-dependent. Most such accounts are phenomenological, but Falk deepens his theory by embedding the needed account in his detailed cognitive science.

Clearly, these chapters introduce enough novel lines of thought to turn philosophies of language and time in new and more fruitful directions, rendering some of the published literature in the 1980s and 1990s "obsolete" in certain important respects.

Chapter Summaries

Since the introductions to parts I and II, written by Richard and Faye, respectively, are substantive essays in their own right and go far beyond the typical "introduction and summary," we take the opportunity to summarize the chapters here to give the reader a concrete impression of the book as a whole.

Section A of part I includes essays by philosophers of language that further deepen and extend extant theories of the semantic content of tensed expressions.

In "Outline for a Truth-Conditional Semantics for Tense," Lepore and Ludwig provide the first systematic treatment of tenses in terms of a *Tarski-style truth-theoretic semantics*. One implication of this treatment is evident from an analogy with Davidson's theory of verbs, adverbs, and events. Davidson originally introduced events as a means of relating adverbs to verbs they modify. He argued that the best semantics for natural language will as a matter of course quantify over events. The strongest argument he advances for the existence of events and their nature derives, surprisingly, from his views on semantics. He claims that a theory of meaning, by providing a viewpoint on the relationship between language and reality, offers substantive answers to the various metaphysical questions about reality. In particular, a theory of meaning will require events in order to explain the semantic (logical) form of action, event, and causal statements. Lepore and Ludwig make a similar case about times and their nature.

Consider the tensed English sentence (1). One obvious candidate for its truth condition is (2):

(1)   John met Bill.

(2)   'John met Bill' is true iff John met Bill.

In (2) language is both mentioned and used, and in this sense (2) "hooks up" language to reality. This hookup remains silent on the nature of reality. It simply tells us that the English sentence (2) requires for its truth that John met Bill. But since there are no specifiable limits on the number of kinds of tenses and tense modifiers that can sensibly attach to sentences like (1), an adequate theory of meaning is forced to read structure into English sentences. So, consider (3)–(5):

(3)   John met Bill before he met Mary.

(4)   John met Bill before midnight.

(5)   John met Bill before midnight on Tuesday.

Treating each distinctively modified sentence as involving a distinct primitive relation threatens to offend against the condition that a semantic theory for a natural language be finite. On the basis of considerations like this, Lepore and Ludwig defend a proposal that reveals the common elements in these sentences, results in the needed semantic truth conditions, and validates the requisite implications (e.g., that (5) implies (4)), and so forth. The idea, roughly, is to assign semantic structure to sentences like (1) and (3)–(5) in such a way that they are "revealed" as harboring existential quantifiers ranging over times. Lepore and Ludwig argue that the thesis that there are times is true because the best semantics for English requires quantification over them. An interesting fact about their use of this truth-theoretic technique is that it sheds light on certain ancient debates about the nature of time.

In "Tense and Intension," Salmon undertakes to develop a novel theory of temporal operators. He proposes a semantic theory of temporal operators to accommodate the thesis (which he defends) that propositions are invariant over time with regard to truth value. He argues that semantic content is doubly indexed both to a context and to a time, which may be other than the time of the context, and in some cases is triply indexed to a context, a time, and a place. Extension is triply (and when necessary, quadruply) indexed to a context, a time, and a possible world (and a place). Salmon indicates that evidence for this theory refutes both the rival theories of Frege and Kaplan. Double indexing of content yields a higher-level semantic value, "content base," which is noneternal and the proper object of temporal operators. Salmon replaces Kaplan's three-tiered semantic structure of character, content, and extension with a four-tiered structure by inserting *content base* on a tier between character and content. He proposes a definition of indexicality based on the four-tiered structure, whereby an expression is indexical if and only if it takes on different content bases with respect to different contexts. Unlike the standard definitions (on which an expression is indexical if and only if it takes on different contents, or even merely different extensions, with respect to different contexts), Salmon's definition differentiates among expressions, like 'the queen of England' (nonindexical) and 'the present queen of England' (indexical), which share the same content with respect to any context of utterance but nevertheless differ in meaning (i.e., differ in "character," as the notion is modified in Salmon's chapter). Salmon argues that the content of a general term, even one that is nonindexical, is a different temporally indexed attribute or concept with respect to each different time, with the result that the content of most words changes over time. Salmon supplements these ideas with an account of pure tenses.

Section B of part I turns from the semantic content of tenses and temporal operators to the cognitive significance (or beliefs) that are associated with this semantic content.

Richard's "Objects of Relief" is more in line with the "direct reference" theory, and he concentrates on the associated notion of cognitive significance, particularly as it pertains to phenomena of tense. On some B-theoretic accounts of tense and temporal thoughts and assertions, they are in one way or another reflexive; their being tensed consists in such reflexivity. For example, one might say that to think (or say) that the meeting starts now is to think that the meeting's beginning is simultaneous with a certain thought (or with the production of some token), one which I therein think (or produce). More generally, some accounts make demonstrative and indexical thoughts reflexive in such ways. For example, some accounts of the first person make first person assertions ones about the very word tokens used in producing them. A putative advantage of such accounts is that they can resolve certain puzzles about our relationships to our thoughts that others seemingly cannot—for example, puzzles about how the thought that I am now hungry can reliably motivate me to seek food. An apparent disadvantage to such accounts is that they seem to have unacceptable semantic consequences. As Richard points out, when I say that I am fatigued, what I am saying might be true without my saying or thinking that I am such.

Recently, James Higginbotham has offered such an account of tensed thoughts, motivating it, in part, through an analysis of the phenomenon of sequence of tense and defending it against the sort of objection alluded to above. Richard argues against Higginbotham's account and suggests that the problems it is meant to deal with are better dealt with otherwise. Richard then discusses some other accounts, which "parameterize" thoughts by introducing into their analysis entities that are not objects of *explicit* reference when being expressed, and that typically vary across thinkers.

In "Tensed Second Thoughts," Higginbotham responds to an example due to Richard. This example shows that in an occurrence of the belief or cognition that is sufficient for being relieved that some painful episode belongs to one's own past, one must take account more explicitly than Higginbotham did in an earlier work of the element of self-consciousness (as Higginbotham now acknowledges). Higginbotham has in mind the element of locating one's present state in one's own present. Higginbotham retains the type of cross-reference between one's current state and the object of one's emotions that he held was essential to being in that state. Higginbotham considers a suggestion by Balaguer that indexical expressions can load their means of fixing reference, as well as their reference, into the linguistic expression of a thought; but he concludes that the role of semantics, as usually understood, cannot extend as far as Balaguer suggests.

In "Tensed Sentences, Tenseless Truth Conditions, and Tensed Beliefs," Brueckner develops a theory of 'present'. If tense is transcendentally ideal, then it functions as the cognitive significance of our talk about a tenseless or B-time world. But Brueckner notes that there are two uses of 'present' and that one of these leads to the idea that tense does not function solely as cognitive significance but has metaphysical import.

In "Need We Posit A-Properties?" Richard responds, arguing that Brueckner's conclusion that tense can be something more than cognitive significance is open to question. The data Brueckner examines can be interpreted in a way that does not require positing A-properties.

In "Time Plus the Whoosh and Whiz," Falk develops a unique theory of the cognitive significance of tense. He argues that if temporal becoming or A-time is mind-dependent, it must be treated as irreducible (unlike most accounts of "mind-dependent temporal becoming") yet as depending for its existence on the mind. Falk develops this theory, not simply by the usual means of giving a phenomenological description of tensed experience, but by examining the workings of the mind and brain from the perspective of a detailed cognitive science, which shows that mind-dependent temporal becoming serves a purpose or function in the organization of mental data. Falk holds the position that there is no "objective becoming" in the physical universe revealed by physics. Previous B-theorists have not provided an account of a sensory mechanism for generating the appearance of temporal passage. Falk criticizes some previous attempts to deal with this problem (e.g., by Mellor and Oaklander) and offers his own theory, which may be seen as an extensive development and modification of the sort of account offered by Grünbaum. An organism, because of the way it acquires its temporal information, will experience temporal flux, or truth indexed to a temporal locus, despite the absence of flux in the world as physics sees it. Unlike other B-theorists, such as Oaklander, Mellor, and even Grünbaum, Falk does not presuppose the distinction between memory and perception in accounting for "the experience of passage" but derives this distinction from a more fundamental level. Falk concludes that there is temporal passage; it is an ingredient of the world at the level of being that contains purposive beings (but not of the subvenient physical world) and is described by some level of scientific theory. In this respect, Falk is more sympathetic to the A-theory of time than are most B-theorists.

Part II focuses on the metaphysics of time, with discussions of the truth conditions, semantic content, or cognitive significance of tenses, temporal indexicals, and operators appearing in a subsidiary role as evidence for or against the tenseless theory of time or a certain version of the tensed theory of time. In section A of part II, philosophers of time introduce new arguments into the debate about whether time is static (the tenseless theory of time) or dynamic (the tensed theory). Le Poidevin and Oaklander present new arguments for the tenseless theory, while Arsenijević vindicates the tensed theory by finding objective features of reality—other than those of pastness, presentness and futurity—that cannot be accounted for in tenseless terms.

Three closely related issues play a central role in recent debates in the philosophy of time: the status of temporal becoming, the analysis of the tenses in ordinary language, and the reference of temporal indexicals such as 'now', 'yesterday', and 'tomorrow'. Oaklander's "Two Versions of the New B-Theory of Language" has two goals. First, Oaklander intends to clarify how the topics of time, tense, and reference are related, and in so doing explicate what is at stake in the debate between A- and B-theories of time. In the course of accomplishing his first goal, Oaklander distinguishes three senses of 'meaning' (reference, token-reflexive, and linguistic) and, correspondingly, three notions of 'truth conditions' (ontological, epistemological, and linguistic). He argues, on the one hand, that keeping these notions of meaning and truth conditions separate can help clarify the movement from the old tenseless theory of time to the new tenseless theory of time and, on the other hand, that confusing them can lead to mistaken criticisms of the new theory, such as those that Oaklander argues are found in the writings of Quentin Smith and others.

Le Poidevin begins "Why Tenses Need Real Times" by arguing that times are necessary in order to give truth conditions for tensed sentences and that times cannot be replaced by temporal relations. This leads to the claim that the truth value of a tensed sentence is always determined in part by the time at which it is tokened. But what are these times? They may be tensed: in some nonrelational sense, past, present, or future. They may be tenseless: ordered by a "later than" relation. Le Poidevin claims that an argument concerning causation implies that these times are tenseless. Consider any tensed sentence reporting causal relations among states of affairs, such as 'It has been raining, and as a result, the pitch is now waterlogged'. Now, substitute the truth conditions according to the four possible theories concerning the truth conditions of tensed statements (basic tensed, token-reflexive, date, and complex tensed) for the two tensed components of the example sentence—(1) it has been raining, and (2) the pitch is now waterlogged—and see which theory succeeds in reporting the intended causal relations. Of the four, Le Poidevin claims, only the date theory does not face the causal objection; that is, it is the only theory that represents the sentence, when its tensed components are replaced by their truth conditions, as a true causal statement. If the date theory is the preferred theory, it naturally suggests the redundancy theory of 'now'. Le Poidevin defends a novel view that 'now' never refers to a time, arguing that 'now' does not have a referential role since no such role is reflected in the truth conditions of the tensed token in which 'now' occurs.

The date theory should also incline us to opt against the reductionist theory of time. That is, at least, times should not be seen as sets of simultaneous events. Times are logically independent of their occupants (according to the realist or substantivalist theory). Le Poidevin's argument for this thesis is fairly straightforward. Consider what happens when we try to combine the date theory with reductionism: the result is that the date theory entails the token-reflexive theory. Accordingly, we must pair the date theory with realism about times. Thus, the causal argument for the date theory is also an argument for realism (as relationism cannot be combined with the date theory and avoid the causal argument). Nowness is not an irreducible A-property that shifts to ever later times.

In "Real Tenses," Arsenijević begins his assessment of the assets and liabilities of the tensed and tenseless theories of time by reconsidering McTaggart's famous argument leading to the conclusion that reality must be timeless. McTaggart's conclusion can be avoided by simply rejecting the tacit assumption that reality is timeless if it is tenseless, and this is precisely what detensers propose to do. Tensers must do more: they have to deny that the world history can ever (even non-relativistically) be represented by simply positioning events onto the one-dimensional time-axis, and they must claim, instead, that the world history differs from time to time in view of pastness, presentness, and futurity, so that it can be represented only by a two-dimensional matrix. The tensed theory squares very well with the commonsense view of time, thereby gaining an initial advantage. However, if the upholders of the tenseless account can provide a detensing analysis of (indicative) tensed sentences, which would make it possible to define the truth conditions of tensed sentences without invoking (monadic) properties of pastness, presentness, and futurity, they would be in a position to apply Occam's razor and deny the objectivity of those properties on the basis of their redundancy. The ball is then in the tensers' court. Given that entities should not be multiplied *praeter necessitatem*, tensers, in order to vindicate their view, must look for some features, other than those of pastness, presentness, and futurity, which, as objective features of reality, cannot be accounted for in tenseless terms. Arsenijević argues that such features are in-the-world-inherent modalities. He cites a typical theorem of a temporal modal logic system that is formulated in terms of a B-series and does not contain tensed operators but whose branching model requires a temporal asymmetry that cannot be accounted for tenselessly. He concludes that detensers lose their main weapon: Occam's razor. Moreover, they arguably have to reinterpret various situations, all of which are straightforwardly dealt with in a branching temporal-modal model, by introducing a sense of 'viewed tenselessly' that, because it means more than 'viewed at any time', is arguably incomprehensible. Arsenijević concludes that tensers are in an apparently advantaged position.

The tensed theory of time receives a more focused treatment in section B of part II, where philosophers of time debate which version of the tensed theory of time is the most viable. Craig and Tooley argue that the future is unreal (and Craig also argues that the past is real), but Tomberlin and Smith argue that the present cannot be the only temporal dimension that is real: the past and future also are real in the senses they specify.

There are at least two versions of the tensed theory of time, the minimalist version (often called 'presentism') and the maximalist version. The minimalist version implies that there are no past or future particulars; what exists are the particulars that can be mentioned in certain present-tensed sentences, such as 'John is sleeping'. The maximalist version implies that there are past particulars, present particulars, and future particulars, and that reference to these particulars can be made in past-tensed sentences, present-tensed sentences, and future-tensed sentences.

In "Reference to the Past and Future," Smith argues that the minimalist (or presentist) version of the tensed theory of time is implicitly logically contradictory and that past- and future-tensed sentences can refer to past and future particulars. (Smith here adopts the current, standard use of the word 'presentism', which differs from his use of this word in *Language and Time* to refer to a particular version of the maximalist tensed theory of time.) After he makes the case that the maximalist tensed theory of time is preferable to the minimalist theory, he defends the maximalist theory against objections made by defenders of the tenseless theory of time. He responds to Oaklander's argument in "McTaggart's Paradox and Smith's Tensed Theory of Time" that his maximalist theory is logically false since it implies McTaggart's paradox. Smith concludes that the old, out-of-fashion doctrine of "degrees of existence" needs to be revived, with the present having the highest degree of existence and with pastness and futurity having lower degrees of existence. Smith then discusses Ludlow's new version of presentism in *Semantics, Tense, and Time*, reductive presentism, which avoids the problems that Smith argues are implied by standard presentist theories. Smith notes that some objections can be made against reductive presentism and concludes that until these objections can be answered, the maximalist tensed theory of time is to be preferred.

In "In Defense of Presentism," Craig offers a detailed account and defense of presentism by way of a critical evaluation of Smith's views on the possibility of successfully referring to past and future concrete objects. The problem of reference to nonpresent entities is part of a broader objection rasied by certain advocates of a tenseless theory of time against the tensed theory of time. The objection is that since only existents can stand in relations and since, on the tensed view of time, past and future entities do not exist (having passed away or not yet come to be), such entities cannot now be relata; that is to say, they cannot now stand in any relations with present (existent) entities. But that implies that one cannot now refer to such entities, which seems implausible.

To avoid this untoward conclusion, the objection goes, one must hold that past and future entities are on an ontological par with present entities—in other words, that the tenseless theory of time is correct.

Craig argues that the basic problem with this argument is the assumption that referring is a relation. He suggests that this assumption is based on a seemingly unsophisticated, almost physical construal of reference as a term's reaching out across space to capture some object as its referent. That such a view is incorrect is evident from the fact that (Craig argues) we routinely refer successfully to nonexistents, as, for example, when we say, 'Santa Claus does not exist' or 'Dragons are creatures of fable'. Craig maintains that the terms of such sentences successfully refer, on the grounds that these sentences are evidently true. Therefore, Craig concludes, either relata need not be existents or else referring is not a relation. In either case, the argument put forward by the defender of a tenseless or nonpresentist theory of time (such as Smith's maximalist tensed theory) is undercut.

Craig argues that Smith's maximalist or A-B theory is unsuccessful since it holds that past items, such as Plato, presently have properties of being referred to. Craig maintains that Smith's thesis that past items can presently have properties is self-evidently false.

The difference between presentist and nonpresentist (or maximalist) tensed theories of time seems to pale in comparison with the striking new version of the tensed theory of time that Tooley defends in "Basic Tensed Sentences and Their Analysis." Developing and adding new ideas to the theory presented in his book *Time, Tense, and Causation*, Tooley begins by asking about the form of basic tensed sentences and whether they are analyzable. Traditionally, advocates of tensed and tenseless approaches to time have agreed that sentences such as 'Event *e* is now taking place' constitute at least one type of basic tensed sentence. They have disagreed, however, on the analyzability issue. Those who accept a tenseless approach to time typically maintain that a sentence such as 'Event *e* is now taking place' involves an indexical term and that, although a translational analysis cannot be given, a truth-conditional analysis can be formulated—one, moreover, where the truth conditions are specified in completely tenseless terms. Those who accept a tensed account, on the other hand, argue that tensed truth conditions are needed. But Tooley argues that a new account is needed, which involves both a dynamic time (in this respect, he sides with the tensers) and a theory that there are only tenseless facts.

In "Actualism and Presentism," Tomberlin offers a criticism of presentism that is quite different from Smith's. Tomberlin appeals to modal considerations (as does Arsenijević), but he arrives at different results. In the metaphysics of modality, actualism is the view that there are no objects that do not actually exist and there are no philosophical problems whose solution demands merely possible but not actual individuals. In the metaphysics of time and tense, presentism is the view that there are no objects that do not presently exist and there are no philosophical problems whose solution calls for non–presently existing objects. There are ample reasons for thinking that we should accept presentism only if we should also accept actualism. Tomberlin mounts sustained arguments against both positions, concluding that any proper ontology must include objects that do not actually exist, as well as objects that do not presently exist.

References

Almog, J., J. Perry, and H. Wettstein, eds. 1989. *Themes from Kaplan*. New York: Oxford University Press.

Anderson, C. A., and J. Owens, eds. 1990. *Propositional Attitudes: The Role of Content in Logic, Language, and Mind*. Stanford, Calif.: Center for the Study of Language and Information.

Chomsky, N. 1995. *The Minimalist Program*. Cambridge, Mass.: MIT Press.

Christensen, F. M. 1993. *Space-Like Time*. Toronto: University of Toronto Press.

Copeland, J., ed. 1996. *Logic and Reality*. Oxford: Oxford University Press.

Craig, W. L. 2000a. *Relativity and the Metaphysics of Time*. Dordrecht: Kluwer.

Craig, W. L. 2000b. *The Tensed Theory of Time*. Dordrecht: Kluwer.

Craig, W. L. 2000c. *The Tenseless Theory of Time*. Dordrecht: Kluwer.

Dorato, M. 1995. *Time and Reality*. Bologna: CLUEB.

Faye, J. 1989. *The Reality of the Future*. Odense: Odense University Press.

Goldblatt, R. 1992. *Logics of Time and Computation*. 2nd ed. Stanford, Calif.: Center for the Study of Language and Information.

Hornstein, N. 1990. *As Time Goes By: Tense and Universal Grammar*. Cambridge, Mass.: MIT Press.

Jokić, A. 1999. Ethics and Ontology: Present Rights of Future Individuals and Property Instantiation. *Journal of Philosophical Research* 24, pp. 473–86.

Kamp, H., and U. Reyle. 1993. *From Discourse to Logic*. Dordrecht: Kluwer.

Le Poidevin, R. 1992. *Change, Cause and Contradiction*. New York: Macmillan.

Le Poidevin, R., ed. 1998. *Questions of Time and Tense*. Oxford: Oxford University Press.

Le Poidevin, R., and M. MacBeath, eds. 1993. *The Philosophy of Time*. Oxford: Oxford University Press.

Ludlow, P. 1999. *Semantics, Tense, and Time*. Cambridge, Mass.: MIT Press.

McCall, S. 1993. *A Model of the Universe*. Oxford: Oxford University Press.

McDowell, J. 1994. *Mind and World*. Cambridge, Mass.: MIT Press.

McInery, P. 1993. *Time and Experience*. Philadelphia: Temple University Press.

Mellor, D. H. 1998. *Real Time II*. London: Routledge.

Oaklander, L. N. 1996. McTaggart's Paradox and Smith's Tensed Theories of Time. *Synthese* 107, pp. 205–21.

Oaklander, L. N., and Q. Smith, eds. 1994. *The New Theory of Time*. New Haven, Conn.: Yale University Press.

Oaklander, L. N., and Q. Smith. 1995. *Time, Change and Freedom*. London: Routledge.

Ogihara, T. 1996. *Tense, Attitudes, and Scope*. Dordrecht: Kluwer.

Øhrstrøm, P. 1996. *Temporal Logic: From Ancient Ideas to Artificial Intelligence*. Dordrecht: Kluwer.

Parsons, T. 1990. *Events in the Semantics of English*. Cambridge, Mass.: MIT Press.

Perry, J. 1992. *The Case of the Essential Indexical and Other Essays*. Oxford: Oxford University Press.

Rakic, N. 1997. *Common Sense Time and Special Relativity*.

Rawls, J. 1971. *A Theory of Justice*. Cambridge, Mass.: Harvard University Press.

Richard, M. 1990. *Propositional Attitudes: An Essay on Thoughts and How We Ascribe Them*. New York: Cambridge University Press.

Salmon, N. 1986. *Frege's Puzzle*. Cambridge, Mass.: MIT Press.

Schlesinger, G. 1997. *Timely Topics*. New York: Macmillan.

Smith, Q. 1993. *Language and Time*. Oxford: Oxford University Press.

Smith, Q. 1998. Absolute Simultaneity and the Infinity of Time. In R. Le Poidevin, ed., *Questions of Time and Tense*. Oxford: Oxford University Press.

Smith, Q. 2002a. Actuality and Actuality at a Time. In L. N. Oaklander, ed., *The Importance of Time*. Dordrecht: Kluwer.

Smith, Q. 2002b. Time and Degrees of Existence. In C. Callender, ed., *Time, Reality and Experience*. Cambridge: Cambridge University Press.

Teichman, R. 1996. *The Concept of Time*. New York: St. Martin's Press.

Tooley, M. 1997. *Time, Tense, and Causation*. Oxford: Oxford University Press.

Wettstein, H. 1991. *Has Semantics Rested on a Mistake and Other Essays*. Stanford, Calif.: Stanford University Press.

I

The Philosophy of Tensed Language

Introduction to Part I

Mark Richard

1 Temporalism and Eternalism

The fundamental semantic question about tensed sentences is a question about what such sentences say. Consider a simple tensed sentence, such as

(1)   Clinton is president.

Obviously, the *sentence's* truth value changes through time. But consider a particular use of (1), say, my use of it on July 4, 1997. Does *what's said* by such a use change truth value through time?

One might reason that it does: temporally disparate uses of (1) say the same thing—namely, that Clinton has a certain characteristic, being president. What (1) says is true when Clinton has the characteristic; otherwise not. Since Clinton is not always president, what's said by a use of (1) changes truth value through time. On this view, sentences that lack temporal modifiers such as 'on July 4, 1997', 'during next summer', or 'yesterday' make claims that are temporally unspecific. Unless facts about the subject matter of such a sentence dictate otherwise, it thus makes a claim whose truth may change with time's passage.[1] Call such a view, of the truth conditions of (what is said by) tensed sentences, *temporalism*.

One might also argue that uses of (1)—indeed, uses of any sentence that says anything at all—make claims whose truth value cannot change over time. Suppose I sincerely utter (1) on July 4, 1997, and go on to sincerely utter its negation on July 4, 2007, when Clinton is no longer president. I do not thereby change my mind about what I said in 1997.

Uttering (1) in 1997 is saying that Clinton is president *then*; uttering it in 2007 is saying something about 2007. Call this view of the truth conditions of tensed sentences *eternalism*. Most of the contributions to part I touch in one way or another on the question, Should we be eternalists or temporalists?

Nathan Salmon's chapter begins by reviewing and defending some arguments for eternalism. In particular, Salmon elaborates and defends an argument for eternalism suggested, in one way or another, by G. E. Moore, William and Marthan Kneale, and myself: Suppose someone believed at a past time *t* that Clinton was president. If the person still believes *that*, she must now believe that Clinton was president *at t*. I will return, at the end of this introduction, to consider such arguments.

Salmon goes on to develop a subtle account of the semantic values of sentences and tenses, on the assumption that the tense of a sentence is a sentence operator. It is natural to think that if tenses are sentence operators, they are semantically akin to operators such as 'it is necessary that'. Indeed, it is natural to think that both 'always' and 'necessarily' "look at" the same thing: a proposition, an intension, or something of the sort. *Necessarily, p*, one thinks, will be true when what *p* provides is necessarily true; *always, p* will be true when what *p* provides is ever true.

However, even if eternalism is correct, sentences with the same possible-worlds intension generally embed differently within tense operators. For example, if eternalism is true, then (relative to July 4, 1997) sentence (1) and

(2)   Clinton is president on July 4, 1997

say the same thing and thus have the same intension.[2] But clearly the sentences

(3)   It is always the case that Clinton is president

and

(4)   It is always the case that Clinton is president on July 4, 1997

differ in truth value. The question thus arises, What stands to a tense operator as possible-worlds intensions stand to the necessity operator? In answering this, Salmon develops an account on which expressions have four sorts of semantic values: extensions, contents (which may be identified with what is said), content bases (on which temporal operators operate), and characters (which may be identified with linguistic meaning).

A complete account of the semantics of tense must account for the wide variety of devices for tensing sentences beyond the simple past, present, and future. There are, for example, the perfect tenses ('Clinton will have been/has been/had been president'), the progressive ('He is writing a novel'), a variety of adverbial constructions ('now', 'yesterday', 'during next summer'), and temporal connectives ('before', 'after'). In their chapter, Ernest Lepore and Kirk Ludwig propose an account of many such constructions within the context of truth-theoretic semantics.

At the heart of their account is the idea that tenses and temporal constructions other than the present generally involve restricted quantification over times. (1) is regimentable as

(1′)   President (Clinton, t^*),[3]

where 't^*' behaves somewhat as does 'now', picking out in any context its time. According to Lepore and Ludwig,

(5)   Clinton was president

and

(6)   Clinton will be president

are regimented as

(5′)   (for some t, $t < t^*$) President (Clinton, t)

and

(6′)   (for some t, $t > t^*$) President (Clinton, t).

In tenses other than the simple present, temporal adverbs are taken to contribute to the temporal quantifier's restriction, as suggested by the regimentation of

(7)   Clinton was president yesterday

as

(7′)   (for some t, $t < t^*$ & t included in yesterday) President (Clinton, t).

In present-tensed sentences, temporal adverbs make the same contribution as they make in other tensed sentences, but are not embedded within a temporal quantifier:

(8)   Clinton is today president,

for example, is regimented as

(8′) t^* is included in today & President (Clinton, t^*).

As Lepore and Ludwig observe, a consequence is that what's said by a tensed sentence at a time t cannot be said in unadorned English at any time other than t. An utterance of (1) or (8) at midnight on Monday says something specific to midnight Monday (and, in the case of (8), Monday itself): as is sometimes said, midnight Monday is a constituent of the proposition expressed. Utterances of (5) and (7) at midnight on Tuesday involve reference to midnight Tuesday. Given that what is said is individuated, in part, in terms of the references made in the saying of, it follows that what's said by (1) and (8) at midnight on Monday are things distinct from what's said by (5) and (7) at midnight on Tuesday. But if we can't resay Monday's sayings with the likes of (5) and (7), it is not clear that we can resay them, period.

There is plausibility in the thought that (7) on Tuesday tells us something—that Monday is past—that (8) on Monday does not. But it is quite counterintuitive that (7) on Tuesday does not resay (8) on Monday. By fiddling with the details of Lepore and Ludwig's account, one can preserve the intuition that in using (7) on Tuesday one resays (8) on Monday, while still granting that (7) on Tuesday says something different from (8) on Monday.

Suppose that we take temporal adverbials to modify that to which tenses apply—untensed verbs—and not the tenses or a tensed verb, as adverbials do on Lepore and Ludwig's account.[4] If so, 'was president yesterday' is "built up" by first applying 'yesterday' to the untensed 'be president', and then applying the past tense to the result. Let A be a temporal adverbial that supplies a temporal interval—for example, 'now', 'yesterday', 'on July 4', 'during next summer'. Note that A contains or is itself an expression that names an interval; use A_n for this expression. Let V be a verb and thus something whose regimentation contains a temporal argument place that is, in simple tensed sentences, occupied either by 't^*' or by a variable bound by a temporal quantifier introduced by the tense. Suppose that we depart from Lepore and Ludwig's account by treating the untensed *VA* so:

(P)   *VA* regiments as *t is included in A_n & (for some t', t' included in A_n) $V(t')$.*

This regiments the untensed 'be president yesterday' as

(9)   *t* is included in yesterday & (for some t', t' included in yesterday) be president (x, t').[5]

Since (P)'s output contains a temporal variable, the tenses apply straightforwardly to it. (7) and (8) will now be regimented as

(7″) (for some *t*, $t < t^*$) (*t* is included in yesterday & (for some t', t' included in yesterday) President (Clinton, t'))

and

(8″) t^* is included in today & (for some t', t' included in today) President (Clinton, t').[6]

Taken relative to a context *c*, (8″) makes a conjunctive assertion. Its first conjunct claims that the time of the context, t^*, is contained in the context's day—that is (so to speak), that today is occurring now. Its second conjunct tells us that Clinton is president on the day in question. Since the initial quantifier of (7″) binds nothing in the scope of its second quantifier, (7″) is *also* plausibly taken as making, in context, a conjunctive assertion. Its first conjunct tells us that the day before the context's time is past—that is (so to speak), that yesterday is past. Its second conjunct tells us that Clinton was president on the day in question. If we set (8″) in a context occupying Monday, and (7″) in a context occupying Tuesday, their second conjuncts make exactly the same assertion. (At least they do, if we individuate what is said in terms of what is referred to and the logical structure of the sentence used.)

On this account, tensed sentences involving temporal modifiers make conjunctive claims. The first part, or conjunct, of such a claim serves to locate the time of utterance relative to the time provided by the modifier; the second part makes a claim about what happens in the interval supplied by the modifier. The tense of a sentence affects only the first claim thus made: the *substantive* claim made on Monday by 'Clinton is president today' (i.e., the claim made by the second conjunct) is identical with the *substantive* claim made by 'Clinton was president yesterday' on Tuesday.[7] It is quite plausible to think that, in assessing whether someone has said today what she said yesterday, we simply ignore the locative role of tense in cases where the speaker explicitly names the interval of time of which she speaks. In this sense, someone who says, or thinks, on July 4, 'Clinton is president today' will say, or think, the very same thing the next day, if she says, or thinks, 'Clinton was president on July 4'.[8]

2   A-Series Properties

Consider the sentence

(10)   The Battle of Hastings is past.

On one view, there is a property, *being past*, that an event has just when it is over; any use of (10) says simply, of the Battle of Hastings, that it has this property. Since use of (10) does not date the time of possessing the property, what (10) says will change truth value over time. Someone who holds this view posits so-called *A-series properties*, such as *being past*, *being present*, and *being future*—and also subscribes to temporalism.

The questions Are there A-series properties? and Is temporalism correct? are independent. In particular, one might hold that there are A-series properties, but that eternalism provides the correct view of tensed sentences, taking (10) to say at a time T what's said then by a sentence along the lines of

(11)   The Battle of Hastings is at t past,

where t names T.[9] And one might, as does Hugh Mellor, deny the existence of A-series properties while holding that what some sentences say changes truth value over time.[10]

Anthony Brueckner's chapter discusses some of Mellor's arguments against the reality of A-series properties. Mellor observes that one can give the truth conditions of sentences such as (11)—and indeed of any tensed sentence—without reference to A-series properties, saying that a use of (11) at *t* is true if and only if the Battle of Hastings ended before *t*. Such truth conditions refer to temporal relations (so-called *B-series relations*, such as being later than) that hold timelessly. Mellor infers that "what makes tensed talk true" are B-series facts. If so, we might conclude, there is no fact about the semantics of tensed talk that requires us to posit A-series properties.[11] Brueckner criticizes this argument, as well as Mellor's view that A-series properties are "transcendentally ideal"—that such properties are artifacts of our way of representing B-series relations and correspond to nothing in reality. Mellor's views are defended by Mark Richard in a brief contribution following Brueckner's chapter.

Arthur Falk's chapter develops a view akin to Mellor's view that time is "transcendentally ideal." According to Falk, the temporal phenomenology of experience—in particular, our experiencing events as present—can be completely explained in terms of the workings of our perceptual apparatus and the way in which we represent (B-series) temporal relations of perceived scenes. Falk concludes that properties like *being present* are "a subjective accretion, a form of egocentric appearance" (sec. 7.1).

Falk develops his view in two extended thought experiments. His central claim is that the kinds of "negative feedback systems" that have in fact evolved—including ourselves—can only have experiences that involve "a sense of passage" (and therefore have experiences that involve "the feeling of presence").

Negative feedback systems are able to act to further goals, receive information from the environment about progress toward goals, and behave (more or less) appropriately on the basis of such information. They have perceptions that represent information about the state of the environment at the time of perception. Suppose such a system perceives, at *t*, a scene. What makes the perception represent what is happening at *t*? According to Falk, the "representational content" of the state does not do this; "[r]ather, the time of the information ... is represented by the time of *the receiving* of the information." That is, the system doesn't explicitly represent when the scene perceived is occurring; it just "assumes" (i.e., behaves in a way consonant with the assumption) that the time of the scene perceived is the time of perception.

It follows, says Falk, that the system (since it acts more or less appropriately) must continually replace perceptual contents with new ones, in order to keep updated about the environment. But, Falk continues, if such a being has experiences at all, this constant updating of perceptual information will be experienced as involving "a sense of passage"; Falk's defense of this claim is that imagining "what it would be like" to be such a system will convince us that it must have such experiences. Since nothing in this argument requires us to suppose that events has A-series properties, we are to conclude that the sense of passage is a result of how we represent the world, not the world represented.

One might wonder about the argument's initial premise, since many of our perceptual experiences (e.g., of the stars) arguably represent past states of objects as past states. Falk is aware of such objections and attempts to meet them. One might also wonder why constant perceptual updating *must* be experienced as involving presentness and pastness. One does not have to be a skeptic about the claim that there is something it is like to be a bat to be simply puzzled as to whether what it is like for the bat to echolocate involves a sense of passage.

Admittedly, if I consider a bat, or some more rudimentary negative feedback system (a bacterium, say), suppose or pretend that there is something it is like to be it, and ask whether such a creature would perceive events as present, I am unable to imagine how it could not. But this may well be an artifact of how I empathize with it. For my empathy seems in good part a matter of my imaginatively equipping myself with its exteroceptors. It is hard to know to what extent such empathy simply imposes my own collection of concepts, including *presentness*, on the creature. For this reason, Falk's thought experiment may be inconclusive.

3   Tense and Cognitive Role

Consider the relation that holds between an object and a time if the first leaves the Denver airport at the second. Let us use *Leave* as a predicate that picks out this relation. Suppose that my flight leaves the Denver airport at 1:30 p.m., July 4. Adopt, for illustration's sake, the account of tensed sentences sketched at the end of section 1. The thought I express if I say to myself,

(12)   My flight leaves now,

is the thought expressed, at the time of thinking, by

(13) t^* is included in now & Leave (my flight, now).

And the thought I would express, if I said to myself,

(14)   My flight leaves at 1:30 p.m., July 4,

is expressed by

(15)   1:30 p.m., July 4, is included in 1:30 p.m., July 4, and Leave (my flight, 1:30 p.m., July 4).

Now suppose that I said (12) to myself at 1:30 p.m., July 4. What difference, if any, is there between the thought I thereby expressed and the thought expressed then by (14)? Clearly, if the only things relevant to the thought expressed by a sentence are what its parts refer to and its logical syntax, there is no difference. But there obviously may be a great difference between thinking to oneself, 'My flight leaves now', and thinking to oneself, 'My flight leaves at 1:30 p.m., July 4'.

Let us speak, somewhat loosely, of a sentence such as (14) being, at 1:30 p.m., July 4, a *detensing* of (12). An example like the above raises two related questions.

Q1:   How, if at all, does what is said by someone who utters at t something that is, at t, a detensing of a tensed sentence S, differ from what is said by someone who at t utters S?

Q2:   Why does the "cognitive role" of a tensed sentence differ so dramatically from the cognitive role of its detensings?

James Higginbotham's "Tensed Second Thoughts" and Mark Richard's "Objects of Relief" are concerned with these two questions.

Some clarification of the notion of cognitive role is in order. Talk of cognitive role often involves the assumption that, given a speaker X and a language L that she understands, X will associate with many sentences of L some collection of

• inferential properties (such as the property 'Pigs run' has, when one is inclined to infer it from 'Pigs and ducks run'),

• behaviorial dispositions (e.g., the disposition most of us have to run upon accepting 'There's a raging fire next to me'), and

• dispositions to accept the sentence when perceiving certain environmental conditions.

Talk of a sentence's cognitive role is often talk of a somewhat vague collection of such properties, often those that are more or less constant across some population of interest (e.g., "typical speakers").

It seems that the tenses and context-sensitive temporal expressions such as 'now' make a distinctive contribution to cognitive role. For example, present-tensed sentences, with or without the modifier 'now', seem distinctively connected to action. It seems obvious enough that there is a difference in the cognitive role of (12) and (14), for only accepting the first is in some sense guaranteed to lead to movement. Again, sentences that "place an event in the past," such as 'My root canal is now over', have a connection to relief and regret that sentences that do not so situate an event ('My root canal is finished as of 5 p.m.') cannot have.

It is often thought that the cognitive role of a sentence (for a person who understands it) is to be explained in terms of what the sentence says, or in terms of the rules that tell us what a particular use of the sentence says.[12] If we accept this view, we will seek some cluster of semantic properties, associated with the tenses and temporal expressions, and determining what tensed sentences say, whose presence is in one way or another responsible for the distinctive cognitive role of tensed sentences. And we will suppose that answers to Q1 will provide, or at least lead to, answers to Q2.

One answer—call it the *simple answer*—to both questions proposes that context-sensitive expressions (and, perhaps, the present tense itself) express "indexical ways of thinking" of times or intervals. On one version of such a view, a sentence's cognitive role is to be individuated in terms of, or even identified with, what the sentence says. Furthermore, what a sentence says is *the same* at different times and in different contexts. In particular, what is said by sentences such as (12) or 'My flight is leaving' is the same at different times. Since expressions such as 'July 4, 1993' express ways of thinking of temporal entities different from those expressed by expressions such as 'now' or the tenses, we may conclude that (12) and (14) express different thoughts, and we may explain their differences in cognitive role as a consequence of the differences in the ways of thinking their constituents express.

Such an account is naturally associated with the view that 'presently', 'now', and so on, ascribe A-series properties, and that sentences such as (12) say things that change truth value across time. On such a view, the objects of assertion and belief can be assigned truth values only relative to a context. Thus, there is a single proposition, *that flight 714 leaves from here tomorrow*, which you and I express (and believe) when we say (sincerely and with understanding),

(16)   Flight 714 leaves from here tomorrow.

This is so, even if you say it in Terminal A on Monday and I say it in Terminal B on Tuesday. Such a view has some counterintuitive consequences. For example, it seems to require us to say that, if you and I utter (16) in the above situations, then there must be a true construal of

(17)   You said that flight 714 leaves from here tomorrow

as spoken by me on Tuesday in Terminal B. One might well wonder if that has to be so, given simply that you uttered (16) on Monday in Terminal A.[13]

A second account—call it the *rule-of-use* account—holds that (12) says different things at different times; indeed, at any time t, (12) says what would be said by a detensing of the form *My flight leaves at T*, where T is any non-context-sensitive name of t. Since the cognitive roles of (12) and the other sentence differ, we thus obviously cannot individuate a sentence's cognitive role simply in terms of what is says in a single context. But we might try explaining (or even identifying) cognitive roles in terms of (with) the rules that tell us how to determine what a sentence's use says in any context.

On a rule-of-use account, the distinctive contribution of 'now' to cognitive role is to be explained by reference to (something like) the fact that to understand 'now' is to know that a use of *It is now true that S* at a time t says something that is true iff S is true *at t*. This strategy is developed, in somewhat differing ways, in the works of David Kaplan and John Perry.[14] Richard's "Objects of Relief" questions whether the requisite notion of rule can be spelled out in a way that will allow the strategy to work. Richard argues further that appeal to the rules of use for a sentence cannot *explain* its cognitive role for a person because there isn't any particularly interesting connection, lawful or otherwise, between a sentence's being governed by a particular rule of use and the sentence's playing a particular cognitive role for a person.

A somewhat different way of answering our two questions begins with Hans Reichenbach's idea that an utterance of a tensed sentence, or of one containing demonstratives or indexicals, involves a sort of reflexivity: such an utterance makes a claim about itself, or about an expression token used therein. To oversimplify madly, Reichenbach's idea was that when one uttered, 'My flight leaves now', one referred to part of one's utterance, saying something like *My flight's departure is simultaneous with my uttering this token of 'now'*.

Observe that it is very difficult to imagine how someone could understandingly utter,

(18)   My flight's departure is simultaneous with this very utterance,

using its last three worlds to refer to that very utterance, but not take the departure of the flight to be present. Analogously, it is very difficult to imagine how one could think to oneself,

(19)   My flight's departure is posterior to this very thinking,

using the last three words to pick out the very thinking one is engaged in, but not take the departure of the flight to be past. Thoughts and assertions that are reflexive in these ways seem to involve locating the time of an event relative to something—the act of assertion or thinking—of whose temporal location the thinker or speaker is "directly aware."

This suggests that if tensed utterances and thinkings are invariably reflexive in the way in which the utterance of (18) or thinking of (19) would be, we should be able to explain their cognitive role in terms of their reflexivity. Notice that this would not require saying that a tensed sentence says something different from its detensings. Suppose I utter (18) now. Suppose I later say (using 'is simultaneous with' tenselessly), 'My flight's departure is simultaneous with that very utterance', using the last three words to refer to the original utterance of (18). The claim made by the latter utterance would be the same as that made by the former, at least if we individuate claims in terms of references made and logical syntax. But the latter utterance is not reflexive, since in making it, I do not refer to the act of uttering I am performing. And thus we need not conclude that it, or the sentence of which it is an utterance, has the same cognitive role as a sentence whose utterance is invariably reflexive.

In recent work, Higginbotham has elaborated an account of tensed sentences and their use along the general lines just sketched.[15] He argues that the account can be at least partially motivated by the behavior of tenses when embedded under verbs such as 'says' or 'believes'. In order to explain the range of readings of sentences such as

(20)   Marsha believed that my cat was ill,

Higginbotham suggests, we do best to see the tense of the embedded sentence as "cross-referenced" with, or anaphoric upon, the tense of the main verb. This will lead us to see a sentence such as 'My cat is ill' as saying something regimentable as

(21)   for some t: t is prior to t^* & Ill (my cat, t),

since such an account allows the tense of the sentence embedded in (20) to be connected appropriately to the tense of the main verb. The justification for taking the quantifier in (21) to range over such things as events of uttering or thinking, instead of over times or intervals, is to be found in the sort of considerations reviewed in the last few paragraphs.

Higginbotham's chapter discusses some objections to this account. One such objection is this: if we accept Higginbotham's account, then an embedding of (12) under a modal operator, as in

(22)   My flight might have left now,

does not say, of what (12) says, that it is possible. This is because (22) says something quite different from what would be said by

(23)   My flight might have left at the time of this utterance.

Higginbotham also defends his account against Richard's claim (chap. 3, this volume) that to think reflexively of a mental state need not involve taking it as present.

Questions Q1 and Q2 are evidently closely connected with questions about the semantics of ascriptions of belief and assertion. Note that one would normally explain someone's running toward the gate, on his thinking (12), by saying,

(24)   He thinks that his flight is leaving.

This is, so far as I can see, one of the primary motivations for the idea that the cognitive role of a sentence is to be explained in terms of what the sentence says, or at least in terms of its semantic properties. One advantage of the simple answer and of Higginbotham's account is that they forge a more or less straightforward connection between what is said by tensed sentences and their motivational properties, thus allowing a more or less straightforward account of how we can explain someone's behavior by ascribing him a belief using a tensed sentence in the complement clause of the ascription. It is thus incumbent on someone like Richard, who denies that there is an interesting connection between what tensed sentences say and their motivational properties, to explain how it is that an ascription such as (24) might be explanatory. In "Objects of Relief," Richard takes up this challenge, arguing that ascriptions such as (24) are explanatory only in the company of (normally reasonable) background assumptions about the ascription's subject.

4   Eternalism Defended

I return to the question, Is what is said invariably temporally specific?

One argument—call it *argument I*—for eternalism is this. Take a simple tensed sentence whose overt lexical material is unambiguous—say, 'Clinton is president'. An utterance of such a sentence says at most one thing. But it seems always possible to correctly portray someone who assertively utters such a sentence as having said something temporally specific. For example, suppose that at midnight, Mary utters the sentence 'Clinton is president', and at dawn, she utters the sentence '[I was wrong,] Clinton was not president at midnight'. At dawn, we can report to Clinton,

(25)   At midnight, Mary said that you were president, but now she
       denies it/that/what she said at midnight.

One denies p only if one utters a sentence that expresses a q such that necessarily p is true if and only if q is not. So, in uttering the sentence 'Clinton was not president at midnight' at dawn, Mary utters a sentence that says something that is, necessarily, not true if and only if what Mary said at midnight is true. Now what Mary said at dawn is such that, necessarily, it is not true if and only if Clinton is not president at midnight. So what Mary said at midnight, when she uttered the sentence 'Clinton is president' is, of necessity, true if and only if Clinton is president at midnight. So what she said is temporally specific. It would seem that a cognate argument could be given for any assertive utterance of a temporally unspecific sentence.

The argument turns on three claims:

1. Utterances of sentences such as 'Clinton is president' express at most one thing.

2. One can always correctly report someone who utters the sentence 'Clinton is president' as having said something temporally specific.

3. Denying p requires asserting something necessarily inconsistent with p.

The first premise might well be denied.[16] Suppose that Susan saw Kate two winters ago and said, 'Darn, she's pregnant'. Suppose that Mindy saw Kate this spring and said, 'She's pregnant'. We can say,

(26)   When Susan saw Kate two winters ago, she swore that Kate was pregnant, and when Mindy saw her this spring, that's what she said, too.

(26) seems to report Susan and Mindy as literally saying the same thing; if they do, presumably they each say something temporally neuter.[17] But we can also construct an example like that involved in argument I around Susan's and Mindy's utterances. For suppose that last spring Susan saw Kate and said to herself, '(I guess that) she wasn't pregnant two winters ago, but she is now'. Then we can surely go to Kate and say,

(27)   When Susan saw you two winters ago, she said that you were pregnant, but now she takes that back/denies that/denies what she said.

All this, it might be said, suggests that when someone utters a tensed, but temporally unspecific, sentence, two distinct reports of what she said will be possible: one reporting her as having said something temporally specific, and one reporting her as having said something temporally unspecific. And this suggests that utterances of temporally unspecific sentences express, or at least typically express, two things, one temporally unspecific, the other specific.[18]

It should be noted in passing that it is not just assertion and its ascription that provide prima facie evidence for the existence of temporally neuter propositional objects. Points cognate to that made by appeal to (26) and (27) can be made by appeal to ascriptions of belief and even of truth:

(28)   Bob went to the monkey house, and now he thinks that he's been infected with the Ebola virus. Every time he goes there he thinks that; he's convinced one of the monkeys is a carrier.

(29)   In the '60s, it was safe to hitchhike, but that's no longer true/the case.

As strong as the prima facie case for the existence of temporally neuter propositional objects is, I am inclined to think that it is a mistake to posit such.[19] This is in part because there is strong prima facie evidence against their existence, in part because the data that suggest there are such things can be explained in other ways.

The evidence against temporally neuter objects is simply that diachronic agreement or disagreement seems to be, of necessity, a matter of agreement or disagreement about something temporally specific. Suppose that at midnight I say to you,

(30)   Smith is awake and she is talking about tense.

Suppose it is now the next morning, and we are at a talk about tense that Smith is giving. Somewhat rudely, we begin arguing with each other about what I said last night. You tell me that you don't believe anything I said last night about Smith; I tell you that everything I said about her last night is the absolute truth. It would seem that if I were to say,

(31)   You and I disagree about everything I said last night about Smith,

I would speak truly. Suppose there is such a thing as the temporally neuter proposition that Smith is awake and talking about tense. If there is, then (a) it is among the things that I said last night about Smith, and (b) you and I certainly both believe it, for we both know that Smith is awake and droning on about tense. So if (31) can be true in the situation in question—which of course it can be—there is no such thing as the temporally neuter proposition that Smith is awake and talking about tense.

Such an argument will be convincing only if we can defuse counter-arguments based upon the apparent truth of (26), (28), and (29). To do this, we need to show that the truth of such sentences is consistent with the claim that what is said or thought is invariably eternal. But the truth of these sentences *is* so consistent, for we may, with a fair amount of plausibility, take the instances of 'that' that occur in these sentences to be, not devices of cross-reference, but devices of ellipsis.

Consider the sentence form

(32)   Mary said that *S*, and Susan said that (too).

Taking 'that *S*' in the first conjunct to be a singular term, an understanding of the second conjunct's 'that' as a device of cross-reference would see it as anaphoric upon 'that *S*' and (thus) referring to whatever 'that *S*' does. Taking 'that' in the second conjunct as a device of ellipsis amounts to taking it as a device for indicating the elision, in that conjunct, of material that is in some sense identical with material in the first conjunct. If we interpret 'that' as a device of cross-reference in

(33)   Mary said that she was going to Portugal next year, and Susan said that (too),

we will say that (33) entails that Susan said that Mary was going to Portugal next year;[20] if we interpret it as a device of ellipsis, we will take (33) as elliptical for

(34)   Mary said that she was going to Portugal next year, and Susan said that she was going to Portugal next year.

(33) itself is ambiguous, but it clearly has a reading on which which it entails that Susan said that Susan was going to Portugal next year. Suppose, as is often done, that we take the sort of identify that licenses us to elide (34) as (33) as one on which occurrences of 'She is going to Portugal next year' may be identical even when their subjects are bound to expressions with different referents. Then the hypothesis that (33)'s 'that' is a device of ellipsis correctly predicts that (33) has a reading on which it entails that Susan said that Susan was going to Portugal next year.

Now consider (26), and suppose that its last 'that' is elliptical for 'that Kate was pregnant'. Suppose further that a quantificational account of tense, like that reviewed above, is correct. Then a tensed sentence contains a variable-like expression that must be either interpreted with a contextually determined time (the norm, when the tense is not embedded) or appropriately bound to another such element (the norm on embedding under verbs of propositional attitude). We will thus take

(35)   that Kate was pregnant

to have syntactic properties suggested by

(36)   that for some t $(t < t^*$ & Pregnant (Kate, t).

Taking (26)'s 'that' to be elliptical for (35), (26) will be elliptical for

(26′)   When Susan saw Kate two winters ago, she swore that Kate was pregnant, and when Mindy saw her this spring, she said that Kate was pregnant.

Given that (35) as embedded in (26″) has syntactic features suggested by (36), and that it is mandatory that (36)'s 't^*' be bound to the immediately governing tense (if it does not receive a contextual interpretation), (26) ends up being understood as making the claim

(26″)   When Susan saw Kate two winters ago, she swore that Kate was then pregnant, and when Mindy saw her this spring, what she said was that Kate was then [i.e., last spring] pregnant.

The upshot is that we explain how (26) can be true without its ascribing the same thought to Susan and to Mindy.[21] The conclusion I draw is that it is tenable, and correct, to suppose that what is said is invariably eternal.

Notes

Thanks to Kirk Ludwig for comments on section 1 and to Jeff King and Ernie Lepore for correspondence on the subject of section 2.

1. Some sentences make claims with constant truth values, regardless of whether they are temporally specific. 'Either there are atoms or there are no atoms' is presumably such a sentence.

2. Actually, this is not quite right. Different versions of eternalism will give different accounts of what is said by tensed sentences. Some will identify what (1)

says with what would be said by appropriately modifying its verb with a qualifier of the form *at t*, where *t* names one or another interval including the time of utterance. Others will identify what is said with some token-reflexive claim, such as (speaking very loosely) the claim that Clinton's being president occurs at the time of this very utterance. Still others will identify what is said with some other temporally specific claim. For present purposes, these differences do not matter.

3. I depart in inessential ways from Lepore and Ludwig's notation.

4. More exactly, the adverbs apply to nonmaximal projections of Vs.

5. In point of fact, the restriction placed upon the quantifier will vary with the interval supplied by *A* and, perhaps, with *V* as well. I ignore this.

6. Exercise: Regiment 'Clinton will be president during 1998' and 'Clinton was president during 1998'.

Conceivably the pattern of regimentation given in (P) will vary according to the verb and the adverb, so that one or the other occurrence of 'is included in' needs to be replaced by 'is identical with'.

7. Note that if temporal order is necessary—that, for example, 1999 could not occur before 1998—the first claim made by a tensed sentence will generally (but not invariably) be necessary, and the second claim will generally (though not invariably) be contingent. ('I was human on my 32nd birthday' is, on somewhat controversial assumptions, an exception to both claims.)

8. The argument in the text assumes that what is said is individuated in part, perhaps wholly, in terms of references made and a logical form associated with the saying. Such a view raises interesting issues familiar from discussions of the paradox of analysis. Consider, for example,

(i) 'Clinton will be president the day after tomorrow' as uttered on Saturday,

(ii) 'Clinton will be president tomorrow' as uttered on Sunday,

(iii) 'Clinton was president yesterday' as uttered on Tuesday,

and

(iv) 'Clinton will be president the day after today' as uttered on Sunday.

Suppose we individuate what is said wholly in terms of references made and logical form. Then it would seem that (i) and (iii) do not say the same thing, for the references made to days are different (one involves reference to Sunday, not Monday; the other to Monday, not Sunday), as are the forms. However, 'tomorrow' and 'the day after today' would seem to be synonymous.

This presumably means (ii) and (iv) say the same thing, since substitution of synonyms preserves what's said. But individuating what's said in terms of form and references made means that (i) and (iv) say the same thing, as do (ii) and (iii). Given that saying the same thing is transitive, we have a contradiction.

My own view is that this argument goes awry when it assumes that 'tomorrow' and 'the day after today' are synonymous in a sense of 'synonymous' in which substitution of synonyms preserves what's said. The relation between the two terms is rather *like* the relation between 'here' and 'the place at which I am located'. The issues are quite orthogonal to the semantics of tense, and so I will not take them up here. For some discussion, see my "Analysis, Synonymy, and Sense," in C. A. Anderson and M. Zeleny, eds., *Logic, Meaning, and Computation: Essays in Memory of Alonzo Church*, pp. 545–71. (Dordrecht: Kluwer, 2001).

9. Salmon's view seems to be close to this view.

10. See D. H. Mellor, *Real Time* (Cambridge: Cambridge University Press, 1981), passim.

11. Of course, there might be some nonsemantic fact that required such properties—say, one that McTaggart's infamous regress argument points to. Such considerations are not at issue in the dispute between Mellor and Brueckner.

12. This idea is sometimes ascribed to Frege. It is not altogether clear that Frege thought that one could explain such things as the connection of belief to action, or the connection between stimulus and acceptance, in terms of sense.

13. One could say that only certain context-sensitive expressions—in particular, temporal indexicals, tenses, and first person pronouns—had indexical senses. This sort of objection would then be less pressing. But one would then want to know why only certain indexical expressions had indexical senses.

A sophisticated view with some affinities to that mentioned in the text is developed by David Lewis in "Attitudes *De Dicto* and *De Se*," *The Philosophical Review* 88 (1979), pp. 513–43. Some further discussion of appeal to A-series properties, in the attempt to explain the cognitive role of tensed talk, is found in Richard's chapter "Objects of Relief."

14. See D. Kaplan, "Demonstratives," in J. Almog, J. Perry, and H. Wettstein, eds., *Themes from Kaplan*, pp. 481–614 (Oxford: Oxford University Press, 1989); J. Perry, "The Problem of the Essential Indexical," *Noûs* 13 (1979), pp. 3–21; J. Perry, "Frege on Demonstratives," *Philosophical Review* 86 (1977), pp. 474–97.

15. See J. Higginbotham, "Tensed Thoughts," *Mind and Language* 10 (1995), pp. 226–49.

16. For that matter, the third premise might be denied. Some discussion of the plausibility of denying this premise can be found in the second section of "Temporalism and Eternalism," *Philosophical Studies* 39 (1981), pp. 1–13. I will not discuss it here.

17. In his chapter, Salmon defends eternalism by observing that it is often the case that an utterance of a sentence of the form α *is F* says something to the effect that α *is F within the interval I*, where the relevant interval is contextually determined. As Salmon correctly notes, this means that nonsimultaneous utterances of a temporally unspecific sentence such as 'Clinton is president' may express the same thing—for example, that Clinton is president in the interval 1993–2001. Salmon observes that, given this, temporalism is not supported by observing that in many cases one retains a belief, expressed at t with 'Clinton is president', from t to a later t' only if one has a belief expressible at t' with 'Clinton is president'.

I think what Salmon says is correct. But I don't think it's sufficient to defend the eternalist view against examples like (26) (or (28)). In any nonbizarre development of example (26), there will be no plausibility whatsoever in the suggestion that there is an interval *i* such that Susan's and Mindy's utterances both say that Kate is pregnant within *i*.

18. It suggests this; it does not entail it. One can imagine the temporalist giving a pragmatic account of the temporally specific saying. It would take us too far afield to evaluate this here.

19. Of course, I am *not* saying that there are not temporally neuter things such as the state of affairs of Clinton's being president (which obtains only between 1993 and 2001) or Salmon's propositional matrices. I am saying that it is a mistake to take such things to be the objects of propositional attitudes such as assertion and belief, or to be among the ("primary") bearers of truth.

20. Actually, this depends on our accepting certain (widely accepted) views about the objects of belief.

21. If this suggestion is to explain the range of data, it will have to be the case that we can plausibly say that, given that the 'that' of

(29)   In the '60s, it was safe to hitchhike, but that's no longer true/the case

is a device of ellipsis, (29) is, or can be, elliptical for

(29′)   In the '60s, it was safe to hitchhike, but it's no longer true that it is safe to hitchhike.

Someone might worry that, given that ellipsis is a matter of suppression of *identical* material, (29) shouldn't be able to be elliptical for (29′), because of the change in tense between complements of the conjuncts.

However, it is clear that such changes in tense are permissible within elided material. The sentence

(i)   When Mary saw Michael on television, she thought that she was taller than him, and if Susan sees Michael on television, she'll think so/that too

Pretty clearly has a reading on which the consequent of the second conjunct elides as 'she'll think that she is taller than him'.

Section A

The Semantic Content of Tensed Sentences

1

Outline for a Truth-Conditional Semantics for Tense

Ernest Lepore and Kirk Ludwig

1.1 Introduction

The use of verbs inflected or modified for tense, and temporal adverbs, indexicals, and quantifiers, pervades everyday speech. Getting clearer about their semantics not only promises to help us to understand how we understand each other, but is also a step toward clarifying the nature of time and temporally located thoughts. The goal of this chapter is to investigate, from the standpoint of *truth-theoretic semantics*, English tense, temporal designators and quantifiers, and other expressions we use to relate ourselves and other things to the temporal order. Truth-theoretic semantics provides a particularly illuminating standpoint from which to discuss issues about the semantics of tense and their relation to thoughts at, and about, times. Tense, and temporal modifiers, contribute systematically to conditions under which sentences we utter are true or false. A Tarski-style truth-theoretic semantics, by requiring explicitly represented truth conditions, helps to sharpen questions about the function of tense and to deepen our insight into the contribution the tenses and temporal modifiers make to what we say by using them.

We are interested in a semantic, rather than syntactic, phenomenon. Although tense is identified traditionally with verb inflection, our concern is with linguistic devices used for indicating a time interval, relative to or in which a state or activity is to be understood to occur or obtain. For ease of exposition, we will press 'tense' into use to cover any verb form used to indicate time intervals in which the event or state expressed by a verb is to occur or obtain. In English, verb inflection, such as adding '-ed' to a bare infinitive, is one such device. But the phenomenon occurs even in languages like Chinese that lack inflection for tense. Though we will be concerned solely with tense in English, we are interested in it as an example of a semantic phenomenon common to natural language. The structure of a semantic phenomenon may be expected to reflect underlying facts about the structure of thoughts about contingent particulars. We expect that all languages share basic expressive resources, even when they are realized by diverse syntactic devices.[1]

Our basic approach, which goes back to Frege (1977) and Russell (1903), treats tense as an indexical device for referring to times or time intervals at which events take place or states obtain. Where the time interval picked out is not the present, tense involves what we will call *indexically restricted quantifiers*. The indexical element functions to pick out a time of utterance as a reference point for indicating quantificationally the relative location of temporally bound states and events. While the central idea is intuitively appealing, it has not been systematically explored within a truth-theoretic framework. It turns out to be particularly powerful in its application to systematizing the often puzzling interaction of tense with other temporal devices. Treating tense as quantificational will make it possible to give a uniform account of tense and temporal modifiers and quantifiers in English, and it can be shown to complement in a compelling way the standard event/state analyses of adverbial modification. If the basic account is correct, in our most ordinary remarks we reveal a commitment to the existence of time intervals. Hence, time is real, or virtually everything we say is false.

We begin in section 1.2 with an overview of how to deploy a truth theory as a compositional meaning theory. We show that the requirement that the theory be *interpersonal* precludes a semantics for tense that employs tense operators. In section 1.3, we present an account of the simple tenses (present, past, future) and of the present progressive, and we discuss several methodological points about tense and semantics. In section 1.4, we give an account of deictic and structured temporal referring expressions. In section 1.5, we consider how our basic account interacts with temporal adverbials, and in section 1.6, how it interacts with 'before' and 'after', used as sentential connectives. In section 1.7, we examine how tense interacts with temporal quantifiers. In section 1.8, we treat so-called habitual sentences. In section 1.9, we examine how our account of tense interacts with the event analysis of adverbial modification. In section 1.10, we consider the interaction of tense in main and complement clauses of indirect discourse reports and attitude sentences. In section 1.11, we apply the account to issues in the philosophy of time, and we discuss the limitations of semantics in metaphysics. Section 1.12 is a summary and conclusion. In the appendix, we show how the account extends smoothly to a truth-conditional semantics for the perfect tenses.

1.2   Truth-Theoretic Semantics

A compositional meaning theory for a natural language L should provide

(R)   from a specification of the meanings of finitely many primitive expressions and rules, a specification of the meaning of an utterance of any of the infinitely many sentences of L.

We confine our attention to declaratives.[2] A compositional meaning theory for a context-insensitive language L—that is, a language without elements whose semantic contribution depends on context of use—would issue in theorems of the form

(M) s in L means that p,

where 's' is replaced by a structural description of a sentence φ of L, and 'p' is replaced by a metalanguage sentence that translates it.

For context-insensitive languages, the connection between a theory meeting Tarski's famous Convention T and a compositional meaning theory is straightforward: a truth theory meets that convention only if it entails every instance of (T),

(T) s is true in L iff p,

where 's' is replaced by a structural description of a sentence φ of L, and 'p' is replaced by a metalanguage sentence synonymous with φ. We shall call such instances of (T) *T-sentences*. The relation between a structural description that replaces 's' and a metalanguage sentence that replaces 'p' in a T-sentence is the same as that between suitable substitution pairs in (M). Therefore, every instance of (S) is true when what replaces 'p' translates the sentence denoted by what replaces 's'.

(S)   If s is true in L iff p, then s in L means that p.

Given a T-sentence for s, (S) enables us to specify its meaning. An advantage of a truth-theoretic approach (over one trying to generate instances of (M) more directly) is its ability to provide the recursions needed to generate meaning specifications for object language sentences from a finite base with no more ontological or logical resources than required for a theory of reference.

In natural languages, many (arguably all) sentences lack truth values independently of use. 'I am tired' is not true or false *simpliciter*, but only as used. This requires discarding the simple accounts above of the forms of theories of meaning and truth. Theories issuing in instances of (M) and (T) for 'I am tired' would yield (1) and (2).

(1)   'I am tired' in L means that I am tired.

(2)   'I am tired' in L is true iff I am tired.

But (1) and (2) express nothing unless relativized to a context of utterance, and what they express in a context depends on who utters them and the time of utterance. This creates two related difficulties. First, theorists employing identical adequacy criteria will arrive at nonequivalent theories, since they will express different propositions by the sentences they use. Second, no one will give the correct account of the meanings or truth conditions of sentences with context-sensitive elements. Were we each to assert (1), one of us would assert that 'I am tired' means that Ludwig is tired at such and such a time, while the other would assert that it means that Lepore is tired at such and such a time. But 'I am tired' means neither.

A semantics for a language should be couched in a context-insensitive metalanguage. We want theories that any inquirer can reach by meeting generally agreed upon theoretical constraints and that can be used to express the same thing in every context. This requires metalanguage expressions, including semantic predicates, to be untensed. This requirement shows why tense operators cannot be employed to give a semantics for English. An operator like 'it was the case that' is *itself* tensed and hence is unsuitable for use in our metalanguage. Tense logics do not provide a semantics for tense expressions in natural languages; rather, they represent a regimentation of them, which itself stands in need of a semantics couched in a context-insensitive metalanguage.

In modifying a compositional meaning theory to accommodate context sensitivity, and a truth theory that serves as its recursive engine, a theorist must choose between two options. The first retains the basic form of the meaning specification, '*x* means in language *y* that *p*', and correspondingly retains within the truth theory a two-place predicate relating a truth bearer and a language. The second adds an argument place to each semantic predicate in the theory for every contextual parameter required to fix a context-sensitive element's contribution when used. Both approaches require metalanguage semantic predicates to be untensed. For concreteness, we will suppose that the fundamental contextual parameters are utterer and time of utterance.[3] On the first option, which adds no argument places to its semantic predicates, a theory must take utterances as the bearers of meaning and truth and will yield theorems of the forms (*M*1) and (*T*1).

(*M*1)   For any speaker *s*, time *t*, sentence φ of *L*, utterance *u* of φ by *s* at *t*, *u* means in *L* that *p*.

(*T*1)   For any speaker *s*, time *t*, sentence φ of *L*, utterance *u* of φ by *s* at *t*, *u* is true in *L* iff *p*.

Since different utterances of the same sentence may take different truth values and express different propositions, what replaces '*p*' can be an open sentence with variables bound by the initial quantifiers. The second option adds argument places to semantic predicates, which issues in instances of (*M*2) and (*T*2).

(*M*2)   For any speaker *s*, time *t*, sentence φ of *L*, φ means$_{[s,t,L]}$ that *p*.

(*T*2)   For any speaker *s*, time *t*, sentence φ of *L*, φ is true$_{[s,t,L]}$ iff *p*.

As a first gloss, we might try to treat 'means$_{[s,t,L]}$' and 'is true$_{[s,t,L]}$' as equivalent to 'means as potentially spoken by *s* at *t* in *L*' and 'is true as potentially spoken by *s* at *t* in *L*'. However, as Evans (1985, pp. 359–60) points out, we cannot read these as ⌜if φ were used by *s* at *t* in *L*, then φ would be true iff/mean that⌝, since, aside from worries about how to evaluate counterfactuals, these interpretations would assign sentences such as 'I am silent' false *T*-theorems. What we need are the readings

⌜if φ were used by *s* at *t* in *L*, as things actually stand φ would be true iff/mean that⌝ or, alternatively, ⌜φ understood as it would be in *L* if spoken by *s* at *t* is true iff/means that⌝. Mutatis mutandis for other semantic predicates.

If either option issues in an adequate meaning theory, so does the other. Both treat actual uses of sentences as fundamental in understanding truth and propositional meaning. We adopt the second because it issues in theorems more directly informative about *sentence* meaning, which is our stated subject. We therefore replace adequacy criterion (*R*) with (*R'*).

(*R'*)   A compositional meaning theory for a natural language *L* should entail, from a specification of the meanings of primitive expressions of *L*, all true sentences of form (*M2*).

The analogue of Tarski's Convention *T* for recursive truth theories for natural languages we shall call Davidson's Convention *D*.

(*D*)   An adequate truth theory for a natural language *L* must entail every instance of (*T2*) such that corresponding instances of (*M2*) are true.

A truth theory for *L* meeting (*D*) with axioms that interpret primitive expressions of *L* (henceforth 'an interpretive truth theory') provides the resources to meet (*R'*). (For a further discussion of the framework for truth-theoretic semantics, see Lepore and Ludwig 2003, pts. I and IV.)

1.3   The Simple Tenses

In this section, we consider the semantics of simple tenses, beginning with state verbs in section 1.3.1 and proceeding to event verbs in section 1.3.2. In section 1.3.3, we will argue that the tradition that treats the progressive as a tense is poorly conceived from the standpoint of truth-theoretic semantics.

1.3.1   Indexicality of Tense for State Verbs

The most salient feature of tense is that its contribution to the meaning of utterances is sensitive to the time of utterance. Each of (3)–(5), in the present, past, and future tense,[4] respectively, may be true when uttered by a speaker at some times but not at others.

(3)   Mary loves Bill.

(4)   Mary loved Bill.

(5)   Mary will love Bill.[5]

This indicates that (3)–(5) each contain a deictic element, either an indexical or a demonstrative device (we will use 'deictic' as generic for context sensitivity). From the standpoint of truth-theoretic semantics, a sentence contains a deictic element if and only if its *T*-sentence has variables on its right-hand side bound by quantifiers that bind contextual parameters in its truth predicate. If the values of the minimal set of contextual parameters alone suffice for understanding what the semantic value of a deictic element is, it is an indexical device; otherwise, it is (in part at least) a demonstrative device.

With (3)–(5), in which tense is the only deictic element, knowing the time of utterance suffices for understanding the contributions of their deictic elements. So the simple tenses are indexicals. This requires that the propositions (3)–(5) express in a context involve direct reference to the time of utterance, since the variable bound by the temporal quantifier in whose scope the biconditional falls is a directly referring term. On the assumption that the proposition expressed by an utterance provides the content of the speaker's belief, every thought expressed using the present, past, and future tense is singular, since it directly refers to the time of utterance.

The case for regarding at least some tenses as quantifying over times is straightforward. When asserting (3), a speaker intends to say that Mary loves Bill then. When using (4), he intends to say that *at some time prior to his utterance* Mary loved Bill. Similarly, when using (5), he intends to say that *at some time after the time of his utterance* Mary will love Bill. In the latter two, clearly, the thoughts expressed quantify, respectively, over past and future times.

Unfortunately, in stating this, we reused the tenses we intend to explain. Even if untensed verbs are used in English, they cannot grammatically replace simple tensed ones.[6] This has an important consequence for the semantics of English: namely, *its semantic theory is unspecifiable in English*. For reasons provided in section 1.2, interpretive truth theories cannot use deictic elements in specifying truth conditions of object language expressions, on pain of being uninterpretive. So providing an adequate interpersonal interpretive truth theory for English requires enriching the metalanguage with tenseless verbs that express relations between objects or events and times. For this purpose, we will use the present tense form, adding a variable in parentheses for the temporal argument place; for example, 'loves(t)' is the tenseless verb in the meta-language corresponding to 'loves' in English.

Treating past and future tenses as indexical quantifiers introduces a second difficulty: namely, the object language lacks explicit markers for temporal variables. Natural language syntax, from the perspective of semantics, is understated. In trying to gain an explicit understanding of how languages work, we inevitably are drawn to paraphrases that yield more explicit syntactic representations of the semantic structures of expressions we study. This is familiar from the study of (other) quantifier phrases in natural languages, whose resources for indicating binding relations show all the marks of having been cobbled together on an as-needed basis. Tense makes this particularly vivid, since, in contrast to the case of more general quantifiers, here even familiar devices of pronominal cross-reference are missing, and binding relations are indicated more subtly.

For present purposes, we will simply specify satisfaction conditions for an extension of English in what we will call *English**. English* includes the usual apparatus for regimenting restricted quantification, as well as tenseless verbs that homophonically translate the tenseless verbs required in the metalanguage to provide tenseless truth conditions. English* also includes a referring term 't^*' with the following reference axiom (stipulated to be interpretive): For any speaker s, time t, $\text{ref}_{[s,\,t]}('t^*') = t$.[7] (While this may seem also to be a natural axiom for 'now', we introduce 't^*' because it is unclear whether they are synonymous (see section 1.4).)

With this as background, leaving implicit the relativization of semantic predicates to English*, we can present satisfaction conditions for (3)–(5) in (6)–(8), respectively.[8]

(6) For any speaker s, time t, function f, f satisfies$_{[s,t]}$ 'Mary loves Bill' iff f satisfies$_{[s,t]}$ 'Mary loves(t^*) Bill'.

(7) For any speaker s, time t, function f, f satisfies$_{[s,t]}$ 'Mary loved Bill' iff f satisfies$_{[s,t]}$ '[There is a time $t_1 : t_1 < t^*$](Mary loves(t_1) Bill)'.

(8) For any speaker s, time t, function f, f satisfies$_{[s,t]}$ 'Mary will love Bill' iff f satisfies$_{[s,t]}$ '[There is a time $t_1 : t_1 > t^*$](Mary loves(t_1) Bill)'.

('$x < y$' and '$x > y$' mean 'x is earlier than y' and 'x is later than y'.) Given the reference clause for 't^*', it is clear that each of (6)–(8) indexes to utterance time. Appropriate reference axioms applied to (6) yield (9), which in turn yields the *T*-sentence (10). Similarly, (8) yields (11).

(9) For any speaker s, time t, function f, f satisfies$_{[s,t]}$ 'Mary loves Bill' iff Mary loves(t) Bill.

(10) For any speaker s, time t, 'Mary loves Bill' is true$_{[s,t]}$ iff Mary loves(t) Bill.

(11) For any speaker s, time t, 'Mary will love Bill' is true$_{[s,t]}$ iff [there is a $t_1 : t_1 > t$](Mary loves(t_1) Bill).

Satisfaction clauses for English tensed and corresponding English* untensed sentences are the same. Since satisfaction conditions for English* sentences present no special difficulty,[9] where appropriate, we will use English* to represent satisfaction conditions of English sentences.

Satisfaction conditions (6)–(8) treat the present tense differently from the past and future tenses. The past and future tenses function as restricted indexical quantifiers, whereas the present tense functions as a simple indexical. We might try to treat the present tense as requiring restricted quantification, as in (12).

(12) [There is a time $t_1 : t_1 = t^*$](Mary loves(t_1) Bill).

But in addition to its being superfluous, considerations about how simple tenses embed in complex expressions provide reasons against the quantification in (12) (see section 1.5).

(7) and (8) reveal that the past and future tenses are, from the perspective of truth-theoretic semantics, restricted indexical existential quantifiers. Existential quantification is required, since utterances in

these tenses reveal only that some event occurred in the past or will occur in the future *at some time or other*. They are *indexical* quantifier expressions because the predicate restrictions on the quantifier in their English* translations contain an indexical.

One important consequence of this treatment is that we can never reexpress in English what we express on a given occasion using a tensed sentence. (This has important consequences for the semantics of indirect discourse and attitude sentences. See section 1.7.) If someone were to assert, 'Mary loves Bill', at *t*, he would express a proposition directly about *t*. To reexpress that same proposition later, it would not do to use the present tense, since any new utterance would be about a *different* time. But using the past tense, even with an adverbial modifier, would still involve direct reference to the time of utterance, which would be later than *t*. Suppose someone were to utter, 'Mary loved Bill at *t*'. Since 'at *t*' determines a time earlier than *the time of utterance* at which Mary is asserted to have loved Bill, the speaker still refers to the utterance time and hence fails to express the original. There is nothing conceptually incoherent about reexpressing a proposition; English* allows us to do so. But this feature of natural languages is surely no accident. Our access to time in thought involves reference to the present time. We step into the river of time only at that point on the bank at which we stand, the perpetual present, and we locate other times fundamentally by reference to that standpoint. Reexpressing the same proposition twice in English* would involve using a directly referring term to pick the time out rigidly. But we would secure the referent of a directly referring term in thought only by describing its relation to the present time.[10]

As we represent tense, the future and past tenses involve quantification. However, unlike explicit quantification, quantification in tense, because it is lexically internal, takes narrow scope with respect to explicit quantifiers.[11] Sentences with explicit quantifiers receive recursive clauses in the truth theory, as in (13) (treating 'everyone' and 'someone' as unrestricted quantifiers for present purposes).

(13)   For any speaker *s*, time *t*, function *f*, *f* satisfies$_{[s,t]}$ 'Everyone(*x*) met someone(*y*)' iff every '*x*'-variant *f′* of *f* satisfies$_{[s,t]}$ '*x* met someone(*y*)'.

In the standard sort of truth theory we are envisaging, both explicit quantifiers in 'Everyone met someone' would be unpacked before the axiom for its verb could be invoked, forcing the quantifier involved in tense always to take narrow scope, as in (14) and (15).

(14)   For any speaker s, time t, function f, f satisfies$_{[s,t]}$ 'Everyone(x) met someone(y)' iff every 'x'-variant f' of f is such that some 'y'-variant f'' of f' satisfies$_{[s,t]}$ 'x met y'.

(15)   For all speakers s, times t, functions f, f satisfies$_{[s,t]}$ 'Everyone(x) met someone(y)' iff every 'x'-variant f' of f is such that some 'y'-variant f'' of f' is such that f'' satisfies$_{[s,t]}$ '[There is a time $t_1 : t_1 < t^*](x$ meets(t_1) $y)$'.[12],[13]

1.3.2   Event Verbs

In contrast to state verbs, event verbs apply to an object at a time only if it is undergoing some change. Neither 'Bill loved Mary' nor 'Bill weighed 145 lbs.' implies that Bill has undergone change; but 'Bill left' implies that Bill underwent a change, minimally, of position. Also, event verbs, in contrast to most state verbs, take a progressive form by concatenating 'is' with the present participle morpheme. Corresponding to 'leave' is 'is leaving'. The same operation on state verbs is generally ill formed; no form 'is knowing' corresponds to 'know'. (This is not uniform, as is shown by 'block', 'stand', and 'occupy'. But these have uses as event verbs as well.)

It is natural to suppose that the simple tenses function uniformly independently of the semantic category of a verb. If so, we should be able to provide a uniform treatment for state and event verbs. While this works smoothly for the past and future tenses of event verbs, it doesn't for the present tense. Compare (16) with (17) and (18).

(16)   Mary loves Bill.

(17)   Mary leaves.

(18)   Mary opens the door.

An utterance of (16) is true if Mary loves Bill at the time of utterance. But it is difficult to find circumstances under which we comfortably assert (17) or (18) unembedded or unmodified (in contrast to, e.g., 'If Mary leaves, I will too' or 'Mary leaves on the 23rd of this month').[14] Even though events typically require more time to complete than utterances of sentences with present-tensed event verbs, this hardly explains the data. (17) is no less odd when said slowly enough for Mary to leave during its utterance. Moreover, many events require no more time than would an assertion that they were occurring (e.g., 'Bill speaks'), but their present tense utterances are no less odd. (We will consider sentences like 'Bill works for a living' in section 1.8. These typically express generality.) We know of no adequate explanation of this aspect of present tense event verbs.

There doesn't seem to be anything conceptually incoherent about a semantics for present tense event verbs that parallels our semantics for present tense state verbs. Moreover, not all natural languages share the awkwardness of present tense event verb sentences with English. This suggests that it is an idiosyncrasy of English and has nothing to do with the fact that these are event verbs per se.

If we are right, present tense event verbs do not index to the time of utterance. Yet from our treatment of past and future tenses, which parallels that for state verbs, it is clear that event verbs express a relation between one or more things and a time. If the implicit argument places for time in present tense event verbs were bound by a quantifier in sentences containing them, there would not be a puzzle about the truth value of their utterances. We suggest, then, that the argument place for time in present tense event verbs is unbound in unembedded and unmodified uses, and that the oddity in uttering (17) and (18) is due to their being open sentences and thereby truth-valueless. If we are right, (17) will receive (19) as its satisfaction clause, where 't'' is a free variable. Satisfaction conditions for past and future tenses for 'leaves', in contrast, are given by (20) and (21).

(19)   For any speaker s, time t, function f, f satisfies$_{[s,t]}$ 'Mary leaves' iff f satisfies$_{[s,t]}$ 'Mary leaves(t')'.

(20)   [There is a $t_1 : t_1 < t^*$](Mary leaves(t_1)).

(21)   [There is a $t_1 : t_1 > t^*$](Mary leaves(t_1)).

(20) and (21) represent past and future tenses with an indexical reference to the time of utterance because of the indexical 't^*' in the restriction on

their quantifiers. The asymmetry in treatments of past and future tenses of event verbs, on the one hand, and present tense, on the other, might be regarded as a defect. But it explains the oddity of utterances of (17) and (18), which an account treating them as parallel to state verbs would fail to do. Whether the proposal is satisfactory depends on how well it integrates into an account of how present tense event verbs interact with temporal adverbials and quantifiers, and on whether a simpler account of the data can be given. While we cannot show that no simpler account is available, we will show in sections 1.4 and 1.5 how to integrate our treatment with one for temporal adverbials and quantifiers.

1.3.3   The Progressive

The progressive is formed by adding '-ing' to (the truncation of) the infinitive of an event verb. The concatenation of 'is' with a gerund has traditionally been treated as a tense. From our perspective, however, classifying the progressive as a tense is a mistake.[15] While 'is leaving' is tensed, since it indexes to time of utterance, its treatment in a truth-theoretic semantics should not distinguish it from the present tense state verbs. The contribution of tense to 'is leaving' (the dimension of variation among 'is leaving', 'was leaving', and 'will be leaving') is represented by the tenseless English* (22).

(22)   Bill is leaving(t^*).

So represented, the present progressive picks out the time of utterance relative to which an implicit argument in the verb is evaluated, just like present tense state verbs. (However, progressives behave like event verbs in their interaction with future-looking or neutral adverbials, like 'noon' or 'on Tuesday'; this appears to be because of the pull of the analogy of form with the future formed from 'to be' + 'going' + the infinitive.)

Treating 'is leaving' as a tense of 'leave' requires exhibiting its satisfaction conditions as derived from those for the untensed verb 'leaves(t)' in English*. This may seem intuitively the right thing to do, since 'is leaving' is clearly related to the infinitive 'to leave'. But this is insufficient to settle whether the connection is conceptual or structural. A virtue of the truth-theoretic approach is that it provides a precise way of distinguishing conceptual from structural connections.

When two verbs are *structurally* related, the same (or a synonymous) metalanguage verb is used in their satisfaction conditions, and the only variation between the satisfaction conditions will be variations in the quantificational apparatus invoked by tense. If the connection is not structural, distinct metalanguage verbs will be used in giving satisfaction conditions.

In light of this, (22) represents appropriate satisfaction conditions for 'is leaving' only if the relation expressed by 'is leaving' ('was leaving', 'will be leaving') is distinct from what is expressed by 'leaves' ('left', 'will leave'). That they are distinct is shown by the fact that someone can be leaving, and not leave, or will be leaving, and never leave. While anyone who leaves the room was leaving, his leaving doesn't require that he left or ever will: he might collapse halfway out the door. He was leaving, even though he never left. The point is even more transparent with other event verbs: someone may be *writing* a book, but never *write* it. These examples help clarify the relation between 'was leaving' and 'left': the former relates an agent to a time interval in which he is *engaged* in an activity that may lead to the kind of event the latter relates an agent to.

If correct, this dissolves the so-called imperfective paradox.[16] This paradox arises on the assumption that the progressive of an accomplishment verb like 'leaves' is a tense. 'Leaves(t)' applies to an object x at a time t only if after t 'x left' applies to it. If 'is leaving' were a tense of 'leave', then 'is leaving' would apply at t to something only if after t 'left' applied to it. This is obviously incorrect. But the pressure to accept the paradoxical result dissipates once we deny that the progressive form of 'is leaving' is a tense of 'leaves'.

Progressives are neither state verbs nor event verbs. They express the occurrence at a time of a portion of a process that, if completed, constitutes an event of the type expressed by the verbs from which they are lexically derived. We shall, following common sense and an earlier tradition, call them *process verbs*.[17]

1.4   Temporal Designators

Temporal designators divide into deictic designators, such as 'now' and 'tonight', and structured designators, such as 'December 7, 1942'.

We begin with 'now' and 'then'. It is natural to treat 'now' as parallel to 'I', and 'then' as parallel to 'that'. Whereas 'I' is used to pick out the speaker of an utterance, 'now' is used to pick out its time. 'That' functions as a demonstrative, and 'then' as a demonstrative restricted to times. A standard reference clause for 'I' is (23); a reference clause modeled on it for 'now' is (24). Likewise, a reference clause for 'that' is (25), and a parallel reference clause for 'then' is (26).

(23)   For any speaker s, time t, $\text{ref}_{[s,t]}(\text{'I'}) = s$.

(24)   For any speaker s, time t, $\text{ref}_{[s,t]}(\text{'now'}) = t$.

(25)   For any speaker s, time t, item x, if s demonstrates x at t with 'that', $\text{ref}_{[s,t]}(\text{'that'}) = x$.[18]

(26)   For any speaker s, times t, t_1, if s demonstrates t_1 at t with 'then', $\text{ref}_{[s,t]}(\text{'then'}) = t_1$.[19]

(25) and (26) assign a referent only if a speaker demonstrates something using the demonstrative expression. This is because even relative to a speaker and a time, a demonstrative sentence has a truth value only if the speaker performs an act of demonstration. In this way, demonstratives differ from indexicals, whose referents are completely determined by contextual parameters.

Treating 'now' as indexing the time of utterance is standard, but inadequate for many of its uses—for example, in issuing commands like 'Do it now, not later', or in sentences like 'Now I have a lot more time to do what I am interested in'. Speakers using such sentences would not intend to be interpreted as referring only to the time of their utterances. Someone who says, 'Do it now, not later', would not be thought to have commanded the impossible. We *may* be able to treat these uses as creating conversational implicatures, but they are so routine that we are inclined to suggest that 'now' has a demonstrative as well as an indexical element. While a use of 'now' refers to a time that includes the utterance time, it can also refer to time extending beyond, and perhaps before, it. To accommodate these uses, we can modify (24) as in (27).

(27)   For any speaker s, times t, t_1, if t_1 is the interval including t referred to by s at t using 'now', $\text{ref}_{[s,t]}(\text{'now'}) = t_1$.

(This could be modified to require that the referent be the utterance time where the speaker lacks appropriate referential intentions.) Natural languages provide an array of descriptive indexical devices for referring to times or time intervals related specifically to the present—for example, in English, 'today', 'tomorrow', 'tonight', 'yesterday', 'last year', 'next year'. A general treatment for descriptive indexical devices is illustrated in (28) and (29).

(28)   For any speaker s, times t, t_1, such that $t_1 =$ the night of t,
       $\mathrm{ref}_{[s,t]}$('tonight') $= t_1$.

(29)   For any speaker s, times t, t_1, such that $t_1 =$ the day before t,
       $\mathrm{ref}_{[s,t]}$('yesterday') $= t_1$.

Temporal indexicals directly refer.[20] In T-sentences derived from axioms like (28) and (29), the descriptive material does not contribute to truth conditions. The T-sentence for 'Tonight is the night', instantiated to speaker s' and time t', where $t'' =$ the night of t', would be (30).

(30)   'Tonight is the night' is true$_{[s',t']}$ iff t'' is the night.

Treating descriptive indexicals as directly referring terms is required because coreferring descriptive indexicals can be interchanged *salva veritate*. We can report your assertion *yesterday* of 'Today is Sunday' by saying *today* that you said that yesterday was Sunday (note the shift in tense: we will discuss tense sequencing in complement clauses in section 1.10).[21]

We might try to treat structured temporal designators such as 'January 1, 2001' either as semantically equivalent to definite descriptions (e.g., 'the first day of January of the 2,000th year after φ', where 'φ' is replaced by a term that picks out an anchor year for the date system—(1 A.D. for the Gregorian calendar) or as having their referents merely fixed by a definite description. We opt for the latter approach. The first approach fails in modal contexts if we substitute for 'φ' a description of an anchor year, such as 'the year of the birth of Christ' (or, more accurately, 'the year thought to be the year of Christ's birth by Dionysius Exiguus', four or five years after the birth of the historical Christ; we will use the shorter description for convenience).[22] Intuitively, 'Necessarily, the year of the birth of Christ was 2,000 years before January 1, 2001' is false. Christ could have been born earlier or later than he was (or Dionysius could have thought him to be born earlier or later). But if 'January 1, 2001' were equivalent to 'the first day of January 2,000 years after the year of the birth of Christ', it would be true, at least on the narrow scope reading. But there is no true reading of the original. To avoid this objection, we could introduce rigidified definite descriptions such as 'the year of the actual birth of Christ', but speakers' competence with the use of date terms does not seem to be contingent on knowing any particular description of the anchor time. We will settle then for a reference clause for date formats, as in (31), using 'Annus Domini' as a *proper name* referring to the year Dionysius Exiguus thought to be the year of Christ's birth.

(31)   For any speaker s, time t, numerals n_1, n_2, month term M, if
$t = $ day $\mathrm{ref}_{[s,t]}(n_1)$ of the month of the year $\mathrm{ref}_{[s,t]}(n_2) - 1$ years
after Annus Domini that satisfies M, then $\mathrm{ref}_{[s,t]}(\ulcorner n_1 \, M \, n_2 \urcorner) = t$.

We follow King (2001) here in treating month terms as predicates of time intervals.[23] 'This month is January' uttered in January 2001 is not, for instance, elliptical for 'This month is January 2001', since one could know what the former is used to express without knowing what the latter is used to express, and thus the 'is' here is the copula. This seems also required for the natural semantic treatment of quantifiers using month terms as nominals, such as 'Every January it is cold' and 'Some Aprils are windy, but not all', which would be represented as '[Every time $t : t$ is January](it is(t) is cold)' and '[Some times $t : t$ is April](t is windy) & ~[All times $t : t$ is April](t is windy)'. Similar remarks apply to day terms: 'Monday', 'Tuesday', and so on. These terms express properties of time intervals they have in virtue of being intervals individuated in a certain way and lying in a certain order in a calendar system.[24]

1.5   Temporal Adverbs and Adverbials

In this section, we discuss relational temporal adverbials such as 'at midnight', 'before noon', 'two days hence', 'yesterday', 'tonight', 'between 2 and 3 p.m.'.[25] Temporal adverbials may be forward looking ('tomorrow', 'next week'), backward looking ('yesterday', 'a month ago', 'last week'), about the present ('now', 'at this moment', 'currently'), or neutral ('on Tuesday', 'in May'). We will call these *future*, *past*, *present*, and *unanchored* adverbials, respectively.[26] A verb's tense restricts what modifiers it can take. The simple past may take past adverbials or unanchored adverbials, but neither present nor future adverbials. 'John slept last week' and 'John slept through May' are fine, but 'John slept right now' and 'John slept in three days' are not. The future tense may be modified by unanchored, present, or future adverbials, but not past adverbials. 'John will sleep on Tuesday', 'John will sleep now', and 'John will sleep tomorrow' are all acceptable, but 'John will sleep last week' is not. An event verb in present tense may be modified by unanchored or future adverbials, as in 'John leaves on Tuesday' and 'John leaves next week', and perhaps by present adverbials, as in 'John leaves now', but it will not accept a past adverbial, as in 'John leaves yesterday'. In contrast, present tense state verbs take only present adverbials. 'I am tired right now' is acceptable, but 'I am tired next week' and 'I am tired last year' are not.

We begin with adverbial modification of sentences in the simple past. We propose a uniform treatment of relational adverbials that will secure entailment relations like those in (32).

(32)   Bill loved Mary yesterday.
        Therefore, Bill loved Mary sometime.
        Therefore, Bill loved Mary.

We are already committed to quantifying over times because of our treatment of simple tenses. 'Bill loved Mary' is equivalent to '[There is a time $t_1 : t_1 < t^*$](Bill loves(t_1) Mary)'. Modifying 'Bill loved Mary' with the adverb 'yesterday' has the effect of specifying the time interval in the past relative to the present when Bill loved Mary—that is, specifying that it is identical with or included in yesterday. This recommends assigning 'Bill loved Mary yesterday' satisfaction conditions equivalent to (33), where '$\subseteq$' is read as 'is included in or identical with'.

(33)   [There is a $t_1 : t_1 < t^*$ & $t_1 \subseteq$ yesterday](Bill loves(t_1) Mary).

We include the adjunct in the restriction on the quantifier because the adverb is intuitively modifying the element contributed by the tense.

Adverbial phrases formed by combining a preposition with a temporal designator receive similar treatment. What varies is the temporal property expressed by the prepositional phrase. 'Bill loved Mary for two hours' is equivalent to '[There is a $t_1 : t_1 < t^*$ & the duration of t_1 is two hours](Bill loves Mary(t_1))'. 'Bill loved Mary before midnight' is equivalent to '[There is a $t_1 : t_1 < t^*$ & t_1 is before midnight](Bill loves(t_1) Mary)'. 'Bill loved Mary in June' is equivalent to '[There is a $t_1 : t_1 < t^*$ & t_1 is in some June/the first June before t^*](Bill loves(t_1) Mary)'. The satisfaction conditions in (33) underwrite the entailments in (32). Our treatment correctly predicts restrictions on modifiers of verbs in the past tense. Future or present adverbials will require the time of an event to be in the future or the present, but the tense of the verb requires it to be in the past. Unanchored adverbials are treated as existentially quantified or implicitly deictic, where neither requires the times of which they are predicated to be in the future, past, or present vis-à-vis the time of utterance.

The future tense receives a parallel treatment (with '$>$' substituted for '$<$'). However, we must say something about the use of 'now' with a future tense verb; to avoid incoherence, this should be understood as sentential and not adverbial modification. 'John will sleep now' should be read as 'It is now the case that John will sleep'. Our discussion of tense in complement clauses will cover this case. For present tense state verbs, satisfaction conditions are illustrated for 'Bill loves Mary now' in (34).

(34)   Bill loves(t^*) Mary & $t^* \subseteq$ now.

Our treatment of past and future tense event verbs exactly parallels that of present and past tense state verbs, but the situation is more complex with present tense event verbs, such as 'leaves' or 'speaks'. One can modify a state verb with a present adverbial, but not with future, past, or unanchored adverbials. In contrast, while present tense event verbs, like present tense state verbs, cannot be modified by past adverbials, they can be modified by future adverbials, and, arguably, present adverbials, though unlike with state verbs it is awkward to do so. (35) is unexceptional, (36) unacceptable, while (37) is awkward.

(35)   John leaves tomorrow.

(36)   John leaves yesterday.

(37)   John leaves now.

We suspect that anyone who finds (37) acceptable is imagining it as a reply to 'When does John leave?', where the reply is expected to indicate a future time, while in fact John's departure is scheduled for the present.

If 'John leaves' is an open sentence, adding a modifier binds the free argument place for time. If (36) and (37) are semantically unacceptable, the quantifier is restricted to future times; if (36) alone is unacceptable, the restriction is to times contemporaneous with the utterance or later. We tentatively assume (37) is semantically acceptable. 'John leaves tomorrow' then receives the following satisfaction conditions:

(38)   [There is a $t_1 : t_1 \geq t^*$ & $t_1 \subseteq$ tomorrow](John leaves(t_1)).

The restriction to present or future times explains the restriction on which adverbials can modify a present tense verb. Present tense verbs modified by unanchored adverbials, such as 'on Tuesday', are likewise interpreted as future looking.

This account treats nonquantificational temporal adverbials as predicates of an implicitly quantified temporal variable. Unacceptable combinations of tense and adverbials are due not to a structural or logical defect, but to semantic incompatibility. Even for unacceptable forms, there is no difficulty in identifying their logical form. What renders them unacceptable is a conflict between the requirement imposed on the event time by tense and what the meaning of the adverbial requires. (Our treatment of temporal adverbials is reminiscent of Davidson's (1980) treatment of event adverbials. However, Davidson treats temporal adverbials as predicates of events as well. In section 1.9, we will argue that this is mistaken.)

1.6 'Before' and 'After'

'Before' and 'after' can function as sentential connectives (as in 'Brutus hailed Caesar before he killed him'), as components in relational predicates flanked by event or temporal designators when concatenated with the copula (as in 'Midnight is before noon'), and as adverbials (as in 'before tomorrow', 'before Mary'). An adequate semantic account of 'before' and 'after' should exhibit them playing the same semantic role in each of these constructions. A simple unified account is suggested by our approach. A sentence such as 'Brutus hailed Caesar before he killed him' will be represented as involving two existential quantifiers over past times relative to the present. 'Before' naturally modifies the verb in the clause preceding it by relating its time to that of the verb used in the clause following it. So 'before' is a relational predicate of times. Satisfaction conditions for 'Brutus hailed Caesar before he killed him' would then be represented as in (39).

(39)   [There is a time $t_1 : t_1 < t^*$][there is a time $t_2 : t_2 < t^*$ & t_1 is before t_2](Brutus hails(t_1) Caesar and Brutus kills(t_2) Caesar).

This suggestion extends to 'after' and other temporal relational terms, such as 'at the same time as' (or simply 'as'), 'until' ('before but not after'), and their modifications, such as 'a few minutes before'. ('Since', which is used with the perfect tenses, is more complicated, but the same idea applies; see the appendix for discussion.) Some relational terms are themselves complex. But there appears to be a uniform contribution of the modifiers of simple relational terms. 'x is M before y' can be unpacked as 'x is before y and INT$(x, y) = M$', where 'INT(x, y)' means 'the interval between x and y'. This licenses general satisfaction conditions for sentences of the form $\ulcorner \varphi\, M\, R\, \psi \urcorner$, where '$R$' is replaced by a simple temporal relational predicate and 'M' by its modifier. This treatment explains why 'before' and 'after' are not truth-functional connectives, for the underlying logical form exhibits 'before' and 'after' as contributing temporal relational predicates.

Occurrences of 'before' and 'after' in adverbials function to relate times as indicated in the previous section. Satisfaction conditions for (40) are given in (41).

(40)   John will leave before tomorrow.

(41)   [There is a $t_1 : t_1 > t^*$ & t_1 is before tomorrow](John leaves(t_1)).

Sentences of the form $\ulcorner \varphi$ before $\alpha \urcorner$, where φ is a sentence and α a noun phrase but not a temporal designator, will be treated as having the underlying form $\ulcorner \varphi$ before $\psi \urcorner$, where φ and ψ are sentences. If α is a predicate nominalization, such as 'being fined', then $\psi = \alpha \,^\frown \text{UNOM}(\alpha, T)$, where UNOM$(x, y)$ yields a predicate of which x is a nominalization with the tense marker y, where y will be the tense of the main verb. UNOM('being fined', future) = 'will be fined', while UNOM('being fined', past) = 'was fined'. If α is a singular term or quantified noun phrase, $\psi = \alpha \,^\frown \text{PRED}(\varphi)$, where PRED$(x)$ is the predicate of x. PRED('John will leave') = 'will leave'. 'John will leave before Mary' has the satisfaction conditions represented in (42).

(42)   [There is a time $t_1 : t_1 < t$][there is a time $t_2 : t_2 < t$ & t_1 is before t_2](John leaves(t_1) and Mary leaves(t_2)).

1.7   Temporal Quantifiers

Natural languages provide a large variety of temporal quantifiers. In English, these include, for example, (1) unrestricted temporal quantifiers such as 'always', 'anytime', 'sometimes', 'once', 'twice'; (2) restricted-interval temporal quantifiers, such as 'someday', 'every day', 'daily', 'weekly', 'monthly', 'yearly', 'two times a day', 'twice a week'; (3) non-specific frequency quantifiers, such as 'seldom', 'often', 'infrequently', 'frequently', 'regularly', and 'intermittently', which do not specify a particular interval, and some of which exhibit topic dependence; and (4) unrestricted temporal quantifiers such as 'when' and 'whenever', which, though adverbs, introduce subordinate clauses and function syntactically as sentential connectives. All of these quantify over times, binding unarticulated argument places in one or more verbs.[27] We treat these four classes in order. This is intended to be an illustrative, rather than exhaustive, treatment of temporal quantifiers in English.

1. The past and future tenses interact with temporal quantifiers differently than the present. We begin with present tense. (43) (typical uses of which would be hyperbole) means roughly that John's hair is a mess at all times, and it can clearly be used on different occasions to express the same proposition.

(43)   John's hair is always a mess.

Although (43) is in the present tense, when modified by a temporal quantifier, it does not function as an indexical. In representing its truth conditions, then, we should treat the unarticulated argument place as bound by the temporal quantifier, rather than as functioning indexically. This leads to (44) (mutatis mutandis for other unrestricted temporal quantifiers).

(44)   [For all times t_1](John's hair is(t_1) a mess).

In contrast, utterances of (45) at different times express different propositions.

(45)   John's hair was always a mess.

An utterance of (45) yesterday would be true if and only if at every time before it John's hair was a mess, but its utterance today would require also that in the intervening time his hair remain unkempt. Similarly for the future tense. Thus, whereas by modifying a present tense verb we can transform a context-sensitive sentence into a context-independent one (other deictic terms aside), past and future tense verbs remain deictic when so modified. This is one reason not to treat the present tense as involving quantification like the past and future, for it would mean treating it as combining with quantificational adverbials differently from the past and future, although they would share underlying structure. The effect of the modification is to replace the default existential quantification over past times with quantification appropriate for the modifier. Satisfaction conditions of (45) then would be represented as in (46).

(46) [For all times $t_1 : t_1 < t^*$](John's hair is(t_1) a mess).

2. Adverbs such as 'someday', 'every day', 'daily', 'weekly', 'monthly', and 'yearly' quantify over specific intervals and indicate that the event expressed by the verb they modify occurs in, as appropriate, some or every (etc.) interval of the appropriate kind. Thus, they supply two quantifiers over time intervals. The first is restricted to quantification over time intervals of a type indicated by the noun from which the quantifier is formed. The quantifier is existential in the first example above and universal in the other examples (indicated by the 'ly' in the last four). The second quantifier is an existential quantifier that binds the argument place for event time in the modified verb, which is restricted to fall within the interval picked out by the first quantifier. Thus, we represent (47) as (48).

(47) John goes to the barber monthly.

(48) [For all months m][there is a time $t : t \subseteq m$](John goes(t) to the barber).

We extend this to the past and future tense as indicated in the shift from (45) to (46); that is, the months would be restricted to times in the past, or future, of the utterance. This treatment extends to complex restricted-interval temporal quantifiers as well, as in 'Most years he vacations in France'; that is, this means that there is a time interval contained in most years during which he vacations in France. A complex restricted-interval quantifier like 'twice a week' introduces two quantifiers. If John washes his car twice a week, then each week there are two times at which John washes his car. Thus, we would represent 'John washes his car twice a week' as in (49).

(49)   [For all weeks w][there are two times t: $t \subseteq m$](John washes(t) his car).

3. Nonspecific frequency adverbials such as 'regularly', 'intermittently', 'frequently', 'often', 'seldom', and 'infrequently' intuitively indicate that the event expressed by the modified verb recurs at intervals of time. In the case of 'regularly', this seems simply to involve intervals of at least roughly the same length. The core meaning of 'intermittently' is not *continuously*, with the implication often of irregularity, though to say something is intermittent but regular is not a contradiction. These adverbs can be treated like 'sometimes' and 'always', namely, as introducing a simple quantifier: 'John woke up intermittently/regularly last night' can be represented as '[There are intermittent/regular times t: $t < t^*$ and $t \subseteq$ the night before t^*](John wakes up(t))'.

For our other examples, the length of the interval is understood relative to the modified verb.[28] For example, someone may fly frequently (twice a week) and comb his hair frequently (every five minutes), though if he combed his hair only as often as he flies, he would not be said to comb his hair frequently. This topic relativity appears to attach to those frequency adverbials from which one can form a comparative, 'more frequent/often than' or 'less seldom/infrequent than'. Thus, suggestively, these frequency adverbials exhibit a kind of topic relativity similar to that of adjectives or nontemporal adverbs formed from comparatives, such as 'large' or 'tall'. A large mouse is not a large animal, but rather *larger than most mice*. Here we can represent the adjective as contributing a conjunct in the representation of the truth conditions that involves quantification over most members of a comparison class. 'Mickey is a large mouse' may be represented as 'Mickey is a mouse and Mickey is larger than most mice' (see Lepore and Ludwig 2001, sec. V). This suggests treating topic-dependent frequency adverbials as involving a comparison of the intervals at which an event recurs to intervals in some appropriate comparison class indicated by the modified verb. In our sample case, 'John combs his hair frequently', we want to compare the frequency with which John combs his hair with that for most hair combers. (It may be that some subset of all the hair combers is typically intended, though since this seems to be something that can shift in context independently of any features of the sentence, it is natural to think that this is the effect of pragmatic factors on interpretation of speaker's meaning.) Since it follows from John's combing his hair frequently that there are times at which he combs his hair (or that John combs his hair; see the next section for discussion of habituals), we want this to be reflected in the representation as well. Thus, we suggest representing 'John combs his hair frequently' roughly as 'There are times at which John combs his hair and his hair combings are more frequent than those for most of those who comb their hair'. More formally, where we make use of plural definite descriptions and plural temporal variables, this sentence is represented as follows:

(50)   [There are times t](John combs(t) his hair) & [the times t: t are
        times of John's hair combings][most x : x are hair combers][the
        times t' : t' are of x's hair combings](t are more frequent than t').

We use 'most' because its vagueness matches that of 'frequently'. 'Seldom' and 'infrequently' are handled in a similar manner. One does *F* seldom/infrequently if one does it but less frequently than most do.

   4. The adverbs 'when' and 'whenever' are syntactically sentential connectives, but should likewise be treated semantically as quantificational. In (51), 'when' and 'whenever' are interchangeable.

(51)   John blushes whenever/when Mary looks at him.

For this reason, we will treat 'when' in such contexts as abbreviating 'whenever'. They are not interchangeable in (52), which requires a separate treatment.

(52)   I did it when he wasn't looking.

The difference is that between a universal and an existential quantifier. (51) is true if and only if at *any* time Mary looks at John, John blushes; that is, (51) is roughly equivalent to a universally quantified conditional with 'whenever' functioning as a quantifier with wide scope binding the unarticulated argument place for time in both verbs. Employing restricted quantifiers, we need not represent (51) counterintuitively as containing sentential connectives, but instead may represent its satisfaction conditions as in (53); treating 'when' as a restricted existential quantifier in (52) yields (54).

(53)   [For all times t_1: Mary looks(t_1) at John](John blushes(t_1)).

(54)   [There is a time $t_1 : t_1 < t^*$ & he is(t_1) not looking](I do(t_1) it).

As above, the past and future tenses remain deictic, though the present of state verbs does not. (It may seem natural to treat 'when' in some contexts as a definite description, as in 'He was electrocuted when he used his hair dryer in the shower', but this is only because we know some things have happened only once. Interpreting 'when' as a definite description cannot be correct, since, for example, 'Caesar defied the Roman senate when he crossed the Rubicon' is obviously consistent with 'Caesar crossed the Rubicon many times'.)

Notice that sentences with mixed simple tenses grammatically conjoined by 'when' or 'whenever', such as 'John blushes whenever Mary looked at him' or 'John blushed when Mary will look at him', have no intelligible interpretation. This is what we would expect if (53) and (54) are correct, since a single quantifier must bind the argument place for time in each verb, which renders restrictions signaled by different tenses unsatisfiable.

1.8   Habitual Sentences and Frequency Adverbials

So-called habitual sentences are about events that occur at (more or less) regular intervals. Many habitual sentences are simply sentences whose event verbs are modified by a restricted interval or frequency adverbial, as in examples (55)–(57).

(55)   Mary often smokes in her office.

(56)   Bill complains frequently.

(57)   Mary lectures three times a week.

If our discussion in the previous section is correct, then the classification of (55)–(57) as habituals just comes to their being sentences with restricted interval or frequency adverbials, which can be treated straightforwardly as contributing temporal quantifiers and, in the case of the topic-dependent adverbs in (55) and (56), a comparative and a quantification over a comparison class. If the proposals of the previous section are correct, it is easy to see why these are called 'habituals', since their truth would typically be grounded in a habit of smoking in the office, or complaining, or lecturing.

However, not all sentences with habitual interpretations contain explicit frequency adverbials modifying the main verb. (58) and (59), for example, are classified as habituals.

(58)   John works for a living.

(59)   Rover barks.

In these cases, though, it is natural to say that we understand speakers to be intending that we read in a contextually appropriate frequency adverbial, more or less specific, perhaps, depending on context. With (58), the adverbial 'for a living' together with the present tense event verb tells us that it is to be understood as quantified. A living cannot be earned from a single event of working, wages being what they are, and the present tense of an event verb typically has no use unless modified by a temporal adverbial. Thus, (58) would usually be interpreted roughly as (60).

(60)   John works *regularly* for a living.

The use of present tense in (59) likewise requires a modifier, and since it is not future or past directed, it is naturally taken to be a frequency adverb of some sort ('often' or 'frequently') or perhaps a vague cardinality quantifier ('a lot [of times]' or 'from time to time') (the speaker could not be intending to convey that Rover barks all the time). Thus, (59) might be interpreted roughly (again, though, depending on context) as (61).

(61)   Rover *often* barks.

These would receive satisfaction conditions appropriate for the implicitly understood adverbials on the model proposed above. (In practice, what adverbial is intended will be no more precise than the context requires.)

Although (58) and (59) employ present tense verbs, it is clear that their future and past analogues may be interpreted habitually as well: in these cases, however, there is an alternative reading of the sentences as existentially quantified, compatible with their modifiers. Discussing Rover's laryngitis, you may remark, 'Don't worry, Rover will bark again'. This would receive the habitual reading. However, if *A*, after remarking to *B* that Rover always barks three times before going to sleep, continues, 'I've counted only two barks so far. Rover will bark again', the same sentence does not receive a habitual reading. Sometimes an adverbial will force a habitual reading, since it is incompatible with the existential reading, given what we know about how things work. This is so for 'will work for a living' and 'worked for a living'. Both would receive the habitual reading, because making a living by working requires, for most, regular application.[29]

Thus, habituals do not need a special semantics, and they do not involve a special tense or aspect.

1.9   Relation to the Event Analysis

In this section, we consider how our account interacts with the Davidsonian event analysis of adverbial modification. The event analysis assigns (62) the satisfaction conditions in (63).

(62)   John walked up the hill at midnight in his dressing gown.

(63)   For any function f, speaker s, time t, f satisfies$_{[s,t]}$ 'John walked up the hill at midnight in his dressing gown' iff there is an '*e*'-variant f' of f such that f' satisfies$_{[s,t]}$ '*e* is a walking by John and *e* is a going up the hill and *e* occurs at midnight and *e* occurs with John in his dressing gown'.

On the Davidsonian account, the temporal adjunct is a predicate of an event, not a time.

(63) does not really avoid treating adjuncts as introducing a predicate of times, because '*e* is a walking by John and *e* is a going up the hill and *e* occurs at midnight and *e* occurs with John in his dressing gown' is tensed, so its satisfaction conditions must be unpacked by tenseless verbs in the metalanguage. (One might insist that these predicates are tenseless, but then they cannot be in English; in any case, reference must be secured to the time of utterance (or its equivalent) to accommodate the sensitivity of tense to time of utterance. See note 30 for further discussion.) Once we do this, we see that 'at midnight' introduces a predicate of times, as in (64).

(64) For any function f, speaker s, time t, f satisfies$_{[s,t]}$ 'John walked up the hill at midnight in his dressing gown' iff there is an 'e'-variant f' of f such that f' satisfies$_{[s,t]}$ '[There is a $t_1 : t_1 < t^*$](e is(t_1) a walking by John) and [there is a $t_1 : t_1 < t^*$](e is(t_1) a going up the hill) and [there is a $t_1 : t_1 < t^*$ & $t_1 =$ midnight](e occurs(t_1)) and [there is a $t_1 : t_1 < t^*$](e occurs(t_1) with John in his dressing gown)'.

(64), however, is inadequate, because it does not require each conjunct to be made true by the same time. For any event in which more than one agent could participate at different times, such as building a house, satisfaction conditions modeled on (64) would be incorrect. We need a single quantifier over temporal argument places for every modifier introduced by an adverbial phrase. So we should treat the main verb as introducing an existential quantifier over times that binds the temporal variable in the main verb and in any other verb introduced by its adverbials. This has an unexpected benefit. Because two quantifiers bind the adjuncts to the main verb (represented as having three places), it becomes possible to treat some adjuncts as modifiers of the agent of the act and not the event he performs. Thus, the awkwardness of treating an adverbial such as 'in his dressing gown' as a modifier of an event can be dispensed with. The result is illustrated in (65).

(65) For any speaker s, time t, function f, f satisfies$_{[s,t]}$ 'John walked up the hill at midnight in his dressing gown' iff there is an 'e'-variant f' of f such that f' satisfies$_{[s,t]}$ '[There is a $t_1 : t_1 < t^*$ & $t_1 =$ midnight](walks(John, e, t_1) & e is(t_1) a going up the hill & John is(t_1) in his dressing gown)'.

Similarly, we are now able to treat what are intuitively adverbials of place (e.g., 'on a mountain top') or of condition (e.g., 'in top form') as modifying objects rather than events (or states). This pleasing result is available only if we treat tense as introducing a quantifier binding argument places in each adjunct introduced by an adverbial.[30]

1.10 Thought and Tense

Sentences used to describe particulars are indexed to the time of their utterance, and the contents of thoughts expressed using them are determined by what they express. Consequently, thoughts about particulars are invariably thoughts directly about the times of the thoughts themselves. Since sentences speakers use to express thoughts express them only once, when speakers want to attribute thoughts or speech acts to others or to themselves at times other than the time of attribution, which sentences they use to articulate their contents must be indexed to the time of the reported thought or speech act. In this section, we consider how this is reflected in the interpretation of tense in complement clauses of indirect discourse and attitude sentences.

We will approach the topic of tense in attitude sentences and indirect discourse as a design problem for constructing reports of attitudes and speech acts, given a straightforward semantics for unembedded tensed sentences. Consider John's potential assertions at t_0 of (66a–c), and their corresponding representations in English* interpreted relative to t_0 in (67a–c).

(66)   a.   Mary was tired.
       b.   Mary is tired.
       c.   Mary will be tired.

(67)   a.   [There is a $t_1 < t_0$](Mary is at t_1 tired).
       b.   Mary is at t_0 tired.
       c.   [There is a $t_1 > t_0$](Mary is at t_1 tired).

We may report John's assertion (or the belief he thereby expresses) either before or after it occurs, or even simultaneous with it. Our temporal position with respect to John's utterance determines the tense of the main verb in our report; the tense of the complement clause, however, must be sensitive to the tense John used to express his belief. Let us consider first a report of what John said from the perspective of a time later than his assertion. The main verb will be in the past tense, but how do we report, given available resources, the content of John's assertion?

Deictic elements in complement clauses are usually interpreted relative to the speaker's context. Thus, although in direct speech we would report that John said, 'I am tired', in indirect discourse we would report the same act by 'John said that *he was* tired'. However, unlike demonstrative pronouns and indexicals, such as 'I' and 'now', which are always interpreted relative to speaker context, just as they are when not embedded in a complement clause, tense is more complex. In reporting an assertion by John of any of (66a–c) at t_0 from the perspective of a later time, it would be inappropriate to interpret a tense in the complement clause relative to speaker context, for that would attribute to the subject an assertion about the speaker's time and not his own. Thus, the tense in the complement clause must have its reference time (the time with respect to which the tense of the complement clause verb indicates the time of the occurrence of the event it expresses) fixed by the tense of the main verb; that is, the argument place that functions indexically when the sentence is unembedded must be bound by the quantifier introduced by the main verb when embedded in an indirect discourse. Then the verb in the complement clause must indicate that the event expressed occurred before, at, or after the time of the reported utterance.

From a design standpoint, it would be simplest to reuse in the complement the tense used by the subject. If the argument place that usually functions indexically were bound by the quantifier the main verb introduces, this would capture the relative present, past, or future directedness of the content of the original assertion. However, while some languages work like this (e.g., Russian, and, though without verb inflection, Chinese and Japanese[31]), English does not: in indirect speech, if the main verb is in the past, the tense of the complement clause *must* shift to the past perfect, past, or past future, respectively, according to whether the tense of the main verb in the reported utterance is past, present, or future.[32] This tense-sequencing rule[33] is illustrated in table 1.1. These reported utterances would be interpreted respectively as (68)–(70).[34]

(68)   [There is a $t_1 < t^*$](John says(t_1) that [there is a $t_2 < t_1$](Mary is(t_2) tired)).

(69)   [There is a $t_1 < t^*$](John says(t_1) that Mary is(t_1) tired).

Table 1.1

Sentence uttered by John	Tense shift in complement clause with past tense main verb
Mary was tired.	John said that Mary had been tired.
Mary is tired.	John said that Mary was tired.
Mary will be tired.	John said that Mary would be tired.

(70)   [There is a $t_1 < t^*$](John says(t_1) that [there is a $t_2 > t_1$](Mary is(t_2) tired)).

The tense of the main verb controls the temporal argument place of the verb in the complement clause, which functions indexically when unembedded. For in order to articulate what John said using (66a), we must represent him as saying at some past time that at some prior time Mary was then tired; this is represented by (68). This has been identified traditionally as the function of the past perfect, namely, to pick out a time prior to some past time indicated by a verb in the sentence. Were the verb in the complement clause to be interpreted relative to the speaker's time, the report would be false of John, since he said nothing about the time of the speaker's utterance. Likewise, to capture what John said using (66b), we must say that there is some time such that John said at that time that Mary was then tired, which is what (69) expresses. To report that in the past John said that in the future relative to the time of his utterance Mary would be tired, the reference time of the embedded verb must be fixed by the time of John's utterance, as shown in (70).[35] If we are right, most indirect discourse and attitude sentences quantify into the complement clause.

The tense-sequencing phenomenon occurs only with the main verb in the past. So reports of John's future speech act use the tense John would use, as in table 1.2. Their interpretations would then be represented as in (71)–(73).

(71)   [There is a $t_1 > t^*$](John says(t_1) that [there is a $t_2 < t_1$](Mary is(t_2) tired)).

(72)   [There is a $t_1 > t^*$](John says(t_1) that Mary is(t_1) tired).

(73)   [There is a $t_1 > t^*$](John says(t_1) that [there is a $t_2 > t_1$](Mary is(t_2) tired)).

Table 1.2

The sentence that will be used by John	Complement clause tense with future tense main verb
Mary was tired.	John will say that Mary was tired.
Mary is tired.	John will say that Mary is tired.
Mary will be tired.	John will say that Mary will be tired.

The tense of the main verb, again, controls the temporal argument places of the verb(s) in the complement clause, which, when unembedded, index to the time of utterance.[36]

Reports of present sayings use the same tense as used by the person whose speech act is being reported, but use the present progressive for the main verb, as illustrated in table 1.3. Here the main verb does not express quantification over times; hence, in complement clauses verbs are simply interpreted relative to the utterance time, which gives correctly the content of John's assertions if he uses those or synonymous sentences. The interpretations are given in (74)–(76).

(74)   John is saying(t^*) that [there is a $t_1 < t^*$](Mary is(t_1) tired).

(75)   John is saying(t^*) that Mary is(t^*) tired.

(76)   John is saying(t^*) that [there is a $t_1 > t^*$](Mary is(t_1) tired).

This provides further support for rejecting the treatment of the present tense in (12).

So far as we can see, there is no deep reason why English must employ a tense-sequencing rule for indirect discourse and attitude sentences when the main verb is in the past tense. Not all natural languages do. Furthermore, the tense-sequencing rule appears to prevent unambiguous reports of certain past speech acts. If a speaker uses a sentence in the past perfect (e.g., 'Mary had been tired') or in the present perfect (e.g., 'Mary has been tired'), no tense can be used unambiguously to report him indirectly, since the past perfect has already been allocated to reporting utterances of sentences in the simple past. In English, the past perfect is used to report speech in the past perfect and the present perfect as well as the simple past, and speakers rely on context for disambiguation. This limitation can be gotten around to some extent by employing adverbial

Table 1.3

Sentence used by John	Complement clause tense with present tense main verb
Mary was tired.	John is saying that Mary was tired.
Mary is tired.	John is saying that Mary is tired.
Mary will be tired.	John is saying that Mary will be tired.

modifiers. We can say, 'John said then that Mary had been tired before some previous time'. This fails to assign content correctly, even if the quantifiers take wide scope, since the modifier is still represented as a conjunct. But such peculiarities of English cannot be philosophically significant, since languages can plainly be designed so as to avoid them.

A brief remark on adverbial modifiers in complement clauses is in order. We take indirect discourse again as our model. By and large, we use the same modifiers as those in the reported utterance. John's assertion of 'Mary left before Jim' would be reported as 'John said that Mary had left before Jim'. This would be represented as '[There is a time $t_1 : t_1 < t^*$](John says(t_1) that [there is a $t_2 : t_2 < t_1$][there is a $t_3 : t_3 < t_1$ & $t_2 < t_3$](Mary leaves(t_2) and Jim leaves(t_3))'. Adverbials that contain deictic referring terms such as 'now' and 'today', however, are evaluated relative to the time of utterance, which forces a shift from the adverbial originally used. Thus, if John said yesterday, 'Mary will leave before the day after tomorrow', he would be reported indirectly today as in (77), which is interpreted as in (78).

(77)   John said that Mary would leave before tomorrow.

(78)   [There is a time $t_1 < t^*$](John says(t_1) that [there is a $t_2 > t_1$ & $t_2 <$ the day after t^*](Mary leaves(t_2)).

Unanchored adverbials, which seem to function deictically when unembedded, such as 'at midnight' and 'by noon', are an exception. In (78), the referent of 'midnight' is determined relative to the time of John's saying, not the time of utterance. Similarly for other expressions that pick out times relative to a day or other standard unit. (79) would be interpreted as in (80).

(79)   John said that Mary had left before midnight.

(80)   [There is a time $t_1 < t^*$](John says(t_1) that [there is a time $t_2 < t_1$ & $t_2 <$ the midnight of t_1](Mary leaves(t_2)).

This fits in with our earlier suggestion that unembedded uses of unanchored adverbials are implicitly deictic or quantified.

The account generalizes straightforwardly to iterated attitude and discourse sentences. In (81), the tense of 'said' governs 'had told', which in turn governs 'would be leaving'.

(81) John said last week that Mary had told him three days earlier she would be leaving tonight.

'Last week' indexes to the present, as does 'tonight', but 'three days earlier' expresses a relation whose second term is suppressed yet is evidently the time of John's report. (81) is represented as in (82).

(82) [There is a $t_1 < t^*$ & $t_1 \subseteq$ the week before t^*](John says(t_1) that [there is a $t_2 < t_1$ & $t_2 \subseteq$ the day three days earlier than t_1](Mary tells(t_2) him that [there is a $t_3 > t_2$ & $t_3 =$ tonight](Mary is(t_3) leaving)).

If 'would say' is embedded in a report with a main verb in the past, the verbs it governs are also governed by the sequencing rule. In (83), the tense of 'would tell' governs 'loved', but 'loved' indexes to the time of the telling, not to a prior time. (83) would be represented as in (84).

(83) John said that he would tell Mary that he loved her by next week.

(84) [There is a $t_1 < t^*$](John says(t_1) that [there is a $t_2 > t_1$ & $t_2 <$ next week](he tells(t_2) Mary that he loves(t_2) her)).

Earlier (note 14), we remarked that event verbs true of speech acts may be used performatively, as in 'I promise I won't be late' or 'I promise to be there'. We suggested that these are understood to be modified implicitly by 'hereby', which refers to the utterance act itself, and that this modifier provides a quantifier to bind what would otherwise be a free variable in the main verb. We can now suggest a representation of the logical form of such sentences in light of our discussion of indirect discourse. We will take 'I promise I won't be late' as our example, which we represent as in (85).

(85) [There is time $t_1 : t_1 = t^*$](I promise(t_1) by this act that it is not the case that [there is a $t_2 : t_2 > t_1$](I am(t_2) late)).

We likewise suggested that sometimes 'now' modifies a sentence, not a verb, as in 'Now he will resign for sure', which is equivalent to 'It is now the case that he will resign' and might be represented as in (86).

(86) [There is a $t_1 : t_1 = t^*$ and $t_1 =$ now](it is(t_1) the case that [there is a $t_2 : t_2 > t_1$](he resigns(t_2)).

The chief moral here is that reports of others' attitudes at times other than the present do not completely report the content of their attitudes, since they involve quantifying into the complement clause. What is conveyed is that some completion of the complement clause gives the content of the speaker's assertion (belief, etc.). There appears to be no way in English to be more precise, since even adding an adjunct does not eliminate quantifying into the complement clause, because the main verb's tense must control verb(s) in the complement clause.[37,38]

1.11   Semantics and the Metaphysics of Time

What light does our account of tense shed on traditional issues in the philosophy of time? A semantic theory for a language by itself has only conditional implications for what there is. It reveals the commitments of the sentences of a language, but nothing follows about what there is independently of which of them are true. Likewise, nothing follows about our commitments independently of our commitment to the truth of some sentences. However, since we are all committed to the truth of what we say using tensed sentences, we can confidently say that we are committed to whatever must be true if most of what we thereby say is true.

A first obvious, though not insignificant, point is that we are committed to times or, time intervals, if the semantics for tense and tense devices proposed here is correct. Not only do we refer to times using temporal referring devices, but we quantify over times as well. So there are times, if most of what we say is true. Moreover, if most of what we say is true, presentism, the view that only the present time is real, must be false, since we quantify over times before and after the present time.

Our account also takes sides in the debate over whether time is an A-series or a B-series, in McTaggart's terminology. Time is a B-series if temporal moments or intervals do not themselves have changing properties, and talk about the present, past, and future is always relativized to some time or other as a reference point. Time is an A-series if times have changing properties of being present, past, or future, where the property of being present is one that each time has in succession. Our semantics for tense is not committed to time's being an A-series in virtue of commitments to what people ordinarily say; indeed, it is not clear that talk of being the present, past, or future time makes sense. Talk about times undergoing change appears to be a category error: if change involves an object's having a property at one time and lacking it at another, for times to change, we would have to treat times as persisting through time! This would confuse times with objects, as one might confuse places with objects located at them and talk of places changing places.

Appeal to use of a predicate such as 'is the present time' is illusory. This predicate is an indexical, since its component verb is tensed. To correctly capture its use, we must exhibit it as being used in accordance with a rule that makes its utterance true of a time if and only if that time is the time of utterance. Its satisfaction clause then can be represented as in (87).

(87)   For any function f, time t, speaker s, f satisfies$_{[s,\,t]}$ 'x is the present time' iff $f('x') = t$.

No property is attributed using the predicate. It would be a mistake to object that 'is the present time' employs the identity sign plus a definite description, for in this case 'present' has no life independent of its use in 'the present time'. (While 'is present' has a use, it is used to mean the same thing as 'is here', and it is not used as a simple predicate of times.) 'The present time' does not function as a complex expression; instead, it functions like 'now'. (Similar remarks apply to 'is in the past' and 'is in the future'.) Likewise, simply using tense-inflected verbs does not commit us to properties of being present, past, or future.[39]

So if the account of tense proposed here is correct, the metaphysics of English—and, presumably, other natural languages—treats time as a B-series (the alternative not only being uncountenanced by compositional semantics, but of doubtful intelligibility: an example of the 'bewitchment of our intelligence by language'). We are left with a variety of puzzles: why we experience times as a succession of instants with a single direction, and why we cannot, as it were, travel in either direction through time the way we can travel in any direction through space. Such puzzles, however, can yield only to conceptual analysis. The project of a compositional semantics is complete after the logical form of the sentences we use to express our thoughts about times has been revealed.

1.12   Conclusion

This chapter sketches a truth-theoretical approach to the phenomenon of tense and temporal modification in English. By treating tense as a device of restricted indexical quantification, we can account for the simple tenses and their modifiers in a way that conforms to our intuitive sense of what we say when we use tensed sentences, and we can show how understanding tensed sentences rests on a finite number of semantic rules. Tense is not very systematic, and we have seen that no simple compositional story can be told about how tenses interact with modifiers and how they behave when embedded. On the other hand, the number of rules required to understand these interactions is small, and we should not expect natural languages to be logically perfect.

While we lack a proof, we still think it would be difficult, compatibly with our methodological requirement that an interpretive truth theory be context insensitive, to give an account of the truth conditions of tensed sentences without treating tense as a quantificational device of some kind. We are aware of only two ways in which to do this: our approach and one that involves quantifying over events or states, as discussed in note 30, in which we also explain why we prefer our approach.

If this approach is correct, then, as noted, a number of conditional consequences can be drawn about the philosophy of mind, language, and metaphysics. First, many of our sentences and thoughts are directly about the present. Second, giving an account of the semantics of propositional attitudes that countenances quantification into their complement clauses is necessary for an adequate semantics for propositional attitudes, for virtually all attitude reports turn out to quantify into the complement clause. Contra Quine, quantifying-in cannot be incoherent on pain of making most of what we wish to say about the attitudes of another incoherent. Third, if much of what we say in ordinary speech is true, times or time intervals are real, and there are past as well as future times. On this condition, irrealism about time and presentism (irrealism about past and future times) are both false. Fourth, the semantics proposed here for tense and temporal referring devices gives no comfort to anyone who views time as an A-series, that is, who views times as undergoing change themselves. The quantificational approach does not treat tense as attributing properties to times at all, but as quantifying over, and indicating relations among, them by means of indexical reference to the time of utterance. Anyone who wishes to maintain that tensed sentences attribute properties to times needs to provide a semantics for tense that achieves as least as much as we have shown is possible with our quantificational approach.

Appendix: Present Perfect, Past Perfect, Future Perfect

In this appendix, we discuss the perfect tenses (or the perfective aspect, as it is often called) and how they differ from simple tenses.[40] Table 1.4 gives the forms of the perfect tenses. The perfect expresses a completed event. The present perfect is used to indicate that an event has been completed as of the present. It differs from the simple past in allowing that the event's terminal point coincides with the time of utterance. One can say, 'John has finished swimming now', but not 'John finished swimming now'. Likewise, one can say, 'John has worked here since 1980', which means that from 1980 to the present John has worked here, but not 'John worked here since 1980', because the simple past requires the time of the event expressed by the verb to be in the past. (Adverbials of the form 'since' $^\frown$ δ, where δ is a temporal designator, are acceptable only with perfect tenses, though there is the idiomatic 'It is a year since we left'.) However, contrary to what some philosophers and linguists claim (see Dowty 1982, p. 27, and references therein), the event need not extend into the present, as shown by the acceptability of 'John has been a lifeguard, but isn't any longer'. The future perfect is used to indicate that something has been completed as of some future time. The past relative to the future reference time may be past relative to the speaker's time of utterance, or it may be completed at any time up to and including the future reference time. If it is true now to say that John sat

Table 1.4

Tense	Form	Example
Future perfect	'will'/'shall' + 'have' + past participle	John will have seen it.
Present perfect	present of 'have' + past participle	John has seen it.
Past perfect	past of 'have' + past participle	John had seen it.

down yesterday, it is true to say that John will have sat down by tomorrow. Likewise, if tomorrow at 3 p.m. one says truly, 'John has finished swimming now', it would be correct to say today, 'John will have finished swimming by 3 p.m. tomorrow'. The past perfect is used to say that something has been completed by some past time. So if John finished swimming at 3 p.m. yesterday, it would be correct to say today, 'John had finished swimming by 4 p.m. yesterday'.

The effect of projecting these future, present, or past reference times relative to which an event is said to have been completed can be accommodated within our framework by introducing another quantifier and a relation restricting the relations among the bound temporal variables. The past perfect of (88a) is illustrated in (88b), and the future perfect of (89a) in (89b).

(88) a. John had seen it.
      b. [There is a $t_1 : t_1 < t^*$][there is a $t_2 : t_2 \leq t_1$](John sees(t_2) it).

(89) a. John will have seen it.
      b. [There is a $t_1 : t_1 > t^*$][there is a $t_2 : t_2 \leq t_1$](John sees(t_2) it).

For convenience, we will adopt Reichenbach's terminology to distinguish among the times represented by 't_1', 't^*', and 't_2', the *reference* time, the *speaker* time, and the *event* time, respectively (see Reichenbach 1947, pp. 287–98). The event time is the time of the action expressed by the main verb, the speaker time is the time of utterance, and the reference time is the time relative to which the event time is located. In (88) and (89), 'have' contributes a restricted existential quantifier that relates its temporal variable, the reference time, to the speaker time as before or after it, depending on whether the tense of 'have' is past or future, and the past participle likewise contributes a restricted existential quantifier binding the variable associated with the event time, which is related to the reference time as before or simultaneous with it. The present perfect of (90a) receives a parallel treatment, as in (90b).

(90) a. John has seen it.
      b. [There is a $t_1 : t_1 = t^*$][there is a $t_2 : t_2 \leq t_1$](John sees(t_2) it).

Though we could simplify (90), it is plausible that the function of combining a tense of 'have' with the past participle is the same in every perfect tense but for the contribution of the tense of 'have'.[41] This leads to a pleasing symmetry in the interaction of perfect tenses with various adverbials.[42]

The utility of the perfect becomes apparent when we consider its interaction with certain adverbial modifiers that (partially) fix the reference time. In 'John will have seen it by tomorrow', 'by tomorrow' modifies the reference time, that is, the future time in the past relative to which the event is said to occur. Similarly for the past perfect and the present perfect. Thus, 'John will have finished swimming by tomorrow' has the representation in (91).

(91) [There is a time $t_1 : t_1 > t^*$ & $t_1 = $ tomorrow][there is a
      $t_2 : t_2 \leq t_1$](John finishes swimming(t_2)).

This explains why 'John will have finished swimming by yesterday' seems ill formed: it would require the reference time, which the quantifier restriction requires to be in the future relative to the utterance time, to be also in the past relative to the time of utterance. Similar remarks apply to the past perfect. One cannot say, 'John had seen it by tomorrow'. The perfect tenses are useful, particularly the past and future perfect, because they allow us to set time boundaries other than the present for events. This is accomplished by adverbial modification on the past or future reference time with respect to which another event is to have occurred in the past relative to it. This explains why unembedded and unmodified uses, or context-free uses, of the perfect (e.g., an unadorned use of 'John had been there') can seem odd. The perfect tenses are almost never used without adverbial modification, or without an appropriate context in which an implicit adverbial modification is provided by the surrounding discourse.

Not all adverbials modifying verbs in a perfect tense modify the reference time; some modify the event time. In 'John had arrived on Tuesday', 'on Tuesday' modifies only the event time. Generally, it appears that adverbials introduced by limiting prepositions, like 'by', 'before', and 'after', modify the reference time. Adverbials that indicate a specific date are used to specify the event time. Often, such modifications will sound odd, as in 'John will have arrived Tuesday next week'. They sound odd because using the perfect tense when the adverbial modifies the event time is usually pointless. 'John had arrived on Tuesday' seems less strange because it is easy to imagine a narrative in which the use of the past perfect would have a point—for example, 'Mary, who arrived on Wednesday, thought she had arrived before John. But John had arrived on Tuesday.'[43]

An interesting test of our proposal is whether it can explain the inter-action of adverbials introduced using 'since' followed by a temporal designator with the various tenses, which seem acceptable only with perfect tenses. While we can say, 'John has/had/will have worked since 1980', we cannot say felicitously, 'John worked/works/will work since 1980'. With the past perfect and the future perfect, 'since 1980' adds that the activity expressed by the verb has taken place in the period from 1980 to the *reference* time; with the present perfect, 'since 1980' adds that the activity expressed by the main verb has taken place in a period from 1980 to the present,[44] but since this is the reference time, we can represent 'since 1980' as requiring for all three that the activity take place between 1980 and the reference time, as illustrated in (92)–(94) (where '$t - x$' means 'the time interval from x to t').

(92)   [There is a $t_1 : t_1 = t^*$][there is a $t_2 : t_2 \leq t_1$ &
        $t_2 = t_1 - 1980$](John works(t_2) here).

(93)   [There is a $t_1, t_2 : t_1 < t^*$][there is a $t_2 : t_2 \leq t_1$ &
        $t_2 = t_1 - 1980$](John works(t_2) here).

(94)   [There is a $t_1, t_2 : t_1 > t^*$][there is a $t_2 : t_2 \leq t_1$ &
        $t_2 = t_1 - 1980$](John works(t_2) here).

So modifying a verb in a perfect tense with 'since 1980' is to say that the *event* time is equal to the time interval between 1980 and the *reference* time. We can see why 'since 1980' does not sit comfortably with the simple tenses. It designates a time interval identified with the event time. But for the simple tenses, the anchor time for determining the time interval would be the time of utterance (i.e., the event time would be identified with $t^* - 1980$), but the requirements imposed on the event time by the simple tenses are incompatible with this. Notice how nicely the account adapts to the embedding of 'since' in other modifiers, as in 'several times since 1980'. The adverbial 'since 1980' modifies 'several times', which quantifies over the event time. So 'John has worked several times since 1980' is represented as '[There is a $t_1 : t_1 < t^*$][several $t_2 : t_2 \subseteq t_1 - 1980$](John works($t_2$))'.

Quantificational adverbials, and 'before' and 'after' used as sentential connectives, likewise modify the event time. Consider (95) and (96).

(95) John had loved Mary long before he said it.

(96) John had never been to Arizona.

'Before' relates event (or state) times; that is, it relates the argument places in the main verbs of the sentences flanking it. In (95), 'long' modifies the state time. (95) is paraphrasable as (97).

(97) [There is a $t_1 : t_1 < t^*$][there is a $t_2 : t_2 \le t_1$][there is a $t_3 : t_3 < t^*$ & t_2 is long before t_3](John loves(t_2) Mary and John says(t_3) it).

The extra quantifier effectively is inert, which explains why (95) and (98) are equivalent.

(98) John loved Mary long before he said it.

The past perfect in (95) serves mostly as a way of emphasizing that John's love was past relative to a relevant time also in the past. The quantifier 'never' in (96) binds the temporal argument place in its main verb. (96) conveys that at no time prior to some former time had John been to Arizona, which does not entail that John has never been to Arizona. (96) is paraphrased as (99).

(99) [There is a $t_1 : t_1 < t^*$][for no $t_2 : t_2 < t_1$](John is(t_2) in Arizona).

'When' may be used with the past perfect, but apparently only if the 'when'-clause is in the simple past. (100) is acceptable; (101) is not.

(100) He had gone when Bill arrived.

(101) He had gone when Bill had arrived.

In (100), 'when' binds the event time for the restricting clause, and the reference time for the past perfect, as shown in (102).

(102) [There is a time $t_1 : t_1 < t^*$ & Bill arrives t_1][there is a time $t_2 : t_2 < t_1$](he goes(t_2)).

When we assigned satisfaction conditions to sentences of the form ⌜φ when ψ⌝, when φ and ψ were in the past tense, we showed that semantically φ shifts to present tense. Now we see that when φ is in the past perfect, it effectively functions like the past, with the argument place that usually functions indexically being bound by 'when'.[45] The problem with (101) is that for 'when' to bind across both sentences, it must bind the reference time in 'Bill had arrived' and what would be the indexical reference to the speaker time in 'He had gone' when unembedded. This yields (103),

(103)   [There is a time $t_1 : t_1 < t^* \;\&\; t_2 < t_1 \;\&$ Bill arrives t_2][there is a time $t_3 : t_3 < t_1$](he goes(t_3)).

which conveys no useful information about the temporal relations between the two event times. 'Whenever', like 'when', is comfortable with the past perfect only when the restricting clause is in the simple past, as in (104), which would be paraphrased as in (105).

(104)   He had tried to buy it whenever he had money.

(105)   [For any time $t_1 : t_1 < t^* \;\&$ he has(t_1) money][for a time $t_2: t_2 < t_1$](he tries(t_2) to buy it).

These examples illustrate how to combine our account of adverbial modification with perfect tenses. There is some interest in looking at the possible combinations of tenses with 'when' and 'whenever', but that would be too involved a task for the present context. Depending on its kind, a modifier will modify either the reference time or the event time. Quantificational adverbials that are not sentential connectives invariably modify the event time. Limiting adverbs invariably modify the reference time. Temporal sentential connectives like 'before' and 'after' invariably connect event times. 'When' and 'whenever' bind the event time in the first clause and the speaker time in the second.[46]

Notes

1. An extensive study of the categories of tense and aspect across languages can be found in Dahl 1985. See also Gabbay and Rohrer 1979 for a comparison of the expressive resources of English and Hebrew.

2. See Ludwig 1997 for an account of how to extend the truth-theoretic approach to nondeclaratives.

3. Though we will not argue for it here, we believe these are the only contextual parameters that are needed to devise an adequate semantics for tense. Throughout, quantifiers over times will range over time intervals, and 'is a time' will be true of time intervals. We will include as a limiting case of a time interval temporal instants. In fact, it seems likely we should construe the restriction to be relative to a speaker's reference frame. Here, we will omit this complication,

which would have more the character of an update of the semantics of English than a description of it.

4. (5) is sometimes said to be untensed (see, e.g., Palmer 1974, pp. 33, 36–38), since its verb is constructed from a modal auxiliary 'will' and an infinitive verb stem and does not involve inflection. As we noted above, our classification is guided not by syntactic but by semantic considerations, and the semantic function of 'will' + infinite verb stem is to indicate that the action or state expressed by the verb occurs or obtains at a time later than the time of utterance, and thus it semantically functions like the present and past tenses.

5. The future tense is also expressed by using 'is' + 'going' + the infinitive, as in 'Mary is going to love Bill'. Since these are equivalent, what we say about the modal + bare infinitive applies equally to the alternative form.

6. Nonfinite verbs, infinitives, participles, and gerunds are said to lack tense. However, they do not function as main verbs, but rather nominally, adjectivally, or adverbially.

7. The expression 'ref$_{[s,\,t]}(y) = x$' is read as 'the referent of y as used by s at $t = x$'.

8. The truth conditions we offer, in broad outline, we believe underlie most thinking about tense in other frameworks. As far as truth-theoretic accounts go, we draw attention to the formulation using restricted quantifier notation, which we think better captures the semantic structure of the past and future tenses. While we will identify some salient differences with other approaches, we will not try to provide a systematic comparison, as that would be a book-length task.

9. The recursive clause for restricted quantifiers has the form (i),

(i)   For any speaker s, time t, function f, f satisfies$_{[s,\,t]}$ $\ulcorner[Qx: Fx](Gx)\urcorner$ iff Q 'Fx'-variants f' of f satisfies$_{[s,\,t]}$ 'Gx'.

where 'Q' is a placeholder for a quantifier, and the metalanguage embeds the object language. 'Fx'-variant f' of f is defined as follows: f' is an 'Fx'-variant of f iff f' differs from f at most in that f' satisfies$_{[s,\,t]}$ 'Fx'.

10. See Ludwig 1996 for a general argument for this view.

11. This neatly handles the need for a potentially arbitrarily large number of independent reference times for events in subordinate clauses, as in 'John saw the man who kissed Mary, who bought a farm from the woman Bill divorced'.

12. As we remarked earlier, metalanguage verbs are tenseless. Object language quantifiers range over every extant object, taken tenselessly (i.e., not relativized to any time). If natural language quantifiers were evaluated relative to the time of utterance, so that their domains were restricted to what existed at that time, this would have to be represented in our semantics by restricting the domain to objects existing at the time of utterance. This is not, however, how quantifiers are used in English: 'Everyone who lived in the nineteenth century suffered from gout' is not vacuously true but rather factually false. As we point out below (note 35), for *restricted* quantifiers the nominal restriction can be interpreted as in a tense other than that of the predicate to which it is attached. We anticipate some

discomfort arising from the reflection that a sentence such as 'Everyone was at the party' will be false on this view because the quantifier will range over people at all times. But this is no more puzzling than that the quantifier is used with an implicit restriction even on the domain of people at the present time.

How does negation interact with tense? Consider 'John did not sleep last night'. If negation can take different scopes with respect to tense, then there should be two readings of this. On one, it would be true if and only if for every past time last night it is not the case that John slept at that time. That is, this reading requires wakefulness the whole night. On the other, it would be true if and only if there is at least one time last night at which John did not sleep. This reading would be true if John woke momentarily in the middle of the night but fell asleep again quickly without waking until morning. Is there then a reading on which an assertion of 'John did not sleep last night' would be true if he woke momentarily in the middle of the night? We might try to imagine a situation in which what is at issue is the effectiveness of a certain sleeping pill. We give it to John at bedtime and wish to know whether it was effective in giving him a good night's sleep. Can John report its failure in the morning by saying, 'I did not sleep last night', if all he means to report is that there is at least one time last night at which he was not asleep? Even in this context it seems to us we would take John's report to be false. In addition, if negation could systematically take narrow or wide scope with respect to tense, we would expect 'That will not turn red' to have a reading on which it is true even if it is also true that it will turn red, so that 'That will not turn red and that will turn red' would not be necessarily false, on one reading, even when 'that' picks out the same thing in both its uses. But there does not appear to be any such reading, We therefore tentatively conclude that negation does not insert itself between the quantifier introduced by tense and the verb.

13. Some authors (see, e.g., Burge 1974; Partee 1973) suggest that simple tenses are implicitly demonstrative. An utterance of 'I didn't turn off the stove' is usually understood to involve a specific past time interval, and not just any past time. Space constraints prevent us from discussing this suggestion fully. While a truth-theoretic approach can easily incorporate devices that work this way, we believe these phenomena are pragmatic and not semantic.

14. There are two exceptions. First, there is the so-called narrative or historical present (or, sometimes, "vividly reporting present"), as in live broadcasts of a sporting event, in which the announcer attempts to convey a sense of immediacy by reporting events in the simple present: 'He hits a terrific serve, approaches the net, and hits a winner down the line to win the game'. (See Visser 1972, p. 724, for a wealth of other examples.) The naked present can also be used in chronological tables: for example, '579 B.C. Nebuchadnezzar takes Tyre'. These are so specialized that we are unsure what weight to grant them. Their aim is clearly to achieve a kind of vividness in reporting that a past tense report would fail to convey. The present tense of event verbs, so oddly used in the present, lies ready to hand: it is no wonder it is pressed into use for such an effect, even if there is something odd about it. But it does seem to be a kind of play with words recog-

nized as a bit odd or out of place, and partly effective for that reason. We are inclined to say this is an *extended* and not a *core* use of the present, despite its appearing throughout the history of English.

The second case is the use of the present tense of event verbs in issuing performatives, as in 'I promise to meet you there' or 'I warn you not to do that'. It is unclear what to say about such uses. It would be odd to interpret them as anything other than promises or warnings, though it is tempting to say that one promises, warns, and so on, by way of asserting one is doing so. But contrast 'I promise to meet you there' with 'I am promising to meet you there'. The latter cannot ordinarily be used to make a promise. So no performative is accomplished by asserting one is perform*ing* the act in question as one speaks. It seems, rather, that utterances of 'I promise to meet you there' intended as promises are implicitly self-referential, that is, are interpreted as 'I hereby promise to meet you there', where 'hereby' makes implicit reference to the utterance; we may treat this modification as introducing a reference to the time of utterance. We will discuss these cases in section 1.10.

15. Though denying that the progressive is a tense is not novel, it is not universally accepted. See Comrie 1985.

16. For discussion, see Dowty 1977; Parsons 1990, chap. 9. It is called the 'imperfective paradox' because 'imperfect' in grammatical usage means 'uncompleted'. The puzzle is how a verb that expresses essentially a complete event can have an imperfect tense, in other words, a tense that implies that the event has not been completed.

17. See Vendler 1967 for a classic discussion of verb classification. According to Vlach (1993, pp. 241–43), progressives are state verbs. So to say that John is leaving is to say that John is in the state of a process of his leaving's being in progress. We see no reason to force the progressive into any category of this dichotomy.

18. See the appendix of Lepore and Ludwig 2000 for detailed discussion of the semantics for demonstratives.

19. (25) and (26) are indexed to the use of the demonstrative because someone can perform more than one demonstration at a time—for example, pointing to a calendar to benefit one interlocutor, while using 'then' to pick out a different time. Further modifications would be required to get it just right, but we omit them here to avoid the distraction an adequate discussion would require. See the appendix of Lepore and Ludwig 2000 for discussion.

20. This explains why temporal indexicals always index to the time of the speaker even when embedded in sentences that otherwise are interpreted relative to a time distinct from the present, as in 'John said that Mary had believed that Bill would be here by now'. Difficulties introduced by such terms (and similar phenomena—see note 37) led to two-dimensional tense logics (see Kamp 1971). In the truth-conditional approach, we can provide a simple and natural explanation of this behavior by treating such terms as singular referring terms and assigning them reference axioms that determine referents relative to the time of a

speaker's use. This cuts through the difficulties Dowty (1982, esp. secs. 4.4.5–4.4.6) encountered working in another framework.

21. Multiple temporal demonstratives and indexicals present an additional complexity, which space constraints force us to touch on only briefly. See Lepore and Ludwig 2000. Sentences such as 'Now isn't now' and 'Now you see it, and now you don't', in which each use of 'now' indexes to a different time, require satisfaction axioms that quantify over times for each occurrence of 'now' as well as for the utterance as a whole, and for each contained sentence (form) in molecular sentences. To accommodate this need, we define a family of relational predicates:

(i)   Def. $\Delta(s, t, t_1, \ldots, t_n, \alpha_1, \ldots, \alpha_n)$ iff $t_1 < t_2 < \cdots < t_n$, and $t_1, \ldots, t_n$ occur in t, and s uses α_1 at t_1, s uses α_2 at $t_2, \ldots, s$ uses α_n at t_n.

The six-place predicate so defined holds between a speaker s, three times t, t_1, t_2, and two temporal designators α_1, α_2 iff $t_1, t_2 \subseteq t, t_1 < t_2$, and the speaker uses α_1 at t_1, α_2 at t_2. We give satisfaction conditions for a two-place predicate, R, expressing a temporal relation as follows: For any speaker s, function f, temporal designators α_1, α_2, and times t, t_1, t_2, such that $\Delta(s, t, t_1, t_2, \alpha_1, \alpha_2)$, f satisfies$_{[s, t]}$ $\ulcorner \alpha_1 \ R \ \alpha_2 \urcorner$ iff ref$_{[s, t_1]}(\alpha_1) \ R(t)$ ref$_{[s, t_2]}(\alpha_2)$. This can be extended to predicates with an arbitrary number of temporal argument places. For molecular sentences, we index the utterance time of the contained sentences. For conjunction: For any speaker s, function f, formulas φ, ψ, and times t, t_1, t_2, such that $\Delta(s, t, t_1, t_2, \varphi, \psi)$, f satisfies$_{[s, t]}$ $\ulcorner \varphi$ and $\psi \urcorner$ iff f satisfies$_{[s, t_1]} \varphi$ and f satisfies$_{[s, t_2]} \psi$. This allows for the possibility of saying truly, 'Though John has not smiled yet, he is smiling now, and now has smiled'.

22. Dionysius Exiguus introduced the anno Domini dating system in Rome in the sixth century A.D.; it became the dominant dating system in the West only after its adoption by Charlemagne.

23. King argues interestingly that day designators are referring terms and not descriptions, but in contrast to our position that they are also nonrigid. King argues that since what the length of a day is depends on the rate of rotation of the earth, and the interval a month term is true of depends on the length of the days it includes, the extension of month terms can differ from possible world to possible world. Thus, 'January 2001' may pick out different time intervals in different possible worlds; similarly, 'January 1, 2001' may pick out different time intervals in different worlds. The same reasoning applies to 'is 2001', since the length of the year depends on how long it takes the earth to rotate around the sun. We are not quite convinced, however, for it is compatible with this that we say that in different possible worlds the same date system would be used to pick out different times, rather than saying that the terms we use pick out different times in different possible worlds. The issue hinges on intuitions about counterfactuals and modal claims that are not easy to adjudicate. We find it odd, for example, to assert, 'January 2001 might not have been January 2001', while there is no puzzle about asserting, for example, 'The president of the United States in January 2001 might not have been the president of the United States in January 2001'.

24. As King (2001) notes, since it may be Monday in the United States but Tuesday in Japan, or January in Tokyo but December in New York, these terms properly express relations between time intervals and locations. We can accommodate this by giving, for example, 'January' the satisfaction clause 'f satisfies$_{[s, t]}$ "x is January" iff January($f(x), s$)', where 'January(x, y)' expresses the appropriate relation between a time interval x and a location picked out relative to a person y. This need not be the speaker's location, since someone may say on the phone, for instance, 'Is it January yet?', intending to ask about whether it is January in his interlocutor's location. Understanding exactly what relation is being expressed requires quite a bit of knowledge of the intricacies of the calendar system. In the division of linguistic labor, most of us rely on a few when we use date names.

25. There is a class of adverbials we will not discuss whose members are used routinely to connect sentences in narratives. These are exemplified by 'three hours later' in the following passage, borrowed from Hinrichs 1986: 'They wheeled me into the operating room and put me under sedation. Three hours later I woke up'. The reference time for 'later' here is understood to be the time the narrator was put under sedation. Examples of this sort, as well as the conventions of narrative more generally, in which times of narrated events are understood to occur in an order indicated by the order of narrative, have suggested to many that the proper unit for semantic analysis is larger than the sentence and that the traditional focus on sentential semantics distorts the semantic structures of natural languages. We will sidestep this debate. Although we think our understanding of narrative can be accommodated by a sentence-level semantics, nothing in our approach prevents our incorporating semantic-level cross-sentential anaphoric reference.

26. We borrow this terminology and classification scheme from Smith 1978.

27. Some uses of temporal adverbials suggest that they are not always used to quantify over times, as in the sentence 'Even numbers are always divisible by 2'. On such grounds, Lewis (1975) argues that they should be treated as quantifying over "cases." This desperate expedient should be resisted. Given that forms of 'to be' in English will have a suppressed temporal argument place, there can be no difficulty in including a temporal quantifier even in sentences that are about abstract objects. Indeed, not supplying a universal quantifier for a sentence such as 'Even numbers are divisible by 2' might be thought to be misleading when a speaker intends to be conveying that this is so necessarily or by definition. The effect of introducing 'always' is to emphasize the noncontingency of the claim, although what is said strictly speaking falls short of what is intended.

28. We are indebted here to comments by Samuel Wheeler.

29. Vlach (1993, p. 231) claims that "[n]o existing framework for temporal semantics provides a general treatment of durative ... and frequency ... adverbials" and that, in particular, none can deal with a sentence such as (i).

(i)   Allen worked out regularly for two weeks last month.

Our account handles this straightforwardly. The frequency adverb is a quantifier that replaces the existential quantifier of the tense of 'worked out', keeping the past time restriction. The duration adverbial 'for two weeks last month' (where 'last month' modifies 'two weeks') modifies the time so bound, which is understood to be within the time so designated, represented as follows:

(ii)   [Regular $t_1 : t_1 < t^*$ & $t_1 \subset$ two weeks last month](Allen works out(t_1)).

Vlach's account of tense (or more properly, tense inflection) is that it makes no truth-functional contribution to sentences in which it occurs, but is like the gender of pronouns, which, he assumes, does not contribute to truth conditions. English speakers are supposed to follow the convention of using 'he' when talking about a male and 'she' when talking about a female, but one may, he asserts, say truly of a woman, 'He is tall'. Similarly, one is supposed to obey a convention of using present and past when talking about the present and the past, but this is no part of the truth conditions of the utterance, taken literally. All the work of semantic temporal reference, Vlach says, is really done by adverbial modification. This is an interesting suggestion, but it certainly swims against the tide! It hardly comports with our intuitive judgments about the truth of utterances using tensed verbs. If one asserts, 'John died', but John is alive and well, one offends not just against usage, but against the truth.

30. Can we account for tense using a quantifier over events and not times? The difficulty is to anchor reference to events to the time of utterance. The only way we can see how to do this is to force every utterance to refer to itself, since each utterance is guaranteed to occur at the time of speech. (Such an approach is sketched in Higginbotham 1995.) For the past tense, we might treat, say, 'John kissed Mary' as equivalent to '[There is an event $e : e < u^*$](Kisses(e, John, Mary)'. Then 'u^*' would receive this reference axiom: For any speaker s, time t, utterance u by s at t, ref$_{[s, t]}$('u^*') = u. It seems counterintuitive, however, to treat every utterance as self-referential. Furthermore, it seems intuitively clear that what one says in uttering, for example, 'It will rain this afternoon', could have been true even if there had been no utterances. It could not have been true, however, if there had been no times. For these reasons, we reject this alternative approach.

31. See Comrie 1985, p. 109, for Russian; and see Ogihara 1996.

32. There are apparent exceptions to this rule—for example, reports of certain states that continue into the present, as in 'I heard last night that Mary is sick' or 'The Egyptians knew that the earth is round' (borrowed from Smith 1978, p. 66). In this case, the present tense is interpreted relative to the speaker's context rather than that of the event or state being reported. This seems acceptable only when the verb is factive or a verb of indirect discourse. One cannot say, for instance, 'I thought that the earth is round'. We suspect that in this case the present tense is used to indicate that the content of the reported state or event is not relativized simply to the time of the reported event or state, but is about a state that would extend from that past time into some indefinite future time that at least includes the time of utterance. (Abusch (1997) gives a different account that makes the

appropriateness hinge on what the speaker believes, but if we wish the reports to be possibly true, the right account should focus on what the reportee knows, hears, says, and the like; one of Abusch's examples, 'John believed that Mary is pregnant', we find hard to interpret!) A related case is 'I asked him who that lady in the tiara is'. Here there is the pull of the demonstrative construction, interpreted relative to the speaker's time, as well as the assumption, forced by the use of the expression in the nominal modifying the demonstrative, that the lady in question is still wearing a tiara. (The example is borrowed from Visser 1972, p. 779, a rich source of examples from Old to Modern English. Visser notes that the use of the present in the complement has been common in all periods of the language, though more recently neglected by grammarians (p. 827). The examples all seem, however, to fit the diagnosis here given. An event or process definitely located only in the past relative to the time of speech is quite unhappily reported in the present in the complement, as in 'He said that he is tired yesterday'.)

33. This terminology is not used consistently in the literature. Sometimes it is used for the semantic phenomenon of the tense in one clause controlling that in another; sometimes to refer to the syntactic phenomenon of back shifting of tense markers. We use it here in the latter sense.

34. We are following traditional rules for sequence of tense in reporting indirect discourse and attitude sentences. No doubt many speakers of English are not so systematic and tend to use the simple past for both the simultaneous reading (69) and the past relative to the time of uttering (68). Higginbotham (1995) assumes this, as does Abusch (1997), who offers examples in which reading (68) would be forced by the narrative context: 'John mostly slept through the sixties. But Joan later claimed that he was active in the antiwar movement' (our example). Locating the saying in the discourse at a time later than the time the mentioned speaker intends to comment on forces an auditor to interpret the discourse as in (68). Our usage seems to track the tradition; but, in any case, tense-sequencing rules are not a deep feature of natural languages, though the underlying semantic structures are.

35. Tense sequencing shows up even without an explicit tense marker governing it, as in Abusch 1997, p. 29: 'Mary's desire to marry a man who resembled her is bizarre'. The past shifting of 'resemble' indicates that the desire is located prior to the time of utterance. This tells us that in its canonical paraphrase, '[The x: x was Mary's desire to marry a man who resembled her](x is bizarre)', the appropriate tense for the copula in the restriction on the quantifier is the simple past. This also points to an account of the acceptability of 'The fugitives are all in jail now' (borrowed from Vlach 1993, p. 259), which, while perfectly acceptable, might seem odd because prisoners are not fugitives. By understanding the predicate introduced by 'fugitives' in the past tense, this unwelcome conflict is resolved.

36. As we remarked earlier, there is a clear reason not to interpret the tense in these sentences relative to the speaker's context: this would guarantee that the report is false since the reportee will not say anything in the future directly about the present time (that has the right structure). We are treating indirect speech

as a model for attitude sentences. But with attitude sentences, there appears to be a counterexample to our analysis, in a sentence noticed by Terence Parsons (reported in Dowty 1982, p. 50).

(i)   One day John will regret that he is treating me like this.

In (i), the tense of the complement verb 'is treating' is independent of that of the main verb; that is, it indexes to speaker time. Loose talk or counterexample? If what one intends to say by (i) is true, John will one day be disposed to report himself by saying, 'I regret that I treated him like that'. But interpreted relative to their respective contexts, sentences in the complement clauses do not express the same proposition, being directly about different times. How then could (i), interpreted as intended, be true? What one intends to convey could have been reported by (ii).

(ii)   One day John will regret that he (has) treated me like this.

This gets it just right. We suggest the following account of the use of (i). A speaker, resentful of John, wishes to emphasize John is mistreating him, and to emphasize the objective wrongness of John's actions by asserting that John will regret (someday) his mistreatment of him (his treating him like this). Our speaker could say, 'John is treating me like this and one day he will regret his treating me like this', but this is a mouthful, and in the heat of the moment, out comes a fusion of the two, natural enough, given that 'his treating me like this' is the nominalization of 'he is treating me like this'. We so interpret him because 'this' is used to pick out a current activity of John's, which requires the tense of 'is treating' to index to the present and not to the time of John's regret. We understand what he intends well enough though he issues an inaccurate report and violates some (well-grounded) rules of usage.

37. Similar binding phenomena occur between the tenses of verbs generally in superordinate and subordinate clauses, where we find the past shifting of tense as a marker of this binding as well. Consider the contrast between (i) and (ii),

(i)   A child was born who would be king.

(ii)   A child was born who will be king.

discussed in Kamp 1971, in which they form part of Kamp's motivation for a two-dimensional tense logic. The effect of the past shifting is to introduce the same kind of binding relation between the tense of the main verb and the tense of the subordinate clause found in complement clauses of indirect discourse. Whereas in (ii) the tense of the verb in the subordinate clause is interpreted relative to the speaker's context, in (i) it is interpreted relative to the time bound by the past tense of the main verb. This can be represented as '[There is a time $t_1 : t_1 < t^*$][there is a time $t_2 : t_2 > t_1$](a child is(t_1) born who is(t_2) king)'. ((ii) is true even if a child was born who at some time after the speech act is king, although, given the availability of (ii), it would be pragmatically misleading to use (i) except when the time of the child's being king precedes the time of speech.) Similarly, the use of the simple past in the superordinate and the past perfect in the subordinate signals that the tense of the main verb controls that of the subordinate. In 'A president was elected who had been jailed', the natural interpretation requires that the event expressed in the subordinate clause occur prior to the event expressed in the superordinate clause. It is not clear that we find the same effect with the simple past in the subordinate clause, however, which, if it followed the pattern of indirect discourse, would index to the same time as the event expressed by the main verb. 'A president was elected who was jailed' does not suggest that the jailing and the election occurred simultaneously; rather, the restriction seems to be that both occurred prior to the time of utterance. The phenomenon occurs with other tenses. Consider 'John will meet a man who has been/is/will be king'. In appropriate contexts, we can force readings in which the tense in the subordinate clause either is independent of the main clause and indexes to speaker time, or is controlled by that of the main clause. It is clearly useful to have both readings, but lamentable that English, in this as in many other cases, provides no means of systematic disambiguation. Using back shifting of tense for verbs in subordinate clauses whose main verbs are in the past can be seen as a half-hearted attempt to disambiguate, which when employed in discourse and attitude sentences leads regrettably to the difficulties we noted with reporting unambiguously past speech acts employing the past and present perfect. But this lack of systematicity should not be too surprising. Natural languages are feral shrubs, untrimmed to the shapes of a logically perfect language.

38. A word may be in order about the implications of our treatment of tense in complement clauses for certain argument forms given in natural language. Consider, for example, this argument: John thought that Mary loved him, and he still thinks that; therefore, John thinks that Mary loved him. (The genre we treat here was brought to our attention by Richard 1981.) The argument is intuitively valid (relativizing both sentences to a set of contextual variables), but what is the function of 'that' in the second conjunct of the first sentence? If it is a referring term, then it cannot be taken to pick out a proposition referred to in the first conjunct, since the only proposition expressed there is that expressed by the full sentence, since the complement clause semantically contains variables bound from outside it. Thus, either we must treat it as something like a pro-sentence, which is to be replaced by 'Mary loved him'; or, if we treat it as a referring term, it looks as if it must refer to the sentence 'Mary loved him'. In favor of the first alternative, perhaps, is the naturalness of replacing 'that' with 'so'. The second alternative, however, could be made to work as well in a sophisticated sententialist account (see Ludwig and Ray 1998).

39. This shows also that modifying our proposal by introducing predicates such as 'Past(t)', 'Present(t)', and 'Future(t)' fails to avoid the result. These must be interpreted indexically, and their analysis treats them as equivalent to '$<t^*$', '$=t^*$', and '$>t^*$'. It might be objected that our account rules out the past and future tensed predicates 'was the present time' and 'will be the present time'. But these are handled by imposing our account of past and present tense onto our analysis of the present tense predicate. So, for the past tense predicate:

(i) For any speaker s, time t, function f, f satisfies$_{[s,t]}$ 'x was the present time' iff [there is a $t_1 < t$](f('x') $= t_1$).

Similarly for the future tense version. No property is attributed in this clause.

40. The reader may wish to compare our account with that of Parsons (1990, chap. 10), who does not analyze the perfect as a tense. Rather, more in the vein of our account of the progressive, Parsons's treats what we call the perfect tenses as perfect *forms* of verbs, which are state verbs that express being in the state of having done or been something (analogous to the structure, subject + tense + 'have' + adjective + noun, as in 'John has red hair') and which can be in the past, present, or future ('had', 'has', 'will have'). This has the same effect as our suggestion below. It is not clear that anything we say rules decisively against this alternative, which could be adopted in the framework we pursue. On the other hand, we are unpersuaded that etymological considerations, which Parsons cites, show that our analysis is incorrect: English speakers use these constructions perfectly ignorant of their history, and there is nothing in their dispositions that would suggest they see a strong analogy with the use of 'have' in state-attributing sentences such as 'John has red hair'. Furthermore, the double quantifier approach interacts in an intuitively compelling way with adverbial modification of perfectives.

41. In this we differ from Taylor (1977), who treats the present perfect as semantically equivalent to the simple past. We already noted it cannot be equivalent to the simple past, which requires that the event expressed occur strictly in the past, while the past perfect does not. We also depart from Taylor in taking syntactic structure as a guide to the semantic structure of the present perfect. Taylor's paraphrases of the perfect tenses employ demonstratives for reference times, for which there is no sanction in the original; in other words, to say that, for example, John had been a major in the army, one does not *need* to have any specific past time in mind relative to which John before that time had been a major in the army, although, of course, one may. Taylor also errs in his treatment of the future perfect in supposing that the event time must lie strictly in the future. This isn't so, as our example in the text shows.

42. An oddity about which adverbials the present perfect will take comfortably is that it does not happily accept adverbials that precisely specify the event time when the time is clearly in the past, though this is not so for the past or future perfect. Although one can say felicitously, 'I have seen her today', one cannot say, 'I have seen her yesterday'. (This fact is discussed in the useful Mittwoch 1988, p. 218.) Our account presents no semantic barrier to this, though it would be pragmatically odd, since given the difference between the present perfect and the past, when an adverbial definitely locates the event time in the past, using the present perfect will seem pointless.

43. Reichenbach (1947, p. 294) incorrectly suggests that such modifiers modify the reference time. In 'John had arrived on Tuesday, a day before Mary', it is not reference time but event time that is in question. Likewise in Reichenbach's example 'I had met him yesterday', 'yesterday' does not modify the reference time, but rather the event time. For we can likewise say, 'I had met him yesterday, but Mary did not meet him until this morning'. So when Reichenbach claims that modifiers modify the event time only when the event and reference time coincide,

he is mistaken. Rather, different modifiers should be taken to modify different times, according to their character.

44. There is another (though less natural) reading, according to which to say that 'John has worked here since 1980' is to say that at some time between 1980 and now, John has worked here. It may be that 'since' is ambiguous. On the other hand, it may be that there is a univocal reading that in standard contexts generates the reading we offered in the text. Three possibilities suggest themselves. First, the sense of 'since' is univocally 'between now and 1980', and it is usually understood as elliptical for 'ever since'. Second, '=' should be replaced with '$\subseteq$', in (92)–(94) and the implication that the period is equal to the whole is pragmatically generated as the most salient period in the conversational context. Third, the latent sense is generated by the possibility of using 'since' in a context in which an implied numerical quantifier modifies it, as in answering 'Has John worked here at any time since 1980?' by saying, 'Yes, he has worked here since 1980'. Nothing fundamental hinges on resolving this.

45. This analysis, together with our treatment of the tenses when unembedded, helps explain the peculiar behavior of an adverb that seems happiest with perfect tenses, namely, 'already'. 'He has already arrived' is felicitous enough, but 'He arrived already' is odd. This is explained by combining the plausible reading of 'already' as conveying that the event time is before the reference time with our analysis. (We cannot treat it as 'before now' because it does not always relate event time to the present, as in 'By the time he had arrived, we had already finished dinner'.) We represent 'John has already arrived' as '[There is a $t_1 : t_1 = t^*$][there is a $t_2 : t_2 \leq t_1$ & $t_2 < t_1$](John arrives(t_2))'.

46. Space constraints prevent us from comparing our account with Reichenbach's celebrated discussion (Reichenbach 1947, pp. 287–98). Reichenbach postulates a speaker, reference, and event time for all tenses, not just the perfect tenses. While we think Reichenbach's basic picture is correct for the perfect tenses, he does not give adequate reasons to postulate a reference time for the simple tenses.

References

Abusch, D. 1997. Sequence of Tense and Temporal De Re. *Linguistics and Philosophy* 20, pp. 1–50.

Burge, T. 1974. Demonstrative Constructions, Reference and Truth. *Journal of Philosophy* 71, pp. 205–23.

Comrie, B. 1985. *Tense.* New York: Cambridge University Press.

Dahl, Ö. 1985. *Tense and Aspect Systems.* Cambridge: Cambridge University Press.

Davidson, D. 1980. The Logical Form of Action Sentences. In *Essays on Actions and Events*, pp. 105–21. New York: Clarendon Press.

Dowty, D. 1977. Toward a Semantic Analysis of Verb Aspect and the English 'Imperfective Progressive'. *Linguistics and Philosophy* 1, pp. 45–77.

Dowty, D. 1982. Tenses, Time Adverbs, and Compositional Semantic Theory. *Linguistics and Philosophy* 5, pp. 23–58.

Evans, G. 1985. Does Tense Logic Rest on a Mistake? In *Collected Papers*, pp. 343–63. Oxford: Clarendon Press.

Frege, G. 1977. The Thought. In P. T. Geach, ed., *Logical Investigations*, pp. 1–30. New Haven, Conn.: Yale University Press.

Gabbay, D., and C. Rohrer. 1979. Do We Really Need Tenses Other Than Future and Past? In R. Bäuerle, U. Egli, and A. von Stechow, eds., *Semantics from Different Points of View*, pp. 15–20. New York: Springer-Verlag.

Higginbotham, J. 1995. Tensed Thoughts. *Mind and Language* 10, pp. 226–49.

Hinrichs, E. 1986. Temporal Anaphora in Discourses in English. *Linguistics and Philosophy* 9, pp. 63–82.

Kamp, J. 1971. Formal Properties of 'Now'. *Theoria* 37, pp. 227–73.

King, J. 2001. Remarks on the Syntax and Semantics of Day Designators. *Philosophical Perspectives* 15, pp. 291–333.

Lepore, E., and K. Ludwig. 2000. The Semantics and Pragmatics of Complex Demonstratives. *Mind* 109(434), pp. 199–240.

Lepore, E., and K. Ludwig. 2001. What Is Logical Form? In P. Kotatko, P. Pagin, and G. Segal, eds., *Interpreting Davidson*, pp. 111–42. Stanford, Calif.: Center for the Study of Language and Information.

Lepore, E., and K. Ludwig. 2003. *Donald Davidson: Truth, Meaning, Language and Reality*. New York: Oxford University Press.

Lewis, D. 1975. Adverbs of Quantification. In E. Keenan, ed., *Formal Semantics of Natural Language*, pp. 3–15. Cambridge: Cambridge University Press.

Ludwig, K. 1996. Singular Thought and the Cartesian Theory of Mind. *Noûs* 30, pp. 434–60.

Ludwig, K. 1997. The Truth about Moods. *ProtoSociology* 10, pp. 19–66.

Ludwig, K., and G. Ray. 1998. Semantics for Opaque Contexts. *Philosophical Perspectives* 12, pp. 141–66.

Mittwoch, A. 1988. Aspects of English Aspect: On the Interaction of Perfect, Progressive and Durational Phrases. *Linguistics and Philosophy* 2, pp. 203–54.

Ogihara, T. 1996. *Tense, Attitudes, and Scope*. Boston: Kluwer.

Palmer, F. R. 1974. *The English Verb*. London: Longman.

Parsons, T. 1990. *Events in the Semantics of English: A Study in Subatomic Semantics*. Cambridge, Mass.: MIT Press.

Partee, B. 1973. Some Structural Analogies between Tenses and Pronouns in English. *Journal of Philosophy* 70(18), pp. 601–9.

Reichenbach, H. 1947. *Elements of Symbolic Logic*. New York: Macmillan.

Richard, M. 1981. Temporalism and Eternalism. *Philosophical Studies* 39, pp. 1–13.

Russell, B. 1903. *The Principles of Mathematics*. Cambridge: Cambridge University Press.

Smith, C. 1978. The Syntax and Interpretation of Temporal Expressions in English. *Linguistics and Philosophy* 2, pp. 43–99.

Taylor, B. 1977. Tense and Continuity. *Linguistics and Philosophy* 1, pp. 199–220.

Vendler, Z. 1967. Verbs and Times. In *Linguistics and Philosophy*, pp. 143–60. Ithaca, N.Y.: Cornell University Press.

Visser, F. T. 1972. *An Historical Syntax of the English Language*, vol. 5. Leiden: E. J. Brill.

Vlach, F. 1993. Temporal Adverbials, Tenses and the Perfect. *Linguistics and Philosophy* 16, pp. 231–83.

2
Tense and Intension

Nathan Salmon

The radical philosopher of flux, Cratylus of Athens, is said to have spurned the use of language altogether in part because, like everything else, our words' meanings are continually changing, making it impossible to convey what we intend. Scholars in the age of "publish or perish" know that language has uses that do not require successful communication, but this seems a weak answer to Cratylus. Whereas diachronic change is inevitable, change in lexical meaning usually takes place over a long enough period that we manage during the interim, now and then, to get our thoughts across. I have come to believe, however, that any viable theory of the semantic content of language—whether Fregean, Russellian, or neither, or both—must accommodate the fact that, in a significant sense, the content or sense of most terms ('red', 'table', 'tree', 'walk') is indeed different at different times. I present here an account of semantic content that is philosophically neutral with respect to the sorts of issues that dominated twentieth-century philosophy of semantics, but that entails this kind of content shiftiness and other interesting consequences concerning the relationship between content and the empire of Time.

2.1   Semantic Content

The primary presupposition of any philosophical theory of semantic content is that the (or at least one) semantic function of declarative sentences is to express a proposition.[1] A declarative sentence may be said to *contain* the proposition it semantically expresses, and that proposition may be described as the *semantic content*, or more simply as the *content*, of the sentence. Propositions are, like the sentences that express them, abstract entities. Many of their properties can be "read off" from the containing sentences. Thus, for instance, it is evident that propositions are not ontologically simple but complex. The proposition that Frege is ingenious and the proposition that Frege is ingenuous are both, in the same way, propositions directly about Frege; hence, they must have some component in common. Likewise, the proposition that Frege is ingenious has some component in common with the proposition that Russell is ingenious, and that component is different from what it has in common with the proposition that Frege is ingenuous. Correspondingly, the declarative sentence 'Frege is ingenious' shares certain syntactic components with the sentences 'Frege is ingenuous' and 'Russell is ingenious'. These syntactic components—the name 'Frege' and the predicate 'is ingenious'—are separately semantically correlated with the corresponding component of the proposition contained by the sentence. Let us call the proposition-component semantically correlated with an expression the *semantic content* of the expression. The semantic content of the name 'Frege' is that which the name contributes to the proposition contained by such sentences as 'Frege is ingenious' and 'Frege is ingenuous'; similarly, the semantic content of the predicate 'is ingenious' is that entity which the predicate contributes to the proposition contained by such sentences as 'Frege is ingenious' and 'Russell is ingenious'. As a limiting case, the semantic content of a declarative sentence is the proposition it contains, its proposition content.

Within the framework of so-called possible-worlds semantics, the *extension* of a singular term with respect to a possible world w is simply its *referent* with respect to w, that is, the object or individual to which the term refers with respect to w. The extension of a sentence with respect to w is its truth value with respect to w—either truth or falsehood. The extension of an n-place predicate with respect to w is the class of n-tuples to which the predicate applies with respect to w, or rather the characteristic function of the class, that is, the function that assigns either truth or falsehood to an n-tuple of individuals, according as the predicate or its negation applies with respect to w to the n-tuple. (Assuming bivalence, the extension of an n-place predicate may simply be identified instead with the class of *n*-tuples to which the predicate applies.) The content of an expression determines the *intension* of the expression. The intension of a singular term, sentence, or predicate is a function that assigns to any possible world *w* the extension that the expression takes on with respect to *w*.

Since ordinary language includes so-called indexical expressions (such context-sensitive expression as 'I', 'here', 'now', 'this', 'she'), the semantic content of an expression, and hence also the semantic intension, may vary with the context in which the expression is uttered. This means that content must in general be "indexed" (i.e., relativized) to context. That is, strictly one should speak of the semantic content of an expression *with respect to* this or that context of utterance, and similarly for the corresponding semantic intension of an expression. This generates a higher-level, nonrelativized semantic value for expressions, which Kaplan calls the *character* of an expression. The character of an expression is a function or rule that determines for any possible context of utterance *c*, the semantic content that the expression takes on with respect to *c*.[2] An indexical expression is then definable as one whose character is not a constant function.

The systematic method by which it is secured which proposition is semantically expressed by which sentence (with respect to a context) is, roughly, that a sentence semantically contains that proposition whose components are the semantic contents of the sentence-parts, with these semantic contents combined as the sentence-parts are themselves combined to form the sentence.[3] In order to analyze the proposition contained by a sentence into its components, one simply decomposes the sentence into its contentful parts, and the semantic contents thereof are the components of the contained proposition. In this way, declarative sentences not only contain but also codify propositions. One may take it as a sort of general rule or principle that the semantic content of any compound expression, with respect to a given context of utterance, is made up of the semantic contents, with respect to the given context, of the contentful components of the compound. This general rule is subject to certain important qualifications, however, and must be construed more as a general guide or rule of thumb. Exceptions arise in connection with quotation marks and similar devices. The numeral '9' is, in an ordinary sense, a component part of the sentence 'The numeral "9" is a singular term', though the semantic content of the former is no part of the proposition content of the latter. I shall argue below that, in addition to quotation marks, there is another important though often neglected class of operators that yield exceptions to the general rule in something like the way quotation marks do. Still, it may be correctly said of any English sentence free of any operators other than truth-functional connectives (e.g., 'If Frege is ingenious, then so is Russell') that its proposition content is a complex made up of the semantic contents of its contentful components.

2.2   The Simple Theory

The *simple theory* is a theory of the semantic contents of some, but not all, sorts of expressions. Specifically, the simple theory is tacit on the controversial question of the semantic contents of proper names and similar sorts of singular terms. According to the simple theory, the semantic content of a predicate (or common noun or verb), as used in a particular context, is something like the attribute or concept semantically associated with the predicate with respect to that context. For example, the content of a monadic predicate may be identified with the corresponding property, while the content of an n-adic predicate, $n > 1$, may be identified with the corresponding n-ary relation. On the simple theory, the content of the sentence 'Frege is ingenious' is to be the proposition consisting of the semantic content of 'Frege'—whatever that may be (man, representational concept, or whatever)—and ingenuity (the property of being ingenious). More generally, an atomic sentence consisting of an n-place predicate π attached to an n-ary sequence of singular terms, $\alpha_1, \alpha_2, \ldots, \alpha_n$, when evaluated with respect to a particular possible context, is held to express the proposition consisting of the attribute or concept referred to by π and the sequence of semantic contents of the attached singular terms. A sentential connective may be construed on the model of a predicate. The semantic content of a sentential connective would thus be an attribute—not an attribute of individuals like Frege, but an attribute of propositions. Similarly, the semantic content of a

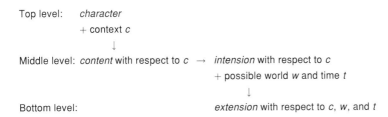

Figure 2.1
Semantic values on the simple theory

quantifier might be identified with a property of properties of individuals, and so on.

One may be tempted to hold that a sentence is a means for referring to its proposition content by specifying the components that make it up. However, a familiar argument due primarily to Alonzo Church and independently to Kurt Gödel establishes that the closest theoretical analogue of singular-term reference for any expression is its extension.[4] Accordingly, the simple theory will be understood to make room for the thesis that any expression refers to its extension, and for a resulting distinction between reference and semantic content.

The simple theory thus recognizes three distinct levels of semantic value. The three primary semantic values are *extension*, *content*, and *character*. On the same level as, and fully determined by, content is *intension*. Semantic values on the simple theory, and their levels and interrelations, are diagrammed in figure 2.1. (Of course, these are not the only semantic values available on the simple theory, but they are the significant ones.) Within the framework of the simple theory, the *meaning* of an expression might be identified with the expression's character, that is, the semantically correlated function from possible contexts of utterance to semantic contents. For example, the meaning of the sentence

(1)   I am writing

may be thought of as a function that assigns to any context of utterance c the proposition composed of the semantic content of 'I' with respect to c (whether that content may be the agent of c, a Fregean sense, or something else) and the property of writing.

2.3 Propositions and Proposition Matrices

Compelling though it is, the simple theory is fundamentally defective and must be modified if it is to yield a viable theory of semantic content. The flaw is illustrated by the following example: Suppose that at some time in 1890 Frege utters sentence (1) (or its German equivalent). Consider the proposition that Frege asserts in uttering this sentence. This is the proposition content of the sentence with respect to the context of Frege's uttering it. Let us call this proposition 'p^*' and the context in which Frege asserts it 'c^*'. The proposition p^* is made up of the semantic content of the indexical term 'I' with respect to c^* and the semantic content of the predicate 'writing' with respect to c^*. According to the simple theory, the latter semantic content is the property of writing. Thus, p^* (the semantic content of the whole sentence with respect to c^*) is a complex abstract entity made up of the semantic content of 'Frege' and the property of writing. Let us call this complex 'Frege writing', or '*fw*' for short. Thus, according to the simple theory, $p^* = fw$. But this cannot be correct. If *fw* is thought of as having a truth value, then it is true if *and when* Frege is writing and false if and when he is not writing. Thus, *fw* vacillated in truth value over time, becoming true whenever Frege began writing and false whenever he ceased writing.[5] But p^*, being a proposition, has in any possible world (or at least in any possible world in which something is determined by the semantic content of 'Frege') a fixed and unchanging truth value throughout its existence, and never takes on the opposite truth value. In effect, a present-tensed sentence like (1) expresses the same eternal proposition on any occasion of utterance as does its temporally modified cousin

(2)   I am writing now.

In this sense, propositions are *eternal*.

   Not just some; all propositions are eternal. The eternalness of a proposition is central and fundamental to the very idea of a proposition, and is part and parcel of a philosophically entrenched conception of proposition content. For example, Frege, identifying the cognitive proposition content (*Erkenntniswerte*) of a sentence with what he called the 'thought' (*Gedanke*) expressed by the sentence, wrote:

Now is a thought changeable or is it timeless? The thought we express by the Pythagorean Theorem is surely timeless, eternal, unvarying. "But are there not thoughts which are true today but false in six months' time? The thought, for example, that the tree there is covered with green leaves, will surely be false in six months' time." No, for it is not the same thought at all. The words 'This tree is covered with green leaves' are not sufficient by themselves to constitute the expression of thought, for the time of utterance is involved as well. Without the time-specification thus given we have not a complete thought, i.e., we have no thought at all. Only a sentence with the time-specification filled out, a sentence complete in every respect, expresses a thought. But this thought, if it is true, is true not only today or tomorrow but timelessly. ("Thoughts," in Frege's *Logical Investigations*, P. T. Geach, ed. (New Haven, Conn.: Yale University Press, 1977), pp. 1–30, at pp. 27–28)

The same sort of consideration is used by Richard Cartwright to show that the meaning of a present-tensed sentence is not its proposition content when uttered with assertive intent, or what is asserted by someone who utters the sentence. Cartwright's argument exploits the further fact that the truth value of a proposition is constant over space as well as time:

Consider, for this purpose, the words 'It's raining'. These are words, in the uttering of which, people often (though not always) assert something. But of course *what* is asserted varies from one occasion of their utterance to another. A person who utters them one day does not (normally) make the same statement as one who utters them the next; and one who utters them in Oberlin does not usually assert what is asserted by one who utters them in Detroit. But these variations in what is asserted are *not* accompanied by corresponding changes in meaning. The words 'It's raining' retain the same meaning throughout.... [One] who utters [these words] speaks correctly only if he [talks about] the weather at the time of his utterance and in his (more or less) immediate vicinity. It is this general fact about what the words mean which makes it possible for distinct utterances of them to vary as to statement made.... They are used, without any alteration in meaning, to assert now one thing, now another. ("Propositions," in R. Butler, ed., *Analytical Philosophy* (Oxford: Basil Blackwell, 1968), pp. 81–103, at pp. 92–94)

Similar remarks by G. E. Moore make essentially the same point about propositions expressed using the past tense:

As a general rule, whenever we use a past tense to express a proposition, the fact that we use it is a sign that the proposition expressed is *about* the time at which we use it; so that if I say twice over "Caesar was murdered," the proposition which I express on each occasion is a different one—the first being a proposition with regard to the earlier of the two times at which I use the words, to the effect that Caesar was murdered before *that* time, and the second a proposition with regard to the latter of the two, to the effect that he was murdered before *that* time. So much seems to me hardly open to question. ("Facts and Propositions," in *Philosophical Papers* (New York: Collier, 1966), pp. 60–88, at p. 71)

Consider again Frege's "thought" that a particular tree is covered with green leaves. Six months from now, when the tree in question is no longer covered with green leaves, the sentence

(3)   This tree is covered with green leaves,

uttered with reference to the tree in question, will express the proposition that the tree is *then* covered with green leaves. This will be false. But that proposition is false even now. What is true now is the proposition that the tree *is* covered with green leaves, in other words, the proposition that the tree is *now* covered with green leaves. This is the proposition that one would currently express by uttering sentence (3). It is eternally true—or at least true throughout the entire lifetime of the tree and never false. There is no proposition concerning the tree's foliage that is true now but will be false in six months. Similarly, if the proposition p^* that Frege asserts in c^* is true, it is eternally true. There is no non-eternal proposition concerning Frege that vacillates in truth value as he shifts from writing to not writing. The complex fw is noneternal, neutral with respect to time. Hence, it is not a complete proposition; that is, it is no proposition at all, properly so-called.

The truths truthsayers say and the sooths soothsayers soothsay—these all are propositions fixed, eternal, and unvarying. Eternal are the things asserters assert, the things believers believe, the things dreamers dream. Eternal also are the principles we defend, the doctrines we abhor, the things we doubt, the things we cannot doubt. The truths that are necessarily true and those that are not, the falsehoods that are necessarily false and those that are not—these are one and all eternal propositions. None of this is to say that the noneternal complex fw is not a semantic value of the sentence Frege utters, or that fw has nothing to do with proposition content. Indeed, fw is directly obtained from the sentence Frege utters in the context c^* by taking the semantic content of 'I' with respect to c^* and the property associated with 'writing' with respect to c^*. Moreover, fw can be converted into a proposition simply by *eternalizing* it, that is, by infusing a particular time (moment or interval) t into the complex to get a new abstract entity consisting of the semantic content of 'Frege', the property of writing, and the particular time t. One may think of the noneternal complex fw as the matrix of the proposition p^* that Frege asserts in c^*. Each time he utters sentence (1), Frege asserts a different proposition, expresses a different "thought," but always one having the same matrix fw. Similarly, in some cases it may be necessary to incorporate a location as well as a time in order to obtain a genuine proposition, for example, 'It is raining' or 'It is noon'. A proposition does not have different truth values at different locations in the universe, any more than it has different truth values at different times. A proposition is fixed, eternal, and unvarying in truth value over both time and space.

To each proposition matrix there corresponds a particular property of times (or, where necessary, a binary relation between times and places). For example, the time property corresponding to the proposition matrix fw is the property of being a time at which Frege is writing. It is often helpful in considering the role of proposition matrices in the semantics of sentences to think of a proposition matrix as if it were its corresponding property of times.

It has been noted by William and Martha Kneale, and more recently and in more detail by Mark Richard, that this traditional conception of semantic content is reflected in our ordinary ascriptions of belief and other propositional attitudes.[6] As Richard points out, if what is asserted or believed were something temporally neutral or noneternal, then from the conjunction

(4)   In 1990, Mary believed that Bush was president, and she has not changed her mind about that,

it would be legitimate to infer

(5)   Mary still believes that Bush is president.

Such an inference is an insult not only to Mary but also to the logic of English, as it is ordinarily spoken. Rather, what we might infer is

(6)   There is some time t in 1990 such that Mary still believes that Bush was president at t.

The reason for this is that what Mary is said by sentence (4) to have believed in 1990 is not the noneternal proposition matrix, Bush being president, but the eternal proposition that Bush is president throughout a particular time period. The point is bolstered if 'know' is substituted for 'believe'.

The length of the time period is a vague matter. For many purposes, it may be taken to be the entire year of 1990. When the time interval involved in a proposition is significantly long, the proposition may mimic its noneternal matrix—for example, in contexts like 'Mary once believed that Bush was a Republican, and she still believes that'—as long as one stays within the boundaries of the time interval in question. Relatively stable properties (like being a Republican, as opposed to being U.S. president) tend to lengthen the time interval in question.[7] (They need not invariably do so.) This point is crucial to the proper analysis of inferences that seem to tell against the argument just considered. Mark Aronszajn, for example, objects to the argument by citing formally similar but evidently valid inferences like the following:

(7)   In 1976, experts doubted that AIDS was transmitted through unprotected heterosexual intercourse, but no experts doubt that today.

Therefore, today no experts doubt that AIDS is transmitted through unprotected heterosexual intercourse.

(8)   In 1990, Mary believed that Bush was president, and in 1992, she still believed that.

Therefore, in 1992, Mary still believed that Bush was president.[8]

The modes by which AIDS is transmitted among humans are presumed to be invariant over a very long period of time (perhaps for eternity). Likewise, a natural interpretation of the second inference has its author ascribing to Mary the belief that Bush was president during the presidential term encompassing the years 1990–92 (as he in fact was). Indeed, if the attributed belief is presumed instead to be merely that Bush was president throughout some shorter period of time (e.g., the year 1990), the inference becomes obviously invalid. In each case, insofar as the inference receives an interpretation on which it is clearly valid, the proposition attributed incorporates a time interval encompassing the indicated passage of time.

2.4   Content and Content Base

Let us call the proposition matrix that a sentence like (1) takes on with respect to a particular context *c* the *content base* of the sentence with respect to *c*. More generally, we may speak of the *content base* with respect to a context of any meaningful expression (a singular term, a predicate, a connective, a quantifier, etc.). The content base of an expression is the entity that the expression contributes to the proposition matrix taken on by (i.e., the content base of) typical sentences containing the expression (where a "typical" sentence containing an expression does not include additional occurrences of such devices as quotation marks or the 'that'-operator).

The content base of a simple predicate, such as 'writes', with respect to a context *c*, is the attribute semantically associated with the predicate with respect to *c* (the property of writing). The content base of a compound expression, like a sentence, is (typically) a complex made up of the content bases of the simple parts of the compound expression. In particular, the content base of a definite description is a complex made up partly of the property associated with the description's constitutive predicate. Since ordinary language includes indexical expressions such as 'this tree', not only the semantic content but also the content base of an expression is to be relativized to the context of utterance. An expression may take on one content base with respect to one context, and another content base with respect to a different context. An indexical expression is properly defined as one that takes on different content bases with respect to different possible contexts.

The simple theory is at odds with the eternalness of propositions. There remains a question of how best to accommodate this feature of propositions within a framework like that of the simple theory. While alternative accounts are available, what is perhaps the path of minimal mutilation from the simple theory centers on its notion of *character*.[9] As defined by Kaplan, the character of an expression is the function or rule that takes one from an arbitrary context of utterance to the expression's semantic content with respect to that context. This may be identified with the expression's *meaning* only insofar as the content is misidentified with its noneternal matrix. Let us now reconstrue character as the function or rule that determines for any possible context c the content base (rather than the content) that the expression takes on with respect to c. This transmutation of the old notion of character forms the heart of a corrected version of the simple theory. An indexical expression is now redefined as one whose character, as here reconstrued, is not a constant function; it is one whose content base varies with context.

The content base of an expression with respect to a context c determines a corresponding function that assigns to any time t (and location l, if necessary) an appropriate content for the expression. (In fact, the function also determines the corresponding content base.) For example, the proposition matrix fw (the content base of 'Frege is writing') determines a function that assigns to any time t the proposition that Frege is writing at t. (This is the propositional function corresponding to the property of being a time at which Frege is writing.) Let us call the function from times (and locations) to contents thus determined by the content base of an expression with respect to a given context c the *schedule* of the expression with respect to c. Since the semantic content of an expression determines its intension, the content base of an expression with respect to a context c also determines a corresponding function that assigns to any time t (and location l, if necessary) the resulting intension for the expression. Let us call this function from times (and locations) to intensions the *superintension* of the expression with respect to c. Accordingly, we should speak of the semantic content, and the corresponding intension, of an expression *with respect to a context c and a time t (and a location l*, if necessary). The simple theory must be modified accordingly. Specifically, the notion of semantic content, by contrast with that of content base, is doubly relativized (in some cases, triply relativized). Significantly, the time to which the content of an expression is relativized need not be the time of the context, although of course it can be. Thus, for example, the expression 'my car' refers with respect to my present context and the year 1989 to the Honda that is formerly mine. The same expression refers with respect to my present context and the year 1996 to the Toyota that is presently mine.

We should also like to speak (as we already have) of the content of an expression (e.g., of the proposition expressed by a sentence) with respect to a context *simpliciter*, without having to speak of the content with respect to *both* a context and a time. This is implicit in the notion of the character of an expression, as defined earlier. How do we get from the content base of an expression with respect to a given context to the content with respect to the same context *simpliciter* without further indexing, or relativization, to a time (and location)?

In the passage quoted above, Frege seems to suggest that the words making up a tensed but otherwise temporally unmodified sentence, taken together with contextual factors that secure contents for indexical expressions such as 'this tree', at most yield only something like what we are calling a 'proposition matrix', that is, the content base of the sentence with respect to the context of utterance, which is "not a complete thought, i.e.,... no thought at all." He suggests further that we must rely on the very time of the context of utterance to provide a "time-specification" or "time-indication"—presumably a specification or indication of the very time itself—which supplements the words to eternalize their content base, thereby yielding a genuine proposition or "thought." Earlier in the same article, Frege writes:

[It often happens that] the mere wording, which can be made permanent by writing or the gramophone, does not suffice for the expression of the thought. The present tense is [typically] used ... in order to indicate a time.... If a time-indication is conveyed by the present tense one must know when the sentence was uttered in order to grasp the thought correctly. Therefore the time of utterance is part of the expression of the thought. ("Thoughts," in *Logical Investigations*, p. 10)

On Frege's view, strictly speaking, the sequence of words making up a tensed but otherwise temporally unmodified sentence like (3), even when taken together with a contextual indication of which tree is intended, does not yet bear genuine cognitive content. Its content is incomplete. Presumably, on Frege's view, the sequence of words together with a contextual indication of which tree is intended has the logicosemantic status of a predicate true of certain times—something like the predicate 'is a time at which this tree is covered with green leaves' accompanied by a pointing to the tree in question—except that (3) thus accompanied may be completed by a time, serving as a specification or indication of itself, rather than by something syntactic, like the term 'now'. Accordingly, on Frege's theory, the content, or "sense" (*Sinn*), of (3) together with an indication of the intended tree but in abstraction from any time would be

a function whose values are propositions, or "thoughts" (*Gedanken*).[10]
Only the sequence of words making up the sentence together with an
indication of which tree is intended and *together with* a time-indication
or time-specification, as may be provided by the time of utterance itself,
is "a sentence complete in every respect" and has cognitive content.

It is not necessary to view the situation by Frege's lights. Whereas
Frege speaks of the cognitive thought content (or *Erkenntniswerte*) of the
words *supplemented by* both a contextual indication of which tree is
intended and a "time-indication," one may speak instead (as I already
have) of the content of the sequence of words themselves *with respect to*
a context of utterance and a time. The content of sentence (3) with respect to a context *c* and a time *t* is simply the result of applying the
schedule, with respect to *c*, of the sequence of words to *t*. This is a
proposition about the tree contextually indicated in *c*, to the effect that it
is covered with green leaves at *t*. In the general case, instead of speaking
of the content of an expression supplemented by both a contextual indication of the referents of the demonstratives or other indexicals contained therein and a "time-indication," as may be provided by the time
of utterance, one may speak of the content of the expression *with respect
to* a context and a time (and a location, if necessary). Still, Frege's conception strongly suggests a way of constructing a singly indexed notion
of the content of an expression with respect to (or supplemented by) a
context of utterance *c simpliciter*, without further relativization to (or
supplementation by) a time, in terms of the doubly indexed locution: we
may define the singly relativized notion of the content of an expression
with respect to a context *c* as the content with respect both to *c* and the
very time of *c* (and with respect to the very location of *c*, if necessary).

In particular, then, the semantic content of a sentence with respect to a
given context *c* is its content with respect to *c* and the time of *c* (and the
location of *c*, if necessary). Consequently, any temporally unmodified
sentence or clause expresses different propositions with respect to different contexts of utterance (*simpliciter*). For example, sentence (3) (more
accurately, the untensed clause 'this tree be covered with green leaves')
contains different propositions with respect to different times of utterance
even though the speaker is pointing to the same tree. Uttered six months
from now, it expresses the proposition about the tree in question that it

is then covered with green leaves. Uttered today, it contains the proposition that the tree *is* covered with green leaves, that is, that it is now covered with green leaves. The existence of this linguistic phenomenon is precisely the point made by Frege and echoed by Moore and Cartwright in the passages quoted in section 2.3.

Let us call this adjusted version of the simple theory the *corrected theory*. The corrected theory is the simple theory adjusted to accommodate the eternalness of semantic content. The adjustment involves only the temporal nature of content. The corrected theory remains neutral with respect to the dispute among Fregeans, Millians, and others concerning the question of what constitutes the semantic content of indexicals and similar expressions.

Within the framework of the corrected theory, the meaning of an expression is identified with its character, now construed as a function from contexts to content bases. This allows one to distinguish pairs of expressions like 'the U.S. president' and 'the present U.S. president' as having different meanings, even though they take on the same contents (or at least trivially equivalent contents) with respect to the same contexts. Their difference in meaning is highlighted by the fact that the latter is indexical while the former is not. More accurately, the character of an expression is the primary component of what is ordinarily called the 'meaning' of the expression, though an expression's meaning may have additional components that supplement the character.[11]

The corrected theory's notion of the content base of an expression with respect to a given context, and the resulting reconstrual of the character of an expression, impose a fourth level of semantic value, intermediate between the level of character and the level of content. The four primary semantic values, from the bottom up, are *extension*, *content* (construed now as necessarily eternal), *content base*, and *character*. There are also two additional subordinate semantic values. Besides intension (construed now as a one-place function from possible worlds) there are *schedule* and *superintension*, both of which are on the same level as, and fully determined by, the content base. Semantic values on the corrected theory, and their levels and interrelations, are diagrammed in figure 2.2. (Notice that character now takes one from a context c to a content base, which still needs a time t in order to generate a content.)

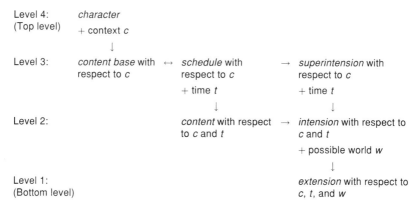

Figure 2.1
Semantic values on the corrected theory

The referent of a complex definite description like 'the wife of the present U.S. president' with respect to a context of utterance c, a time t, and a possible world w is semantically determined in a sequence of steps. First, the character of the expression is applied to the context c to yield the content base of the expression with respect to c. The latter is something like the time-neutral concept of uniquely being a wife of whoever is uniquely U.S. president at c_T, where c_T is the particular time of the context c. (The temporal indexing to c_T is provided for by the term 'present', which is interpreted here in its indexical sense.) This yields the schedule of the expression with respect to c, which assigns to any time t' the concept of uniquely being at t' a wife of whoever is uniquely U.S. president at c_T. This schedule is applied to the particular time t to give the eternal semantic content of the expression with respect to both c and t. This semantic content, in turn, yields the expression's intension with respect to c and t, which assigns to any possible world w' the individual who is uniquely a wife at t in w' of whoever is uniquely U.S. president at c_T in w'. (Since this is not a constant function, the description is not a rigid designator.) Finally, this intension is applied to the particular world w to yield the wife at t in w of the U.S. president at c_T in w. On the corrected theory, the extension of an expression with respect simply to a given context of utterance, without further relativization to a time or a possible world, is the result of applying the intension of the expression with respect to that context (which in turn is the result of applying the superintension of the expression with respect to that context to the very time of the context) to the very possible world of the context. Thus, where c_W is the possible world of c, the referent of 'the wife of the present U.S. president' with respect to c itself is none other than the wife at c_T in c_W of the U.S. president at c_T in c_W.

2.5   Tense versus Indexicality

It may appear that I have been spinning out semantic values in excess of what is needed. We need a singly indexed notion of the semantic content of an expression with respect to a context and, as a special case, a notion of the content of a sentence with respect to a context. This led to the simple theory's identification of meaning with a function from contexts to contents. But we have just seen that this function has no special role to play in determining the semantics for an expression like 'the wife of the actual U.S. president'. In getting to the content, and ultimately to the extension, we are now going by way of the content base instead of the content. With regard to 'the wife of the actual U.S. president', and similarly with regard to an entire sentence like (1) or (3), the content base with respect to a context is neutral with respect to time whereas the content with respect to the same context is eternal, somehow incorporating the time (and location, if necessary) of the context. If the rule of content composition is that the content of a complex expression, like a sentence, is constructed from the contents of the simple contentful components *together with* the time (and location, if necessary) of utterance, then why bother mentioning those partially constructed propositions I am calling 'proposition matrices'? Singling out content bases as separate semantic values generates the doubly indexed notion of the content of a sentence with respect to both a context c and a time t, and thereby the new construal of character. What is the point of this doubly indexed notion, and of the resulting reconstrual of character? Are we not interested only in the case where the time t is the time of the context of utterance c? Why separate out the time as an independent semantic parameter that may differ from the time of utterance?

Semantic theorists heretofore have gotten along fine by indexing the notion of content once, and only once, to the context of utterance, without relativizing further and independently to times. For example, in discussing the phenomenon of tense, Frege also considers various indexicals—'today', 'yesterday', 'here', 'there', and 'I'—and suggests a uniform treatment for sentences involving either tense or indexicals:

> In all such cases the mere wording, as it can be preserved in writing, is not the complete expression of the thought; the knowledge of certain conditions accompanying the utterance, which are used as a means of expressing the thought, is needed for us to grasp the thought correctly. Pointing the finger, hand gestures, glances may belong here too. ("Thoughts," in *Logical Investigations*, pp. 10–11)

Following Frege, it would seem that we can handle the phenomena of tense and indexicality together in one fell swoop, with tense as a special case of indexicality, by simply relativizing the notion of semantic content once and for all to the complete context of utterance—including the time and location of the utterance as well as the speaker and his or her accompanying pointings, hand gestures, and glances. Any aspect of the complete context of utterance may conceivably form "part of the expression of the thought" or contribute to the content. Once content is relativized to the complete context, including the time of utterance, gestures, and so on, there seems to be no need to relativize further and independently to times.

It has been known since the mid-1970s that the phenomenon of tense cannot be fully assimilated to temporal indexicality and that the presence of indexical temporal operators necessitates "double indexing," that is, relativization of the extensions of expressions—the reference of a singular term, the truth value of a sentence, the class of application of a predicate—to utterance times independently of the relativization to times already required by the presence of tense or other temporal operators.[12] (Something similar is true in the presence of an indexical modal operator such as 'actually' and in the presence of indexical locational operators such as 'it is the case here that'.) Here is an illustration: The present perfect tense operator functions in such a way that for any untensed clause S (e.g., 'Frege be writing'), the result of applying the present perfect tense operator to S ('Frege has been writing') is true with respect to a time t (roughly) if and only if S is true with respect to some time t' earlier than t. Similarly, the nonindexical operator 'on the next day' + future tense functions in such a way that the result of applying this operator to any untensed clause S is true with respect to a time t if and only if S is true with respect to the day next after the day of t. For example, suppose that instead of uttering sentence (1), Frege speaks the following words (perhaps as part of a larger utterance) in his context c^*:

(9)   I will be writing on the next day.

This sentence, in Frege's mouth, is true with respect to a time t if and only if Frege writes on the day after the day of t—whether or not t is the time of c^*. Indeed, our primary interest may be in some time t other than that of c^*—for example, if Frege's complete utterance in c^* is of the sentence

(10)   Regarding December 24, 1891, I will be writing on the next day.

On the other hand, the indexical operator 'tomorrow' + future tense functions in such a way that the result of applying it to any untensed clause S is true with respect to a context c and a time t if and only if S is true with respect to c and the day after c, forgetting about the time t altogether. If in c^* Frege had uttered the sentence

(11)   I will be writing tomorrow,

the sentence, in Frege's mouth, would be true with respect to any time if and only if Frege writes on the day after c^*.

   To illustrate the need for double indexing, consider how one might attempt to accommodate 'on the next day' + future tense using relativization only to possible contexts of utterance, without independent relativization to times. Let us try this: Say that the result of applying this operator to S is true with respect to a context c if and only if S is true with respect to some possible context c' just like c in every respect (agent, location, etc.) except that the time of c' is one day later than that of c. For example, 'I will be writing on the next day' will be regarded as being true with respect to a context c if and only if its untensed operand

(1$'$)   I be writing

is true with respect to a possible context c' whose day is the day after c, but which involves the same agent as c to preserve the referent of 'I'. (We assume for the time being that an untensed clause such as (1$'$) is a mere surface grammar variation of its present-tensed counterpart, so that (1) and (1$'$) share the same semantics.) This singly indexed account seems to yield the correct results until we consider sentences that embed one temporal operator within the scope of another. Consider the following sentences:

(12)   The U.S. president is a Republican,

(13)   The present U.S. president is a Republican,

(14)   Sometimes, the U.S. president is a Republican,

(15)   Sometimes, the present U.S. president is a Republican.

Sentences (14) and (15) result from applying the temporal operator 'sometimes' to sentences (12) and (13), respectively. According to the singly relativized account, (15) is true with respect to a context of utterance c (roughly) if and only if there is some time t', which need not be c_T (the time of c), such that the U.S. president at t' is a Republican at t' (in the possible world of c). But this is the wrong truth condition for the sentence. In fact, it is the correct truth condition for the wrong sentence, to wit, the *nonindexical* sentence (14).

Sentences (14) and (15) differ in their truth conditions. Suppose both sentences are uttered in 1996, when the U.S. president is a lifelong Democrat though previously the presidency had been held by the Republicans. Sentence (14) is then true whereas sentence (15) is false. Sentence (15) is true with respect to a context of utterance c (roughly) if and only if there is some time t' such that the U.S. president at c_T (the time of the context c) is a Republican at t' (in the possible world of c). The temporal operator 'sometimes' directs us to evaluate its operand clause with respect to all times t'. The operand clause (13) is true with respect to the same context c and a time t' if and only if the description 'the present U.S. president' refers to something with respect to c and t' to which the predicate 'is a Republican' applies with respect to c and t'. In computing the referent of the description with respect to c and t', the indexical operator 'present' directs us to seek an object to which its operand phrase 'U.S. president' applies with respect to c_T, the very time of the context of utterance itself, forgetting about the time t'. Thus, in evaluating sentence (15) with respect to a time of utterance c_T, we are concerned simultaneously with the extension of 'U.S. president' with respect to c_T and the extension of 'is a Republican' with respect to a second time t'. The truth value of the whole depends entirely and solely on whether the unique object to which the phrase 'U.S. president' applies with respect to c_T is something to which the predicate 'is a Republican' applies with respect to t'. It is for this reason that a systematic theory of the extensions of the expressions of a language containing indexical temporal operators requires double indexing; that is, in general the notion of the extension of an expression (e.g., the truth value of a sentence) is relativized to both a context and a time, treated as independent semantic parameters.

A systematic singly indexed theory gives the wrong results. Frege's theory, for example, must regard the indexical description 'the present U.S. president' as extensionally semantically equivalent to the nonindexical 'the U.S. president'. Both would be regarded as expressions that are incomplete by themselves (hence, refer by themselves, in abstraction from any context, to functions), but that when completed by a "time-specification" or "time-indication" (as may be provided by the time of utterance) refer to the individual who is U.S. president at the specified or indicated time. Using extensional semantic considerations alone, Frege's theory is unable to find any difference with respect to truth or even with respect to truth conditions between the indexical sentence (15), taken as uttered at a certain time, and the nonindexical (14), taken as uttered at the very same time.[13]

This example illustrates that where an indexical temporal operator occurs within the scope of another temporal operator within a single sentence, the extensions of expressions are to be indexed both to the time of utterance and to a second time parameter, which may be other than the time of utterance and not even significantly related to the time of utterance. Temporal operators determine which time or times the extension of their operands are determined with respect to. In the special case of indexical temporal operators, the time so determined is a function of the time of the context of utterance. What is distinctive about indexical expressions ('I', 'this tree', or 'the present U.S. president') is not merely that the extension with respect to a context c varies with the context c, or even that the intension or semantic content with respect to a context c varies with c. That much may be true of even a nonindexical expression, such as 'the U.S. president' or 'Frege is writing'. What makes an expression indexical is that its extension with respect to a context c and a time t and a possible world w varies with the context c even when the other parameters are held fixed. This is to say that its superintension, and hence its content base, with respect to a context c varies with c. It is precisely this that separates 'the present U.S. president' from its non-indexical cousin 'the U.S. president'.

Though it is less often noted,[14] it is equally important that double indexing to contexts and times (or triple indexing to contexts, times, and locations, if necessary) is required at the level of semantic content as well as at the level of extension. For illustration, consider first the sentence

(16)   At t^*, I believed that Frege was writing.

By the ordinary laws of temporal semantics, this sentence is true with respect to a context of utterance c if and only if the sentence

(17)   I believe that Frege is writing

is true with respect to both c and the time t^*. This, in turn, is so if and only if the binary predicate 'believe' applies with respect to c and t^* to the ordered pair of the referent of 'I' with respect to c and t^* and the referent of the 'that'-clause 'that Frege is writing' with respect to c and t^*. Hence, sentence (16) is true with respect to c if and only if the agent of c believes at t^* the proposition referred to by the 'that'-clause with respect to c and t^*. The 'that'-clause in (16) refers with respect to c and t^* to the proposition that is the content of the operand sentence 'Frege is writing'. But which proposition is that?

If content is to be singly indexed to context alone, it would seem that the 'that'-clause 'that Frege is writing' refers with respect to c and t^* to the content of 'Frege is writing' *with respect to* c, forgetting about t^* altogether. This is the proposition that Frege is writing at c_T, where c_T is the time of c. However, this yields the wrong truth condition for (16). This would be the correct truth condition for the sentence

(18)   At t^*, I believed that Frege would be writing now.

Sentence (16) ascribes a belief at t^* that Frege is writing *at* t^*. Assuming that content is singly indexed to context alone, we are apparently forced to construe the 'that'-operator in such a way that a 'that'-clause $\ulcorner$that $S\urcorner$ refers with respect to a context c and a time t' not to the content of S with respect to c but to the content of S with respect to a (typically different) context c' exactly like c in every respect (agent, location, etc.)

except that its time is t'. (The contexts c and c' would be the same if and only if t' were the time of c.)

This account appears to yield exactly the right results until we consider a sentence that embeds an indexical temporal operator within the 'that'-operator and embeds the result within another temporal operator. Consider the following:

(19)   In 2001, Jones will believe that the present U.S. president is the best of all the former U.S. presidents.

This sentence is true with respect to a context c if and only if Jones believes in 2001 the proposition referred to by the words 'that the present U.S. president is the best of all the former U.S. presidents' with respect to c and the year 2001. On the singly indexed account of content, sentence (19) comes out true if and only if Jones believes in 2001 that the U.S. president in 2001 is the best of all the U.S. presidents before 2001. But this is the truth condition for the wrong sentence, namely,

(20)   In 2001, Jones will believe that the then U.S. president is the best of all the former U.S. presidents.

Sentence (19) ascribes, with respect to c, a belief that the U.S. president at c_T is the best of all the U.S. presidents before 2001. In order to obtain this result, the 'that'-clause in (19) must be taken as referring with respect to c and the year 2001 to the proposition that the U.S. president at c_T is the best of all the U.S. presidents prior to 2001 (or to some proposition trivially equivalent to this). This cannot be accommodated by a singly indexed account. It requires seeing content as doubly indexed: to the original context c and to the year 2001.

2.6   Temporal Operators

Two sorts of operators are familiar to philosophers of language. An *extensional* operator is one that operates on the extensions of its operands, in the sense that an appropriate extension for the operator itself would be a function from *extensions* appropriate to the operands (as opposed to some other aspect of the operands) to extensions appropriate to the compounds formed by attaching the operator to an appropriate operand. An extensional sentential connective (such as 'not' or 'if ..., then ...') is truth functional; an appropriate extension would be a function from (*n*-tuples of) truth values to truth values, and hence an appropriate semantic content would be an attribute of truth values. An *intensional* or *modal* operator is one that operates on the intensions of its operands. An appropriate extension for a modal connective like 'it is necessarily the case that' would be a function from (*n*-tuples of) sentence intensions (functions from possible worlds to truth values) or propositions to truth values, and an appropriate semantic content would be an attribute of intensions or propositions—for example, the property of being a necessary truth.

David Kaplan forcefully raises an objection to the conventional conception of propositions as eternal in connection with the applicability of intensional operators. He writes:

> Operators of the familiar kind treated in intensional logic (modal, temporal, etc.) operate on contents.... A modal operator when applied to an intension will look at the behavior of the intension with respect to [possible worlds]. A temporal operator will, similarly, be concerned with the time.... If we build the time of evaluation into the contents (thus ... making contents *specific* as to time), it would make no sense to have temporal operators. To put the point another way, if *what is said* [i.e., if the proposition asserted by a speaker] is thought of as incorporating reference to a specific time,... it is otiose to ask whether what is said [the proposition] would have been true at another time ... ("Demonstratives," pp. 502–3)

He elaborates in a footnote:

> Technically, we must note that [temporal] operators must, if they are not to be vacuous, operate on contents which are neutral with respect to [time]. Thus, for example, if we take the content of [(1)] to be [an eternal, time-specific proposition rather than its noneternal, temporally neutral matrix], the application of a temporal operator to such a content would have no effect; the operator would be vacuous. ("Demonstratives," pp. 503–4 n.)

Continuing this line of thought in the text, he writes:

> This functional notion of the content of a sentence in a context may not, because of the neutrality of content with respect to time and place, say, exactly correspond to the classical conception of a proposition. But the classical conception can be introduced by adding the demonstratives 'now' and 'here' to the sentence and taking the content of the result. ("Demonstratives," p. 504)

It is not otiose in the least to modify a sentence like (1) by applying a temporal operator, like 'yesterday' + past tense. The attached operator is anything but vacuous. It does not follow, however, that the content of (1), with respect to a given context, is something temporally neutral. Claiming that temporal operators operate on contents, and having defined the content of a sentence as the proposition asserted by someone in uttering the sentence, or *what is said*, Kaplan is forced to construe the proposition expressed by a sentence like (1) as something that may change in truth value at different times and in some cases even at different places. But this yields an incorrect account of propositions. Propositions, qua objects of assertion and belief, are eternal. As Frege, Moore, and Cartwright pointed out—and as Kaplan seems to acknowledge—propositions do not vacillate in truth value over time or space.

Consider the temporal operator 'sometimes'—or more accurately, 'sometimes' + present tense, which applies to an untensed clause S to form a new sentence. Is this an extensional operator? Certainly not. With respect to my actual present context, the sentences 'It is cloudy' and '$2 + 2 = 5$' are equally false, though 'Sometimes, it is cloudy' is true whereas 'Sometimes, $2 + 2 = 5$' is false. Nor is the 'sometimes' operator intensional, in the above sense. As with (1) and (2), sentences (12) and (13), uttered simultaneously, have precisely the same intension—indeed, they share the same proposition content (or at least trivially equivalent contents that are very nearly the same). But their temporal existential generalizations, (14) and (15), uttered simultaneously, have different contents, even different truth values. On the relevant reading (the Russellian secondary occurrence or narrow scope reading), (14) is true whereas (15) is false. (In fact, (15) is false on both the narrow scope and wide scope readings.) Thus, 'sometimes' is not a content operator either. As Kaplan points out, a temporal operator, if it is not to be vacuous, must operate on something that is temporally neutral. Contrary to Kaplan, what follows from this is that temporal operators do not operate on propositions. When a temporal operator is applied to (12), it is the matrix of the proposition expressed by (12), not the proposition itself, that is the proper object upon which the operator operates. In short, temporal operators like 'sometimes' are superintensional operators.[15] An appropriate extension for 'sometimes' with respect to a context c, a time t, and a possible world w would be the function that assigns truth to a proposition matrix (or to its corresponding schedule or superintension) if its value for at least one time (the resulting proposition or sentence intension) itself yields truth for the world w, and that otherwise assigns falsehood to the proposition matrix.

Kaplan comes close to recognizing that the objects of assertion and propositional attitude are eternal propositions when he shows ("Demonstratives," p. 500) that *what is said* in uttering a temporally indexical sentence like (2) at different times is different. His argument for this is that if such a sentence is uttered by me today and by you tomorrow, then

[if] what we say differs in truth value, that is enough to show that we say different things. But even if the truth values were the same, it is clear that there are possible circumstances in which what I said would be true but what you said would be false. Thus we say different things.

This is indeed correct. But the same argument can be made with equal force for a nonindexical tensed sentence. Thus, it is not surprising to find the following analogous argument given earlier by G. E. Moore:

It seems at first sight obvious that, if you have a number of judgements [i.e., utterances] with the same content, if one is true the rest must be.

But if you take a set of judgements [i.e., utterances] with regard to a given event A, [using words to the effect] either that it is happening, or that it is past, or that it is future, some of each set will be true and some false, which are true and which false depending on the time when the judgement [i.e., utterance] is made.

It seems a sufficient answer to say that a judgement [i.e., an utterance of a sentence of the form] "A is happening" made at one time never has the same content as the judgement [i.e., an utterance of the sentence] "A is happening" made at another. ("The Present," Notebook II [*c.* 1926], in *The Commonplace Book 1919–53*, Casimir Lewy, ed. (New York: Macmillan, 1962), p. 89)

Consider again sentence (1). Mimicking Kaplan, and following Moore, one may argue that if Frege utters it at t^* and again on the next day, and if what he asserted on the two occasions of utterance differ in truth value (across time), as indeed they may, that is enough to show that he asserted different things. This is precisely because it is known that what is asserted is not the sort of thing that can switch back and forth in truth value from one moment to the next. Since what is asserted on the one occasion is different from what is asserted on the other, it is not this content but its matrix, fw, upon which temporal operators operate.

In order to obtain the correct results, one must regard a sentential temporal operator such as 'sometimes' as operating on some aspect of its operand clause that is fixed relative to a context of utterance (in order to give a correct treatment of temporally modified indexical sentences like (15)) but whose truth value typically varies with respect to time (so that it makes sense to say that it is *sometimes* true, or true at such and such time). Once it is acknowledged that content is eternal, there simply is no such semantic value of a sentence on the simple theory's three-tiered array of semantic values. Nothing that is fixed relative to a context is also time sensitive in the required way. In order to find an appropriate semantic value for temporal operators such as 'sometimes' + present tense to operate on, one must posit a fourth level of semantic value.

The result of applying 'sometimes' to a sentence S may be regarded as expressing, with respect to a given context c, a proposition concerning the content base of the operand sentence S with respect to c. For example, the sentence

(21)   Sometimes, I am writing

contains, with respect to Frege's context c^* (or any other context in which Frege is the agent), the proposition about the proposition matrix *fw* that it is sometimes true. Accordingly, an appropriate semantic content for a temporal operator such as 'sometimes' would be a property of proposition matrices—in this case, the property of being true at some time(s).

2.7   Predicates and Quantifiers

An important point about predicates, quantifiers, and certain other operators emerges from the four-tiered corrected theory, and from the distinction between semantic content and content base in particular. The content base of a predicate with respect to a given context of utterance c is a concept or attribute (property or relation). This, together with a time t, determines the semantic content of the predicate with respect to c and t. In turn, the semantic content of a predicate with respect to c and t, together with a possible world w, determines the extension of the predicate with respect to c, t, and w. It follows that the semantic content of a predicate such as 'writes' (or 'be writing') with respect to a context c and a time t is not just the concept or property of writing (or anything similar, such as the function that assigns to any individual x the proposition matrix x *writing*). The concept or property of writing, together with a possible world w, cannot determine the extension of 'writes' with respect to both the world w and the time t, that is, the class of possible individuals who are writing at t in w. The property of writing, together with a possible world w, determines only the class of possible individuals who are writing *at some time or other* in w (or at most, the function that assigns to any time t the class of possible individuals who are writing at t in w). The semantic content of 'writes' with respect to a time t must be such as to determine for any possible world w the class of (possible) individuals who are writing *at the given time t* in w. Only some sort of complex consisting of the concept or property of writing *together with the given time t* will suffice to determine for any possible world w the extension of 'writes' with respect to both w and t. The semantic content of 'writes' with respect to a given time t is not merely the concept or property of writing but a *temporally indexed* concept or property: the concept or property of *writing at t*.

In general, the semantic content of a predicate with respect to a time t (and a location l, if necessary) is not the same attribute as the content base of the predicate but is the temporally indexed attribute that results from taking the content base of the predicate together with the time t (and location l, if necessary). Semantic content for predicates like 'writes' thus varies with time. Exactly analogous remarks apply to quantifiers, other second-order predicates, the definite-description operator 'the', and a variety of other operators.

This usually unrecognized fact about predicates allows us to retain, at least as a sort of general guide or rule of thumb, the principle that the semantic content of a compound expression, such as a sentence or phrase, is a complex made up solely and entirely of the semantic contents of the contentful components that make up the compound. In particular, the content of sentence (1) with respect to a context of utterance c may be thought of as made up of the semantic contents of 'I' and 'am writing' with respect to c. There is no need to introduce the time of the context as a third and separate component, for it is already built into the semantic content of the predicate (the property or concept of writing-at-c_T, where c_T is the time of c).

Since the semantic content of an expression with respect to a context c *simpliciter* is the semantic content with respect to both c and the time of *c* (and the location of *c*, if necessary), it follows that the semantic content of a typical predicate varies with context—even the content of non-indexicals like 'writes', 'red', 'table', 'tree'. To this extent, Cratylus was right on the money. It is this usually unnoticed feature of predicates that accounts for the fact that the sentence 'Frege is writing' takes on not only different truth values but also different contents when uttered at different times, even though the sentence contains no indexicals and is not itself indexical. It is also this feature of predicates that accounts for the fact that certain noneternal (i.e., temporally nonrigid) definite descriptions, such as 'the U.S. president', take on not only different referents but also different semantic contents when uttered at different times even though the description is not indexical. Recall that the distinctive feature of an indexical like 'I' or 'the present U.S. president' is that it takes on different content bases in different contexts. The semantic contents of the definite description 'the U.S. president', of the word 'writes', and of the sentence 'The U.S. president is writing' each varies with context. Yet none of these expressions is indexical; each retains the same content base in all contexts.[16]

The account of the semantic contents of temporal operators as properties of proposition matrices (or other content bases) makes for an important but usually unrecognized class of exceptions to the general principle that the semantic content of a compound expression is made up of the contents of its contentful components. Where *T* is a monadic temporal sentential operator (e.g., 'sometimes' + present tense or 'on July 4, 1968' + past tense), the content of the result of applying *T* to a clause *S* is made up of the content of *T* together with the content base rather than the content of *S*. In general, if *T* is a temporal operator, the content of the result of applying *T* to an expression is a complex made up of the semantic content of *T* and the content base rather than the content of the operand expression. Ordinarily, the content of an expression containing as a part the result of applying a temporal operator *T* to an operand expression is made up, in part, of the content base of the operand expression rather than its semantic content. (For complete accuracy, the notion of semantic content with respect to a context, a time, and a location, for a language *L* should be defined recursively over the complexity of expressions of *L*.)[17]

It is instructive to look at how the four-tiered corrected theory treats a simple, untensed clause, such as (1′) and various complex sentences built from it. The character of (1′) is given by the following rule:

(22)   For any context c, the content base of (1′) with respect to c is the proposition matrix c_A *writing*, where c_A is the agent of c. This proposition matrix is made up of the content bases of 'I' and of 'be writing' with respect to c. The latter may be taken to be the property or concept of writing.

The schedule of (1′) with respect to a given context c is thus given by the following rule:

(23)   For any time t, the semantic content of (1′) with respect to c and t is the proposition made up of the content of 'I' with respect to c and t (i.e., the result of applying the schedule of 'I' with respect to c to the particular time t) and the property of writing-at-t (the result of applying the schedule of 'be writing' to t). This may be taken to be the proposition that c_A is writing at t, where c_A is the agent of c.

The semantic content of (1′) with respect to a context c *simpliciter* is therefore the proposition that c_A is writing at c_T, where c_T is the time of c.

We may contrast this with the indexical sentence (2). Its character is given by something like the following rule:

(24)   For any context c, the content base of (2) with respect to c is the higher-order proposition made up of the content bases of (1′) and of 'now' + present tense with respect to c. The former may be taken to be the proposition matrix c_A *writing*, and the latter the property of proposition matrices of obtaining (or being true) at c_T, where c_A is the agent of c and c_T is the time of c.

This rule reveals the fact that the content base of the eternal sentence (2) is in fact already a full-fledged, eternal proposition, rather than a non-eternal proposition matrix. The schedule of (2) with respect to a context c is thus a constant function from times to the higher-order proposition about the proposition matrix c_A *writing* that it obtains at c_T. The content of (2) with respect to a context c *simpliciter* is this same higher-order singular proposition, whereas the semantic content of the simpler (1') with respect to c is the proposition that c_A is writing at c_T. Since, c_A is writing at c_T if and only if the proposition matrix c_A *writing* obtains at c_T, the semantic contents of (1') and (2) with respect to any context of utterance are trivially equivalent. If we assume that sentence (1) is merely a surface transformation of (1'), then *what is said* by a speaker uttering either (1) or (2) at the same time is very nearly the same, as long as the speaker is the same. Still, the content bases are very different. With respect to any context c, the content base of (1) is noneternal, neutral with respect to time, whereas the content base of (2) is eternal. As Kaplan notes, only the former can be felicitously operated upon by temporal operators.

Contrary to Kaplan, since the contents, *what is said*, are trivially equivalent, the function of 'now' cannot be primarily to affect what is said in context. Its effect on content is in fact nil (or virtually so). Rather, the function of 'now' is primarily to affect the content base of its operand, eternalizing it and thereby sealing it off from the influence of external occurrences of temporal operators. For example, attaching 'sometimes' to sentence (1), whose content base with respect to any context is noneternal, aptly yields sentence (21), whose content base is eternal. By contrast, 'sometimes' is at best superfluous in

(25)   Sometimes, I am writing now.

Compare also the role of 'present' in (15).

Analogously, the schedule of a sentence like 'I will be writing tomorrow', as uttered by a speaker c_A at time c_T, is the constant function that assigns to any time t the eternal proposition that c_A *writing* obtains on d^+, where d^+ is the day after the day of c_T. The schedule of the sentence 'I will be writing on the next day', with respect to the same context, is a nonconstant function that assigns to any time t the proposition that c_A *writing* obtains on the day next after t_D, where t_D is the day of t. Despite the close similarity between the contents of the two sentences with respect to any context (*what are said*), the schedules are very different, and only the latter sentence may be felicitously operated upon by temporal operators. Compare 'On December 24, 2001, I will be writing on the next day' with 'On December 24, 2001, I will be writing tomorrow'.

2.8   Pure Tenses

A considerably richer semantic theory of temporal operators may be obtained by drawing a three-way distinction among *quantificational* or *general* temporal operators, *specific* or *singular* temporal operators, and *pure tense* operators such as simple past or future tense. Quantificational or general temporal operators include such operators as 'sometimes', 'always', present perfect tense (as in 'I have been writing' in the sense of 'I have sometimes been writing'), 'it will always be that' + present tense, 'twice before' + past tense, and so on. Specific or singular temporal operators include 'it is now the case that', 'on December 24, 2001' + future tense, 'when Frege wrote "Thoughts"' + past tense, and so on. (Compare 'possibly' with 'actually'.) The difference between these two sorts of temporal operators lies in their accompanying semantics. Roughly, a specific sentential temporal operator T is one such that there is some specific time t semantically associated with T, with respect to a context (and a time and a possible world), in such way that the result of applying T to a sentence S is true with respect to a time t' if and only if S is true with respect to t, and t stands in some appropriate temporal-order relation to t'. For example, 'On December 24, 2001, I will be writing' is true with respect to a context c and the year 1996 if and only if both of the following conditions obtain: (a) clause (1') (or sentence (1)) is true with respect to c and December 24, 2001; and (b) 2001 is later than 1996. A general sentential temporal operator T is a nonspecific temporal operator such that there is some specific property P of classes of times semantically associated with T (with respect to semantic parameters) in such a way that the result of applying T to a sentence S is true with respect to a time t' if and only if the class of times with respect to which S is true and that stand in some appropriate temporal-order relation to t' has P. For example, in the case of the present perfect tense, the property P is that of being nonempty, and the appropriate temporal-order relation is the earlier-than relation.[18]

Now consider ordinary past or future tense, as in 'Frege was writing' or 'Frege will be writing'. Past tense is often treated as though it were a quantificational temporal operator, so that the displayed sentence is regarded as being true with respect to a time t if and only if 'Frege is writing' is true with respect to some time or other earlier than t. (See, for example, the quotation from G. E. Moore in section 2.3.) While a simple past-tensed sentence is sometimes used in this way (roughly, as equivalent to the corresponding present-perfect-tensed sentence), it generally is not. Ordinarily, a simple past-tensed sentence like 'Frege was writing' is used with implicit reference to a specific (though perhaps vaguely delineated) time, so that if Frege was not writing at the relevant time, then what is said is false even if Frege was writing at some time or other prior to the utterance. Compare 'I asked Frege to come along, but he was writing' with 'I have sometimes asked Frege to come along, but he has sometimes been writing'. Analogous remarks apply to future tense.

Most simple sentential temporal operators require, in idiomatic English, an appropriate adjustment in the tense of the operand. For example, if I wished to apply the temporal operator 'at 3:00 p.m. on August 24, 1996' to sentence (1), at the time of my writing these words—which happens to be 2:55 p.m. on August 24, 1996—I must accompany it with a shift from present to future tense. If I wait six minutes and forever thereafter, I must instead use past tense. It is not sufficient to say when my writing occurs; I must also specify whether the time of my writing is now, or previously, or still to come. The content base of each sentence is eternal, and the same proposition (or at least very nearly the same propositions) would be asserted at each time, and yet grammar compels me to indicate besides the indicated time, the temporal direction of that time—either earlier or later—from the time of utterance. What I say is that (a) my writing occurs at 3:00 p.m. on August 24, 1996; and (b) 3:00 p.m. on August 24, 1996, is future (or present or past, depending on the tense used). It is not enough simply to date the described state of affairs. One is linguistically required also to place the state of affairs described within what J. M. E. McTaggart called the *A-series*—the ever-changing manifold divided into past, present, and future, in which each element in the third of these three categories eventually finds itself temporarily in the second before coming to rest in the first. In this sense, the specific temporal operator 'at 3:00 p.m. on August 24, 1996' is *incomplete*. Simple past tense and simple future tense are complementary incomplete temporal operators, which modify an untensed, temporally unmodified clause like (1′) to form a sentence that may now be modified by an incomplete specific or incomplete general temporal operator. The tense operator primes the atomic clause for the application of a specific or general (incomplete) temporal operator. An incomplete specific or general temporal operator combines with a pure tense operator to form a complete temporal operator. The complete temporal operator applied to (1′) is 'at 3:00 p.m. on August 24, 1996' + future tense. The extension of a complete temporal operator is a function from proposition matrices (or minimally, from sentence superintensions) to truth values, and the content of a complete temporal operator is accordingly a concept or property of proposition matrices.

It is instructive to regard ordinary past tense as a superintensional operator with the following distinguishing property: its extension with respect to a time t and a possible world w is the function that assigns to any proposition matrix m (alternatively, to any sentence schedule or superintension—i.e., any function from times to sentence intensions) not a truth value, but the class of times $t′$ earlier than t at which m obtains in w (or equivalently, the characteristic function of this class of times). An analogous construal is possible for the future tense operator, replacing 'earlier' by 'later'. A past-tensed or future-tensed but otherwise temporally unmodified sentence would thus have as its extension not a truth value, but a class of times. For example, the extension of the simple past-tensed sentence

(26)   I was writing,

with respect to a context c, a time t, and a possible world w, would be the class of times $t′$ earlier than t such that the component untensed clause (1′) is true with respect to c, $t′$, and w. An unmodified past-tensed sentence like (26) may be represented formally as

(27)   *Past Tense*[*Be Writing*(I)].[19]

Such a sentence essentially stands in need of completion by an incomplete temporal operator, either specific or general, in order to achieve truth value. The extension (with respect to a context, a time, and a possible world) of an incomplete specific temporal operator, like 'at 3:00 p.m. on August 24, 1996', may be taken to be simply the indicated time, rather than the corresponding function from proposition matrices (or sentence schedules or superintensions) to truth values. Where T is any incomplete specific temporal operator without an accompanying tense operator, the result of applying *T* to a past-tensed sentence such as (26) is representable as

(28)   *T(Past Tense[Be Writing(I)])*.

This is a complete sentence, whose extension is a truth value. The sentence is true (with respect to semantic parameters) if and only if the extension of *T* is an element of the extension of the operand past-tensed clause *Past Tense[Be Writing(I)]*. It is thus as if the past tense operator in (26) transformed its operand clause (1') into the corresponding predicate

(29)   is a past time at which I be writing.

An incomplete specific temporal operator such as 'at 3:00 p.m. on August 24, 1996' attaches to the tensed sentence as if the operator were a singular term to which a monadic predicate attaches. The complete temporal operator 'at 3:00 p.m. on August 24, 1996' + past tense is a one-place connective. Its extension may be regarded as a function from proposition matrices to truth values.

In ordinary use, a past-tensed but otherwise temporally unmodified sentence like (26), standing alone as a declarative sentence in a piece of discourse, may be regarded as involving an implicit, specific, demonstrative temporal operator 'then', or 'at that time', in order to obtain a complete sentence, 'I was writing then'. This ordinary sort of use of (26) would thus be represented formally as

(30)   *Then(Past Tense[Be Writing(I)])*

and would be taken to mean something like *That time is a past time at which I be writing*. If the time implicitly designated in an utterance of (26) (standing alone as a declarative sentence in a piece of discourse) is not one at which the speaker writes, what is said is false even if the speaker has written at other times prior to the utterance. Analogous remarks apply to 'I will be writing'.[20]

Taking the extension of an incomplete specific temporal operator like 'at 3:00 p.m. on August 24, 1996' without an accompanying tense operator to be simply the indicated time, in order to obtain a complete sentence whose extension is a truth value from an incomplete specific temporal operator and an untensed clause like (1') as operand, a tense operator must be supplied as a bridge connecting the content base of the operand clause with respect to a context *c* to the extension with respect to *c* of the temporal operator, thereby achieving truth value. Which tense operator is appropriate will depend on the direction of the indicated time, earlier or later, relative to the time of *c*. This account thus accommodates the fact that the appropriate complete temporal operator typically shifts its constitutive tense from future to past with the passage of time.

On a Fregean approach, incomplete specific temporal operators like 'now' and 'at 3:00 p.m. on August 24, 1996' would be taken as expressing as the operator's semantic content (*Sinn*), a certain concept or property of the time so designated. On a Millian approach, by contrast, the semantic contents of these operators may again be regarded as simply the indicated time. On either approach, the content of a specific temporal operator like 'when Frege wrote "Thoughts"' may plausibly be regarded as analogous to that of the corresponding definite description 'the past time at which Frege writes "Thoughts"'. (The word 'when' in such constructions is the temporal analogue of the definite-description operator 'the'.) To repeat, the corrected theory is completely neutral regarding such issues and is consistent with either approach.

In earlier work, I have advocated a Millian version of the corrected theory, on which the semantic content of 'now' with respect to a context is taken to be the time of the context itself rather than a concept or property (*presentness*) of that time (see *Frege's Puzzle* and "Tense and Singular Propositions"). It does not follow, contrary to an argument of Quentin Smith,[21] that my nonneutral approach is committed to a rejection of McTaggart's A-series of time in favor of the B-series—in which any element is past, present, or future not per se but only relative to some (another or the same) element of the series—and hence to a "tenseless" theory of time, according to which the distinction among past, present, and future is unreal, illusory, relational (to a particular speech act or thought act), merely subjective, or carries no special metaphysical or cosmological significance.[22] Nor does it follow that tensed sentences like (1), (2), and (26), on my approach, locate particular states of affairs within the B-series but not within the A-series. On the contrary, even the corrected theory, which is itself neutral with regard to the contents of specific temporal operators—and of which my Millian account is a special version—explicitly recognizes, for example, that (26) places the speaker's writing in the past. On a Millian version of the corrected theory, this is not accomplished by the implicit 'then' in (26). On any version of the corrected theory, it is accomplished by the explicit 'was'. The A-property of pastness is overtly expressed in (26), by the very presence of past tense. Similarly, futurity is expressed by future tense.[23]

Just as an incomplete specific temporal operator may be plausibly treated as a singular term, so an incomplete quantificational temporal operator may be plausibly treated as a corresponding quantifier. The extension of 'sometimes', for example, may be taken to be the class of all nonempty classes of times (or equivalently, the characteristic function of this class), and its semantic content may likewise be taken to be the corresponding higher-order property of being a nonempty class of times. A quantificational temporal operator thus also requires an accompanying tense as a bridge connecting the superintension of its operand clause to its own extension. The result of applying a quantificational temporal operator to a tensed sentence is true if and only if the extension of the tensed sentence (which is not a truth value but a class of times) is an element of the extension of the quantificational temporal operator. Thus, for example, the sentence 'Sometimes, Frege was writing' is true with respect to a time t if and only if the class of times earlier than t at which Frege is writing (the extension of 'Frege was writing' with respect to t) is nonempty—that is, if and only if some time t' is a time earlier than t at which Frege is writing. (The complete quantificational temporal operator 'sometimes' + past tense provides a roughly correct, albeit somewhat strained, definition of one use of the present perfect tense, as in 'Frege has been writing', as well as of language theorists' alternative use of simple past tense.) Incomplete quantificational temporal sentential operators such as 'sometimes', 'always', and 'twice before' are thus regarded as attaching to tensed sentences in the way that quantifiers such as 'something', 'everything', and 'exactly two smaller things' attach to monadic predicates, whereas incomplete specific temporal operators such as 'on August 24, 1996' and 'when Frege wrote "Thoughts"' are regarded as attaching to tensed sentences in the way that singular terms are attached to by monadic predicates.[24]

There are complications involved in extending this account of temporal operators to cases in which temporal operators such as 'sometimes', 'always', 'now', and 'today' are applied directly to present-tensed sentences, as in any of the examples (2), (14), (15), and (21). The account would suggest that such instances of present tense be regarded as instances of a pure tense operator, analogous to past or future tense except that its extension with respect to a time t and a possible world w is the function that assigns to any proposition matrix m the class of times t'—whether earlier than, later than, or overlapping with t—at which m obtains in w. Such an operator is required, on the account being considered here, in order to prime a temporally unmodified clause such as (1′) for an operator such as 'sometimes' or 'today', to bridge the superintension of the unmodified clause with the extension of the incomplete specific or general temporal operator.

Strictly speaking, (1) probably should not be regarded as the atomic sentence formed by attaching the temporally unmodified predicate corresponding to the naked infinitive phrase 'be writing' to the term 'I', as represented formally by

(31)   *Be Writing(I)*.

What this represents is not (1) but (1′). Although (1′) is not a grammatical sentence of English, it is complete in itself. Its extension (with respect to appropriate semantic parameters) is a truth value; it is true with respect to a context c, a world w, and a time t if and only if the agent of c is writing at t in w. What, then, becomes of (1)?

On the account of temporal operators under consideration, the result of applying present tense to (1′), represented formally as

(32)   *Present Tense[Be Writing(I)]*,

is not a complete sentence of English, capable of truth value standing alone. Its extension is a class of times rather than a truth value. Yet surely one who wishes to assert what is encoded by a simple, atomic clause like (1′) uses a tensed sentence, namely, (1). How are we to accommodate the fact that (1) is capable of achieving truth value when standing alone as a declarative sentence without an additional temporal operator?

On this theory, such uses are regarded as involving an implicit specific, indexical temporal operator such as 'now'. For example, sentence (1) standing alone would be seen as elliptical for (2), represented formally as

(33)　*Now*(*Present Tense*[*Be Writing*(*I*)]).

This account of simple present tense is exactly analogous to the treatment suggested above of simple past tense according to which a simple past-tensed sentence such as (26) or 'Frege was writing', standing alone as a declarative sentence in a piece of discourse, is elliptical for a temporally indexical completion, for example, 'Frege was writing then'. We may call this the *ellipsis theory of present tense*.[25] It is not my purpose here to fill out the details of the ellipsis theory or to cite linguistic evidence either in favor of or against this general account of the simple tenses. It is adequate to my purpose merely to indicate the richness of the apparatus of the corrected theory for dealing with complete and incomplete temporal operators.[26]

It is interesting to note that on the ellipsis theory, a present-tensed sentence such as (3) is taken to be an incomplete sentence standing in need of completion, much as if it were the corresponding predicate 'is a time at which this tree be covered with green leaves'. At the level of semantic content, the present tense operator thus converts the content base of its untensed operand clause into something like its corresponding property of being a time at which the tree in question is covered with green leaves. This theory of the pure tenses thus mimics Frege's construal of a present-tensed sentence as standing in need of completion or supplementation, typically provided by the time of utterance. Frege's theory works remarkably well as a theory of tense. Unfortunately, as we saw in sections 2.5 and 2.6, it fails as an account of temporal indexicality.

Notes

Portions of my book *Frege's Puzzle* (Atascadero, Calif.: Ridgeview, 1986, 1991) and of my chapter "Tense and Singular Propositions," in J. Almog, J. Perry, and H. Wettstein, eds., *Themes from Kaplan* (Oxford: Oxford University Press, 1989), pp. 331–92, have been incorporated into the present chapter. Where those presentations presuppose a Millian (or neo-Russellian) semantic theory, this presentation, by contrast, is deliberately neutral regarding all such issues. I am grateful to Steven Humphrey, Aleksandar Jokić, Takashi Yagisawa, and my audience at the Santa Barbara City College conference "Time, Tense, and Reference" for their comments.

1. Throughout this chapter, I am concerned with discrete units of information that are specifiable by means of a 'that'-clause—for example, that Socrates is wise. These discrete units are *propositions*. Following the usual practice, I use the verb 'express' in such a way that an unambiguous declarative sentence expresses (with respect to a given possible context c) a single proposition, which is referred to (with respect to c) by the result of prefixing 'the proposition that' to the sentence. A declarative sentence may express two or more propositions, but if it does so, it is ambiguous. Propositions expressed by the proper logical consequences of an unambiguous sentence are not themselves expressed, in this sense, by the sentence. The proposition that snow is white and grass is green is different from the proposition that snow is white, though intuitively the latter is included as part of the former. The sentence 'Snow is white and grass is green' expresses only the former, not the latter.

2. Whereas Kaplan introduces his notion of character in connection with his version of a direct reference theory, the general idea of relativizing content to context, and the resulting notion of the character of an expression, can easily fit within a Fregean (or "anti–direct reference") conception of content.

Throughout this chapter, I use a quasi-technical notion of the *context* of an utterance which is such tht for any particular actual utterance of an expression, if any facts had been different, even if only facts entirely independent of and isolated from the utterance itself, then the context of the utterance would, ipso facto, be a different context—even if the utterance is made by the very same speaker in the very same way to the very same audience at the very same time in the very same place. To put it another way, although a single utterance occurs in indefinitely many different possible worlds, in every possible world in which the same utterance occurs it occurs in a new and different context—even if the speakers, his or her manner of uttering, the time of the utterance, the location of the speaker, the audience being addressed, and all other such features and aspects of the utterance reamin exactly the same. Suppose, for example, that it will come to pass that a Democrat is elected to the U.S. presidency in the year 2000, and consider a possible world w that is exactly like the actual world in every detail up to January 1, 1999, but in which a Republican is elected to the U.S. presidency in 2000. Suppose I here and now utter the sentence

(i)　Actually, a Republican will be elected to the U.S. presidency in 2000 A.D.

In the actual world, I thereby assert a proposition that is necessarily false. In w, on the other hand, I thereby assert a necessary truth. In uttering the very same sequence of words of English with the very same English meanings in both possible worlds, I assert different things. If we were to use the term 'context' in such a way that the context of my utterance remains the same in both worlds, we would be forced to say, quite mysteriously, that the sentence I uttered is such that it would have expressed a different proposition with respect to the context in which I uttered it if w had obtained, even though both its meaning and its context of utterance would remain exactly the same. The content of the sentence would emerge as a function not only of the meaning of the sentence and the context of utterance but also of the apparently irrelevant question of which political party wins the U.S. presidency in the year 2000. Using the term 'context' as I do, we may say instead that although I make the very same utterance both in *w* and in the actual world, the context of the utterance is different in the two worlds. This allows us to say that the sentence I utter takes on different information contents with respect to *different* contexts of utterance, thereby assimilating this phenomenon to the sort of context sensitivity that is familiar in cases of such sentences as 'A Republican is presently U. S. president'.

3. The latter clause is needed in order to distinguish 'Bill loves Mary' from 'Mary loves Bill', where the sequential order of composition is crucial. This succinct statement of the rule connecting sentences and their contents is only an approximation to the truth. A complicated difficulty arises in connection with the latter clause of the rule and with quantificational locutions. Grammatically the sentence 'Someone is wise' is analogous to 'Socrates is wise', though logically and semantically they are disanalogous. In 'Socrates is wise', the predicate 'is wise' attaches to the singular term 'Socrates'. As Russell showed, this situation is reversed in 'Someone is wise', wherein the restricted quantifier 'someone' attaches to the predicate 'is wise'. Thus, whereas grammatically 'someone' is combined with 'is wise' to form the first sentence in just the same way that 'Socrates' is combined with 'is wise' to form the second sentence, the semantic contents of 'someone' and 'is wise' are combined very differently from the way the contents of 'Socrates' and 'is wise' are combined. A perhaps more important qualification to the general rule is noted in the next paragraph of the text. Yet another important qualification concerns overlaid quantifiers. For details, see *Frege's Puzzle*, pp. 155–57.

4. See A. Church, "Review of Carnap's *Introduction to Semantics*," *The Philosophical Review* 52 (1943), pp. 298–304, at pp. 299–301; K. Gödel, "Russell's Mathematical Logic," in P. A. Schilpp, ed., *The Philosophy of Bertrand Russell*, (New York: Tudor, 1944), pp. 125–53, at pp. 128–29. The general argument is applied to the special case of monadic predicates in my *Frege's Puzzle*, pp. 22–23, and in greater detail to the special case of common nouns in my *Reference and Essence* (Princeton, N.J.: Princeton University Press, and Oxford: Basil Blackwell, 1981), pp. 48–52.

5. This forces a misconstrual of the intension of sentence (1) with respect to Frege's context c^* as a two-place function that assigns to the ordered pair of both a possible world w and a time t a truth value, either truth or falsehood, according as the individual determined by the semantic content of 'Frege' is writing in w at t or not.

6. See W. Kneale and M. Kneale, "Propositions and Time," in A. Ambrose and M. Lazerowitz, eds., *G. E. Moore: Essays in Retrospect* (New York: Humanities Press, 1970), pp. 228–41, at p. 235; Mark Richard, "Temporalism and Eternalism," *Philosophical Studies* 39 (1981), pp. 1–13.

7. This is similar to a point made by Kneale and Kneale, "Propositions and Time," pp. 232–33. Compare my *Frege's Puzzle*, p. 157 n. 3. On the most natu-

ral interpretation of past-tensed belief attribution sentences ⌜α believed that φ⌝, such a sentence is true with respect to a particular time t if and only if there is a salient time t' earlier than t and a salient interval t'' including t' such that the referent of α with respect to t' believed at t' the proposition expressed by φ with respect to t''. (This semantics involves a slight departure from that proposed by Richard.)

8. See M. Aronszajn, "A Defense of Temporalism," *Philosophical Studies* 81 (1996), pp. 71–95. Aronszajn's actual examples invoke the past progressive in place of the simple past tense (specifically, 'AIDS was spreading among heterosexuals' in place of 'AIDS was transmitted through unprotected heterosexual intercourse'), and the attribute of being up to no good as president in place of merely being president. Aronszajn's examples strike me as significantly less plausible than the ones provided here. If experts in 1976 believed that AIDS was not spreading among heterosexuals, but they have since changed their minds about that, then what they no longer believe is that AIDS was not spreading in 1976 among heterosexuals. It is logically possible, and even consistent (albeit irrational), for such experts to believe that AIDS was spreading among heterosexuals in 1976 (having changed their minds in exactly the manner described) and at the same time to believe that as a result of recent educational efforts AIDS is no longer spreading among heterosexuals. Likewise, though Mary in 1990 believed Bush to be up to no good, and though she held fast about that two years later, she may well have believed by then that Bush was no longer up to no good. Imagine, for example, Mary saying the following: 'In 1990, I believed on the basis of reliable sources that Bush was abusing the power of his office through illegal wiretaps, directing the IRS to persecute his enemies, and more. Two years later, I received confirmation of that very same abuse in the 1990 White House and so continued to believe that, though I also believed that Bush had cleaned up his act by then and was finally behaving properly. I have just received evidence that such abuse in fact continued through 1992'.

It should be noted that the anaphoric pronoun 'that' in examples like those under consideration here need not always refer to the proposition referred to by its antecedent. In some uses, it may refer instead to another proposition related to the antecedently referred to proposition by having the same matrix. Analogously, the conjunction 'Johnny believes that he is the strongest boy in the class and so does Billy' may be used to report agreement between Johnny and Billy concerning who is strongest, or alternatively to report a disagreement between them. On the latter reading, the anaphoric pronoun 'so' does not refer to the act of believing the particular proposition referred to in the first disjunct, but to the act of believing the proposition expressed by 'I am strongest'. (Compare 'Naturally, Johnny believes that he is the strongest boy in the class. At that age, nearly every boy believes that'.)

9. A somewhat different approach is adopted in my *Frege's Puzzle*, pp. 24–43, and in "Tense and Singular Propositions." Compare M. Richard, "Tense, Propositions, and Meanings," *Philosophical Studies* 41 (1982), pp. 337–51. The burden of this chapter is to show that one can consistently hold that propositions

are eternal while temporal sentential operators operate on noneternal semantic values of sentences, by holding that temporal sentential operators operate on two-place functions from contexts and times to eternal propositions. These two-place functions are similar to (and determined by) sentence characters. Indeed, Richard calls his two-place functions the 'meanings' of sentences. The claim that temporal operators operate on the "meanings" of expressions, however, is at best misleading. When each of Richard's two-place functions is replaced by its corresponding one-place function from contexts to one-place functions from times to eternal propositions, it emerges that temporal operators operate on something at a level other than that of character.

Richard also apparently misconstrues to some extent what Kaplan (and others) mean in saying that an operator "operates on" such-and-such's. In general, to say that a given operator operates on the such-and-such of its operand is to say that an appropriate extension for the operator would be a function from such-and-such's appropriate to expressions that may serve as its operand to extensions appropriate to the compounds formed from the operator together with the operand. For example, to say that a modal sentential operator operates on the content or on the intension of its operand sentence is to say that an appropriate extension for a modal operator would be a function from propositions or from sentence intensions (functions from possible worlds to truth values) to truth values.

10. On Frege's theory, the domain of this function would consist of senses that determine times, rather than the times themselves.

There is no reason on Frege's theory why the time-indication or time-specification that supplements the incomplete present-tensed sentence could not be verbal, as in 'At 12:00 noon on July 4, 1983, this tree is covered with green leaves'. This aspect of Frege's theory allows for a solution to the problem of failure of substitutivity of coreferential singular terms in temporal contexts—a solution very different from Frege's solution to the parallel problem of failure of substitutivity in propositional attitude contexts. Consider the following example. The expressions 'the U.S. president' and 'Bill Clinton' refer to the same individual with respect to the time of my writing these wods, but the former cannot be substituted *salva veritate* for the latter in the true sentence 'In 1991, Bill Clinton was a Democrat'. The result of such substitution is 'In 1991, the U.S. president was a Democrat', which is false on the relevant reading (the Russellian secondary occurrence or narrow scope reading). Frege may solve this problem, not implausibly, by noting that the expression 'the U.S. president' is incomplete and requires supplementation by a time-specification, such as may be provided by the time of utterance, before it can refer to an individual. The description 'the U.S. president', supplemented by the time of my writing these worlds, refers to the same individual as the name 'Bill Clinton'. Supplemented by the year 1991, or by a verbal specification thereof, it refers to George Bush. The result of the substitution includes a verbal time-specification, 'in 1991', which, we may assume, supersedes the time of utterance in completing any expression occurring within its scope in need of completion by a time-specification. Compare Frege's treatment of substitutivity failure in propositional attitude contexts. On Frege's theory, a propositional attitude operator such as 'Jones believes that' creates an oblique context in which expressions refer to their customary contents ("senses") instead of their customary referents. On the Fregean solution to substitutivity failure in temporal contexts presented here, by contrast, the referent of 'the U.S. president', as occurring within the context 'in 1991, ____', is just its customary referent.

11. For example, the meaning of the term 'table' might include, in addition to its character, some sort of conceptual content, such as a specification of the function of a table. If so, it does not follow that this sort of conceptual entity is any part of the semantic content of the term. Nor does it follow that it is *analytic*, in the classical sense, that tables have such and such a function. What does follow is that in order to know fully the meaning of 'table', one would have to know that the things called 'tables' are conventionally believed to have such and such a function.

12. The need for double indexing was apparently first noted in 1967 by Hans Kamp in unpublished material distributed to a graduate seminar while Kamp was a graduate student at U.C.L.A. See his "Formal Properties of 'Now'," *Theoria* 37 (1972), pp. 227–73. Kamp's results were reported in A. N. Prior, "'Now'," *Noûs* 2 (1968), pp. 101–19.

13. This is partly a result of Frege's principle of compositionality (or interchange) for reference. (See note 1.) On Frege's theory of tense and indexicality, both 'the U.S. president' and 'the present U.S. president' refer, in abstraction from context, to the function that assigns to any time t the individual who is U.S. president at t—like the functor 'the U.S. president at time ____'—except that the expression may be completed by a time rather than by a verbal time-specification (the time of utterance acting as a self-referential singular term). By Frege's compositionality principle for reference, it follows that any complete sentence built from 'the U.S. president', without using oblique devices (e.g., 'In 1996, the U.S. president was a Republican'), has the same truth conditions, and therefore the same truth value, as the corresponding sentence built from 'the present U.S. president'.

14. But see Richard, "Tense, Propositions, and Meanings," pp. 346–49. The idea of double indexing content to both contexts and times is Richard's.

15. Modal operators on the so-called branching worlds (or "unpreventability") interpretation emerge as superintensional operators.

16. On this account, the sentence 'Rain is falling' typically expresses, with respect to a context of utterance c, the proposition that rain is falling at c_L at c_T, where c_L is the location of c and c_T is the time of c. (An exception arises if, for example, the sentence is used as a shorthand for 'Rain is falling there', with implicit reference to some location other than that of the context.) No actual reference is made, however, either explicitly or implicitly, to either c_L or c_T. Instead, assuming that the sentence is subject-predicate, the predicate 'is falling' expresses as its semantic content the spatially and temporally indexed concept or property

of falling at c_L at c_T, and the extension determined is the class of things that are falling at c_L at c_T in the world of the context. This contrasts with the account proposed by Mark Crimmins and John Perry. See their "The Prince and the Phone Booth: Reporting Puzzling Beliefs," *Journal of Philosophy* 86 (December 1989), pp. 685–711, at pp. 699–700; and Crimmins's *Talk about Beliefs* (Cambridge, Mass.: MIT Press, 1992), pp. 16–18.

17. The content base of the result of attaching a content operator (such as 'necessarily' or the 'that'-operator) to a sentence is a complex made up of the content base of the operator and the content base of the sentence, rather than its content. Thus, for example, the content base of the 'that'-clause 'that Frege is writing' with respect to any context c does not involve the content of 'Frege is writing' with respect to c (which is the proposition that Frege is writing at c_T). Instead, it is something like the ordered pair of two elements: (a) a certain abstract entity, analogous to a property, which is the operation of assigning any proposition to itself (this operation—call it 'O_p'—is the content base of the 'that'-operator); and (b) the proposition matrix *fw*. Thus, the content base of 'that Frege is writing' has the structure $\langle O_p, \langle$Frege, writing$\rangle\rangle$. The content of 'Sometimes, Frege believes that he is writing' has the following structure, where 'Σtimes' designates the property of proposition matrices of being true at some time(s):

(i) $\langle\langle$Frege, O_p, $\langle$Frege, writing$\rangle$, believing$\rangle$, Σtimes$\rangle$.

(For further details, see appendix C of *Frege's Puzzle*.)

18. These explications of the notions of specific and general temporal operators cannot be regarded as strict definitions and are intended only to convey a general idea. The operator 'when Frege wrote "Thoughts"' + past tense is to count as a specific temporal operator even if it should turn out that Frege did not write "Thoughts." Also, given a sufficiently liberal notion of a property of a class, some precaution must be taken if a specific temporal operator is to be precluded from being a general temporal operator. It may be appropriate to define a general temporal operator as a *nonspecific* temporal operator of a certain sort. (A similar difficulty is encountered in defining ordinary quantifiers in such a way as to preclude ordinary singular terms.) More importantly, the explications provided here are appropriate for what I shall call *complete* temporal operators below, although the terminology of 'specific' or 'singular' and 'quantificational' or 'general' temporal operators will be used also for the components of these, which I shall call 'incomplete' temporal operators below (e.g., 'when Frege wrote "Thoughts"' without an accompanying tense operator). These various notions can be made precise, though it is preferable to leave them at an intuitive, informal level in motivating the account under consideration here.

19. The naked infinitive phrase 'be writing' might be represented further as

(i)   *Progressive Tense*(*Write*).

The word 'writing' itself is functioning here adjectivally.

20. See W. V. O. Quine, *Word and Object* (Cambridge, Mass.: MIT Press, 1960), pp. 170–71.

21. See Q. Smith, *Language and Time* (Oxford: Oxford University Press, 1993), especially pp. 44–48; L. N. Oaklander and Q. Smith, eds., *The New Theory of Time* (New Haven, Conn.: Yale University Press, 1994), especially pp. 12–19, 51–54, 136–53.

22. Those (such as myself) who accept the A-series as veridical need not deny that the dating of an event or state of affairs within the series, or indeed that the whole series itself, is relativized to a "frame of reference." They may hold that, relative to one's frame of reference, the division among past, present, and future is real, with the present enjoying a special metaphysical status and each time eventually having its turn at it.

23. Furthermore, even if the particular word 'now' does not express any concept as its semantic content, a relevant concept of presentness may be semantically contained elsewhere in other expressions. In my "Existence," in J. Tomberlin, ed., *Philosophical Perspectives*. Vol. 1, *Metaphysics* (Atascadero, Calif.: Ridgeview, 1987), pp. 49–108, I suggest that the English word 'current', as in 'the current U.S. president', exemplifies an ambiguity analogous to David Lewis's distinction between the primary (indexical) and secondary (nonindexical) English senses of 'actual'. (Consider 'In 1989, current interest rates were higher than present rates'.) The secondary sense of 'current' is a concept of precisely the sort that Smith misinterprets me as rejecting (note 21 above).

   On the other hand, on the corrected theory a tensed sentence is translatable, in some relevant sense, into an untensed sentence that places the described state of affairs in the B-series. According to the corrected theory, in uttering the sentence 'At t^*, Frege was writing', one asserts that (a) *fw* obtains at t^*, and (b) t^* is past. This is an A-determination, rather than a B-determination, in virtue of the second conjunct. But since propositions are eternal, the second conjunct is not the proposition matrix t^* *being past* (which obtains only after t^*, not at t^* itself or at any earlier time), but the eternal proposition that t^* is past *at* c_T, where c_T is the time of utterance. And this proposition is tantamount to the B-determination that t^* is earlier than c_T. For this reason, it is a conceptual mistake to pose the question of whether "time is tensed" (i.e., whether the A-series is cosmologically veridical or objective, etc.) in terms of the untranslatability of tensed A-statements into tenseless B-statements. And indeed, it is a philosophical mistake to infer from the translatability (in this sense) of A-statements into B-statements that the A-properties of pastness, presentness, and futurity are somehow unreal or illusory, and so on. Doing so is analogous to claiming to have discovered a cure for baldness, which consists in paraphrasing any statement ascribing baldness to Jones into a statement asserting the binary relation of *being bald at*—not a property—to hold between Jones and the time of utterance. Though Jones may rejoice in his loss of the property of baldness, he still has no need of shampoo. (Hegelians, who love a synthesis, will probably conclude that he wears a wig.)

24. A problem for this account arises in connection with such constructions as 'Frege always was busy', which does not mean that every time is a past time at which Frege is busy. The sentence seems to mean instead that every past time is a

time at which Frege is busy. But on the account proposed here, the past tense operator operates on the value base of the untensed clause 'Frege be busy' and the incomplete operator 'always' attaches to the result (i.e., to the past-tensed 'Frege was busy'), apparently resulting in the incorrect former reading for the sentence. The alternative reading would seem to require seeing the past tense operator as somehow modifying the 'always' rather than the untensed clause.

Whereas the latter reading of the sentence is closer to the actual meaning than the former (clearly a misreading), it also does not seem exactly correct. The sentence in question generally is not used with this meaning (although, of course, it *can be* so used). As with a simple past-tensed sentence, a sentence such as 'Frege always was busy' is ordinarily used with implicit reference to a particular (perhaps vaguely delineated) period or interval of time in mind, so that what is said is true as long as Frege is busy throughout that period even if at some other times he is not busy. This feature of such constructions can be accommodated on the present account by taking incomplete quantificational temporal operators, such as 'always', to involve implicit reference to a particular period or interval—very much in the manner of implicitly relativized uses of quantificational constructions in English (such as, the 'everything' in 'Everything is in order' or the 'everyone' in 'Is everyone here?'). A sentence such as 'Frege always was busy', standing alone as a declarative sentence in a piece of discourse, may thus be taken to mean something like the following: Every time during *that period* is an earlier time at which Frege is busy (with reference to a contextually indicated period of time).

25. One alternative to the ellipsis theory is the theory that the English construction represented by '*Writing*(*I*)' is simply sentence (1). Indeed, it is commonplace in most discussions concerning logical form to assume that (1) is, at least as typically intended, an atomic sentence constructed from the singular term 'I' and the simple predicate 'am writing', while regarding the present tense of the latter not as a separate component of the sentence but as somehow built into the predicate. In an effort to facilitate understanding of the general theory of temporal operators presented here, much of the preceding discussion was based on the presumption of some such theory. However, if verb tenses are to be taken seriously in accordance with the general theory of temporal operators presented here—as semantically significant contributions to sentences in themselves—this alternative theory ultimately requires the postulation of a systematic semantic ambiguity in the present tense, so that a simple, present-tensed sentence like (1) is ambiguous between the complete

(i)   *Writing*(*I*)

and the incomplete (in need of supplementation by an incomplete specific or general temporal operator)

(ii)   *Present Tense*[*Writing*(*I*)].

The first would be an instance of the *tenseless* use of present tense, the second of the *tensed* use. The tenseless (1) has a truth value for its extension and would be an appropriate operand for any complete temporal operator, whereas the tensed (1) would be the result of applying a certain tense operator (viz., present tense qua tense operator) to the tenseless (1). The more complex logical form of the latter would have to be regarded on this theory as going entirely unrepresented in the surface grammar. We may call this the *ambiguity theory of present tense*.

Certain general considerations tend to favor the ellipsis theory over the ambiguity theory of present tense. In general, when attempting to explain apparently divergent uses of a single expression or locution, if an ellipsis account is available, it is to be preferred over the postulation of a systematic semantic ambiguity—although, of course, some third alternative may be preferable to it. See S. Kripke, "Speaker's Reference and Semantic Reference," in P. French, T. Uehling, and H. Wettstein, eds., *Contemporary Perspectives in the Philosophy of Language* (Minneapolis: University of Minnesota Press, 1979), pp. 6–27, especially p. 19.

26. It is important for a full theory of the simple tenses to take account of the fact that the proper operands of tenses in English seem to be not whole clauses but simple predicates (or, more accurately, verbs). It is largely a simple problem of formal engineering to transform the theory of pure tenses presented here into a theory of tenses as operators on the content bases of simple predicates rather than on the value bases of whole clauses. For example, in accordance with the spirit of the general theory of tenses presented here, a past-tensed predicate such as 'was writing'—which results from applying the past tense operation to the simple predicate (naked infinitive) 'be writing'—may be regarded as having for its extension, with respect to a possible world w and a time t, not a class of individuals (or its corresponding characteristic function from individuals to truth values), but the function that assigns to each (possible, past, present, or future) individual i the class of times before t at which i is writing in w.

It may also be important to recognize that the 'that'-operator, which transforms a sentence into a singular term (typically) referring to the sentence's semantic content, may be attached in English to a tensed but apparently otherwise temporally unmodified sentence, for example, 'When Frege wrote "Thoughts," he knew that he was writing'. It may be necessary to regard such 'that'-clauses as involving an implicit 'then' or 'now' operator. See note 17.

Section B

The Cognitive Significance of Tensed Sentences

3

Objects of Relief

Mark Richard

The beliefs expressed by tensed sentences, such as 'Smith was sad' or 'My plane is leaving', obviously have a cognitive role quite different from those expressed by untensed sentences such as 'The time of my plane's departure is 7:00'. A familiar sort of example: given that I do not know that it is 7:00, I will run if I think my airplane is leaving, but not if I think it is leaving at 7:00.[1] A closely allied point is that whether an emotional reaction like relief or anticipation is sensible seems to depend on belief's being tensed. The point is famously made by Prior:

One says, e.g., "Thank goodness that's over!", and ... says something which it is impossible that any use of a tenseless copula with a date should convey. It certainly doesn't mean the same as, e.g., "Thank goodness the date of the conclusion of that thing is Friday, June 15, 1954", even if it be said then. (Nor, for that matter, does it mean "Thank goodness the conclusion of that thing is contemporaneous with this utterance". Why should anyone thank goodness for that?) (Prior 1959, p. 17)

That tensed belief—that is, belief expressed by tensed sentences—has such properties can seem puzzling. After all, believing that the airplane is leaving is presumably believing that it is leaving now; and if it is now 7:00, that is, on a broadly Russellian conception of belief, believing that it is leaving at 7:00. Some explanation of the distinctive properties of tensed beliefs seems called for.

Some would give such an explanation in terms of the states of affairs that are the objects of tensed thoughts: they involve, it is said, *temporal transients*, properties like *being present* and *being past*, which attach to states of affairs, events, or propositions at some times and not others; that tensed belief has such an object explains its distinctive properties.

This view seems to imply that (in some motivationally important sense of 'state of mind') the states of mind that realize tensed beliefs are ones we can be in only if we are thinking about temporally transient properties.

Reasons to be suspicious about this claim arise, once we notice that thinking about a temporal transient *in and of itself* cannot be what is responsible for the motivational properties of tensed belief. Suppose I am introduced to a property of events, being serp, by being told the following:

(D1)   Let midnight, January 1, 2001, be called t_m; call the present time t_i. At t_i, a claim p is serp iff p is true at t_m. In general, a claim p is serp at a time t_e iff p is true at t_e plus the difference between t_m and t_i.

(In notation familiar from Kaplan 1989, this cashes out so:

(C)   For any t_j and t_e: $t_j[\text{Serp}(A)]t_e$ iff $t_j[A]t_e + (t_m - t_i)$.)

If, as it happens, t_i is t_m, then being serp is (at least from a tense-logical perspective) the temporal transient being present. If I understand the way in which 'serp' is introduced, I understand such sentences as 'The millennium is serp' and thus can think that the millennium is serp. This is so, even if I did not realize that the time I learned the term 'serp' was the millennium. So thinking, of the millennium and the property of being present, that the first has the second, does not, in and of itself, have the motivational powers of the tensed thought that the millennium is present.

The way in which one thinks of a (putative) state of affairs has as much to do with the motivational powers of one's thought as does the state of affairs of which one thinks. Given this, it is unclear why we should think that invoking temporal transients would have any special explanatory power. After all, we will have to invoke ways of thinking of the transients, as well as the transients themselves. And since it is the way of thinking, not the referent, that does the psychological heavy lifting, the temporal transient will tend to drop out of the explanation.[2]

This suggests looking for a more or less Fregean explanation of the cognitive role of tensed beliefs, claiming that tensed belief's distinctive cognitive role flows from the ways of apprehending states of affairs that we deploy in such belief. For example, some say the state of affairs that my plane is leaving (i.e., leaving now) obtains (or not) timelessly. When I believe that my plane is leaving, that state of affairs is apprehended under an "indexical mode of presentation"; the latter is responsible for tensed belief's motivational role.[3]

This chapter examines two attempts to explain the motivational role of tensed belief in a more or less Fregean manner. I will suggest that neither of these explanations is quite right. Section 3.1 takes up an interesting proposal about the nature of tensed thought and the semantics of its ascription due to James Higginbotham. Higginbotham's view is (not unfairly understood as) one that attempts to explain tensed belief's distinctive role as resulting, not from the propositional object of a tensed belief, but from the "way it is apprehended." Higginbotham's proposal can be construed in two ways; neither, I argue, accounts for the facts. Section 3.2 discusses the idea, familiar from the works of David Kaplan, that the character of a sentence (or of a belief state realized by tokening a sentence) both determines the semantic properties of the sentence (state) and is responsible for its cognitive role. I argue that while there is a regular connection, in the case of indexicals, between character and cognitive role, character cannot be seen as *explaining* cognitive role. Section 3.3 sketches my own views of the matter; section 3.4 discusses the relations between ascriptions of tensed beliefs and ascriptions of the motivational properties of such beliefs.

3.1   Higginbotham on Tensed Thought

If right now I think that I am flying home today, I think of a day— today—in a certain way. In order to think of the day in this way, I must stand in a certain relation to it—I must be "located in it" at the time of the thinking. If I demonstrate Maggie and say with understanding, 'She's a Jungian', there is (arguably) a way I think of Maggie, associated with the sentence's demonstrative use; to think of Maggie in this way requires that I stand in a particular relation to Maggie—I must, inter alia, perceive her.

One feels a generalization hovering: to apprehend a proposition under a particular mode of apprehension is, inter alia, to bear a certain relation to what the mode presents. For Frege, the relation seems to have been invariably conceptual. But one can certainly broaden Frege's idea to allow for nonconceptual relations to help constitute sense. One might hope that by finding the right "sense-making" relations, be they conceptual or non, one could give an account of the distinctive role of tensed thought.

James Higginbotham has made a proposal about tensed thought that can be seen as an implementation of this strategy. According to Higginbotham, a state of having a tensed thought is "reflexive": it is a state of thought whose object contains that very state as a constituent. Specifically, such a state involves temporally locating an event or situation (that which the thought is intuitively about) as simultaneous with, before, or after that very state. For example, when I am relieved that my root canal is over, "the thought that I think is indicated in (1):

(1)   ($\exists s$) s is the situation of my root canal's being over & (the time of)
         s includes (the time of) e." (Higginbotham 1995, p. 228;
         numbering altered here and for subsequent examples)

Here, s includes s' if all the times at which s' obtains are ones at which s does; 'e' names my thinking the thought in question.

Higginbotham grants that one might, in principle, think this thought at any time one exists, and that thinking it is not "intrinsically relieving." One might anticipate that there would be a first time one would be relieved that the impending root canal was over, christen that state of relief 'Anton', and think to oneself,

(2)   ($\exists s$) s is the situation of my root canal's being over & (the time of)
         s includes (the time of) Anton.[4]

But in such a case, of course, the thought state one was in would not be Anton himself, but some other thought state. But things are different, Higginbotham tells us, if (2) is the object of Anton himself:

The point of reflexivity emerges when we consider that the thought that I would express by saying (3) essentially involves cross-reference between (the time of) my state and (the time of) the presence of a situation:

(3)   I think that my root canal is over.

We thus distinguish between

(4)   the thought that e is a state of my thinking that my root canal is over as
         of e

and

(5)   the thought that *e* is a state of my thinking that my root canal is over as of *e'*

which is not cross-referential, even when $e = e'$. When I am relieved that my root canal is over, I think (4). (Higginbotham 1995, p. 229)[5]

There are two questions one could raise: Is thinking that *s* is present thinking that *s* is simultaneous with one's so thinking? If so, will this help us to explain the distinctive cognitive role of tensed thought? Here, I will pursue only the first question, for I think its answer is negative.

We need to get a bit clearer about the sort of cross-reference that is supposed to lie at the bottom of tensed thought. According to Higginbotham, tenses encode temporal relations, thereby making possible the temporal cross-reference that occurs in belief reports; it is this sort of cross-reference that occurs in the tensed thoughts such reports report. Higginbotham's account of this cross-reference is set in a broadly Davidsonian framework, in which predicates have implicit argument places for situations (i.e., events or states). Tensed utterances are taken as token reflexive, so that an utterance *u* of 'Smith's sad' says, roughly, that the sadness is simultaneous with *u*.

Ignore the Davidsonian embedding and token reflexivity for a moment, and replace the implicit argument places for situations with ones for temporal intervals. Then the proposal assigns

(6)   Smith is sad

and

(7)   Smith was sad

the forms

(6') $(\exists t)(\text{includes } (t, \text{now}) \ \& \ \text{Sad } (\text{Smith}, t))$

and

(7') $(\exists t)(t < \text{now} \ \& \ \text{Sad } (\text{Smith}, t))$.

Here, inclusion is the relation an interval *t* bears to an interval *t'* if all of *t'* is in *t*; '$<$' names the precedence relation, which *t* bears to *t'* if all times of *t* are before all in *t'*. The proposal assigns the ambiguous

(8)   Mary said that Smith was sad

the logical forms

(8′)   a. $(\exists t)(t < \text{now} \ \& \ \text{Say (Mary, } t, \text{ that } (\exists t')(\text{Sad (Smith, } t') \ \& \ t' < t)))$

b. $(\exists t)(t < \text{now} \ \& \ \text{Say (Mary, } t, \text{ that } (\exists t')(\text{Sad (Smith, } t') \ \& \ t' \text{ includes } t)))$.

Replacing the temporal reference of 'now' with a reference to one's utterance (use 'u' for this), replacing the quantification over and predication of times with quantification over and predication of events, and taking inclusion and precedence as relations between situations, we obtain the forms Higginbotham in fact assigns (8):

(8″)   a. $(\exists e)(e < u \ \& \ \text{Say (Mary, } e, \text{ that } (\exists e')(\text{Sad (Smith, } e') \ \& \ e' < e)))$

b. $(\exists e)(e < \text{now} \ \& \ \text{Say (Mary, } e, \text{ that } (\exists e')(\text{Sad (Smith, } e') \ \& \ e' \text{ includes } e)))$.[6]

Here, '$\text{Say}(a, b, c)$' says that b is a's making an assertive utterance whose content is c.

Cast in this format, Higginbotham's idea is that an utterance U of

(9)   I am relieved that my root canal is over

has the logical form

(10) $(\exists s')(s' \text{ includes } u \ \& \ \text{Relieved (I, } s', \text{ that } (\exists s)(\text{over (my root canal, } s) \ \& \ s \text{ includes } s')))$,

where 'u' picks out U. That is, to put it crudely, an utterance of (9) says that I have a state of relief whose object is that that very state of relief is contemporaneous with the root canal's being over.

One understanding of Higginbotham's proposal is that there is something "intrinsically relieving" about being in such a state, at least given a strong distaste for root canals. That is, (a) where U is an utterance of (3) (named by 'u'), the logical form of (3) is

(11) $(\exists s')(s' \text{ includes } u \ \& \ \text{Believe (I, } s', \text{ that } (\exists s)(\text{over (my root canal, } s) \ \& \ s \text{ includes } s')))$;

(b) if I am in the state described by (11) and dislike root canals, I will be relieved. That is, given that (11) or

(11′) $(\exists s') (\text{Believe (I, } s', \text{ that } (\exists s)(\text{over (my root canal, } s) \ \& \ s \text{ includes } s')))$

is true ((11′), since I might have the belief without speaking) and that I have a strong distaste for root canals, (9) will be true.

Suppose that I anticipate that my root canal will be over at 4:00 p.m., and that I anticipate that I will then think, with relief, that it is over. Suppose, being the christening kind, I introduce 'Glenn' as a name of the first (occurrent) state of belief I have, concerning my root canal, after 4:00 p.m. Later, in the dentist's chair, I suddenly think to myself,

(12)   There is a state of affairs s such that my root canal is over by s and s includes Glenn.

I am, sadly, *in medias rootcanalis*, and the thought causes me no relief.

But if the time of my thought was just after 4:00 p.m. and there was no other thought of root canals occurrent when I had it, then the state of believing I was then in was Glenn. And so it would seem that

(12′)   Believe (I, Glenn, that there is a state of affairs s such that my root canal is over by s and s includes Glenn)

must be true at the time of my thinking. But existentially generalizing on 'Glenn' here yields (11). So, it would seem, on the current construal of Higginbotham's proposal I must be relieved. The problem is that a state of believing can apparently be a constituent of its propositional object in virtue of two kinds of relations: either in virtue of "direct" relations—as when, as it were, I think to myself, 'This very thinking I am currently doing is some thinking about the government'; or in virtue of "indirect" ones, as when I have a name that picks out a token judgment j, and that name figures in j itself.

One response—I do not think it would be Higginbotham's—would be to simply deny that a mental state could think about itself indirectly. This is tantamount, it seems to me, to denying that we can name our mental states, and seems most implausible.

A more interesting response holds that I have subtly misdescribed what occurs in the dentist's chair at 4:00 p.m. My objection, in essence, was that one might reflexively think one's root canal over but in an "untensed way." The response is that if I am thinking anything at all when I mentally rehearse (12), I am having a tensed thought: (12)'s first 'is' is in the present tense. So what I am thinking is something conveyable so:

(12″)   Consider the state of affairs: there being a state of affairs *s* such
that my root canal is over by *s* and *s* includes Glenn. *That* state
of affairs includes (and is thus temporally simultaneous with) my
current state of thinking.

Call the state of affairs that is the subject of this thought (the one picked
out by 'that') 'Ed'. Ed is tenseless in the sense that he either always
obtains or always fails to do so, depending upon whether Glenn occurs
after the ending of my root canal. (12″) is the thought that this state of
affairs obtains—speaking as I might at the time of the thought—*right
now*. Since Ed is tenseless, it is no wonder that thinking (12″)—that is,
(12)—yields no relief. But since the thought in question is not the one
that would be expressed by 'My root canal is over', this is not a problem
for Higginbotham's account.

To give this response is, in effect, to deny that one can *have* untensed
thoughts; if it is to be seriously advanced, one must be ready to say, for
example, that to think that $2 + 2 = 4$ is to think that $2 + 2$ is presently 4,
or that the state of affairs that $2 + 2 = 4$ is something that obtains *right
now*. For the response is to insist that the main verb of (12) is tensed and
thus involves, when I think (12), reference to my thought; if this is true of
(12), it surely is true across the board.

I think this view is implausible. Here are two reasons. (a) Surely there
can be languages that make claims that are untensed. Arguably, interpreted versions of first-order logic, which have sentences that are naturally read as is

(13)   Smith is tired at time *t*,

are such. We understand such languages. Understanding them requires
being able to think the thoughts their sentences express. But on the current response we cannot think them, as they are untensed. (B) Surely it
is *possible* for you and me to literally think the same thought. Not so,
on the current response. For example, no matter what we might try,
we will end up, if we try to think what (13) says, thinking things that
are not even metaphysically, much less logically, equivalent. For when
you try to think what (13) says, you will think something that involves
reference to your mental states, and I will think something involving reference to mine. Since one of us could have existed without the other,

one thought could be true without the other's being so. While there is no formal incoherence in any of this, it is, well, strange.[7]

There is another interpretation of Higginbotham's account. It identifies tensed beliefs with states of believing that are reflexive "in the right way." We posit a relation—let us call it *awareness*—that a state s realizing a propositional attitude of an agent x can bear to a mental state s' of x. One stipulates that one can be aware of one's mental states only when they occur; it is to be understood that awareness of a state involves "taking it as present." Strictly, we should speak of a state of belief s being aware of a mental state s' as it occurs (at a particular locus) in an object of a propositional attitude. Write

Ref (s^*, s, p)

for

s^* is a state of s bearing the awareness relation to the state that occupies the tense position of the thought p,

it being understood, for example, that the tense position of the thought

(14) $(\exists s)$(over (my root canal, s) & s includes s')

is that occupied by s'. We say that tensed belief involves "reflexive awareness" and that there is a "subatomic" reference to the relation Ref in a belief ascription; sentence (3) is to be ascribed the logical form, or is at least necessarily equivalent to,

(11*) $(\exists s')$(s' includes u & Believe (I, s' that $(\exists s)$(over (my root canal, s) & s includes s')) and $(\exists s^*)$(s' includes s^* & Ref $(s^*, s', $ that $(\exists s)$(over (my root canal, s) & s includes s')))).

Roughly put, this says that there is a state s' of my believing, its object is that it itself includes my root canal's being over, and s' bears the Ref relation to itself, as it occurs in that object.[8]

I will express two reservations about this proposal. (1) As I see it, states of thinking, like other states, can endure through time. For example, I may spend a few minutes thinking, 'Eventually the millennium will come'; if so, there is a single state of my thinking that lasts several minutes. But now consider what I am supposed to think when I think, say, that Smith was sad. On Higginbotham's view, I think,

(15) $(\exists s)(s < s' \ \& \ \text{Sad (Smith, } s))$,

where s' is my state of thinking this. But given that s' might commence before the onset of Smith's sadness, (15) can be false, even though it is true that Smith was sad.

It may be felt that we need only to tinker with the logical form. Why not say that the content of my belief is not (15) but

(16) $(\exists s)(s < \text{the current moment of } s' \ \& \ \text{Sad (Smith, } s))$,

with, again, s' being my very thought thereof? But this seems to finesse all the interesting questions, with its insertion of 'current' into the specification of my belief. To meet the objection, one must do one of three things: (a) find a way to specify the relevant time of s' without introducing either a tensed expression such as 'now' or an untensed one such as 'the moment of s that is identical with my 45th birthday'; (b) say that the constituent of my thought that Smith is sad is not my state of thinking it, but a temporal slice thereof; (c) deny that states of thought can endure. Since it is *states* of thought that are under discussion, I do not see how we cogently take the third route; the first appears hopeless.

I am not sure we should rest happy with the second option. Suppose I think (15) at t, with the value of 's'' being some previous temporal slice of the state of thinking I am in at t. Then (15) may still be false, though 'Smith was sad' is true. (Suppose as before that I started thinking, 'Smith was sad', a bit before Smith began to be sad and that I continued in that state of mind as he became sad; and take s' to be the slice at which my thinking commenced.)

Perhaps we should say that at a time t a state of thinking can only be aware of its current temporal slice, ascribing to (3) a logical form along the lines of

(11**) $(\exists s')(s'$ includes u & $(\exists s'')(s''$ is a temporal slice of s' & Believe
         $(I, s',$ that $(\exists s)(\text{over (my root canal, } s) \ \& \ s$ includes $s''))$ and
         $(\exists s^*)(s'$ includes s^* & Ref $(s^*, s',$ that $(\exists s)(\text{over (my root canal,}$
         $s) \ \& \ s$ includes $s''))))$.

We might gloss this so: some state s' of my thinking has as object that s''—which is in fact a temporal slice s'—is after my root canal, and s' Refs s'' as it occurs in that object. Given that necessarily, if s' is aware of

s'' at t, then s'' is a momentary temporal slice of a mental event that occurs at t, this seems to solve the problem of getting the truth conditions of tensed thoughts right.

I see no formal problem with this proposal. But I think we should be uncomfortable with it. It builds into tensed belief and the semantics of its ascription a very restrictive notion of acquaintance, since the proposal will succeed only if we insist that we cannot be aware of (non-instantaneous) mental states and that we cannot be aware of the temporal parts of mental states we remember. It is simply not obvious that there is a relation that will do the work that needs doing here. Furthermore, we would apparently have to ascribe to thinkers to whom the proposal applies the ability to discriminate (momentary) temporal parts of states from those states themselves. For the idea here is that the content of my thought at t that Smith was sad is given by

(17) $(\exists s)(s < s'' \ \& \ \text{Sad (Smith, } s))$,

where the value of 's''' is the temporal slice of that state of thought which is my thinking this content. *Something* has to make it the case that when I think that Smith is sad, I am picking out just the momentary slice of my thinking, and not the temporally whole enchilada. I am not sure what would make it the case that it was plausible to ascribe this sort of ability to an ordinary thinker. When I think to myself, 'This very thinking has taken a few seconds', I don't sense that I am caught up in necessary falsehood, or that I make tacit reference to some function from temporal parts to wholes.

(2) If it is the reflexivity of tensed belief that accounts for its distinctive cognitive properties, this is because of the truth of something like

(18) I must be aware, if I think reflexively of a state s of mind, that s is presently occurring.

One can think of a relatively straightforward argument for (18): Whenever I am thinking, I know that I am thinking—that is, presently thinking. Thus, if I think reflexively of my thinking, I know that what I think of is simultaneous with something presently occurring. Thus, a reflexive state "knows" that it is present. Thus, the reflexivity of tensed thought guarantees that it is thought that locates an event, for the thinker, relative to her present, since it locates the event relative to something the believer knows is occurring in the present.

An obvious upshot is that Higginbotham's account fails on its own terms, if it is possible for someone to reflexively think that her thinking is simultaneous with an event *e*, but not believe that her so thinking is presently occurring. That is, the account requires that it be impossible that there be a state of thinking *s* (a) whose object is that *s* is simultaneous with some event *e*, (b) that is reflexive, but (c) that is such that *s* "as it is presented in *s*" is not presented as present.

Now, 'think' and allied expressions are ambiguous between something like 'believe' and 'entertain'. Conditions (a) through (c) are possible, if 'think' is understood as 'entertain'; for it is possible to "reflexively entertain" the claim that event *e* is simultaneous with one's so thinking without thereby taking one's entertaining the claim to be presently occurring.

Suppose that I am given to particularly vivid recall of things that have happened in the past. For example, I at times recall (without trying to recall) the tolling of the midnight bells so vividly that I need to reflect in order to determine that my experience is a memory, not a present event. Not only do I on occasion so recall external events, but on occasion I have, or at least believe that I have, such recollections of my internal reactions to them. For example, I at times recall (without trying) hearing the tolling of the midnight bells and occurrently thinking, 'This [the bells' tolling] marks midnight'. On some such occasions, I take the entire episode to be a memory, of my experience of the bells and my mental reaction thereto; on other, I am unsure whether I am recalling something past or not.

Suppose that I know that a certain sound is characteristic of the dog's clawing at the door to gain entrance. Suppose the dog claws, I hear it, and that causes me to think,

(19)   The dog's wanting entrance is simultaneous with my hearing this
         [I intend the clawing] and with my so thinking.

I know how I often vividly recall the past. And so, at the same time I think (19), I take myself (mistakenly) only to be recalling (quite accurately) something that happened several weeks ago; consequently, I don't go to the door to let the dog in, which I would if I thought the dog was *now* clawing.[9]

Let *t* be the state that is my thinking (19) to myself on hearing the dog. *t* is a state with propositional content. Its content is that of (19) when tokened therein. So *t* is a state in which I entertain (what's said by *t*'s tokening of) (19). And *t* seems reflexive, given that my tokening of (19) is my thinking, 'The dog wants entrance *while this (i.e., t) happens*'. But I do not take the reference of 'my so thinking' in my tokening of (19) to be present, since I (mistakenly) take myself to be recalling something that happened in the past. Thus, *s* is a reflexive state of thinking, but in *s*, *s* is *not* presented as presently occurring. In *s*, *s* is simply presented as simultaneous with some other events, events that I also take to be past. So here we have an example of a state that satisfies conditions (a) through (c) above. This seems to show that what makes a propositional attitude tensed is not its being reflexive.

It might be objected that *t* itself is not a propositional attitude. My propositional attitude, it might be said, is a state that takes *t*, or constituents thereof, as objects. After all, what I *believe* is that *that thinking* (i.e., *t*) *was* simultaneous with the noise, not that *this thinking* (i.e., *t*) *is* so simultaneous. In response: to grant the point about belief is not to grant the objection. Note that if *t* occurred "in a different mental environment"—one in which I did not take myself to be merely recalling something—*t* would obviously be an entertaining of the content (19). The fact that *t* is embedded as it is does not rob its constituents of their semantic values. And *t*, in its actual mental setting, involves "apprehending" the content (19). So it would seem to be a propositional attitude.

It might be objected that *in t itself* I take my thinking (i.e., *t*) to be present; it is just that I have another mental state that "overrides" this apprehension. After all, *t* is a state "engaged" in the activity of thinking. How, then, can *t* not "recognize" the fact that what it "is doing" (i.e., thinking) it is presently doing?

In a sense, this objection just reiterates Higginbotham's position: to think reflexively, we are told, just is to take one's thinking as present. But as I see it, we have no very strong reason to think that this is so. In thinking that *this very thought* is such and such, I focus on a thought. I do not conceptualize or pick it out by its temporal location. Rather, I "mentally demonstrate" it. The default assumption, about such demonstration, is that what's demonstrated is present, for how else could I demonstrate it? But that assumption is quite separable from the act of demonstrating itself. I don't need to make the assumption to demonstrate; I just need, so to speak, to point. And of course the point of the example is that the demonstrating can occur without the assumption's coming into play.[10]

Finally, one might respond that the example does not show that Higginbothams' account fails for attitudes that involve belief: if I believe (what I express when I token) (19), it might be said, then my belief is realized, not by the tokening t of (19), but by some other occurrent mental state. After all, I am reflecting upon t. I take it to be a veridical memory of something that once happened. It is my so taking it (call the token state of my so taking it t') that makes it the case that I believe what (19), when I token it, says. But then the belief I have whose object is what (19) says when I token it is not a reflexive belief, since the state that realizes the belief is not t, but t'.

The observation about the nonreflexivity of the belief in (19) (as opposed to the entertaining of (19)) is perhaps correct. However, it raises another question: why is t, my tokening of (19), not itself a state of my believing what (19)-as-tokened-by-me says? It would seem, after all, that if I didn't have an erroneous belief about t's causal history, t would be a present tense belief.

It seems to me that what keeps t from itself being a present tense belief is that in so tokening (19) (i.e., in t), I do not take the state of mind I represent with the words 'my so thinking'—t itself—to be present. In order that t realize a present tense belief, I must take the state of mind I am representing in t (t itself) to be one presently occurring. And what the example shows is that it does not follow from the sort of reflexivity t exhibits that I so take it.

What makes Higginbotham's account plausible is the fact that a reflexive state indeed is *normally* one that presents itself as present. But, as I hope the argument has made clear, thinking reflexively of a state is only normally, not necessarily, thinking of it as present.

3.2   Character and Cognitive Significance

David Kaplan's and John Perry's work suggests accounting for the cognitive role of tensed thoughts in terms of "indexical modes of thinking," modes indexical because (unlike traditional Fregean senses) they present different things in different contexts. Such views often distinguish between two "objects of belief." One, a proposition, is identified with the object of assertion and bearer of truth. The other, which provides a "way of grasping" the first, is held to (contextually) determine the first, and to determine the cognitive properties of a state of belief.

A Kaplanesque version of this view identifies modes of grasping with Kaplan's characters, functions from contexts to propositional constituents. It encourages us to think of "using" a mode m of grasping a proposition as having a belief in virtue of accepting a sentence with m as its character. It claims that the special motivational role of my belief that I am flying home today is to be explained in terms of my accepting a sentence with the character of 'I am flying home today'; analogously for the explanation of why I might be relieved when I think, 'I am flying home today', as opposed to 'I am flying home on February 9, 1997'.[11]

As with Higginbotham's account, we can pose two questions. Is the identification of thinking that e is present with thought held under a certain character plausible? If so, can the psychological properties of tensed thought be explained in terms of its semantic ones? I shall eventually allow that the first question can (probably) be answered yes, but the second cannot.

Whether the first question *can* be answered affirmatively depends upon the exact nature of character. If the picture sketched a paragraph ago is correct, then my accepting any sentence with the character of 'I am flying home today', and thereby having a belief, should have, all else being equal, the same motivational upshot as the belief realized by 'I am flying home today'. But doesn't this idea trip over the problem raised at the beginning of this chapter, concerning temporal transients and being serp? Suppose I am taught a word 'yadot' on a day d, being told,

(D2)   Today, 'yadot' names Sunday, February 9, 1997. And each day, 'yadot' names the day immediately succeeding (immediately preceding) the day it named the day before (it names on the next day).

So long as I understand these instructions, I understand 'yadot'. And so when I accept 'I am flying home yadot', I will be in a belief state in virtue of that acceptance. Suppose I was told the above on Sunday, February 9, 1997, but I didn't know that the day was Sunday. Then in accepting 'I am flying home yadot', I am accepting a sentence with the character of 'I am flying home today' and am in a belief state individuated by its character. But of course the belief state does not have the motivational properties of the belief state that I am flying home today.

In a way, the preceding misinterprets Kaplan.[12] Kaplan *represents* the character of an expression as a function from contexts to propositional constituents. But he explicitly says that character is a *rule* and observes that representing characters as functions will result in the identification of distinct characters (Kaplan 1989, p. 505). Isn't that what is going on in the preceding argument? There are (at least) two *rules* one might associate with 'yadot', (D2) and something like

(D3)   In any context, 'yadot' names the day of the context.

Given that the rules are different and that it is (D3) that corresponds to the character of 'today', the above is no counterexample to the claim that the distinctive properties of tensed belief can be explained by reference to the character of (the sentence that realizes) the belief.

In what sense do (D2) and (D3) determine different rules? Well, one might say, to give a rule is to write out a sentence that refers to some functions, individuals, properties, and relations, and that determines a "procedure" (via the sentence's syntax); to follow the rule is to apply the procedure to the functions, and so on. (D3)'s rule is thus something like this: Find the context; apply the *day-of* function thereto; the result is the referent (in the context) of 'yadot'. (D2)'s rule is quite different, requiring a computation on, among other things, February 9, 1997. Call the picture of rules and rule following suggested in these sketchy remarks the *procedural* picture of rules.

The picture does not meet the problem we are considering. Consider the yad function, which maps contexts to days. It is defined as follows:

(D4) For any context c,
  a. yad(c) is February 9, 1997, if the day of c of today;
  b. if the day of c postcedes today, yad(c) is one day later than yad(c^*), for any context c^* whose day is one day earlier than c's;
  c. if the day of c precedes today, yad(c) is one day earlier than yad(c^*), for any context c^* whose day is one day earlier than c's.

What function (D4) defines is a matter of when it is introduced; if it is introduced on February 9, 1997, it of course defines the function *the day of context c*. Suppose (D4) is introduced on February 9, 1997, and subsequent to that introduction, the following rule is introduced:

(D5) In any context, 'yadot' names the yad of the context.

On the procedural sense of rules, it would seem, (D3) and (D5) encode the same rule, namely: To discover what 'yadot' names, figure out what the day of the context is.

If the suggestion that character determines cognitive significance is to succeed, the requisite sense of procedure must be more fine grained than that introduced above, in which the rule encoded by a sentence is something one follows if one, understanding the sentence and applying the procedure straightforwardly determined by its syntax, arrives at a result. For no matter what set of instructions we might write down, there will be various ways of implementing those instructions, as there will be various ways of "grasping" the functions, properties, and individuals mentioned therein. Different ways of implementing the instructions will (or at least can) correspond to (or determine) different motivational properties. So, no matter what instructions we write down, there will be a straightforward sense in which one can understand the instructions, but not know how to follow the rule (i.e., the character) that the instructions are supposed to give—*at least given that motivational properties are to supervene on character*. If it determines motivational properties, character is, in a certain sense, ineffable.

How, then, are we to explain the requisite notion of rule? One account—we might call it the *evidentiary*—proposes that such rules are (sometimes, and in part) individuated in terms of an epistemic notion, like that of evidence. Consider, for example, Gareth Evans's suggestion that to give an account of a way of thinking of something "is to explain how [its possessor] knows what object" the sense presents. In the case of the sense of 'today', "this knowledge at least partly consists in a disposition to judge the thoughts [involving the sense] as true or false according to how things observably are upon" the day in which the thought is had: "we can test very easily whether someone, in this interpretation of a sentence, is thinking of the day in the right way be seeing if he is disposed to judge the sentence as true or false according to how things observably are on that day" (Evans 1990, p. 81).

Adapting the idea for Kaplan's purpose, we might propose that there is a way C of thinking of contexts such that, for any context c, an expression as used by the agent of c expresses that way of thinking of c if and only if (in part), where w expresses the way of thinking in question, the person is disposed to accept ... w ... as true or false depending upon how things observably are (to the person) in c. We might go on to give an account, in terms of evidence, of what it is to grasp the day-of function. We would then have identified an indexical way of thinking of contexts, C, and a way D of thinking of the day-of function. Fusing all this with the idea that ($D3$) gives the (form of the) rule for the character of 'today', we might say that the character of 'today' is the rule that someone follows when, thinking of the day-of function in way D and thinking of the context she occupies in way C, she applies the function to the context and thereby identifies a day. Arguably, this account is immune to the sort of objection raised above.

Character is a semantic notion; according to Kaplan, the character of a sentence is its meaning:

The character of an expression is set by linguistic conventions and, in turn, determines the content [i.e., propositional contribution] of the expression in every context. Because character is set by linguistic conventions, it is natural to think of it as *meaning* in the sense of what is known by the competent language user. (Kaplan 1989, p. 505)

Given this, there are two worries one might have about the evidentiary account of character we are considering.

First of all, one might well question whether evidential criteria ought be built into a semantic notion. The character of an expression is the rule that determines its contribution to what's said. If we think of such contributions in the way Kaplan counsels us to—in a broadly Russellian fashion—the addition of an epistemic layer to character seems completely gratuitous. Isn't the rule that determines the contribution to what's said for 'today' simply the *procedural* rule (D6)?

(D6)   For any context c, 'today' in c contributes the day of c to what's said.

Someone who has mastered that rule, however she understands the day-of function and so forth, will associate the same Russellian assertion with a use of 'Today is sunny' as do we. Building the notion of evidence into the notion of character may help save the thesis that the semantic properties of tensed language determine its cognitive properties. But one feels that this thesis is being saved by fiat, by simply *calling* an epistemic phenomenon—which has nothing to do with the determination of a sentence's truth conditions or assertoric content—a semantic one.

A related worry is that on the evidentiary account, character is not plausibly identified with meaning, at least given fairly natural assumptions concerning meaning. People who (apparently) are able to understand one another's tensed utterances—indeed, who very obviously *mean* the same thing by their tensed utterances—need not associated the same evidentiary rules with tensed sentences. Sentence meaning is less fine grained than such things as evidentiary role.

I elaborate. On the current account, for an expression to have (say) the character of 'now' for a certain person would be (in part) for that person to take perceptual evidence as especially relevant to (certain) sentences in which the expression occurs. Understanding 'Someone is now in the room' of necessity involves being disposed to take one's current perceptions as evidence for or against its truth. But a person could believe that at any time t her experiences—at least her experiences of external objects—were experiences, not of those objects at t, but of those objects as they are at some other time—say, k seconds in the future: she thinks that her perceptions are consistenly of how things will be in just a little while. When you ask her a question, she consistenly waits k seconds before answering; if she hears the telephone ring, she waits k seconds before answering it; and so on. She in fact complains about her cursed luck, of being perceptually out of touch with the present, saying things like, 'I know that you are in the room now, because I saw that you were *k* seconds age'.

As I understand Evans's suggestion, for a person to use an expression α with the normal sense of 'now', it must be true of the person that, at least so far as an "observation sentence" *F*α is concerned, at each time *t*, the person is normally disposed to take the perceptual evidence she has at *t* to be (potentially) conclusive, as to whether *it is now the case that F*α is true or false. But while I think the person I have just described could use 'now' and 'in *k* seconds' with the semantics we do, this person would not take her perceptual evidence at *t* as potentially conclusive for the truth of *it is now the case that F*α; she would take it as potentially conclusive for *in k seconds it will be the case that F*α.

Indeed, I am inclined to think that such a person could *mean* what we do with 'now'. We would understand the person, the person would understand us. We would not think the person to suffer from any *linguistic* deficit. If, as Kaplan suggests, character is meaning, it follows that the person, since she has beliefs realized by sentences synonymous with 'now'-sentences, has beliefs under the character of 'now'-sentences. But those sentences do not have the distinctive evidentiary role of present tense beliefs. Such a person would obviously have present tense beliefs— beliefs realized and expressed by sentences that mean what present tense sentences mean—but those beliefs would not have the evidentiary role that a belief expressed by a present tense sentence would have to have, on an account like Evans's. It follows that it is in no sense necessary that if a sentence has the character of a present tense sentence as I use it, the sentence will have the (ordinary) cognitive role of that sentence. So cognitive role is not determined by character; it does not "supervene" thereon, in that it is in some interesting sense necessary that if an expression α has the character of 'now' or of the present tense as I use it, then it has what is ordinarily the cognitive role of 'now' or the present tense.

As I see it, attempts to "thicken" the notion of character-as-a-procedural-rule, by adding one or another epistemic overlay to the notion, make it implausible that character is a semantic notion—at least given the widespread and natural assumption that speakers who understand one another and appear, to themselves and others, to share a language, normally do share a language, in the sense of using forms with the same meanings. But it is implausible that one could in any interesting sense explain the cognitive significance of present tense belief merely in terms of the character-as-a-procedural-rule under which such beliefs are held. I conclude that, insofar as character is a semantic notion, it will not be of much help in explaining the cognitive role of present tense beliefs.

3.3   Cognitive Role and Tensed Thoughts

In speaking of the cognitive significance of a (type of) belief, I intend—as I think are usually intended—salient and typical aspects of the belief's evidential and motivational role, as well as salient and typical aspects of its inferential role. Somewhat more precisely: the cognitive significance of a type of belief is given by a set of salient properties, having to do with evidence, inference, and action, which are typically possessed by belief states of the type. The typicality is typicality relative to a (presupposed) way of individuating the states and within a (presupposed) population. Suppose that we identify present tense beliefs with those beliefs that are realized (in us) by present tense sentences. Then to say that a token state s has the cognitive significance of a present tense thought is to say that there is a cognitive role (i.e., a family of evidential, inferential, and motivational properties) R that are typically possessed by the thoughts expressed (in a certain class—say, adult humans) by present tense sentences, and s has (enough of) R. I think it is tolerably clear what the properties in question are. They are imputed by banalities such as

(P1)   If at t one has an experience as of rain, then one normally accepts 'It is (now) raining' and thereby believes at t that it's (then) raining

and

(P2)   If at t one believes that one's plane is (then) leaving (and one wants to catch it), then one normally moves toward where one takes the plane to be located.

Now, what would it be to explain the fact that present tense beliefs have the role they have by reference to their character—that is, by reference to the character of the sentences that realize them? The most obvious way in which one would explain the other is for the latter to be in some straightforward sense a result or consequence of the former, with consequence being understood in some sense of necessity: in some sense of 'necessary', it is necessary that, normally, if something has a rainy experience (and it understands a sentence with the character of 'It's raining'), it will accept it; necessarily, it is normally the case that if one believes (under the right character) that one's plane is leaving, one will move toward where one takes the plane to be located.

I have argued that the ordinary cognitive role of tensed thoughts is not, in this sense, explained by the character (cum procedural rule)[13] of the sentences that realize those thoughts: that is, character does not determine (normal) cognitive role. It could be the case that everyone knew that 'yadot' named the yad of the context, but no one knew that yadot is today. It is not normally the case that the woman who believes she perceives the future thinks, on having a rainy experience, that it is raining.

I do not deny that semantic properties like character can be said to be the "bearers" of cognitive role, if by this is meant only that there is a regular or normal connection between the semantic and the cognitive roles of beliefs and other attitudes. But to say this is not to say that there is a way to explain the cognitive properties of beliefs in terms of their semantic properties: there is, after all, a regular connection (in English speakers) between the present tense syntactically conceived and its cognitive role; but no one, I hope, will be tempted to explain the latter by reference to the former.

To say that character is the bearer of cognitive role in this sense is to assimilate the relation between the semantic and cognitive role of temporal expressions to that between such roles of nonindexical expressions. There is, for example, a cluster of evidential and motivational properties normally associated with (sentences in which) 'fire' (occurs). It borders on the cognitively pathological to understand 'fire' (and thus "have the concept of fire") but not take fiery experiences as evidence of the presence of fire; it borders on the behaviorally pathological to understand and think true 'There is a fire in the house' (and thereby think that there is a fire in the house) but not be moved to put it out. But presumably both are straightforwardly possible; we cannot explain the cognitive properties of someone's belief that there is a fire in the house by pointing to its semantic properties.

If the semantics of a tensed belief do not explain its cognitive role, what does? Well, what we have learned and the way in which we are constituted seem good starting places. In learning to speak (and thus developing our ability to think), we acquire the disposition to form present tense beliefs upon appropriate visual stimulation: upon seeing a dog running at me, I think, 'A dog is running at me', not 'A dog runs at me on Sunday', even if I know it's Sunday. We acquire dispositions to act in certain ways when we have present tense beliefs and desires. And so on, for other familiar aspects of the cognitive role of tensed belief. Given that these dispositions serve us well and involve no particular irrationality, why should any more explanation be called for?

The distinctive role tensed thoughts play in our psychology is best characterized in terms of a large collection of principles such as (P1) and (P2). For "constructions" (or aspects of belief states) to have the conceptual role of the tenses in someone's mental economy is for "sentences" (belief states) in which the constructions "occur" (to which the aspects attach) to satisfy enough of the principles about tensed attitudes that have as humdrum a status as (P1) and (P2). That a construction has such a role for someone is an important fact, but it is not to be explained by reference to truth conditions, or a mode of presentation thereof. If we choose to call what determines the role 'sense', we should be clear that it is a sort of sense that has nothing to do with reference.

3.4   Cognitive Role and Attitude Ascription

I will suppose that one way in which we can individuate states of belief and the other attitudes is sententially. I also suppose that for each character C there is a more or less mundanely determined collection S of principles that determine a conceptual role, CR_C. Using bracketing to form a name of a sentence's character, examples of such principles of 'It is raining' might include

(P3)   If someone has an experience as of rain, she normally accepts a sentence with [it is raining]

and

(P4)   If someone accepts a sentence with [it is raining] and desires to keep dry, she normally seeks shelter.

Such principles determine a cognitive role for sentence types in a straightforward manner. For instance, the two just mentioned determine a role that a sentence S plays for x just in case (1) if x has an experience as of rain, she normally accepts S; and (2) if x accepts S and desires to keep dry, she normally seeks shelter.

Since we would not require, in order that a state have the conceptual role for you that 'It is raining' has for me, that our states satisfy *exactly* the same platitudes, we might best understand talk of conceptual role in terms of satisfying "enough" of the platitudes. Continuing to suppose that for each character C, there is a set C^* of mundane principles like the above that determines a conceptual role, we then say that a sentence S plays the conceptual role CR_C for x provided S plays for x a role defined (in the way just indicated) by enough of the members of C^*. I leave it open for today as to when enough is enough.

If what I have said thus far is correct, there are at least three accounts possible of the connection between an ascription of a tensed belief, such as

(20)   Mary believes that Smith is sad

and the ascription of the typical cognitive role of a tensed belief. Each has (20) entail that Mary is in a state of belief whose content is that Smith is sad.[14] But the stories differ so:

(S1)   It is sufficient for (20)'s truth in a context c that Mary be in a state with the content that Smith is sad at t, where t is the time of c.

(S2)   It is necessary for (20)'s truth in c that Mary be in such a state *and* that, for some a that refers to Smith and some predicate F that refers to the property of sleeping, the state have [a is F].[15]

(S3)   It is necessary for (20)'s truth in c that Mary be in a state with the content that Smith is sad and that has for Mary $CR_{[a\ is\ F]}$, for some a and F as in (S2).

(*S3*) has (20) entail that Mary is disposed to behave in certain ways characteristic of having a present tense belief. On (*S2*), (20) does not entail this, but it does imply that she is in a state that is normally accompanied by a disposition to behave in these ways, at least given that beliefs realized by sentences with a character of a sentence of the form *a is F* are normally accompanied by such dispositions. (*S1*) has neither of these implications.

If the argument above was correct, (*S3*) is to be rejected because one could have a belief realized by (a sentence with the character of) 'Smith is sad' but, because of a disruption of the normal relations between such beliefs and action and evidence, not be disposed to act in ways characteristic of a present tense belief. Since someone who has a belief expressed by the English 'Smith is sad' can be ascribed that belief using 'Smith is sad', (*S3*) must be rejected.

(*S1*), in my opinion, must be rejected as well. For it certainly seems to be true that, for example,

(21)   Normally—that is, in all but the most exceptional cases—if someone believes (at a time) that Smith is (then) sad and has a standing desire to comfort those who are sad, that person will try to comfort Smith.

But the truth of this does not seem to be consistent with (*S1*), as it is not, or at least need not be, at all exceptional for someone to believe at a particular time *t* that Smith is sad at *t* by accepting *Smith is sad at T*, where *T* names *t*, while not realizing that *T* names the time of belief.

This leaves us with (*S2*).[16] If we accept (*S2*), we will say that when we ascribe a belief using tensed language, what we say (semantically) implies something about "how" the belief is realized—we say that the belief is realized by a tensed construction with a particular kind of character. And given the facts about those to whom we normally ascribe beliefs— in particular, that for us these characters normally carry a particular conceptual role—what we say will have certain implications about the behavior of the believer. But these implications can only extracted by invoking background assumptions—in particular, that the believer is, like most of us, someone in whom the tenses are associated with a particular conceptual role.

If something like (S2) is true, what shall we say about the semantics of ascriptions of tensed beliefs? I shall sketch an answer. It piggybacks upon Higginbotham's account of the tenses as involving quantificational cross-reference, one that I find attractive. I think the account to be sketched could be embedded in other syntactic proposals about tense, but I shall not investigate that here.

I have assumed that beliefs and other attitudes are realized sententially, and I will continue to do this. Under this assumption, it makes sense to speak of a natural language sentence "translating" someone's belief. I am going to simply assume that we should say that

(22)   Mary believes that S

is true or false depending upon whether or not S adequately translates one of Mary's beliefs. I have argued for this view elsewhere (see Richard 1990). I think that in adequate translation referential structure is always preserved, so that (R1) is a requirement on adequate translation in belief ascription:

(R1)   If q in *a believes that* q is, relative to context c, an adequate
        translation of a belief p of the agent of a context c^*, then the
        syntactic structures of p and q are isomorphic, and their
        constituents have, pointwise and in their respective contexts, the
        same semantic values.

I have made much in the past of the idea that what counts as an adequate translation may vary with context. This would explain why in some contexts we allow substitution of 'Hesperus' for 'Phosphorus' within 'She believes that Phosphorus is rising', but in others we do not, even if the contexts do not differ in whose beliefs are being discussed or in what the conversants know about the subject's belief states. Here, I want to observe that by adopting this picture of attitude ascription, but holding that the translation of tenses is *not* variable across contexts in this way, one can account for tensed ascriptions of belief.

Recall Higinbotham's proposal. It regiments utterances of

(23)   Smith is sad

and

(24)   Smith was sad

as

(23′) $(\exists t)$(includes (t, t^*) & Sad (Smith, t))

and

(24′) $(\exists t)(t < t^*$ Sad (Smith, t)).

For Higginbotham, the t-variables range over events and states, 'includes' and '$<$' pick out temporal relations between events and states, and 't^*' picks out the utterance. I propose to adopt the regimentation's form, but to understand the variables as ranging over intervals. Let us call the first arguments in 'includes (t, t^*)' and '$t < t^*$' the *locating* arguments (since variables co-bound with them serve to locate an event or state of affairs in time); call the second arguments in these predicates *anchoring* arguments (since, when unembedded, these arguments will in one way or another be assigned, or replaced with, something that picks out a time, thus "anchoring" the sentence as a whole in time). Higginbotham's idea is that when embedded as in an ascription of belief, the anchoring variables in (23′) and (24′) are (appropriately replaced with new variables and) bound to the locating variables of the superordinate tense, as in the regimentations of

(25)   Mary believes that Smith is sad

and

(26)   Mary believed that Smith was sad

as

(25′) $(\exists t)$(includes (t, t^*) & Believe(Mary, t, that $(\exists t')$(includes (t', t) & Sad (Smith, t'))))

and

(26′) $(\exists t)(t < t^*$ & Believe(Mary, t, that $(\exists t')(t' < t$ & Sad (Smith, t')))).

(26′) gives the "past over past" reading of (26); to achieve the reading, on which Mary is said to have believed something she would have voiced in the present tense at the time of belief, Higginbotham invokes a principle according to which presents embedded within pasts may be realized phonetically by the past tense, yielding

(26″) $(\exists t)(t < t^*$ & Believe(Mary, t, that $(\exists t')(t'$ includes t & Sad (Smith, t')))).

Let us accept this syntactic proposal here. Note that on this proposal, *all* beliefs realized by a tensed sentence contain a "present tense constituent." For example, to think, 'Smith was sad', is to think, '$(\exists t)(t < t^*$ & Sad (Smith, t))', with 't^*' picking out the present time. If we take the latter sentence to give the "logical form" of the former, then we will say that 't^*', as it occurs in an unembedded occurrence of (23′), has the character of 'now', since (when (23′) is unembedded) 't^*' therein will, taken relative to any context, rigidly denote the time of the context. Thus, all belief realized by a tensed sentence will, in a certain sense, be present tense belief with the "present tensing" realized by a constituent with the character of 'now'.

How, given this much, should the embeddings of tensed sentences be understood? If we accept what I said above about belief ascription, we will say that (25′), (26′), and (26″) are true, taken in context, provided that, in context, the sentences following 'that' are acceptable translations of one or another of Mary's beliefs at the appropriate time. If we accept story (S2), we will say that (25′) implies that Mary's belief is realized by something with the character (of a sentence of the form) α *is F*; (26)'s two readings require, respectively, that in the past, Mary had beliefs realized with the character α *was F* and α *is F*. (25) and (26) have such truth conditions, given that the following is involved in specifying the translation relation invoked by verbs like 'believes':

(R2)   If q, taken relative to a belief ascription B (*a believes that q*), is, in context c, an adequate translation of a belief p of the agent of a context c^*, and the anchoring argument of q's (main) tense is in B bound with the locating argument of the immediately superordinate tense, then the expression in p that occupies the position of the anchoring argument of q's main tense has [now].

More simply: If the tense of q in *a believes (believed, will believe) that q* is bound to the tense of 'believes' ('did believe', 'will believe'), then the bound element translates something that is present tense.

How does this work? Well, consider (26)'s two readings, given by (26′) and (26″). Take (26′) first. For my present use of this to be true, there must be some past time, T call it, and some belief b Mary had at T, such that when T is assigned to 't' in

$(26'^*)$ $(\exists t')(t' < t$ & Sad (Smith, t'))

$(26'^*)$ adequately translates b. Suppose belief b is indeed so translated by $(26'^*)$. By $(R1)$, this means that b is "referentially isomorphic" with $(26'^*)$—b must look something like

$(26'^{**})$ $(\exists u')(u'\,R\,u$ & Sad $(s, u'))$,

with the parts of $(26'^{**})$, in their context, having the same references as those of $(26'^*)$ in its context. So, in particular, 'R' in $(26'^{**})$ picks out the earlier-than relation, and u picks out the time T. And by $(R2)$ and the fact that $(26'^*)$'s 't' is bound to the superordinate tense, 'u' as it occurs in $(26'^{**})$ must for Mary have the character [now]. So if, on the current proposal, (26) construed as $(26')$ is true, then at some time in the past, T, Mary had a belief, the referential content of which was that at some time before T, Smith was sad, and this belief was realized by something whose tense position was present tense—that is, occupied by something with [now]. Given that Mary is like the rest of us, it follows that the sentence realizing the belief had, for Mary at T, the motivational powers of a sentence like 'Smith was sad before now'. And this is exactly the result we are looking for. An analogous argument establishes that $(26'')$ gets assigned the right truth conditions.[17]

Summing up: I have found fault with two broadly Fregean accounts of tensed thought. Against Higginbotham, I have argued that tensed thoughts cannot be identified with certain reflexive thoughts; against the followers of Kaplan, that plausible accounts of meaning cum character cannot support the idea that the semantics of a tensed sentence secures its cognitive properties.

More positively, I have suggested that to have a present tense belief is to have a belief whose realization has a certain sort of semantics. Sentences with such semantics typically (in us) have a certain sort of cognitive role. To ascribe a tensed belief is to say that someone has a belief that has a realization of a certain semantic sort; the sort in question typically has (in us, as a matter of contingent fact) a certain kind of cognitive role. There is this much connection between the semantics and psychology of tensed thought. But this much does not imply that there is an interesting explanatory connection between the two. So far as I can see, there is not.

Notes

I'm grateful for the comments of participants at the conference "Time, Tense, and Reference" held at Santa Barbara City College in April 1997, especially those of my commentator, Mark Balanguer. Thanks also to Jason Stanley and Jeff King for comments on temporal parts hereof.

1. Perry 1979 is the classic development of such examples.

2. One might deny that temporal transients, qua constituents of tensed thoughts, are to be identified with temporal intensions—functions from times, or worlds and times, to extensions. But, one might continue, (D1) "acquaints" us only with a temporal intension, not with the property of being present that is a constituent of the thought that my plane is leaving at present. Alternatively, one might concede that (D1) "acquaints" us with a property (in a sense of property other than that in which temporal intensions are properties), but say that the property it acquaints us with is but (necessarily) coextensive with presentness, and is not presentness itself.

This does not by itself meet the general point behind the argument in the text. It would seem that we can be "acquainted" with or "grasp" a property in a number of ways, just as we can be acquainted with an individual in a number of ways. Given this, and failing an argument that one can only be acquainted with presentness in ways that guarantee that we ascribe it to what "seems present," appeal to temporal transients alone has no explanatory utility in the present context.

These issues are pursued further in section 3.2

3. I am, of course, departing from Frege in making the reference of a sentence a state of affairs or Russellian proposition.

4. The example is mine, not Higginbotham's, though I imagine he would approve.

5. A natural objection to this proposal is that it makes false predictions about the truth conditions of embeddings of tensed sentences. For example, one might observe that on Higginbotham's view, the thought that I think, if I think that my root canal is over, is the thought that a certain state of thinking postcedes the end of my root canal. Modal arguments, however, suggest that this identification is incorrect. Here is Higginbotham's version of such an argument:

Consider the utterance

(C1)   My root canal might not have been over (now)

This utterance should be capable of expressing the thought

(C2)   Possibly: not: ($\exists s$) (over (my root canal, s) & s includes s').

... [But] whether I ever happen to think anything again ... Is irrelevant to (C1) ... [Not so, for]

(C3)   My root canal might not have been over as of my so thinking.

... [These] familiar observations constitute a demonstration that when I say 'My root canal is over', I cannot express the thought [that my root canal is over as of my so thinking]. (Higginbotham 1995, pp. 241–42, with inessential notational changes)

Higginbotham responds:

[An argument such as that involving (C1–3)] evidently depends upon the assumption that embedding under modality does not discard information. But it may be that it does, and even necessarily so, though of course we would want to know why. (p. 242)

Many of our thoughts, and ... Virtually all of the contents of our utterances, are reflexive.... Their reflexivity is often suppressed, however, when these thoughts are viewed as the objects of other thoughts or utterances; for thoughts that are common knowledge, or thoughts that one can carry through time, will not in general be reflexive. It is perfectly in order to consider a thought denuded of reflexivity. (pp. 245–46)

As I understand the proposal, it is that sentences like

(C4)   My root canal is over (now)

and

(C5)   My root canal is over as of this thinking

express the same thought if uttered by me in isolation, but embed differently in modal and (sometimes) belief contexts. No mechanism for how embedding proceeds is suggested, but, as observed, there may be perfectly good reasons for a language to work in this way. I do not see why one could not work out the details more or less systematically. Most simply, one could assign a pair of objects, a thought and a "modal proposition," to a sentence. The latter would be controlled by the material explicitly occurring within a sentence, so that (C5)'s modal proposition contained a mental state while (C4)'s did not. I do not think such a proposal incoherent. I propose, therefore, not to press objections like the above.

   One might also object that the proposal, taken to apply quite generally to tensed thoughts, implies that (1) the argument

(i)   I am relieved that my root canal is over. You are relieved that my root canal is over. So, there is something about which we are both relieved.

must be invalid; (2) a sentence like

(ii)   You and I are both relieved that my root canal is over

cannot be true.

I think Higginbotham is simply stuck with implication (1), at least on natural construals of the propositional quantifier. Note 7 suggests a way to evade implication (2).

6. I have departed from Higginbotham, in ways irrelevant here, in the form of the content-specifying clause.

7. I am not here objecting that Higginbotham, if he adopts the response, makes it impossible for both of us to have the same thought—that is, that he make sentences of the form

(i)   You and I both think that S

invariably false. Higginbotham would say that whether

(ii)   You believe that S

is true or not depends upon whether you have a belief with a content similar to that of the complement as uttered; he can say that similarity is usually computed by adjusting for the mental state component. My objection here is not to this, but to the idea that it is in principle impossible for us to literally think the very same thing.

8. Some of Higginbotham's remarks suggest he intends to be understood in some such way. See especially Higginbotham 1995, pp. 247–48.

9. One might deny that I can "vividly recall" internal occurrent thinkings. Even if that were so, which I doubt, it suffices for the present case simply that I be disposed to take some occurrent thinkings as memories of such.

10. I am indebted, in the last two paragraphs, to comments from Jason Stanley.

11. In fact, Kaplan *identifies* the cognitive significance of a thought with the character under which it is held.

12. Kaplan has emphasized this point in conversation.

13. Henceforth, it goes without saying that it is this notion of character that is at issue.

14. By this I mean something like: The content of Mary's belief state is the Russellian proposition that Smith is sad.

15. I will henceforth not be prissy about distinguishing character as a property of sentences from character as a property of belief states.

16. Of course, one might look for an option other than (S1), (S2), or (S3). I will not explore this possibility here.

17. As I have spun story (S2), it is part of the semantics of claims like (26) that they imply something about the character of Mary's belief. I remark that it is possible to slightly weaken (S2). One might hold that *normally* in ascribing tensed beliefs to others, (R2) is one of the constraints on the translation relation. This would allows one to say that sentences like (20) normally imply that a belief is held in a certain way, while allowing that in certain cases (e.g., ascriptions of beliefs to animals), the implication is absent. Whether this is to be preferred to the account just sketched is a matter I shall not pursue here.

References

Evans. 1990. Understanding Demonstratives. In P. Yourgrau, ed., *Demonstratives*, pp. 71–96. Oxford: Oxford University Press.

Higginbotham, J. 1995. Tensed Thoughts. *Mind and Language* 10, pp. 226–49.

Kaplan, D. 1989. "Demonstratives." In J. Almog, J. Perry, and H. Wettstein, eds., *Themes from Kaplan*, pp. 481–614. Oxford: Oxford University Press.

Perry, J. 1979. The Problem of the Essential Indexical. *Noûs* 13, pp. 3–21.

Prior, A. N. 1959. Thank Goodness That's Over. *Philosophy* 34, pp. 12–17.

Richard, M. 1990. *Propositional Attitudes*. Cambridge: Cambridge University Press.

4

Tensed Second Thoughts

James Higginbotham

In Higginbotham 1995, I discussed an issue raised by Arthur Prior, concerning the objects of states such as relief, regret, and anticipation, as expressed by ordinary English tensed sentences. For a subject to be in any of these states involves having a conception of the position of other states or events in one's temporal experience. In the case, for example, of relief that some painful episode is concluded, it is crucial that one conceive the episode as lying, not merely in a time that is in fact past, but in one's own past, or its being over and done within one's own present. To bring out this feature of the state of relief, I proposed that it necessarily involved cross-reference between the state and a constituent of its object, thus making relief what I called a *reflexive state*. On the view I suggested, what the semantics for English delivers as the truth conditions of my utterance u of 'I am relieved that my root canal is over' is (1).

(1)　$(\exists s')$ {relieved(I,that $(\exists s)$ [over(my root canal,s) & s includes s'],s') & s' includes u}

Or, in paraphrase, there is a state of my being relieved, whose time includes that of my utterance u, and whose content is that my root canal's being over includes that state. The reflexivity of the state of relief is thus shown in the cross-reference marked by 's''. Since the time of my root canal's being over includes that of my state, which in turn includes the time of my speech, my root canal itself precedes that time and thus lies in my own past.

In his chapter "Objects of Relief," Mark Richard proposes as one interpretation of my view that, disliking root canals as I do, his $(11')$, reproduced here as (2), should express a sufficient condition for me to be relieved.

(2)   (∃s′) [believe(I,s′,that (∃s) (over(my root canal,s) & s includes s′))]

That is, it should be sufficient that I am in a state of belief whose content is that my root canal is over as of my being in that state. Relief should follow that belief. But Richard then constructs a scenario on which (2) is true—indeed, one in which I might even be said to know its content—but I am not relieved, being at the time in the dentist's chair and actually undergoing the root canal.

Now, (2) exhibits the kind of cross-reference that I conjectured was essential to states such as relief and anticipation. But neither its truth, nor, where s^* is a state, the truth of (3), is a sufficient condition for me to be relieved—even obviously so, because s^* has not been located with respect to my position in time.

(3)   Believe[I,s^*,that (∃s) (over(my root canal,s) & s includes s^*)]

Hence, any commitment to the sufficiency of (2) or (3) to bring about the state of relief that my root canal is over would constitute a fatal defect for my account. To his objection, Richard conjectures one response that he finds implausible, and then a more complex view, which involves a considerable elaboration of the rather elementary apparatus that I gave. I think that the issue to which Richard calls attention begins farther back. Distinguish first of all the thought at which one is relieved (that a painful or distasteful episode lies in one's past) from the emotional state of relief, which has that thought for its object. Having the thought, or believing or knowing it, is insufficient for the emotional state, as Richard rightly observes. But then what state of belief or cognition would be sufficient? Evidently, one that locates that state itself in one's present, and so locates the state of the painful episode's being over also in one's present, and the painful episode therefore in one's past. On the assumptions in force, for the case of *saying*, 'I believe that my root canal is over', the location of the state is given by its relation (simultaneity with, or temporal inclusion of) the utterance itself. Belief is then sufficient for relief. But for the case of merely *thinking* that my root canal is over, the location is not automatic; or so I take Richard as suggesting. Thus, he gives his (11), reproduced here as (4), as sufficient for being in the state of relief, but then proposes that "since," as he puts it, "I might have the belief without speaking," his (11′) (= (2) above) alone should be sufficient, which of course it is not.

(4)   (∃s') {believe(I,that (∃s) [over(my root canal,s) & s includes s'],s')
      & s' includes u}

What Richard's considerations bring out, I think, is that there must, in the occurrence of the belief or cognition that is sufficient for relief, be an element that plays the role of the utterance u in the avowal of that state. In my article, I had glossed over this point, remarking only that the presentness of a present mental state was, in Shoemaker's (1968) formulation, "immune to error through misidentification," so that given (5) in analogy to (4), where e is a mental particular, there was no question of the falsehood of 's' includes e'.

(5)   (∃s') {believe(I,that (∃s) [over(my root canal,s) & s includes s'],s')
      & s' includes e}

What then is e? By analogy to the case of asserting, 'I think my root canal is over', where my own consciousness of myself as making the assertion through the utterance u locates my state of belief in my present, we may take e to be the event of my affirming the content of (5) itself. Then the thesis becomes: although the content of (2) is not sufficient for relief, that of (5) is sufficient. In affirming (2) I merely affirm, in effect, 'There is such a thing as my believing that my root canal is over'; but in affirming (5), I affirm that there is such a thing temporally coincident with my affirmation. The latter implicates the feeling of relief, the former not.

If only (5), which incorporates tense in the clause 's' includes e', will suffice, does it follow that we cannot but think in tenses, or, as Richard puts it, are incapable of untensed thoughts? No; but it does follow that the feeling of relief presupposes an element of self-consciousness, an element that is masked when one considers only public utterances, which by their nature are self-conscious acts. Evidently, relief, anticipation, and regret presuppose belief if not knowledge. If I am right, however, they presuppose more than this, namely, the capacity to locate one's own belief states with respect to one's current affirmations or other mental events.

I have argued above that the account of the truth conditions of utterances expressing relief that some painful episode lies in one's past carries over to the thought itself, that one is relieved. The state of being relieved involves the state itself as a constituent of the object of relief, and demands also the location of that state as present—that is, as coincident with one's own self-consciousness of the state. But now that the latter point has been made explicit, it may be questioned whether the apparatus of cross-reference was essential to begin with. Why not say simply that the object when I am relieved is just (6) rendered as (7)?

(6)   My root canal is over now.

(7) $(\exists s)$ [over(my root canal,s) & s includes now]

The word 'now' contributes to (7) nothing but its reference, the time of utterance or, in the scenario lately envisaged, of inner affirmation. If, however, I am affirming it, then we can let that affirmation e, or its time $T(e)$, serve without cross-reference between the state of belief and its object, obtaining instead of (5) the formulation (8).

(8) $(\exists s')$ {believe(I,that $(\exists s)$ [over(my root canal,s) & s includes e],s') & s' includes e}

For the particular case of present avowals, indeed, there is nothing much to choose between (5) and (8): on either rendition, the time of the critical state includes that of my avowal, directly in the case of (8), by swift implication in the case of (5). But notice that, even if (8) is chosen, my state of belief, hence of relief, continues to be reflexive, although so to speak at second remove, through the cross-reference marked by 'e' between my affirmation and the object of my belief.

When we turn to embeddings under the past tense, however, the situation changes. As I argued in Higginbotham 1995, for interpretations in which a subordinate past tense is taken as expressing the past relative to the past state in the superordinate tense, or where as in classical *consecutio temporum* it is taken as nonpast but expressing simultaneity with the superordinate state, there is an anaphoric relation between the state-arguments. Thus, (9) may be taken either as (10) (asserting the existence of a past belief state whose content was that my root canal's being over preceded that state) or as (11) (asserting the existence of a past belief state whose content was that my root canal's being over included that state).

(9)   I believed (then) that my root canal was over.

(10) $(\exists s')$ {believe(I,that $(\exists s)$ [over(my root canal,s) & $s < s'$],s') & $s' < u$}

(11) $(\exists s')$ {relieved(I,that $(\exists s)$ [over(my root canal,s) & s includes s'],s') & $s' < u$}

If so, then we should recognize as a general principle that the anaphoric connections run from the coordinate s', the first coordinate of the superordinate tense, to the second coordinate of the subordinate tense, as in the original formulation (5). The crucial case is that represented in (11), where (9) is taken as asserting the existence of a past, intuitively present-tensed state, my belief in which was sufficient for me to have then felt relieved.

Throughout, I have assumed that indexical words contribute to what is expressed nothing but their reference; but it may be proposed (as by Mark Balaguer (1997)) that since (12) and (13) differ in that assertions of the latter, but not the former, will be accompanied by the feeling of relief, their objects express different thoughts, even under circumstances guaranteeing that they will be true or false together.

(12)   I believe that my root canal will be over then.

(13)   I believe that my root canal is over now.

These examples are useful in expounding more fully the view I defend here. If u_1 and u_2 are my utterances of (12) and (13), respectively, then (12) is as in (14), and (13) is as in (15).

(14) $(\exists s')$ {believe(I,that $(\exists s)$ [over(my root canal,s) & $s > u_1$ & then(s)],s') & s' includes u_1}

(15) $(\exists s')$ {believe(I,that $(\exists s)$ [over(my root canal,s) & s includes s' & now(s)],s') & s' includes u_2}

If s_1 is a state that makes true the existential quantification in (15), then the objects of belief—namely, the contents (16) of (14) and (17) of (15), respectively—are certainly going to be different in their structure.

(16) $(\exists s)$ [over(my root canal,s) & $s > u_1$ & then(s)]

(17) $(\exists s)$ [over(my root canal,s) & s includes s_1 & now(s)]

That my belief in the content of (16) does not bring relief follows at once from the fact that the state s follows my self-conscious utterance u_1; but to bring out that (17) does suffice, the information that s is located in my present must be recoverable from my use of 'now'. How is this to be done?

The adverb or the present tense morpheme in (13) must not only refer to the time of my speech, but also place the state of my root canal's being over in temporal coincidence with it. But then the modal statement (18)

(18)   My root canal might not have been over now.

must ignore this very feature of the adverb and the tense; for its truth is obviously independent of what I may happen to utter or to think. Could there be a conception of indexical meanings or concepts that can look both ways, on the one hand incorporating information about the agent's temporal position, on the other allowing the simple semantics for the modal statement, to which this information is irrelevant? It is not clear that there could: explication of 'now' as *the present time* simply pushes the problem back a step, and indeed (19), like (18), is indifferent to all but the value of that time, and so indifferent to whether the speaker thinks of it as "present."

(19)   My root canal might not have been over as of the present time.

In my original article, I left the dual behavior of indexical expressions, as sometimes importing into content the principles that govern their use, but sometimes banishing those very principles from content, in the in-determinate state where the data seemed to place it. More recently (Higginbotham, forthcoming), I have elaborated the possibility that the proper form of a theory of truth for indexical expressions will systemat-ically imply the banishment of the content-determining rules from con-tent. On this view, indexicals are governed by rules of use, whose content figures in the antecedents of conditional truth conditions of whole sen-tences. The rule of use for 'now', for instance, is that it is to be deployed as a predicate expressing the simultaneity or inclusion of one's own utterance (or its time) in another state as given by the sentence. As ap-plied to (6), this account gives the conditional truth conditions in (20), where 'A' abbreviates the contribution of the linguistic material apart from the adverb (and for simplicity I have abstracted away from the first person and the present tense).

(20)   If u is an utterance of (19), and the speaker s of u uses the utterance of 'now' therein as a predicate P true of just those states that temporally include u, then u is true iff $(\exists s)\ [A(s)\ \&\ P(s)]$.

Given an utterance of (6) satisfying the antecedent of (20), and instantiating so as to detach the biconditional consequent

u is true iff $(\exists s)\ [A(s)\ \&\ P(s)]$,

the right-hand side contains nothing of the application of the rule of use for 'now' but the value of the predicate P. Thus, we capture the modal behavior of (6), or the proper truth conditions of (19), but lose the information necessary to set up a content that, apprehended by the speaker, becomes an object of relief. Suppose that, as far as semantics goes, the relevant parts of the whole story about (6) are as in (20). What consequences are there for a general account of the relations between the words we utter and the thoughts we express? If I am right about the general form that semantic theory should take, and also about the structure of thought that is necessary to bring out the circumstances under which we are in states such as relief, then we should construe the representations of thought expressed as extending beyond the narrowest truth-conditional conception of semantics, to include the circumstances of our deployment of indexical concepts. The words we use do robustly express our thoughts; but to see them as so doing, we should take account of the principles that set up our assertions, and not just what we assert.

References

Balaguer, M. 1997. Indexical Senses. Ms., California State University, Los Angeles. Presented at the conference "Time, Tense, and Reference," Santa Barbara City College, Santa Barbara, Calif., April 1997.

Higginbotham, J. 1995. Tensed Thoughts. *Mind and Language* 10, pp. 226–49.

Higginbotham, J. Forthcoming. Competence with Demonstratives. In J. E. Tomberlin, ed., *Philosophical Perspectives*, vol. 16. Oxford: Blackwell. To be reprinted in M. Hahn and B. Ramberg, eds., *Festschrift for Tyler Burge*. Cambridge, Mass.: MIT Press.

Shoemaker, S. 1968. Self-Reference and Self-Awareness. *The Journal of Philosophy* 65, pp. 555–67.

5

Tensed Sentences, Tenseless Truth Conditions, and Tensed Beliefs

Anthony Brueckner

I would like to raise some questions about the semantics of tensed sentences and about the beliefs they express. I have found it fruitful to pursue these questions in connection with D. H. Mellor's tenseless theory of time and his correlative view that tense is *transcendentally ideal*.[1] I would like to consider his recent arguments to show that 'present' does not express a metaphysically significant A-series property.

The sentence 'The Battle of Hastings is present' can, according to Mellor, be used to express what he calls a *seriously tensed proposition*. Mellor holds that such a proposition is to be conceived as a function from times to tenseless truth conditions. Such a proposition, according to Mellor, can take on different truth values at different times. But a *tenseless* proposition, such as that the Battle of Hastings occurs at t (where 't' names a specific time), has a *fixed* truth value. Thus, we must conclude, says Mellor, that seriously tensed propositions cannot be *identified* with tenseless ones.

I believe that we can formulate a position very close to that just described without having to conceive of propositions as changing their truth values over time. We could hold that the meaning of a seriously tensed *sentence* determines a function from contexts of utterance to propositions that have fixed truth values—propositions that can be expressed by tenseless sentences. This is like David Kaplan's view that the *character* of a sentence is a function from contexts to what he calls *contents*; some sentences, for example, tensed ones, have a character that is not a constant function.[2]

Let us turn to Mellor's denial of the reality of A-series properties such as *being present*. It appears that Mellor's main argument for this position in the paper under discussion proceeds from the claim that seriously tensed propositions are made true by tenseless facts (e.g., the fact that a certain tenseless truth condition holds, or is satisfied, where this truth condition falls in the range of one of Mellor's functions from times to truth conditions). Let us consider again the sentence 'The Battle of Hastings is present'; forget about whether this sentence is used to express a Mellor-style proposition-cum-function that somehow changes in truth value, or rather a number of distinct propositions each with fixed truth value. Either way, we can formulate something very close to Mellor's view as follows: the *sentence* in question is true as uttered in context *c* if and only if the Battle of Hastings is simultaneous with t_c, the time of the context.[3] This *tenseless* truth condition concerns a *B-series* fact. So a seriously tensed sentence is made true by a tenseless, B-series fact.

How exactly does this plausible point about semantics help establish the tenseless theorist's metaphysical claim that *being present* is not a real property of events? What is it, anyway, to deny the reality of putative A-series properties? There are two well-known ways of denying the reality of putative *moral* properties. According to the *noncognitivist*, sentences such as 'The assassination was wrong' are not fact-stating. They lack truth conditions, and so they are not even candidates for truth or falsity. Instead, they have some sort of prescriptive function. On the other hand, according to the *error theorist*, moral discourse *is* 'truth apt', in Crispin Wright's phrase.[4] Sentences that appear to attribute moral properties to acts *are* in the business of doing just that. The problem is that the truth conditions of such sentences are never satisfied, since no act has a moral property.

Neither of these routes is embraced by Mellor. He provides truth conditions for seriously tensed sentences, and those provided are often *satisfied*. So Mellor's denial of the reality of putative A-series properties must be different in character from the familiar ways of denying the reality of moral properties.

Take a sentence that appears to attribute a real property to an individual, such as 'John is thinking'. We can state truth conditions for this sentence that do not involve the explicit attribution of the property apparently attributed by the sentence (viz., the property of thinking). For example, a functionalist might hold that 'John is thinking' is true if and only if John is in functional state F. But, granting the correctness of the functionalist's statement of truth conditions, it obviously does not follow that thinking is not a real property of individuals. The same may well hold for the A-series property apparently attributed to the Battle of Hastings by our seriously tensed sentence.

Mellor will protest that I am missing his point. The defender of the reality of A-series properties, Mellor will say, attributes a special metaphysical status to such properties. However, it has turned out that A-series sentences are made true by boring old B-series facts that are *relational* in character. So since A-series sentences are not property-attributing at all, it cannot be that they attribute exciting *A-series* properties to events, properties with some special metaphysical status.

As against this, the proponent of the A-series would maintain that when an event figures in a relational B-series fact such as that the Battle of Hastings is simultaneous with t_c, that event possesses an A-series property at the pertinent time. In this case, the Battle had at t_c the property of being present.

Consider a parallel case. 'The Battle of Hastings is actual' is true as uttered in c iff the Battle of Hastings is part of, or exists in, w_c, the world of the context. David Lewis argues from the correctness of these truth conditions to the conclusion that *being actual* is not a special, distinguished property possessed by just one possible world.[5] However, Lewis himself draws a distinction between two senses of 'actual', a primary one and a secondary one. The foregoing example involved the primary sense. The secondary sense is found in sentences such as 'If Fred ate less, he would actually enjoy himself more'.[6] In such a sentence employing the secondary sense, the pertinent world for truth value evaluation of an utterance of the sentence is *not* the world of the context of utterance, in contrast to sentences employing the primary sense of 'actual'. Instead, the pertinent world is some world with respect to which the antecedent is true. This opens up the possibility, suggested by Nathan Salmon, that the secondary sense of 'actual' *does* express a metaphysically significant property that is possessed by just one possible world.[7]

Maybe the situation is parallel for sentences that appear to attribute A-series properties. That is, maybe Mellor is right about sentences employing the *primary* sense of 'present'. But what if some A-series sentences involve a *secondary* sense of A-series predicates? Consider the sentences (1) and (2).

(1)   In 1996, the present U.S. president was a Democrat.

(2)   In 1996, the current U.S. president was a Democrat.

(1) is false as uttered now, because George W. Bush is the president at the time of the context, and he was never a Democrat. However, there might well be a reading of (2) on which it comes out true, since Clinton was in 1996 the then current president.[8] Consider also sentence (3).

(3)   In 1996, the then present U.S. president was a Democrat.

Supposing that this sentence is legitimate English, it does not involve the primary sense of 'present'. If it did involve that sense, we would need to consider the person who is president at the time of the context in evaluating the truth value of an utterance of the sentence. But in (3), it seems that the pertinent president is the 1996 one.

What about the sentences that are standardly used to explain the alleged distinction between the A-series and the B-series? I say, 'In 1065, the Battle of Hastings was future; then at a time in 1066, the battle was present; and in 1067, the battle was no longer present but was rather past'. If there is no secondary sense of 'present', then the foregoing sentence is nonsense. But if the A-theorist's sentence makes sense, then there *is* a secondary sense of 'present'. And in that case, Mellor's remarks about the *primary* sense of 'present' do not go any way toward establishing the unreality of A-series properties.

In asserting the transcendental ideality of putative tensed facts (which status we will discuss soon), Mellor says (p. 37) that "tense is just a way of representing the temporal locations of things"; but, in Kant's phrase, tense "in itself, apart from the subject, is nothing." Tense, as Kant says of time, "... does not ... remain when abstraction is made of all subjective conditions of ... intuition." *Which* way of representing things is Mellor talking about here? Presumably, a way of representing things that has no corresponding real property, on Mellor's view. But then this way of representing things is presumably expressed by the *secondary* sense of A-series predicates.

I will conclude by considering some questions about tensed beliefs. This discussion raises some issues concerning the cognitive significance of tense.

One way to understand the claim that putative A-series facts and properties are unreal is to think of tense as being *transcendentally ideal* in much the same way that the phenomenal world of spatiotemporal objects is, for Kant, transcendentally ideal. One way of understanding *that* Kantian claim is as follows. When we abstract from the constituting activities of minds and consider things as they are in themselves, supremely independently of *us*, we do not find spatiotemporal objects. A parallel view applies to tense, according to a Mellor-style transcendental idealist about putative tensed facts.

But why think that tense is somehow "contributed" by us, in something like the way spatiotemporality is, for Kant, contributed by our faculty of intuiting objects? Prior to asserting the transcendental ideality of tense, Mellor argues that successful timely action requires true *tensed belief*, that is, belief of a proposition expressed by a seriously tensed sentence. For example, if my aim is to start running when the gun fires, it won't suffice to have the correct belief that the gun's firing is simultaneous with a particular time *t*. I need to believe that the gun's firing is *present*. Maybe the suggestion is that tense is transcendentally ideal in that tensed belief is just an artifact of the human condition, which happens to involve timely action and hence tensed belief. However, successful timely action also requires the existence of a systematic causal structure in nature, and *that* is obviously not, on Mellor's view, transcendentally ideal.

I want to look a bit more closely at Mellor's claim that true tensed beliefs are indispensable for successful timely action. Mellor says that we must be able to acquire tensed beliefs when they are true and to lose them when they are false. Let us unpack this claim. A true tensed belief is a belief of a true tensed proposition. Such a proposition, according to Mellor, is true at some time (or times) and false at others. This is because tensed propositions are functions from times to truth conditions. So let us consider the function, construed as a set of ordered pairs, that is associated with the proposition-expressing sentence 'The Battle of Hastings is present'. This set contains the following ordered pairs:

$\langle t_1, t_1$ simultaneous with Battle of Hastings$\rangle$

$\langle t_2, t_2$ simultaneous with Battle of Hastings$\rangle$

The values of the function are truth conditions. Suppose that the truth condition involving t_2 is among those that in fact hold, or that are in fact satisfied. Then that truth condition *always* holds (is always satisfied). So to say that our tensed proposition is true at t_2 is not to say that the truth condition in question is satisfied at t_2 (because the truth condition is satisfied at all times, but the proposition, according to Mellor, is not true at all times). Instead, to say that the tensed proposition is true at t_2 is to say that t_2 is one of the arguments of our function that has as its value a truth condition that is in fact (timelessly) satisfied. In other words, a tensed proposition is true at a time if and only if its truth condition for that time is timelessly satisfied. (Applying this to tenseless propositions, we could think of them as *constant* functions from times to truth conditions. So if such a proposition is true at any time (i.e., if its truth condition for that time is timelessly satisfied), then, since each time determines the same truth condition, the proposition is true at all times.)

Believing a tensed proposition when it is true is to be conceived as follows. Anyone who sincerely assents to the sentence 'The Battle of Hastings is present' believes the same proposition. But that proposition has various different truth conditions. Believing the proposition when it is true is believing it at a time whose corresponding truth condition is timelessly satisfied.

As noted earlier, in asserting the transcendental ideality of putative tensed facts, Mellor says that tense exists solely as a way of representing the temporal locations of things but is nothing in itself, apart from the subject. This suggests that the tensed propositions that, according to Mellor, must figure in beliefs causing successful timely action involve modes of conception that apply to nothing in reality. So these modes of conception presumably purport to apply to A-series properties that allegedly characterize events at some times but not at others. However, it appears that such modes of conception do *not*, according to Mellor, figure in the content of the tensed propositions cum functions we have just been discussing at some length. That content is, or is represented as, a Mellor-style function from times to tenseless truth conditions. So it is hard to see how a consideration of the role of Mellor-style tensed beliefs in timely action can help to establish the transcendental ideality of tense. That is, on Mellor's view, tensed beliefs do *not* involve A-series modes of conception that apply to nothing in reality. So: either (1) the content of tensed beliefs is correctly represented by Mellor's apparatus, in which case such beliefs are irrelevant to the alleged transcendental ideality of tense, or (2) tensed beliefs *are* relevant to showing the transcendental ideality of tense, in which case Mellor has incorrectly represented their content, leaving out the allegedly problematic A-series modes of conception.

Notes

I would like to thank Nathan Salmon for helpful discussions of many of the points in this chapter.

1. See Mellor's "Transcendental Tense," in *Proceedings of the Aristotelian Society*, Supplementary Volume 72 (1998), pp. 29–43.

2. See Kaplan's "Demonstratives," in J. Almog, J. Perry, and H. Wettstein, eds., *Themes from Kaplan* (New York: Oxford University Press, 1989), pp. 481–563.

3. Strictly, the truth condition is that some time during the duration of the Battle of Hastings is simultaneous with t_c.

4. See Wright's *Truth and Objectivity* (Cambridge, Mass.: Harvard University Press, 1992).

5. See Lewis's *On the Plurality of Worlds* (New York: Basil Blackwell, 1986).

6. See Lewis's "Anselm and Actuality," *Noûs* 4 (1970), pp. 175–88.

7. See Salmon's "Existence," *Philosophical Perspectives* 1 (1987), pp. 49–108.

8. See again Salmon's "Existence."

6

Need We Posit A-Properties?

Mark Richard

Hugh Mellor argues against the reality of A-properties, such as the putative property of being present, which an event has when and only when it is occurring.[1] He observes that one can give the truth conditions of sentences such as

(1) The Battle of Hastings is past

—and indeed of any tensed sentence—without reference to A-series properties. After all, it is beyond debate that a use of (1) at t is true if and only if the Battle of Hastings ended before t. Such truth conditions refer to temporal relations (so-called B-series relations, such as being later than) that hold timelessly. Mellor infers that "what makes tensed talk true" are B-series facts. If so, we might conclude, there is no fact about the semantics of tensed talk that requires us to posit A-series properties.[2]

As Anthony Brueckner observes in his chapter "Tensed Sentences, Tenseless Truth conditions, and Tensed Beliefs," defenders of the A-series will find this argument less than compelling, since it is perfectly consistent with all that Mellor says, not only that there are A-series properties, but also that predicates such as 'is past' ascribe them. Brueckner goes on to point to certain sentences, such as

(2) In 1996, the current U.S. president was a Democrat

and

(3) In 1996, the then present U.S. president was a Democrat,

which arguably have true readings, and which, if they have such readings, seem to require that 'present' and 'current' have senses on which they express the A-series property *being present*.[3] And indeed, as Brueckner observes, sentences such as 'The Battle of Hastings was present but is no longer' seem senseless—certainly they are not true—if 'present' doesn't have such a sense.

One might find some of Brueckner's examples, such as 'The battle was future' somewhat strained. But suppose that Brueckner is correct that the sentences have true readings. Does this mean that Mellor's argument has been defused?

The debate about A-series properties is of interest only on a view of properties on which they are (much) "sparser" than functions from worlds, or worlds and times, to extensions, for there is obviously a property-cum-possible-world-times-intension of being present. While it is far from clear what the basis is for asserting that "sparse" properties exist, on many views whether a putative property P can do (causal-) explanatory work looms large in justifying the claim that P exists. It is such a conception of properties that Mellor seems to have in mind when he says that believers in A-series properties hold they are "real non-relational differences between ... things ... much like temperatures; and just as temperature differences make things different in other respects, so ... other differences depend on differences in" A-series properties.[4]

Given that the debate is over whether there are "sparse" A-series properties in the sense gestured to above, it is not clear that Brueckner disarms Mellor's line of argument. For suppose that a claim is explanatory in virtue of its truth conditions and that, as Mellor claims, the truth conditions of any claim can be given adequately in terms of B-series relations. Then there is nothing about explanation that forces us to suppose that there are A-series properties. If this is correct, and B-series properties are "explanatorily indispensable," then Mellor does have grounds for denying the reality of A-series properties.

Mellor holds that A-series properties are "transcendentally ideal" in something like Kant's sense. On this view, A-series properties are artifacts of our way of representing B-series relations, and they correspond to nothing in reality. Brueckner argues that this view sits poorly with Mellor's view of propositions, on which they are functions from times to (tenseless—i.e., eternal) truth conditions, such a proposition being true at just those times t at which its value is (eternally) true. (For example,

(1) expresses the proposition that maps *t* to a truth condition that (timelessly) obtains if and only if the Battle of Hastings occurred before *t*.)

Brueckner argues that if tense is transcendentally ideal in Mellor's sense, then the propositions expressed by tensed sentences must involve "modes of presentation" of A-series properties, though those modes of presentation present nothing real. But the functions from times to eternal truth conditions just mentioned involve no such modes of presentation: the truth conditions to which the claim made by (1) maps a time *t* involve no such thing; neither is the claim itself such a mode of presentation. So either Mellor is wrong about the nature of tensed beliefs, or he is wrong about the transcendental ideality of tense.

There are certainly ways of elaborating the claim that tense is transcendentally ideal that avoid this dilemma. The A-theorist thinks there is a property that 'is present' ascribes in any context. The anti-A-theorist thinks this is a mistake: the role of 'is present' is, instead, to ascribe at *t* the relational property *happens at t*. Suppose the anti-A-theorist is correct. Then A-theorists misunderstand the representation 'is present'; properties like being present are "in themselves, nothing" at all; the illusion that there are such properties is generated by the way in which we represent—the from of words we use to represent—the temporal relations of things. 'Is present' seems to have a property-ascribing role like 'is purple', but it does not. If this *is* what it is for tense to be transcendentally ideal, then tense can be ideal—and thus an artifact of representation—without tensed propositions containing "empty modes of presentation."

So far as I can see, Mellor's view—that we have no need to posit A-properties, and that they are but an artifact of our representation of the B-series—survives Brueckner's criticisms.

Notes

1. See, for instance, Mellor's *Real Time* (Cambridge: Cambridge University Press, 1981), passim.

2. Of course, there might be some nonsemantic fact that required such properties—say, one that McTaggart's infamous regress argument points to. Such considerations are not at issue in the dispute between Mellor and Brueckner.

3. Brueckner's idea is presumably that (1) the logical syntax of 'In 1996, the current U.S. president was a Democrat' is something like

(i)   It is true in 1996 that (the x such that it is currently the case that x is president is a Democrat);

(2) for (i) to be true, 'it is currently the case that' must have a sense on which it is redundant: *it is currently the case that S*, taken relative to a time t, is true relative to a time t' iff S, taken relative to t, is true at t'; (3) if the operator 'it is currently the case' has such a sense, the predicate of 'The Battle of Hastings is present' has such a sense.

4. See Mellor, *Real Time*, P. 4.

7

Time Plus the Whoosh and Whiz

Arthur Falk

If the theory that time is McTaggart's B-series (the B-theory) is to be justified, there needs to be an account of the appearance of passage (whoosh and whiz). Hinton and later authors gave a clue for such an account, by conceiving of substances as world-lines in a four-dimensional spacetime and of selves as experiencing passage instead of experiencing the spacetime. But they gave no account of any sensory mechanism for generating the appearance of whoosh and whiz. In this chapter, I only intend to point out this hiatus in the B-theorist's case, criticize five previous attempts to fill it, and then fill it myself. My success should be a relief to the B-theorist and leave the A-theorist chagrined, especially one whose commitment to A-theory rests on the failure of B-theory to account for experience. I also show how an account of human deliberation and agency can take the tensed contents of perceptions and intentions, regrets, and expectations seriously and nonreductively, consistently with the tenets of B-theory.

The cognitive significance of tensed language (i.e., the sense or meaning of tense) is usually explicated in semantics (e.g., as in Kaplan's theory), but there are psychological aspects of cognitive significance, some of which underlie its semantic manifestation and others of which supervene on it, as Richard remarks in his chapter "Objects of Relief." Our semantic competence grows from our animal psychology and in turn nurtures our human psychology. So the semantics should be informed by psychological insights and goes awry if it is not so informed. I focus on these psychological aspects, first the ones more primitive than semantic cognitive significance, and then the ones dependent on that significance. The primitive aspects ground reflexivity in semantics (e.g.,

Higginbotham's semantics). The human aspects are probed in a science of agency.

This procedure departs from the more common way philosophers of language explicate the cognitive significance of tense (e.g., Kaplan, Salmon, Yourgrau, Castañeda, Wettstein, and others), since I do not take my cue from ordinary English, but from innate biological and psychological mechanisms in humans. We should not try to "read off" the solution to the problem of the cognitive significance of tense or the experience of passage from an examination of ordinary public languages, which are just collections of conventions (Chomsky 2000, pp. 44–45). We need to explore the psychological and biological mechanisms that underlie the surface phenomena of ordinary language. My general approach is more similar to Peter Ludlow's (1999), despite our being on opposite sides of the issue; I explain the cognitive significance of tense by examining the "innate computational/representational system that is part of our biological endowment" (Ludlow 1999, p. 14). Ludlow's A-theoretic approach to tense is to examine the human representational systems; my B-theoretic approach involves dealing with more primitive animal systems as well. I shall examine the underlying perceptual mechanisms, those that humans share with other animals as well as the distinctively human ones, which together create the cognitive significance of tense.

The goal of this chapter is to answer the question, If the tenseless or B-theory of time is true, what explains our experience of passage and the cognitive significance of tensed language? Since my goal is to provide an answer to this question, not to argue that the B-theory is true and the A-theory false, the background of my discussion is the ontological assumption that the B-theory describes the mind-independent physical world. However, there is a sense in which I am arguing for the B-theory of time and not merely assuming it. For unless the B-theory can explain the cognitive significance of tense, the B-theory is not adequately justified. Many A-theorists argue the B-theory is false since it cannot explain the cognitive significance of tense (e.g., Smith 1993; Craig 1996, 2000); my aim is to rebut this argument.

Other B-theorists have aimed at rebutting it (e.g., C. Williams 1992). I think, however, that I deliver a more convincing rebuttal by showing how there can be an explanation of time's passage and the cognitive significance of tensed discourse that is consistent with and supports the B-theory. A successful explanation requires that we trace the cognitive significance to primitive psychological mechanisms, thus grounding, at least in part, the semantics of tense in psychology and even biology. Grice and Schiffer (in his early book, *Meaning* (1972)) argued that semantics is reducible to psychology and developed a program in the philosophy of language that came to be known as 'intention-based semantics'. But their psychology remained at the level of iterative propositional attitudes, that is, attitudes about attitudes. I think we need to theorize at a more basic level, in terms of the biological mechanisms of perception, which belong to all animals and not merely to humans. The semantics of tense is not reducible to the psychology of tense, but this semantics is based, at least in large part, on primitive psychological mechanisms. The distinctively human cognitive significance of tensed language emerges from this more basic level of the experience of passage.

7.1 The Presupposition of a B-Theoretic Description of Time

As background for addressing the question this chapter aims to answer, namely, If the B-theory is true, what explains time's passage and the cognitive significance of tensed discourse?, I adopt the familiar B-theoretic assumption that time is just a dimension of extensiveness. Some of its elements are named by dates, construed broadly to include clock readings and enough descriptors to ensure that some of the times, that is, the elements of time, do not share all their names with another time. Hereafter, by a date I mean a name of a single time only. A calendar orders dates. Objective time is just what the calendar measures; I call it *calendar time*.

According to the B-theoretic ontology I am adopting, times are related by the relation-schema of one being later than another by *n* units; the relation of one being later than another by some units is abbreviated as one being later than another. The relation has the properties that induce on the set of times a serial ordering, which is time's arrow. The relation might itself be defined in terms of the physical anisotropy in time of causal order, for example, in terms of the greater entropy at later dates.

Then times would have to be defined accordingly as being the terms in such physical relations, and time would necessarily be a concomitant only of change, as physicists understand change, fluxlessly. I leave this matter aside. If anisotropy is a by-product of increasing entropy merely, or is merely a statistical property of elementary events such as kaon decays, is the one and only time to be anisotropic for aggregate events but isotropic for the elementary events making up the aggregate, as mechanics seems paradoxically to suggest? Or is anisotropy rather a property of something other than the time itself? I do not answer this question, and either answer is compatible with this chapter's thesis. But it may help you make the distinctions needed to understand the thesis, if you assume that time is anisotropic really: time's arrow (supposing it is time's) *is* antecedent in definition to time's passage, which is an optional add-on. If passage is added on, the arrow constrains it to pass one way only. The assumption of real anisotropy helps avoid the conceptual trap of treating the A- and B-theories as merely contrasting theories of temporal order. As theories of order, they are equivalent. They differ not on time's arrow, but on time's passage, on the seemingly objective evanescence of times within the now—affirmed by A-theory, not by B-theory.

Some B-theorists postulate an ontology of events; others work with continuant substances. I take the approaches to be intertranslatable, and I opt for the latter approach here. Things are located in places at times. The three-word phrase 'located … in … at' does not represent three dyadic relations, but a single triadic one. A relation of location is a three-placed relation between a thing, a spatial position, and a time: the thing *occup[ies]* the place *at* the time named by a date. Brackets on the verb's suffix indicate a tenseless mode of expression. The times are in the domain of relata along with the spaces and things. The relation is as "outside of time" as is the relation of squares to rectangles, which is the relation of being members of sets related by set inclusion, $\subset$. Here is another untensed relation: one time [is] later than another time.

The language we use is invented, as set theory's is; we think with the learned.[1] We reject equations of grammatical categories to ontology; we circumvent mandatory features of ordinary grammar by bracketing them. Tenses, like the indexical 'now' and the past, present, and future, are foreign to calendar time, that is, B-time. They are part of the whoosh and whiz I call *now-based time*, that is, A-time. (The zippy words are D. C. Williams's (1951) for time's flow or passage, borrowing from C. I. Lewis's "the jerky and whooshy quality of transience." Other phrases of Williams's are the "flow and go," the "rearing and charging," and the "grace and whiz" of now-based time.) Time is such as our formal analysis and empirical science find it to be: just calendar time without whoosh and whiz. My chief contrast will be between time (i.e., calendar time) and time plus whoosh and whiz (i.e., now-based time). Because time is calendar time, now-based time with all its whoosh and whiz is a subjective accretion, a form of egocentric appearance.

7.2   A Concession to A-Theory on Temporal Perception

I archly assume all this, knowing full well it's controverted, for I want to explain how the mind adds the whoosh and whiz (sections 7.4–7.7). But we should not treat the whoosh and whiz as illusion merely. A science of ourselves as deliberators and agents will treat agents and a deontologized now-based time as co-supervening on cybernetic systems working in calendar time, for the reality of agency depends on the agent's having propositional attitudes toward now-based time (section 7.8). On the other hand, the adding of whiz is not an evolved adaptation either, as are our brains and hands; it's rather an evolutionary trap we are caught in. It's like that other evolved but nonadaptive trap, selfhood, which developed like a pearl: however adaptive the later accretions may be, at its core is some junk. But, although the parallel is close between selfhood and time's flux, between I and now, that's not the story I wish to tell here.

Our creative hypothesis-forming powers gave us the thought of a calendar time without the whoosh and whiz, and formal analysis and empirical science support the hypothesis's truth. Nevertheless, there is the challenge to the completeness (adequacy) of calendar time. In D. C. Williams's words, "[W]e *find* passage,... we are immediately and poignantly involved in the whoosh of process, the felt flow of one moment into the next" (1951, p. 299). It is not enough to declare reason superior to the senses in this respect. Reason should tell us *why* the senses are not to be trusted. The primary problem is the perception of things in flux, the whoosh and whiz. This trait of perception is not the same as an awareness of nowness. The former has objects at the center of attention, the latter has time itself. The mind-dependence of the flux is more than the fact that it would not exist if minds did not. In that sense, tables and chairs are mind-dependent, since we make them. For something to be mind-dependent in the proper sense is for it to be unable to exist except as the object of a mental act, or as a property of a mental act that can be made the object of a reflective mental act. Calendar time theorists must demonstrate this proper sort of mind-dependence of whoosh, and defend it against the now-based time theorists who claim the whoosh and whiz are objective.

Many defenders of now-based time accept the theory of relativity as Einstein presented it. So they concede that the whoosh is a frame-dependent phenomenon and not as objective as, for example, the speed of light through a vacuum, which is frame-invariant; but they explain time's flow nevertheless by appeal to physics and not to the creative powers of the mind. They note that I, for instance, have access at any one time t to the information that defines in spacetime the surface of a hypercone, that is, the four-dimensional analogue of a three-dimensional cone, with my t-segment being at its apex, and its surface opening out around my past. Electromagnetic radiation carr[ies] the information along that surface to me in the time that it travel[s] through a vacuum; other slower signals that reach me at the same time must fall within that hypercone at angles to its surface that are set by the speeds of the signals. Thus, my "now" receives new (i.e., heretofore inaccessible) information about my past; how far into the past depends on how far away it was and how fast the information traveled to me. My perceptually accessible present is highly localized. Once the t-segment of me is superseded by a later segment of me, the signals at t are necessarily not accessible to the later me. Just in that physical fact is the whoosh and whiz, according to these theorists of now-based time. If my t-segment retains old information about my past from my prior segments, that will be episodic memory in the t-segment. The rest of the universe at t divides for me into my future and my spacelike elsewhere. So the past, local present, and future do not exhaust all there is from my frame; it is no big deal to admit a fourth category, the elsewhere.

These defenders of now-based time, the A-theorists, charge their opponents, such as me, of confusing frame-dependence with mind-dependence, and so mistakenly asking psychology for answers that physics supplies. The confusion I am supposed to be guilty of is abetted by the Minkowski spacetime diagram, which is not a license for us to adopt the "view from nowhere and nowhen" unconstrained by hyper-cones; it is rather a way to see how the many perspectival and localized now-based times are introduced physically into the world. It's not the mind's measuring, but the spatiotemporally limited availability of the information to be measured at any one time and place, that constrains the measurer to divide her time into a past, present, future, and the else-where that is none of these. At the beginning, I mentioned that time's arrow may not be an objective feature of time, but few think that it is introduced into thermodynamics by an illusion that is purely mind-induced. A similar moral should be drawn about time's flow. So argue many now-based time theorists.

Calendar time theorists, the B-theorists, respond in various ways (Sellars 1962, sec. 16; Grünbaum 1967, p. 70; Mellor 1998, pp. 53–57). I respond to the now-based time theorists by conceding all except their characterization of my position as the claim that time's flow is an illusion *purely* mind-induced. For flux *is* constrained by the physical facts represented by the hypercone. It is more like the experience of a secondary quality, a product of an interaction of subjective and objective constraints where neither makes the other otiose. As brown is to color in the world (sc., light wave frequency), so flux is to the time in spacetime. Later, I prove that the frame-dependency of whoosh does not make its mind-dependency otiose, any more than brown's dependency on light waves makes otiose its dependency on visual systems. Thus, my reply is that the now-based time theorist foists off a false dichotomy between frame-dependence and mind-dependence to insist on one side, whereas I want both sides.

Against the more metaphysical now-based time theorists, I deny ontological weight to the evanescence of the now-experience; there is no wave of becoming-real washing through the spacetime manifold along a time axis from earlier to later. For a frame-independent wave of becoming is inconsistent with relativity theory, and a frame-dependent one is, if not ego-logy, then not ontology either (Putnam 1967; *pace* Sklar 1977, pp. 272–75). Now-based time's objective side is only the limitation of perceptually accessible information to whatever arrives at the hyper-cone's apex. The illusion of whoosh is the overinterpreting that limita-tion and the imputing to the world of an objective flux of being.

7.3   A Critique of Prior B-Theoretic Analyses of Perception

Before I present my account, let us review the efforts of five other calen-dar time theorists. They failed to explain the process that makes for this evanescence of now-experience.

Charles Hinton (1880, 1904; also Broad 1935) showed how now-based time may be an illusion analogous to the spatial illusion that the sun moves around the earth and that the earth is not rotating. Although he only showed a possibility, he showed *thereby* that there is no phe-nomenological proof of objective whoosh, just as Aristarchus showed there was no phenomenological proof of the sun's revolving around the earth, for visual appearances and even the absence of kinesthetic sensa-tions were consistent with the earth's rotating. Hinton's result is impor-tant, for it shows that the calendar time theorist does not have the burden of proof to show that the now-based time theorist's claims of objectivity are false. The now-based time theorists do not even have an argument to objectivity from appearances. So the two theories start off on equal footing as far as phenomenology goes.

Briefly, Hinton argued from the concept of an object in four dimen-sions. He reconceptualized substances as events stretched over time, a way of thinking prefigured in Locke's concept of personal identity. The idea became fixed in its canonical form in 1908 with Minkowski's anal-ysis of the geometry of the spacetime manifold. Not only did now-based time have no place in the manifold except locally, but substances were divided by time into proper parts, so that only a part of any substance existed during any interval of its life span. The concept of a substance is of a hypervolume in four dimensions. See figure 7.1.

The earth over time is a hyperhelix wrapped around a hypercylinder (not really a cylinder, but a hyper-Bernini column, since they each re-volve about the common center of mass). On the surface of a small time-

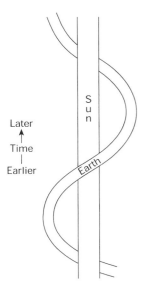

Figure 7.1
The earth's world line in spacetime is a hyperhelix, and the sun's is a hyper-cylinder, relatively to each other, according to general relativity theory. This figure portrays about fifteen months of the existence of the earth. Redrawn from Perlman 1970, p. 580.

slice of this hyperhelix there is a tiny wormlike hypervolume, its length being in time. (I am that spacetime worm.) The worm doesn't experience hypervolumes; it is subject to the illusion of whoosh and whiz instead. But Hinton gives no account of any sensory mechanism for generating the appearance of whoosh and whiz to that spacetime worm.

D. C. Williams (1951) incorrectly believed that the calendar conception of time directly predicts the now-based time. He correctly thought that our act of comparing our experience to the scientific map of things at some time and place is itself on the map. But he concluded that "the perspectivity of the view is exactly predictable from the map" (p. 300). If this means predicted directly, without the intermediation of indexical truths, it is just false, as work on the essential indexical has shown. For a perspective may not be unique (Burks 1949), and in any case, given just the map and calendar, I could not tell which perspective was mine (Prior 1959; Perry 1979). A better argument of Williams's is that a pure intelligence could have expected or predicted the perspectival nature of the experiences it would have after being incarnated into the form of a human spacetime worm. It had learned "the design of the human spacetime worm, with its mnemic organization, its particular delimited but overlapping conscious fields, and the strands of world history which flank them" (p. 301). However, Williams fails to tell us just what the pure intelligence learned about the organization of this worm that enabled it to expect the now-based perspective upon its incarnation.

Adolf Grünbaum's account fares no better, for Grünbaum's is not a theory of the mechanism either. Nor does it concern itself with perception of the whoosh and whiz, but at most with an awareness of presentness. Grünbaum (1969b, pp. 155–56) says, "M's experience of the event at time *t* is coupled with an awareness of the temporal coincidence of his experience of the event with a state of knowing that he has that experience at all." Question: Is what is known a tensed fact, as the word 'has' suggests? He continues, "In other words, M experiences the event at *t* and knows that he is experiencing it." The answer to my question is yes; the tense of what is known is present in the progressive aspect: "I am experiencing it." He continues, "Thus presentness or nowness of an event requires conceptual awareness of the presentational immediacy of the experience of the event." But the presentational immediacy is what was to be generated from a condition describable in calendar time. Grünbaum (1969a) concedes the circularity, but denies that it is vicious for his purpose, which is to state a necessary condition for a becoming that is obviously mind-dependent. For my purposes, his necessary condition would be viciously circular.

D. H. Mellor's early account was circular. He said (1981, p. 171), "So much for our perception of the flow of time, which we see to be nothing more than an accumulation of memories." If Mellor has not misused 'flow' to mean 'arrow', then not much work is done by the truism that a recollection is later than the experience recollected. A distinction exists between perception and episodic memory, only because of the now-based time in which recalled experiences are tagged with pastness. One must explain episodic memory in tandem with perception, and so memory cannot explain its own explanation. Can the convexity of one side of a curve explain the concavity of its other side? No, nor can memory explain the presentness of experience. I will later explain what it is about us that makes the distinction between perception and memory necessary in us, by contrast with a possible being I call a scheduler for whom no such distinction is necessary. Meanwhile, you might think of God. L. Nathan Oaklander (1993, p. 349) repeats Mellor's early question-begging approach when he says, "[I]t is just this succession of different psychological attitudes toward the same event (first anticipation, then consciousness, then memory) that gives rise to the impression of time's flow …"

Mellor's recent account is like the one I will defend: "[C]hanges in our A-beliefs would correspond exactly to the changes A-theorists take to constitute the flow of time" (1998, pp. 68–69). But why his emphasis on belief rather than perception? Perhaps because of what he says next: "And similarly for all other perceptible examples of time flowing. We can experience all of them just as easily—and as truly—without the flow of time as with it" (p. 69). But is perception tied to the whoosh and whiz only extrinsically? I doubt it, because I for one cannot have non-A-perceptions. Nor is the A-ness of my perception induced by my having A-beliefs about it or any other reflective attitudes such as feelings about it (contra Mellor 1983). Any theory that makes the flow of experience depend on something extrinsic to the sensing is not in accord with the phenomenological facts. For surely we must not aspire to perceive like animals with less developed minds, thinking they perceive whoosh-lessly because they cannot be reflexively aware of their perceptions! No, presentness is an inextricable part of all sensory appearance, theirs and ours, and A-theorists are right to insist on an account of the experience of presentness that does not appeal to any reflexivity (e.g., Smith 1988, p. 354).

7.4   The First Thought Experiment: The Negative Feedback System

Let us see if I can do any better. I claim that calendar time embodies all the objective temporal information in our experience. The rest is a by-product of our way of perceiving and acting. My proof will be two thought experiments: the thought experiment of the negative feedback system,[2] and the contrasting thought experiment of the scheduler.

The first of the two major thought experiments will proceed incrementally. The increments may be either a simulation of evolution from the simplest knowers to ourselves or a progression from our own most abstract structure to our more detailed structure as knowers. Either way, we start with a negative feedback system. We look not to the most advanced types of awareness, but to the most rudimentary types and build from there. The experiment has four steps.

1. The simplest minds create the foundations for the appearance of passage, and they are feedback systems tracking their own agency. A negative feedback mechanism can initiate action to reach a goal and correct its action in response to information (the feedback) about its progress. We start with a system that has no memory and no capacity to detect motion. As the experiment progresses, we will add the perception of motion, the perception of patterned motion, and memory.

Animals are at least negative feedback systems; that follows from their being agents. What is the information about time in the feedback of a negative feedback system? We distinguish two possibilities: (1) time indications included in the content of the feedback, distinguished from (2) time indications not included in the content of the feedback, but otherwise conveyed. The latter alternative, noninclusion, is the case with all living things. The time of the information is not conveyed in the way the rest of the information is, that is, by representational content. Rather, the time of the information, as well as the sequencing of bits of information, is represented by the time of *the receiving* of the information. (So much can be found in Locke 1690, II, chap. 14 (cf. Aristotle, *Physics*, IV.11 (219a5ff, 27ff.)). He traced all our acquaintance with time to the succession of our ideas in our minds. But he did not believe that now-based time was subjective. So he did not see how his theory of our acquaintance with time entailed that the mind *added* the whoosh and whiz.)

For an example, let the feedback content be about overheating: "Too darn hot!" The attribute of being too darn hot is *directly attributed* (in Chisholm's (1979, 1981) sense and D. Lewis's (1979) sense of self-ascription) to a double subject, the one who is predicating and the time of the predicating, in a way that does not require the predicator's cognitive access to either subject. For an attribute is predicated directly to a subject if the attribute is predicated of it without being concatenated with a singular term. The subjects of the predication are fixed, despite the lack of singular terms for them, by their being that which is moved by the predication at the time of the predication (Falk 1987; Mellor 1989). The system's predication is of itself and of the time of predication because it cools itself off then. A system need not have the ability to report its direct attributions, but if it could report the attribution, it would say, "I am overheated now." The act of direct attribution does not require command of indexical terms; only the public expression of direct attribution requires that. Another example of feedback (Cooney 1991, pp. 54ff.): In a bacterium, an enzyme's concentration falls below a critical level and a gene turns on, leading to the production of more enzyme. In effect, the system is directly attributing enzyme deficiency to itself at that time. Engineers would say the error signal is positive. When certain end products of the metabolic process reach a certain concentration, the gene turns off. The error signal has returned to zero; the system no longer directly attributes enzyme deficiency to itself.

The concept of direct attribution has been around for over twenty years, and it's time for us to put it to use in the debates over time. The obstacle has been that the paradigm of the attributed entity is a linguistic predicate, and we fail to generalize. It was David Kaplan, I believe, who broke the hold of the paradigm by noting that, when we say the national anthem goes like this [and then we hum], it is legitimate to claim the humming is the predicate of the anthem. If we say of someone that he looked like that, and point to a portrait, it is legitimate to claim a look is being predicated of the person. In that vein, I ask you to think of perception as a kind of self-ascription or direct attribution. Perceptual input is simply the perceptual direct attribution of a pictorial sort of attribute. Despite our eyes' and ears' focus on objects, the perspectival nature of our perceptual inputs shows us that their subjects of attribution are oneself and one's place and time (Humphrey 1992).

We should note two things about the matter of attributes. First, the attribute itself is not perspectival; a fortiori it is untensed, which is another way of saying the time is not in the content. For part of perceptual recognition is the ability to recognize a reoccurrence of the same from a different perspective. Perceptually directly attributing is accepting a pictorial predicate as true of oneself from the perspective of here and now. The same predicate may be accepted at another time and place as true of oneself then and there also. Second, putting the stress now on the contents' being attributes, the contents of our perceptions are not facts or propositions, a fortiori not tensed facts or propositions. Perceptual contents are attributes, and the perceiving is the attributing of them directly to the perceiver and the time of the perceiving.

Times are not part of the content attributed either by dates or by tenses; they are rather among the subjects of attribution. We who have learned the biological, even metaphysical, lesson reflected in the essential indexical (Perry 1979; Falk 1987, 1995b; Mellor 1989) and who also believe that time is just calendar time must take seriously that times are as much the subjects of direct attribution as are the persons doing the attributing. For the word 'now' is as essential an indexical as the word 'I' is. Times are nows just at the times when perceptual direct attributions are made to them. Calendar time theorists can maintain that perceptual direct attribution creates nowness just as it creates I-ness.[3]

How do we get to the perceptual content's being present, that is, present-tensed, from a tenseless attribute's being perceptually directly attributed to the time of attribution? From the time of the attribution to its being the time of the content attributed, that is, from a property of the representation to its being a property of the represented: here's the primordial use-mention confusion, and nature never selected against it! If the world had been different, nature would have selected against it. If information in radiation were always of the sort that codes for a TV picture, organisms like us would have had trouble using it. For the temporal order of the TV transmissions mostly signifies the spatial array on the picture tube, not time sequence. Fortunately, it's not nature's way to be so devious. So, considering just a simple negative feedback mechanism, the absence of a time indication from the content of its feedback does not hurt it, since it acts on any error signal upon its reception forthwith, and the timing of the signal is indicative of the time of the signaled content. Since immediate response is the mode of its timing of action relatively to input, the action is typically appropriate to its circumstances. The confusion is serendipitous in simple organisms. The concept of the serendipitous use-mention confusion is Quine's (1974, p. 68).

Anticipatory and preemptive action in more sophisticated organisms, as well as appropriate delays in action, are built up from this base in a makeshift way by evolution. Thus, I claim that evolution never corrects this basic feature of feedback content, but only works around it. That is ever evolution's way; witness the blind spot in the vertebrate eye. The use-mention confusion's being uncorrected by natural selection is obvious: astronomers watching sunspots through telescopes use their intellects to correct their eyes and convince themselves the events in their perceptual nows really happened nine minutes before. Intellectual correction does not dispel the nowness of the content perceived, however.

We have derived the now as the opening of a viewpoint in perception by virtue of direct attribution. There was no appeal to reflective acts of awareness. With the now comes the whoosh, which is the flushing and freshening of the now. Let me explain.

The capturing of temporal information by direct attribution has the effect that information must be continuously *flushed* from the rudimentary feedback system and replaced by the information appropriate for the new time. For, in order for the perception to be true of the time it is about, it can only last as long as that time does. If the perceiver is not to be deceived, the information about a date can only *be* information for it when (i.e., at the same time as) the perceiver is *at* that date. The information must *not be* information for it when it is at a later date. The perceiver is a continuant, a worm in spacetime, and so is at many dates, but its perceptual information about a date is not information for it at all its temporal locations. The information must be flushed soon after it is received, or at least it must not be actively retained, but allowed to decay quickly.

Now I ask you to momentarily endow it with a what-it-is-like-to-it-for-it-to-collect-and-flush-information and then empathize. Go into the inner life of such a being. How could this flushing of information be achieved except at the price of creating a sense of passage? Flushing is something the mind does at every date to the input from the previous date. The truth about a time is only in consciousness during the time it is about, not before or after. So the mind experiences a flux. Veridicality for such perceivers requires time-blinders. A horse wears blinders so that it only reacts to information in front of it. We too wear blinders that delimit a now.

The system need not act at any time to prevent its perceiving some information about a later time, since perception depends on the causal propagation of the information, a process that cannot perceptualize information about a time later than the time of its reception. Here, the objective fact of the hypercone is constraining the experience of passage. So the freshening is caused objectively. Continuous *freshening* of input cannot be the whole of the experience, however. Consider this disanalogy: A black object's temperature is the result of its intercepting light, let's say. But since it cannot flush or reset its temperature at any moment, its temperature is useless as an indicator of the intensity or frequency of the light that it has just intercepted. Experience is unlike temperature in that it matches the freshening with a flushing. The flushing returns the system to the kind of state that can register new information. The flushing is caused subjectively.

Flushing is a change to be analyzed using the tenseless language proper to calendar time. It is simply the system's both being aware of an undated content at a date and not being aware of it at a very close later date. The agent at *t* lose[s] from perceptual consciousness one bit of information that lack[s] a time indication, and take[s] in an incompatible bit of information that also lack[s] a time indication. For example, picture the slide of consciousness over the hyperhelix (in figure 7.1) as a window onto a small temporal slice of the hyperhelix. (You might cut a window in a sheet of paper, put it over the diagram, and slide the diagram along underneath the paper.) The system takes in some information about the hyperhelix at the later edge of its four-dimensional window to the hyperhelix while flushing some of it at the earlier edge. The window is an effect of the intaking and flushing of direct attributions, however, not a preexistent, despite my way of expressing it. Since we can describe the changes in the perceiver in a tenseless language, C. W. K. Mundle (1967, p. 136) was simply confused when he argued that, in order for the perceiver to change, the perceiver could not be in four-dimensional spacetime, "and one would still have to acknowledge a [real] time dimension other than the one which has been spatialized, in which our states of consciousness are successive." Not so, for spacetime has succession in the sense of one moment's being later than another; but succession as whoosh is an appearance generated for any spacetime worm-perceiver as a concomitant of the way it collects and discards temporal information, and the genesis of the appearance does not require a second whooshy time dimension.

Here is another objection: The intentional standpoint objectualizes the bits of information received as third terms in the eternal relations between perceivers and dates. Intentionalistically, bits of information are entities to which the perceiver is related at one time by consciousness and not so related at another time. Now-based time theorists would like to make them the objective carriers of whoosh and whiz, especially since they are reported in tensed sentences.[4] But calendar time theorists have at least two strategies available to parry this attack. The Platonistic one will treat the perceptual bits of information as eternal entities; the Aristotelian one will reanalyze the account of flushing so that the bits of information are part of the relation between a perceiver and a date, and not independent third terms.[5] Both accounts will resist importing the time indications of tensed reports into the content of the experiences reported.

My theory of time perception, augmenting the scientific evidence against objective now-based time, has the consequence that the whoosh and whiz are mind-dependent. A first approximation of what is happening is that a property of the mental acts of acquiring information is being mistaken for a property of the events which the information is about. In the classic "sun rising, sun setting" type of thinking, which attributes to the sun our own motion, the mind attributes the resulting passage to the object, because it does not sense *itself* as in contrary relations to dates, only the *other* things' being in contrary relations to dates. But this way of describing things is excessively Parmenidean in its skepticism about the senses; we are noticing something objective in noticing flux, namely, the contours of hypervolumes. It is truer to think of the flushing as like our seeing the color brown; both are secondary qualities.

2. So far, the thought experiment is too simple. We should take it further, since we do perceive succession whenever we perceive movement. We do not see a succession of positions and infer motion, when a scene is continuously lit. (We do see a succession of positions when the scene is lit by a strobe light, also when we look at an object moving in front of a lit computer monitor. Motion is inferred in these cases.) Fur-

thermore, perception of movement is extremely primitive. Direction of movement is detected in the third layer of neural processing in our eyes (Poggio and Koch 1987). In other words, some of the signals entering the optic nerve from the eye already contain information about the direction of the motion being seen. So what must we add to the Lockean account that I gave?

We must first say what the now has turned out to be: Using tenseless language by bracketing the mandatory tense, a time [is] a now to any negative feedback system, if and only if that time [is] the time of some directly attributed feedback to the system, and that time represent[s] the time of the feedback's wide content (environmental information) to the system, there being nothing in that content to indicate the time. The time that is predicated-of is the time of the predicating. But the idea of a durationless instantaneous now is incredible in any sense other than as a mathematical idealization, even without taking into consideration our perception of movement. Surely the visual now of the motion-seer endures long enough to encompass many perceptions, each briefer than the now. The finger wiggled in front of a lit computer monitor or a TV screen or a movie screen shows about four or five co-occurring, that is, temporally overlapping, positive, quickly vanishing afterimages over the movement's trajectory. These are an extract of what is seen ordinarily within a single now. Ordinarily there are so many such images that they form a blur in the trail of the moving object, like a comet tail. The TV screen background to our wagging fingers lets us glimpse an excerpt from what is going on in vision when we see movement lit ordinarily.

The key addition to our previous thought experiment is a more extensive now. The now is not a point-instant. The more encompassing now is not an idea of succession, just the embracer of a succession. While the more encompassing now is a form of retentiveness, it is not memory, since it does not entail a sense of pastness and it is brief. (Memory is introduced later in our series of thought experiments.) How long is the now? I mean something briefer than James's specious present, which encompasses several seconds. It endures for at least 30 milliseconds. The duration of a now is an artifact of the flushing: the time from input to flushing. Experiments with motion perception show that a duration or a minimal perceivable speed is context dependent; we can see a slower movement if some fixed object is nearby (Wallach 1959).

Let us now consider the possibility of partial flushings of the input, feature by feature, within that interval of an expanded now. If the partial flushings of an input also delimit partial nows within the interval before its final flush, we can have a now that encompasses a succession.

"Stop there! Aren't you smuggling in whoosh?" No, dear attentive reader; nothing here escapes description in calendar time, as I will show. "Process" in the sense of the progressive aspect of verbs, as distinct from the perfect/imperfect and habitual/continuous contrasting aspects, does become an object of a system's awareness with my admission of partial flushings. But calendar time can fully accommodate aspect, which is independent of tense, contrary to what both A-theorists and B-theorists have assumed. Let's not confuse it with tense, which does record the whoosh of now-based time.

Although aspects and tenses both attach to propositions, "aspects are different ways of viewing the internal temporal constituency of a situation" (Comrie 1976, p. 3). The internality is what distinguishes aspect from tense. Tense is external, in the sense that it is indexical, always referring the time of the situation described to the present time in one way or another. Aspect describes the temporal structure of an event (the verb's referent) without referring to another time that's external to the event. After the references to times in the tense, the further references to times that differentiate the aspectual forms are not relative to the context of the speech event. Aspect is sensitive to such semantic distinctions between situations as nondynamic states, in contrast to complete events, in contrast to processes in progress (Comrie 1976, p. 13). Ter Meulen (1995) offers an alternative idea of aspect as a way speakers control the flow of information. On either conceptualization of it, aspect can vary independently of tense. I can point to English syntax as exhibiting this independence. It is more marked in English syntax than in the Romance languages, whose grammars have treated aspect confusedly under the heading of tense (Comrie 1976, p. 1 n. 1), a tradition that philosophers follow uncritically.

Some philosophers suggest that aspect is fully captured by iterated tenses. The suggestion does not work. The future perfect, as in 'I shall have eaten', is not fully explicated in an iteration of future and past tense operators operating on a present-tensed core, 'It will be that it was theretofore that I eat then'. If it were fully explicated, the past perfect, as in 'I had eaten', would be explicated by an iteration of two past tense operators, 'It was that it was theretofore that I eat then'. This iteration is equivalent to the simple past, yet 'I ate' is not equivalent to 'I had eaten'. (For example, contrast 'When he arrived, I ate' with 'When he arrived, I had eaten'.) In linear time, there are fifteen nonequivalent tenses if we count iterations of tense operators but not their negations (Øhrstrøm and Hasle 1995, p. 178). To express all fifteen, we never need more than a pair of tense operators, and even some of the pairs are equivalent to a simple tense. As expressive as these iterative tenses may be, they do not express all that aspect expresses.

I think the attempt to reduce aspect to combinations of tenses stems from the failure of Reichenbach's (1947, sec. 51) unified treatment of tense and aspect. His account required indexicality to be at the core of the treatment. It had not only the perspective of the time of utterance, but also another perspective on the content, a time defined as simultaneous with, or earlier or later than, the time of utterance. Prior (1967) pointed out how gratuitous his choice of two perspectives was and demonstrated its inadequacy in yielding some of the aspects. By contrast, his own preferred view—namely, the iteration of tenses—was demonstrably limited to a pair of tenses. But we have seen this fails too. Aspect simply is not indexical. Therefore, any unified treatment of it and tense is confusion.

McCawley (1993, sec. 12.2) put us on the right track when he introduced the distinction between points of time and intervals of time in his account of tense and aspect. Aspect is best thought of as dealing with intervals of time and the internal relations of the times within the interval that distinguish the various aspects. Then the tense relates the interval to an instant of time related to the present. For example, the simple perfective aspect marks an interval as filled with an event without any further delineation of it: 'I worked once'. The progressive aspect notes that an interval has an event filling a subinterval within it: 'I was working'. The interval for the progressive is the extended now, when the tense is the present.

I will add more in a positive vein in section 7.7. For now, it suffices to note that a verb like 'find' does not take the progressive aspect (except when it takes a predicate adjective). That is because finding is not a motion. So it's good that our thought experiment uncovers one of the origins of aspect; motion is, after all, something with an imperfective, continuous, and progressive aspect. But we must look to tense for whoosh. Nevertheless, even if the experience of becoming is a hybrid of whoosh and progressive aspect, we must account for it.

For the phenomenal basis of the progressive aspect, I go back to Helmholtz, who published in 1867 the idea that perception represents time with time[6] much as maps represent space with space. Within the extended now is a manifold of time wherein a succession of contents is perceived. This innovation extends Locke's succession of ideas, so that it occurs even *within the confines of* the now. *A time* represents a time, precisely because the informational content does not. There are three ways of reconciling this idea with the preliminary calendar time account of what the now is.

The first of the three ways to put this innovation into calendar time talk would require that the awareness relation be relative to a stopwatch in effect. The person [is] aware of a content afresh at t, while the person [is] aware of a similar content for a bit, and while the person [is] aware of a less similar content for a bit longer. The stopwatch ensures a first-in, first-out flushing of awarenesses while allowing some temporal overlap. This account has the consequence that contradiction occupies consciousness, unless the different stopwatch indications are counted in the contents. But the finger wiggled in front of the computer monitor just is contradictory—multiple positions for a finger, however briefly (Paton 1929). So to make this account work, the content at the fresh point must be the only content that conveys conviction at that instant about the position of the thing in motion. There is first a partial flush; the conviction about position is jettisoned. The simultaneously occurring positive afterimages must reveal themselves as ghosts of departed entities, and of departed convictions about position. They only convey conviction at that instant about a velocity vector associated with the thing in motion.

Alternatively, to analyze the perception of motion we may say that the flushing relation comes in degrees. At the date a person [is] aware of a content, she [is] half aware then of the content she [is] fully aware of on the close previous date; she [is] a quarter aware then of the content she [is] half aware of on the close previous date; and so on. This second way may allow the now to be instantaneous, but it has the disadvantage that all partial flushings lead to false belief—false despite all the false ones being only partially believed.

Are we hung on the dilemma of falsehood or contradiction? No. Either way, the perceived content is transformed from its initial occurrence to its lingering phase, when it is a positive afterimage. Also, the awareness of the afterimage does not cause conviction about a thing's position. Why doesn't a lengthened now reveal the hypervolume instead of reinforce the appearance of whoosh and whiz? It would reveal the hypervolume, if it were not for the fact that the extended now of motion-perception is not one enduring percept, but a succession of them.

A third solution is that the awareness relation is to differences of contents. The now for the perceiver of movement would be: within certain temporal limits, the perceiver's brain detects the physical, *nontemporal differences* of its representings and preconsciously attributes the differences of the representings to the nonsimultaneity of the undated scenes represented. As mentioned above, the initial layers of processing outside the brain detect direction of motion, which the brain can use to sequence the accompanying inputs. It prepares for a perceptive consciousness having some duration, the span of a now during which there will be a succession of displays. At this point in my argument, I appeal to the phenomenon as I experience it: the now endures so that I experience succession now, and yet I experience the succession now by way of a succession of experiences *within* the now. So I perceive the scene changing and moving. The span of the now that is sufficient to encompass succession is the key: the motion-perceiver's now is lengthened. Using calendar time to describe the experience, the perceiver self-locates-at-t_2 in some interval, $t_2 - t_1$, less than or equal in duration to the now, simultaneously with the differences of [scene y − scene x].[7] The subtraction could be literal, if information about each scene is stored as entries in a matrix. Further, if the intervals are small, and approximations to a limit are made, the resultant experience will have the smoothness of continuous becoming.

3. Let us complicate our thought experiment further by adding the perception of *patterned* motion and change. If any case is to refute Helmholtz's idea, it is our perception of music and meaningful speech.

For we sense the whole series that constitutes a phrase or clause of speech, as well as the temporal order of its parts (Royce 1901, lec. 3). We have the experience of succession and not just a succession of experiences (Volkmann, quoted in James 1890, p. 629). This experience of succession would fill up the span of a now with *one* experience. So we are conscious of the experience of succession (James 1890, pp. 609–10), rendering the succession of experiences derivative, revealed to us upon reflection, not the primary thing it is for the more primitive system we just considered (Pöppel 1997).

Of course, we need not choose between succession of experiences and experience of successions. It's a case of having both a succession of experiences within the span of a now and contemporaneously one experience summing up the now. Even if a unitary duration is phenomenologically basic for *us*, Locke's and Helmholtz's ideas are still appropriate for primitive beings and our primitive substructure. I think our perception of the pattern in movement is a matter of second-order awareness. A person is aware, second order, of her current first-order content as having a certain mode or weight because of the contents that preceded the current first-order content in awareness. This extends Locke's idea, that we get our idea of duration by reflection on the succession of ideas in our minds. However, I do not mean consciously reflexive as Locke did; it's the brain's preconscious reflexive processing of information. Also, the duration is patterned. Pattern is essentially a predictive property, and so it is valuable in action. For example, a mongoose wins its fights with cobras, matching its feints to the cobra's sways, and its success implies that it has this predictive sense of pattern. Further, the second-order preconscious reflection is not confined to reflection on the extended now of motion perception, but takes into consideration the contents over the span of the several seconds that James identified as the specious present. The progressive aspect covers this interval and more.

4. When the second-order experience goes beyond the now and beyond the specious present, and draws on memory to yield a sense of familiarity or a measure of equal durations, we reach a further complexity. So our thought experiment's third complication will be to add memory to our negative feedback system: If the system must preserve information, then the flushing of it is in conflict with that need. That

which is to be preserved must be segregated from incoming information, thus forcing some such distinction as perception and memory. We may define perception as that way of acquiring information in which the time known about is represented by the time of the representing, as the time-spread of a drama represents the time-spread of the events dramatized. Then somehow, in episodic memory a rudimentary now-based time indication is incorporated into the content recalled: pastness. The innovation of including a time indication in content gave us memory. But even perception of motion requires comparison over time, which is not a matter of memory or sensed pastness. The difference is that perceptual comparisons over time do not make time a part of the content, whereas memory does. There is a whoosh-like character within memory, namely, the episodes remembered receding ever deeper into the past. But I don't think this is a matter of the conscious imagery of recall. I do not myself find degree of pastness marked by degree of faintness or anything phenomenological like that. I simply know when I am recalling something recent or something remote.

It is wrong, perhaps, to treat the development of episodic memory as later than the perception of patterned motion. One might argue that, just as episodic memory requires a past time indicator to be incorporated into the content, so the predictive uses of the perception of patterned motion require a future time indicator to be incorporated into the content of our expectations. In that respect, they involve the same innovation, time indicators in the content. I will return to this idea, but for now beware of taking the further step of supposing a present time indicator in the content of perception. Perception is more primitive than either memory or expectation, for perception can exist without them, but they cannot come to be unless there is perception already. Let its primitiveness reside in its lack of a time indicator in its content.

This concludes (for the time being) our first thought experiment. It has revealed five concepts for understanding the whoosh in the perception of time. First, perceivers directly attribute perceptual attributes to themselves and the times of the attributing. By a serendipitous use-mention confusion they attribute the time of the perceiving to the perceived. Second, this entails the flushing and freshening of content. They perceive succession by way of a succession of perceivings (Locke's idea). Third, the now is enough of a duration to permit succession within it, so that time can represent time (Helmholtz's idea) and generate the experience expressed in the progressive aspect. Fourth, we can add to this basic structure a second-order perception of the pattern in the motion perceived (another of Locke's ideas). Fifth, we reconcile the flushing of information with the need to retain it by having a way of storing flushed information with a marker of its having been flushed, namely, its pastness. The five concepts account for the whoosh and whiz.

Empathically grasping the intentional content of our perceiver's perceptual states, and supposing yourself able to express yourself in either a tensed or tenseless language (perhaps by bracketing the mandatory tense of English), you see the system's content must be for it of a form that you would have to express by choosing the present tense. If it perceives movement, our reports of its experiences would have to use the progressive aspect. Elaborating on an idea of David Schenk (n.d.), we can define the being's temporal perspective at a time as the conjunction of its perceptually directly attributed contents at that time.

Note the irony in the experiment. I have you empathize from without with the state of the simplest possible perceiver. But such beings as these are we. Evolution has not corrected this basic plan of any perceiver.

Notice that my account posits A-qualities, of presentness in the use-mention confusion, of pastness in the innovation of memory, and of futurity in the perception of patterned motion. The A-qualities are mind-dependent ones in the way secondary qualities are, not as hallucinations are. We experience items as being now (not merely simultaneous with some event), being past, or being future because the flushing of information takes place. The flushing and other quirks of perceptual information processing, all properly B-theoretic, cause the A-qualities to be *instantiated*, not reduced or eliminated. They are not reduced because they contain more information than the flushing accounts for, as I conceded in section 7.2. But they are instantiated only subjectively in the experiences organisms have, and they play no role in canonical statements of the objective truth conditions for the organisms' beliefs. (A canonical statement is a statement in the ideal scientific theory.) I would say the same of secondary qualities. So much for the canonical status of '"Snow is white" is true iff snow is white'! More on this at the end.

7.5   The Second Thought Experiment: The Scheduler

The second major thought experiment is imagining a being I call the *scheduler*. This experiment contrasts the feedback system with a scheduler and so is a major backup to the empathic experiments I just described. A scheduler would come upon information with a date attached that represents the time, not the time of receipt, but the time that the information is about. It would perceive things as we perceive a TV displaying a time in the corner of the picture—suppose the picture is live, and the time in the image originates with the rest of what's pictured. Thus, the date would be part of the content that a scheduler perceived. The scheduler is not a direct attributer as we are. Whereas we directly attribute properties to the time at which the attribution occurs, it assents to dated singular propositions.

Try empathizing with the scheduler. You will see the following features emerge. A scheduler does not have to receive information about events in any particular order. Its order of receiving information could be temporally scrambled, yet it would not be confused about sequence. Furthermore, it would not have to distinguish perceived information from remembered information. It would not have to flush information about a time in order to receive more information about another time. Why? The dates would provide all the temporal information. A scheduler would not even have to receive information sequentially. It could receive it all at once. Unlike your empathy with the primitive organism that perceives by negative feedback, your empathic grasp of the scheduler's intentional content shows it is not tensed.

It is easier to empathize if we let the experiment be unconstrained by the hypercone of relativity theory that I described in section 7.2. But if one reintroduces the constraint of the hypercone on the scheduler, it still does not unleash any whoosh.

Furthermore, a scheduler would not experience the now as I defined it. However, according to Oaklander's (1993, p. 346) misstatement of a sufficient condition of the now-experience, the scheduler would have to have the experience of presentness, but it does not. He says, "[I]f I am conscious at t_1 of an experience that occurs tenselessly at t_1, and if, as a matter of tenseless fact, it is t_1, then I know the experience is present."

To see Oaklander's error, put the date in the content of the experience and omit time itself representing time, since it would be otiose for this being. Your empathy should reveal that no presentness is involved.

A scheduler could sequence an action and coordinate it with events, for it could have an internal clock telling it the date, which it could compare to dates in intentions. But it must delegate the performance to a negative feedback system; it could not itself be a timely agent unless it could see its representations of times coincide with the times represented. We bang up against the essential indexical when we focus on action being guided by information.

A scheduler could perceive hypervolumes. No whoosh, gee whiz. This is one way to think it has the thought of a succession without having a succession of thoughts. A scheduler with access to information without limits of space and time is ... aw, telling's no fun. But if Godlike knowing is possible, the scheduler is a possible being who contrasts radically with all living things, except only our own power of theoretic insight into nature. Come to think of it, the scheduler is the two gods that Lewis discusses (1981, p. 139). Their cognitive blind spot concerns 'I'; the scheduler's concerns 'now'; in each case, the blind spot exists because of an incapacity for direct attribution.

7.6   A Concession Concerning Brainwork

I must now face a problem that is thought to undermine the cogency of the above experiments, namely, the problem of brainwork prior to perceptual consciousness. Time itself represents time in the perception of movement, but that is not to say that objective time is simply transferred through from the stimulus situation to consciousness. No. First, it takes time to become conscious of information, up to half a second from the time of being stimulated near the threshold level of intensity, and to about a fifth of a second for normal intensities of stimulation. Second, the brain has reconstructed the sequencing in consciousness. James and Dennett wrongly find reason here to reject the Locke-Helmholtz approach to the perception of temporal succession, rather than simply adjust the approach, which is what even Helmholtz did. (See the quotation in note 6.)

I accept four principles of brainwork. They are all consistent with time itself representing time in the final conscious product. First, brainwork can create seamless consecutivity in subjective experience even where there are objective skips according to objective time, and vice versa. The principle is illustrated in our seeing a movie as continuous, not as a succession of stills, which is what a movie is. Our segmenting a continuous stream of speech into words is an example of the vice versa. Second, brainwork can create equal units of subjective time even where there are unequal units of objective time, and vice versa. I think Reid was the first to see this, when he criticized Berkeley's making the succession of ideas in our minds into an internal clock. Third, brainwork can create an order in subjective time using objective contents that did not come in that order. Sometimes it makes consecutive that which comes simultaneously. "If we can hear forty-five phonemes per second, the phonemes cannot possibly be consecutive bits of sound; each moment of sound must have several phonemes packed into it that our brains somehow unpack" (Pinker 1994, pp. 161–62). Sometimes, it makes simultaneous that which comes consecutively, especially when the time lapse between the consecutive events is less than 25 milliseconds. Thus, a red light quickly followed by a green light is seen as one yellow light (Geldard and Sherrick 1986). Perhaps brainwork changes order. Experiments concerning the hearing of extraneous clicks during listening to speech suggest this; the brainwork places the clicks in a perceived sequence where they are not in the sequence of stimuli (Fodor and Bever 1965; Bever 1970). (A caveat: If awareness is a neglectful penumbra around an attentive focus, the focus of attention at some time could be events that were in neglectful awareness a second or so earlier. So the clicks may have been in neglectful consciousness in the right order, but we attend to them out of order.) A fourth principle is that small time separations between stimuli may retroactively mask the earlier stimulus or cause its saltation, that is, its being perceived as spatially closer to the later stimulus than it actually was (Geldard and Sherrick 1986). All this brainwork is consistent with the idea that the brain lets the temporal sequencing of its perceptual output stand proxy for the sequence of the objective events perceived. What it makes doubtful is naive realism about perceived sequence.

7.7   A B-Theoretic Description of Agency

Recall that the scheduler could not act directly. What then about agency? Our thought experiments show how our perceptual processes are responsible for adding the whoosh and whiz to time. But the whoosh and whiz are also implicated in any agency, including our own. We tack on a fifth step to our first thought experiment to distinguish the whoosh in agency from the whoosh in perception. The simple negative feedback system coordinates its actions with environmental events by timing its initiation of actions to coincide with the incoming of the information that guides the actions. The actions of a system without memory are always corrective to reduce the influx of unwelcome information about its current self.

The nexus between an agent's intention and its action requires that all the directly guiding information be direct attributions, which would be expressed in indexical format, as Prior (1959), Perry (1979), and others (e.g., Falk 1987) working on the essential indexical have shown. 'I must go now' expresses a belief that is effective for me when the belief expressed by 'Arthur must go at noon' is not. Generalizing the point to all negative feedback systems, a system's instructions to its executive parts for them to take corrective action would be direct attributions with volitive force. Their expression in a public language would use a first person volitive or imperative in the present tense to express that the command is for it and its parts to carry out forthwith, urgently. (Sanskrit has such a form, by the way.)

These action-initiations must also be flushed, along with the perceptions, since any command is prompted by, and corrective of, the information that is just past. Thus, instructions are discharged or displaced as the new feedback that confirms their effects modifies them into new instructions. The calendar time description of flushing can be tailored to agency: the agent at t delete[s] from volitive consciousness one instruction that lack[s] a time indication and create[s] an incompatible instruction that also lack[s] a time indication. Our empathic understanding of this being shows us that it experiences itself as striving.

To understand the calendar time theorist's account of this volitive experience, we must return to the distinction between aspect and tense, and to the distinction within aspect between perfective and imperfective (or progressive). Aristotle called attention to acts that are perfective of potentialities, such as seeing and understanding. He used a grammatical test to identify them: X-ing is an actualization (energeia) if to X is to have X-ed (*Metaphysics*, IX.6). Thus, seeing is an actualization, since to see an object is to have seen it. He did not mean that anytime it's true that I see an object, it's also true that I saw it earlier. Verb aspect, not verb tense, is in play in Aristotle's test: anytime I see an object is a time at which I have seen it.

Linguists distinguish the perfective from the imperfective aspect, and within the imperfective the habitual from the continuous aspect, and within the continuous the nonprogressive from the progressive aspect (Comrie 1976, p. 25). For example, the perfective: 'had worked' and 'had been working'; the habitual: 'used to work'; the progressive: 'was working'; the nonprogressive: 'worked', as in 'I worked all day'.

Tense operations apply globally to sentences that already have aspect. All these forms are in the same past tense, namely, 'it was the case that ...' applied to the present-tensed form of the aspect. For example, 'I had been working' is 'it was the case that I have been working'. Only the past-tensed 'I used to work' must resort to an adverbial ambage to operate on the present tense of the habitual aspect, for which English has no syntactic marker: 'it was the case that I habitually work'.

After the references to times in the tense, the further references to times that differentiate the aspectual forms are not relative to the context of the speech event. Aspect is sensitive to such semantic distinctions between situations as nondynamic states in contrast to complete events, in contrast to processes in progress (Comrie 1976, p. 13). Thus, aspect can vary independently of tense. B-theory simply incorporates aspect; it is a part of calendar time.

We now set up an analysis of whoosh in agency by adding tense to aspect. Consider first achievements such as seeing. According to Aristotle's account of seeing, the simple and perfect aspects spuriously distinguish two ways for this special kind of act to be; there's no difference between to see and to have seen, tense being the same. The identity of the two aspects in the case of this kind of act shows the total absence of effort or of distance between the act and the success state of the act.

These acts are inertial, so that for them to occur at any time is for them to *have* occurred at *that* time without necessarily having occurred at any earlier time, since they occur at their success state if they occur at all. If the use of 'have ... ed' to indicate perfective occurrence, not past time, is confusing, calendar time theorists can adopt alternative ways of indicating aspect, such as this adverbialization: for the act to occur simply is for it to occur perfectively.

So far, the link to whoosh is not obvious. We need a contrast. Aristotle made another use of aspect, in this case the equivalent of English's progressive aspect, in noting that "makings" contrast with "seeings." Makings are such that anything that [is] made at a time [was] theretofore in the process of being made (*Physics*, VI.6 (237b10)). The term 'process' can be cashed out in terms of tenseless descriptions of incomplete stages of the making. Thus, this progressive aspect also is consistent with a calendar time that does not recognize a wave of becoming, as my tenseless version of the Aristotelian definition of the aspect shows (*pace* Cooney 1991, chap. 4).

Linguistic aspects are rooted in types of experience. Because the definition of a making mentions many times, whereas the definition of a seeing or finding mentions only one, there is a distinctive what-it-is-like-to-a-being-for-it-to-undergo-a-making, in contrast to what-it-is-like-to-a-being-for-it-to-act-perfectively. The contrast makes the former a part of the whoosh and whiz because to experience it is to have a unitary experience of many times seriatim, that is to say, flushed successively. The experience is at level 4 in our first thought experiment. Our strivings as agents are of this type. The ontologizing of now-based time tempts one most persistently there in the progressive aspect.

7.8   A B-Theoretic Account That Legitimates Agency

We should not conclude from section 7.7 that calendar time is irrelevant to agency, having no use in deliberation. In human beings, the virtues of foresightful prudence and delayed gratification are based on reasons, unlike the virtues of the instinctive squirrels. Thus, human agents struggle with temptation intellectually, while squirrels only vacillate. To understand the persuasiveness of reasons for resisting the temptation to indulge in instant gratification, we must attribute to ordinary human beings a calendar theory of time with their various life stages entered into the calendar dates (Nagel 1970, pt. 2), because their reasons refer to these stages and weight them equally. So calendar time enters into our theory of human agency.

Calendar time cannot be the whole story of time in agency, however. Deliberation is impossible if the outcome of the deliberation is known to the deliberator. It is pointless even if the deliberator believes it is already settled what will be, although she does not know what that is. Futurity is essential to deliberation, for (as Aristotle said in the *Nicomachean Ethics*, VI.2 (1139b5ff.)) no one deliberates about having sacked Troy: intention presupposes that the act intended is to be carried out now or later. Some illocutionary acts, like promising, concern the future. Deliberative agency requires an agent to have a perspective on the events that come after the ones in her perceptual window, or might come after them, especially on those events that might bring pleasure or pain with them. So, the way we come to know about the time of our information—there being no time indication in the content—has the consequence of creating deliberative agency as well as memory. As episodic memory marks the recalled information with pastness, so agency marks the contents of desire and decision with futurity. So let us try to save a de-ontologized now-based time as part of a B-theory of deliberative agency—"de-ontologized" so that time is no more than calendar time.

Some have doubted the compatibility of agency with the physical. Whitrow (1961, p. 350) describes the causal anomaly at any supposed border between events ruled by now-based time and events ruled by calendar time thus:

In purely physical causation [in calendar time] an effect would not actually be produced [made to come into being] by its cause; it would merely be further on in time. However, mental causation of a physical event—such as deciding to drop a stone into a pond—would mean that a cause (in this case, a decision to drop the stone) suddenly comes into being, but the effect (the splash when the stone strikes the water) would not; it would just be.

The nondualistic solution is to see how physical science can describe the conscious events in calendar time, despite their appearance of occurring in now-based time. For physical science, the sequence of your conscious experiences is expressed in the following way, using brackets to remind you of the tenseless expressions: you [are] aware of x but not y at t_1; you [are] aware of y but not x at t_2; if y is your decision to drop a stone, you [are] aware of it at t_2 but not before t_2. The relation of your being aware of it, indeed your making it, holds at one time but not at another. That is all its coming into being amounts to. There's no border.

The science of agency takes now-based time into account, first by *quoting* the tensed sentences *within* calendar time statements, and second by applying the truth conditions for those tensed utterances, also stated within calendar time statements. For example, you believe[ ] at a time a tensed sentence, 'p'. Your use of tenses can be described in calendar time: you [are] not aware of t_2 at t_1, and you [say] at t_1, "Not yet, but it will be"; you [are] aware of t_2 but not t_1 at t_2, and you [say] then, "No longer t_1, it was, but now it is t_2." When you [are] aware of t_3 as your now at t_3, you [say], "t_1 was earlier than t_2." But this tensing of the earlier-than relation is distinct from its tenseless use in stating calendar time. When we deliberate, we reflect on ourselves and the events we want to affect in ways that may necessarily impute passage to the events. But a physical description in calendar time of our tensed ascriptions of passage will only quote them, not endorse them. So the description is compatible with them. In this way, we can describe both the mental and the physical without any disparity of the sort Whitrow fears.

The science of agency, which supervenes on physical science, can endorse tensed statements as well as quote them. An agent's belief in a tensed sentence, a direct attribution to the agent's now, may be true. For the purpose of assessing truth, the calendar time theorist adopts Prior's semantics of tenses. In ordinary language, the elementary statement (or direct attribution of a property, in Lewis's and Chisholm's analyses of belief) is by default present tensed, because all tense expresses direct attribution to the now. The elementary statement [is] true at a time—the time of interest for a statement that's not part of a compound is usually the time of its utterance—if and only if its predicate directly attribute[s] to that time what [is] the case then. All the other tenses are operators on present-tensed propositions or on operations on those, recursively. The operators do not mean temporal or time-dependent ontological properties; they only show how to think of the semantic valuation of the statement they operate on. Thus, a past-tensed sentence [is] true at a time if and only if the internal sentence, the one operated on, [is] true at a time earlier than then. (Needless to say, the internal sentence need not have been uttered then in order for it to have been true of then. Semantic valuation is not a matter of doing anything.)

This approach yields a recursive definition of a well-formed tensed sentence and a recursive definition of truth, whereas the alternative of attaching properties of being past, present, or future to propositional contents does not (Prior 1967, pp. 14ff). Also, the theorist can give truth conditions for tensed sentences without recourse to the properties of being past, present, or future. It is important to calendar time theorists of agency to have this option, since to interpret tenses as referring to those properties or similar ontologically contentious ones would be for them to have self-contradictory ontic commitments. So their semantic metalanguage is the untensed language we have been using. The metalanguage could assume an event ontology, but we have been assuming the common ontology of continuants and relativizing predicates to dates, that is, upping their adicity to include a term for dates by incorporating an 'at' or similar particle indissolubly into the predicate. Quine explains both options; for the event ontology, see 1960, sec. 36, and 1974, sec. 34; for upping the adicity of predicates of continuants, see 1965, sec. 37.

The truth predicate, as applied to tensed statements, has a greater adicity than it would have, were it applied to an eternal sentence, that is, a sentence in a form such that, if it is ever true anywhere, it is always true everywhere. The truth predicate for eternal sentences is absolute; for tensed statements, truth is a relation to a time. The adicity of truth increases further when we resort to Lewis's and Chisholm's analyses of belief as direct attributions of properties. As applied to a property, truth (or its converse, satisfaction) is indexed to all the elements that would complete the property and yield a proposition. We must note the matter of adicity in order to block challenges from the proponents of now-based time, challenges such as the following:[8] Let $S =$ 'It is now 1980'; let $T =$ [S occurs in 1980]. Then S is true if and only if T. Also, 'T' is true if and only if T. So S (disquoted) if and only if T. We block the discomfiting inference of a necessary and sufficient condition for being 1980 when we see the absolute truth predicate is misapplied to tensed sentences. S is *true at* 1980, where 'true at' is a single dyadic relation, not a conjunction of a monadic 'true' with a dyadic 'at'—that conjunctive analysis would lead to contradiction, given a sentence true at one time and false at another. Another error is equating context of sentence-utterance with context of sentence-evaluation. It's false that *S* is *true at* 1980 only if *T*. Note that the printed occurrence of *S* in quotation marks above, which did not exist in 1980, is *true at* 1980. Being 1980 is truly directly attributed to 1980. The separation of context of utterance from context of evaluation permits the sentence 'It was the case that it is 1980 B.C.' to be true today. The internal present-tensed sentence was true then, although it was certainly never uttered then.

A systematic body of calendar time truths, a B-theory, should predict and explain all the phenomena of agency. Since it must endorse or reject various tensed claims as either true or false, it must use, not merely mention, the tensed expressions of now-based time. It would not undermine this science to say that agency is based on a nonadaptive concomitant (indexicality) to an adaptation (information collection). But it would undermine this science to say that agency is a fiction, which would lead to a totally dehumanized reductionism. The middle ground between being a part of the scientific image and being a fiction is that of secondary quality; agency belongs there.

Notes

My thanks to Quentin Smith for gracious remarks on drafts of the chapter, which espouses a position he has argued so resolutely against. Indeed, he authored five paragraphs of the chapter that draw the reader's attention to strengths of my position, which I had left unemphasized. That's philosophy, the virtue. My thanks also to Brian Cooney for uncovering much sloppy thought in a draft. Four scattered paragraphs come from Falk 1995a with revisions. Sections 7.4–7.6 appear as chapter 5 in Falk 2003. The thought experiment is there exploited to yield insight into spatial consciousness.

1. And speak differently with the vulgar, although not so differently if we speak one of the languages in the Sino-Tibetan group, or even a language like Wintu (California) or Dyirbal (Queensland), none of which make grammaticality depend on tensing. My Chinese student, Wang Feng, informs me, quite correctly I think, that anyone who says, 'English sentences must have tense,' is refuted out of his own mouth, since English sentences with auxiliary 'must' have no tense (unlike 'will', 'shall', or 'can', which are present, in contrast with their past-

tensed forms). Teichmann (1998) argues that all the sentences of any possible language are tensed at least semantically, if not syntactically. For my attempt to anticipate and refute his argument, see Falk 1998.

2. A negative feedback mechanism can initiate action to reach a goal and correct its action in response to information (feedback) about its progress. Good introductions to this concept can be found in many places, for example, *The Oxford Companion to the Mind*, entries under 'biofeedback', 'cybernetics, history of', and 'feedback and feedforward'. For a recent account, see Falk 1995c.

3. Chisholm (1981, app.) rejects this, although he is clearly one who has learned the metaphysical lesson underlying the essential indexical. My explanation of his dissent is that he has not learned the lesson of contemporary physics that time is more like space than like modality. The analogy between time and modality is built into our language; times and possible worlds can be given analogous treatments; 'now' can be treated like 'actually' rather than like 'here'. Chisholm goes this route, but the old analogy is to be resisted. Time is calendar time, and calendars are like maps.

4. See Smith 1993 for principle D1 (p. 209) and its application (p. 230). My Platonist and Aristotelian strategies provide alternative motivations for rejecting principle D1. For more criticisms of it, see Nerlich 1997.

5. I incline to the Aristotelian alternative, because I see no reason even to postulate contents except as shorthand for knowers' acts and dispositions toward the things they know.

6. Southall translates section 26 (p. 22): "The external events, like their perceptions, proceed in time; and so the temporal relations of the latter may be a faithful reproduction of the temporal relations of the former." A few sentences later he admits, "not quite a faithful reproduction." Compare Hertz 1895, introd. and sec. 428: for Hertz, the fundamental realism-guaranteeing principle of thought was that what follows upon our image of a thing should be an image of what follows the thing that was imaged. My confining the idea to the compass of a now is my own. James (1890, p. 628) criticizes the idea not so much for being false as for being incomplete. Compare Dennett 1991, sec. 6.2.

7. 'Self-locating' is Perry's (1979) term for what Chisholm (1979) calls direct attribution and D. Lewis calls self-ascription. Here is Lewis's point about the logical form of beliefs: the objects of one's believings are properties, not propositions, and the properties are self-ascribed for the time of the ascribing. And here is Chisholm's way of stating it: we directly attribute properties to ourselves at a time without benefit of a self-denoting singular term; there are no singular propositions (Chisholm 1989).

8. Derived from Smith's (1993, p. 69) criticism of Mellor's (1981, p. 74) proposal. Smith justly criticizes Mellor, but he also writes as if the difference between a tensed sentence and an eternal sentence aimed at expressing the same fact must be in the differing senses of the expressions (e.g., p. 50). But differences of sense cannot explain the difference between a tensed and an eternal sentence, as work on the essential indexical shows. Elsewhere (1994, p. 19), he concedes that the

name 'now' does not refer by way of a sense, but it predicates a property of presentness as well as directly refers. Here he has made a distinction from Fregeanism without a difference.

References

Aristotle. *Nicomachean Ethics, Physics*, and *Metaphysics*.

Bever, T. G. 1970. The Cognitive Basis for Linguistic Structures. In J. R. Hayes, ed., *Cognition and the Development of Language*, pp. 279–362. New York: Wiley.

Broad, C. D. 1935. Mr. Dunne's Theory of Time in "An Experiment with Time." *Philosophy* 10, pp. 168–85. Reprinted in *Religion, Philosophy and Psychical Research*, pp. 68–85. New York: Harcourt, Brace, 1953.

Burks, A. 1949. Icon, Index, and Symbol. *Philosophy and Phenomenological Research* 10, pp. 673–89.

Chisholm, R. 1979. The Indirect Reflexive. In C. Diamond and J. Teichman, eds., *Intention and Intentionality: Essays in Honour of G. E. M. Anscombe*, pp. 39–53. Ithaca, N.Y.: Cornell University Press.

Chisholm, R. 1981. *The First Person*. Minneapolis: University of Minnesota Press.

Chisholm, R. 1989. Why Singular Propositions? In J. Almog, J. Perry, and H. Wettstein, eds., *Themes from Kaplan*, pp. 145–50. Oxford: Oxford University Press.

Chomsky, N. 2000. *New Horizons in the Study of Language and Mind*. Cambridge: Cambridge University Press.

Comrie, B. 1976. *Aspect*. Cambridge: Cambridge University Press.

Cooney, B. 1991. *A Hylomorphic Theory of Mind*. Frankfurt am Main: Peter Lang.

Craig, W. L. 1996. The New B-Theory's *Tu Quoque* Argument. *Synthese* 107, pp. 249–69.

Craig, W. L. 2000. *The Tenseless Theory of Time*. Dordrecht: Kluwer.

Dennett, D. 1991. *Consciousness Explained*. Boston: Little, Brown.

Falk, A. 1987. Reference to Myself. *Behaviorism* 15, pp. 89–105.

Falk, A. 1995a. Bewusstsein, Indexikalität, und der Fluss der Zeit. Paper presented at the conference "Indexikalität und Bewusstsein," Hannover. Published in M. Kettner and H. Pape, eds., *Indexikalität und sprachlicher Weltbezug*. Paderborn, Germany: Mentis-Verlag, 2001.

Falk, A. 1995b. Consciousness and Self-Reference. *Erkenntnis* 43, pp. 151–80.

Falk, A. 1995c. Gaia = Māyā. *History and Philosophy of the Life Sciences* 17, pp. 485–502.

Falk, A. 1998. Review of Roger Teichmann, *The Concept of Time*. *Philosophical Books* 39, pp. 54–56.

Falk, A. 2003. *Darwinism and Philosophical Analysis*. New Delhi: Decent Books.

Fodor, J. A., and T. G. Bever. 1965. The Psychological Reality of Linguistic Segments. *Journal of Verbal Learning and Verbal Behavior* 4, pp. 414–20. Reprinted in L. Jakobovits and M. S. Miron, eds., *Readings in the Psychology of Language*, pp. 325–32. Englewood Cliffs, N.J.: Prentice-Hall, 1967.

Geldard, F. A., and C. E. Sherrick. 1986. Space, Time and Touch. *Scientific American* 255 (July), pp. 90–95.

Grünbaum, A. 1967. The Status of Temporal Becoming. *Interdisciplinary Perspectives of Time: Annals of the New York Academy of Sciences* 138, art. 2, pp. 374–95. Reprinted in J. Zeman, ed., *Time in Science and Philosophy*, pp. 67–87. Amsterdam: Elsevier, 1971. Page references are to reprint.

Grünbaum, A. 1969a. Are Physical Events Themselves Transiently Past, Present and Future? A Reply to H. A. C. Dobbs. *The British Journal for the Philosophy of Science* 20, pp. 145–53.

Grünbaum, A. 1969b. The Meaning of Time. In N. Rescher, ed., *Essays in Honor of Carl Hempel*. Dordrecht: Reidel.

Helmholtz, H. von. 1867. *Treatise on Physiological Optics* (1856–1867), vol. 3. 3rd ed. Translated by J. P. C. Southall. Rochester, N.Y.: Optical Society of America, 1925.

Hertz, H. 1895. *The Principles of Mechanics*.

Hinton, C. H. 1880. What Is the Fourth Dimension? In *Scientific Romances*. London: Swan Sonnenschein, 1884. Reprinted in Rudolf v. B. Rucker, ed., *Speculations on the Fourth Dimension: Selected Writings of Charles H. Hinton*, pp. 1–22. New York: Dover, 1980. According to the preface, the article was originally published in 1880.

Hinton, C. H. 1904. The Fourth Dimension. In *The Fourth Dimension*. London: Swan Sonnenschein. Reprinted in Rudolf V. B. Rucker, ed., *Speculations on the Fourth Dimension: Selected Writings of Charles H. Hinton*, pp. 120–41. New York: Dover, 1980.

Humphrey, N. 1992. *A History of the Mind*. New York: Simon and Schuster.

James, W. 1890. *Principles of Psychology*, vol. 1. New York: Henry Holt.

Lewis, D. 1979. Attitudes *De Dicto* and *De Se*. The *Philosophical Review* 88, pp. 513–43. Reprinted with postscripts in *Philosophical Papers*, vol. 1, pp. 133–59. Oxford: Oxford University Press, 1983. Page references are to reprint.

Locke, J. 1690. *An Essay Concerning Human Understanding*.

Ludlow, P. 1999. *Semantics, Tense, and Time*. Cambridge, Mass.: MIT Press.

McCawley, J. D. 1993. *Everything That Linguists Have Always Wanted to Know about Logic*. 2nd ed. Chicago: University of Chicago Press.

Mellor, D. H. 1981. *Real Time*. Cambridge: Cambridge University Press.

Mellor, D. H. 1983. MacBeath's Soluble Aspirin. *Ratio* 25, pp. 89–92. Reprinted in L. N. Oaklander and Q. Smith, eds., *The New Theory of Time*, pp. 312–15. New Haven, Conn.: Yale University Press, 1994.

Mellor, D. H. 1989. I and Now. *Proceedings of the Aristotelian Society* 89, pp. 79–94. Reprinted in *Matters of Metaphysics*, pp. 17–29. Cambridge: Cambridge University Press, 1991.

Mellor, D. H. 1998. *Real Time II*. London: Routledge.

Minkowski, H. 1908. Space and Time. In H. A. Lorentz, A. Einstein, H. Minkowski, and H. Weyl, *The Principle of Relativity*, pp. 75–91. New York: Dover, 1952.

Mundle, C. W. K. 1967. Time, Consciousness of. *Encyclopedia of Philosophy*, vol. 8, pp. 134–39. New York: Macmillan.

Nagel, T. 1970. *The Possibility of Altruism*. Princeton, N.J.: Princeton University Press.

Nerlich, G. 1997. Time as Spacetime. In R. Le Poidevin, ed., *Essays on 'Language and Time'*, pp. 119–34. Oxford: Oxford University Press.

Oaklander, L. N. 1993. On the Experience of Tenseless Time. *Journal of Philosophical Research* 18, pp. 159–66. Reprinted in L. N. Oaklander and Q. Smith, eds., *The New Theory of Time*, pp. 344–50. New Haven, Conn.: Yale University Press. Page references are to reprint.

Øhrstrøm, P., and P. Hasle. 1995. *Temporal Logic*. Dordrecht: Kluwer.

Paton, H. J. 1929. Self-Identity. *Mind* 38, pp. 312–29.

Perlman, J. S. 1970. *The Atom and the Universe*. Belmont, Calif: Wadsworth.

Perry, J. 1979. The Problem of the Essential Indexical. *Noûs* 13, pp. 3–21. Reprinted in *The Problem of the Essential Indexical, and Other Essays*, pp. 27–44. Oxford: Oxford University Press, 1993.

Pinker, S. 1994. *The Language Instinct*. New York: HarperPerennial.

Poggio, T., and C. Koch. 1987. Synapses That Compute Motion. *Scientific American* 256 (May), pp. 46–52.

Pöppel, E. 1997. The Brain's Way to Create 'Nowness'. In H. Atmanspacher and E. Ruhman, eds., *Time, Temporality, Now: Experiencing Time and Concepts of Time in an Interdisciplinary Perspective*, pp. 107–20. Berlin: Springer.

Prior, A. 1959. Thank Goodness That's Over. *Philosophy* 34, pp. 12–17. Reprinted in *Papers in Logic and Ethics*, pp. 78–84. London: Duckworth, 1976.

Prior, A. 1967. *Past, Present and Future*. Oxford: Clarendon Press.

Putnam, H. 1967. Time and Physical Geometry. *The Journal of Philosophy* 64. Reprinted in *Mathematics, Matter, and Method*, pp. 198–205. 2nd ed. Cambridge: Cambridge University Press, 1979.

Quine, W. V. 1960. *Word and Object*. Cambridge, Mass.: MIT Press.

Quine, W. V. 1965. *Elementary Logic*. Rev. ed. New York: Harper and Row.

Quine, W. V. 1974. *The Roots of Reference*. LaSalle, Ill.: Open Court.

Reichenbach, H. 1947. *Elements of Symbolic Logic*. New York: Macmillan.

Royce, J. 1901. *The World and the Individual*. New York: Macmillan.

Schenk, D. (n.d.) On the Egocentric Experience of B-Time. In *Proceedings of the Philosophy of Time Society*. Drake University, Center for the Humanities.

Schiffer, S. 1972. *Meaning*. Oxford: Clarendon Press.

Sellars, W. 1962. Time and the World Order. In H. Feigl and G. Maxwell, eds., *Scientific Explanation, Space, and Time*, pp. 527–616. Minneapolis: University of Minnesota Press.

Sklar, L. 1977. *Space, Time, and Spacetime*. Berkeley and Los Angeles: University of California Press.

Smith, Q. 1988. The Phenomenology of A-Time. *Diálogos* 52, pp. 142–53. Reprinted in L. N. Oaklander and Q. Smith, eds., *The New Theory of Time*, 351–59. New Haven, Conn.: Yale University Press, 1994. Page references are to reprint.

Smith, Q. 1993. *Language and Time*. Oxford: Oxford University Press.

Smith, Q. 1994. Introduction: The Old and New Tenseless Theories of Time. In L. N. Oaklander and Q. Smith, eds., *The New Theory of Time*, pp. 17–22. New Haven, Conn.: Yale University Press.

Teichmann, R. 1998. Is a Tenseless Language Possible? *The Philosophical Quarterly* 48, pp. 176–88.

ter Meulen, A. 1995. *Representing Time in Natural Language*. Cambridge, Mass.: MIT Press.

Wallach, H. 1959. The Perception of Motion. *Scientific American* 201 (July), pp. 56–60. Reprinted in *Perception: Mechanisms and Models*, pp. 310–14. San Francisco: W. H. Freeman, 1972.

Whitrow, G. J. 1961. *The Natural Philosophy of Time*. London: Nelson. 2nd ed. Published Oxford: Clarendon Press, 1980. Page references are to 2nd ed.

Williams, C. 1992. The Phenomenology of B-Time. *Southern Journal of Philosophy* 30, pp. 123–37. Reprinted in L. N. Oaklander and Q. Smith, eds., *The New Theory of Time*, pp. 360–72. New Haven, Conn.: Yale University Press, 1994.

Williams, D. C. 1951. The Myth of Passage. *The Journal of Philosophy* 48, pp. 457–72. Reprinted with slight additions to notes in *Principles of Empirical Realism*, pp. 289–307. Springfield, Ill.: Charles Thomas, 1966. Page references are to reprint.

II

The Metaphysics of Time

Introduction to Part II

Jan Faye
[With insertions by Quentin Smith]

Part II presents the second half of this book's project of exhibiting a relevant and close similarity between philosophers of language and philosophers of time, thereby providing readers with the metaphysical ideas that can be used, in various ways, to construct a synthesis of a theory of language and a theory of time (of the sort exemplified in Ludlow's (1999) *Semantics, Tense, and Time*). Here, philosophers of time will present theories that have clear implications for the philosophies of language and specifically of the semantics of tense that were discussed in part I.

The aim of this introduction is to develop a theoretical framework that will allow the metaphysical issues raised in Part II to be viewed from a critical perspective.

The metaphysics of tense concerns whether reality consists of only tenseless facts (or B-states of affairs) or whether it consists of tensed facts (or A-states of affairs) and, as a separate issue, whether it does or does not consist of temporal becoming. Usually these two issues are identified, but I will suggest they are distinct.

[Talking about whether reality is tensed or tenseless should present no problem. Since the interchange between Mellor and Priest in *Analysis* in the late 1980s (including an article called "Tense, *Tense* and TENSE"), it has become more common for philosophers of time to talk about tensed or tenseless propositions, truths, facts, situations, times, worlds, and so on. 'Tensed' and 'tenseless' have become technical philosophical terms, and the "objection" that "in ordinary language, it is correct or proper to say that only linguistic items are tensed or tenseless" has been more or less relegated to the museum of the "ordinary language philosophy" of the 1940s and 1950s. *QS*]

Let us begin with a review of some familiar ideas and new distinctions (early presented in my work (1981, 1989)). The past, present, and future have been considered by most people to be identical with time itself and thus taken as essential features of reality as such. But then what are the past, present, and future, more precisely? Some philosophers, like Zeili-covici (1986) and Shimony (1993), have argued that the notion that time is identical with the past, present, and future should not be taken to mean that pastness, presentness, and futureness are temporal attributes. These distinctions are not properties at all, they say, in the same way as existence, according to Kant, is not a property. Their ascription to events adds nothing to the specification of these events.

But their claim could be questioned by A-theorists in different ways. One obvious way would be by arguing that it really makes a difference in the description of, say, the causal powers of an event with respect to present events whether the event itself is past, present, or future.

Many philosophers see these temporal characteristics as taking part in the constitution of facts about a temporal event. Any theory that seeks to give an account of events in terms of such irreducible, intrinsic prop-erties, the so-called A-theories, regard tense as something that relates to every entity with respect to its possible location in time. Thus, the A-theorist holds that there are tensed facts (i.e., things or events having tensed properties) and that these facts endow tensed sentences with a truth value.

Nonetheless, quite a few philosophers, particularly in the twentieth century, have argued that the difference between past, present, and future does not represent objective properties of events but may instead reflect a projection of our subjective awareness onto the events of the world. Their view is that any appropriate account of time, a so-called B-theory, could be expressed in terms of later-than, earlier-than, and simultaneous-with relations. Thus, the B-theorist denies that anything objectively real can be tensed, and therefore that there are tensed facts making tensed sentences true or false.

This part of the metaphysical debate becomes therefore a discussion about which of these theories, the A-theories or the B-theories, gives the appropriate explanation of the temporal and other matters connected with existence in time. Although the debate first and foremost is ontological in nature, it is also a common assumption of analytical philosophy that the discussion of language and what makes sentences true or false provides us with an insight into the correct ontology. It is tacitly presumed that semantic arguments can help reveal the proper view concerning reality.

For a long time, B-theorists hoped to give grounds for their ontological position by showing that the meaning of tensed sentences could be reduced to the meaning of appropriate tenseless sentences. Today, it is generally agreed that such a semantic reduction is not possible. Since the early 1980s, however, a vivid discussion has been going on about the force and the scope of a new tenseless theory of time, as it has been called. This new B-theory was, to the best of my knowledge, first put forward in Andersen and Faye 1980, Faye 1981, 1989, and independently in Mellor 1981. The basic insight is that tensed sentences are not translatable as tenseless sentences: they differ in meaning, but, nevertheless, tensed statements have tenseless truth conditions. But, in contrast to Mellor as his views are interpreted by Dyke (2002), Andersen and I argued that tensed and tenseless sentence tokens have the same truth conditions. Consequently, there are no objective facts about the world other than tenseless ones that make tensed statements true or false.

Since a particular tensed sentence token has the same truth conditions as a particular tenseless sentence token, the difference in their meaning cannot be captured by their truth conditions. Instead, Andersen and I argued that the difference in meaning has something to do with a possible difference in the belief state of a person who expresses a certain temporal opinion in terms of a tensed and a corresponding tenseless sentence. The two types of tokens express different epistemic attitudes toward the world, something reflected by the fact that tokens of a tensed sentence have variable truth values depending on the time of utterance, whereas tokens of a tenseless sentence are invariably true or false independently of the time of utterance. Inspired by the works of Kaplan (1978) and Perry (1977, 1979), we urged that the sense of a tensed sentence contains two components: the content, which changes from one token to another; and the linguistic meaning (character), which is constant within tokens of the same type and which determines how the content is fixed by the context.

If B-theorists are right that tenses are merely in our heads as features of our representation of temporal reality rather than features of temporal reality itself, they apparently face a serious problem of how such a representation can be explained in detail. This is because they argue that tensed beliefs as mental events have a causal role to play in the explanation of human action. So how can tensed beliefs qua being tensed cause actions without tenses' being objectively real? In answering the question, is it then possible for B-theorists to uphold the mind-dependence of tenses and the causal efficacy of tensed beliefs and still to remain neutral as to the philosophy of mind and personal identity they espouse?

Dorato (1996) argues that in such a case, advocates of the B-theory cannot subscribe to eliminationism or to supervenience, but must embrace some sort of dualism. I don't think he is right, but I agree that B-theorists should pay much more attention to this problem, which could be the chink in their ontological armor.

What A-theorists who criticize the new tenseless theory of time had to do, apparently, was to establish that truth is not a timeless or tenseless property of sentence tokens or of other truth bearers. Priest (1986a) defended its legitimacy in a very simple way. What Priest did was in direct opposition to the new tenseless approach. He argued that tenseless facts might be unreal since it is possible to endow both tensed and tenseless sentences with tensed truth conditions. The truth conditions of tensed and tenseless tokens can be specified in terms of tensed truth; that is, the numerically same token—say, 'I am now working on this introduction', stated on October 11, 2001, at 2:30 p.m., may lack any truth value as long as this time still lies in the future, be true as of this instant, and again lack any truth value (or be false) when it becomes part of the past.

Thus, the dispute between the new tenseless view of time and the tensed view of time seems to boil down to a disagreement about whether contingent facts are tensed or tenseless, and hence whether or not truth is sensitive to the difference between past, present, and future.

In his summary of the above discussion, Dorato (1995) concludes that the debate between the tensers and the detensers seems to end in a stalemate, since tensed (as well as tenseless) sentences can be given both tensed and tenseless truth conditions by relying on a tensed or a tenseless theory of truth. The tenser who follows Dorato's argument on this matter therefore thinks that the metaphysical issue concerning objective becoming cannot be settled by semantic arguments.

Is Dorato right, or is it possible to avoid such a conclusion? In his chapter, Le Poidevin seeks to evade it. He distinguishes four possible theories about truth conditions: (1) the basic tensed theory, (2) the token-reflexive theory, (3) the date theory, and (4) the complex tensed theory. According to Le Poidevin, both (1) and (4) consider tensed tokens to have tensed truth conditions; the contrast is that (1) holds that the same token has changing truth values, whereas (4) denies it. On the other hand, (2) and (3) take tensed tokens to have tenseless truth conditions; but here the difference is that (2) includes a reference to the token in the specification of these truth conditions, something that (3) does not. Then he tests all four theories by seeing how they can handle tensed causal sentences. He concludes that they all fail except (3).

It is with a certain satisfaction that I state this—regardless of Dyke's (2002) new argument against the date theory in favor of the token-reflexive theory—since the date theory is basically the one I hold myself (Andersen and Faye 1980; Faye 1981, 1989).

Thus, if Le Poidevin's analysis is correct, it shows, inter alia, that the debate between the tenser and the detenser does not end in a stalemate. It appears to me, however, that Dyke's (2002) demonstration of the possible failure of the date version of the tenseless truth conditions is very much a result of the chosen formalization. In her truth-conditional schema (6a), $\forall u \forall t (Sut \rightarrow (Tut \leftrightarrow Set))$, where T is the truth predicate, S is the simultaneous-with relation, and e is the event referred to by the token u in question, the truth predicate is really assigned to a proposition qua all of its tokens *simpliciter*. But one could argue that the assignment of the truth predicate should instead be to a token vis-à-vis a certain time t. Using a similar notation, my alternative proposal may be spelled out as '$(\forall u \in A)(Sut)$ is true' $\leftrightarrow \exists(t)\exists(e)(Set)$ under the assumption that t on the left-hand side is a constant. Why could the advocate of the date theory not urge this suggestion as a sound candidate for the correct formalization of the tenseless truth conditions of present-tensed sentences? Such a reading, a more plausible one I believe, would not face the same objection, and Dyke's argument would therefore not be an insurmountable obstacle to the date theory. [If we want to integrate Lepore and Ludwig's theory from chapter 1 into a broad-based linguistic/metaphysical theory, such as Ludlow's (1999), some of these arguments may be used to justify their assumption that the date theory is true. Richard, who assumes the tenseless token-reflexive theory in chapter 3, may hope that Dyke's development of her argument for this theory will prove successful. A Richard/Dyke combination may be another example of synthesis of philosophy of language and metaphysics that Ludlow suggests is desirable. Richard's various distinctions in his theory of language may in turn prove invaluable to the development of the linguistic premises of Dyke's argument. *QS*]

It is also worth noticing that among the tenseless theories, (2) corresponds to the relational or reductionist view, according to which times and temporal relations subsist on events and their relations, whereas (3) instead considers times and temporal relations as intrinsic and absolute as being logically independent of their contents. It appears that this sort of contrast is not found between (1) and (4).

Let me add an argument which I believe proves that the basic tensed theory (the one Priest puts forward) in combination with the theory of objective becoming is not a viable possibility. This is more particular than the argument in Tomberlin's chapter against presentism in general. Take a briefly enduring sentence token like the spoken utterance 'Caesar crosses the Rubicon now'. Call this utterance u, and call the fact that makes it true S. Then we can describe the situation of how tensed facts may attribute different truth values to the same numerical token in different perspectives. Now:

The truth maker perspective

In the tensed case, S as a fact about a particular event, caused by a human action, does not come into being until it becomes present, and perhaps even goes out of being again when it becomes past. We therefore have a changing truth value of u, because S is the truth maker that makes u true when, and only when, S is present; otherwise, S cannot make u true. Hence, truth must be tensed.

The truth bearer perspective

If u is a truth bearer that changes its truth value from being false/lacking a truth value, to being true, and again to being false/lacking a truth value, then it has to exist in the past, present, and future in order for the numerically same *u* to have different truth values.

The challenge

Since *u* by itself is an event caused by a human action, it does not become real until the present and then, whenever it becomes past, perhaps ceases to exist again.

The conclusion

Tensed truth involves a contradiction because something that is not real cannot carry a truth value.

As far as I can see, the basic tensed theory along with the dynamic theory of time is an incoherent position. Only if the tenser holds the complex tensed theory, or denies objective becoming, is it possible to avoid such a conclusion.

Indeed, the basic theory could be combined with presentism if the advocate of such a view were to argue that only presently stated present-tensed sentences are true. Since neither the past nor the future exists, sentence tokens in the past and the future cannot exist either. Therefore, they cannot be true or false. Similarly, since presently stated past- or future-tensed sentences refer to something that does not exist, neither can they be true or false. Only a presently stated present-tensed sentence can have a truth value.

Presentists may, however, advocate a complex tensed theory of truth conditions. It means that they would say that any presently stated past- (or future-) tensed sentence, like 'It rained yesterday', is now true or false, not because a tensed fact exists in the past making it true or false, but because in the present there exists a tensed fact that it was raining yesterday or a fact that it wasn't raining yesterday. This is the sort of view suggested in the chapter by Craig. Of course, one could argue in this manner, but it would be an argument based on a notion of facts that we don't know how to identify in any other way than by the propositional content of sentences. This view seems to open up the possibility for all kind of facts: negative, counterfactual, modal, hypothetical, universal, and probabilistic facts as well.

[Furthermore, Craig allows that past-tensed truths have "truth makers" (in Craig's sense, not Faye's sense), as well as truth conditions (the abstract states of affairs that presently exist), and that the truth makers are often concrete objects or situations that used to exist. I also posit such truth makers, and it would be interesting to see how Craig could reconcile his ontological posits with his claim that the past, concrete objects or truth makers that I posit are not on the ontological map. Both Craig and I would say, for example, that 'Hegel was writing a book' contains a name that refers to a concrete object that used to exist. But this is what I mean by a maximalist tensed theory of time, which Craig argues is mistaken since "only the present is real." How could Craig differentiate his presentism from my maximalist tensed theory if both he and I agree that *the concrete object Hegel used to exist and can now be referred to*? If Craig argues that reference is not a relation to Hegel, but is a monadic property of the person who is referring, then Hegel is not being referred to, since the concrete person, Hegel, who used to exist, is not a monadic property or a part of a monadic property of the speaker. Suppose we go the adverbial route. If I am conscious Hegely (so to speak), I have no conscious relation to Hegel; even worse, this would mean that a concrete person, who no longer exists, is presently a property or operator on my consciousness. But this is unacceptable. I can safely assume that the person, Hegel, who used to exist, is not attached to my consciousness as a property or an operator. Further, if reference is a monadic property and not a relation to something distinct from myself, it seems hard to imagine how I can escape solipsism. As I said, both Craig and I would agree to 'The concrete object Hegel used to exist and is now being referred to'. I offer an ontological analysis of what makes sentences of this sort true, an analysis that Craig forcefully criticizes; but Craig does not explain what he means by such sentences or offer an ontological analysis of its truth maker to replace my ontology. Craig explains his "states of affairs" but does not explain how a name can now refer to a concrete person who used to exist (consistently with the presentist doctrine that "nothing is real but the present").

But focusing on this one issue gives a wrong impression of Craig's chapter. In his chapter, Craig undeniably has made much progress developing a presentist ontology. Craig can certainly be credited, with Ludlow, for developing a presentist ontology much more than other presentists who have followed in Prior's tradition that "only the present is real." *QS*]

Some more general observations can be made. Up to this point, we have been treating tensed truth conditions as if truth comes about because truth-making facts are things or events having tensed properties. But most presentists would argue that things or events cannot be said to be past or future as a fact of the present; they will maintain that tenses should be read not in a *de re* but in a *de dicto* manner, ascribing instead tensed properties to a proposition. Thus, tensed truths are concerned with propositions and the evaluation of such propositions; that is, a sentence like 'Caesar has crossed the Rubicon' should be read as meaning that it was once true that Caesar crosses the Rubicon. Smith argues in his chapter, however, that the *de dicto* presentist cannot coherently believe both in a correspondence theory of truth and in a truth value link between presently stated past- and future-tensed sentences and pastly or futurely stated present-tensed sentences without also believing in *de re* tensed states of affairs. The latter would, nonetheless, jeopardize the entire idea behind the *de dicto* approach.

One possible way of getting off the hook is to treat truth differently from correspondence—for instance, by saying that any truth ascription to a proposition or a sentence has only illocutionary purposes.

When I say it was true that Caesar crosses the Rubicon, I don't assert a certain past state of affairs, I only express that my consent to 'Caesar crosses the Rubicon' once would (or might) have been affirmative. If one wants to hold on to the correspondence theory of truth, one should give up the *de dicto* approach and argue in favor of a maximal theory of tenses, as Smith does, assuming that events have the real property of being past, present, or future.

A distinct metaphysical problem concerns the objectivity of becoming. By saying this, I am also indicating my view that the existence of tenses, or tensed properties, is logically independent of the nature of becoming of which presentism is *only one* possible theory. In other words, the dispute between A-theorists and B-theorists about tensed statements, having tensed or tenseless truth conditions does not necessarily imply a static or a dynamic view of time.

This may seem like a surprising claim, but consider some distinctions. Following Fitzgerald (1968), we could name the four different ontological theories concerning the objectivity of becoming as (1) the instant view of time, or as it is often called, presentism; (2) the empty view of the future; (3) the half-full view of the future; and (4) the full view of the future. (1) assumes that what exists now is the only reality; (2) takes both past and present events to be real, but no future events are so, whereas (3) holds that past and present events as well as causally determined future events are real; and (4) assumes that every event is real irrespective of whether it occurs in the past, present, or future. The first three approaches see becoming as a dynamic feature of the world, in contrast to the fourth approach, which sees time only as a static one.

Oaklander says in his chapter that the status of temporal becoming is the fundamental issue in the philosophy of time. But I don't think the question of objective becoming can be easily identified with the question of whether tenses are real or not, and therefore whether the truth conditions of tensed sentences are tensed or tenseless. Objective becoming does not, according to my mind, necessarily involve a change from one A-series position to another. In other words, if we can prove the unreality of tenses, we have not thereby proven the nonexistence of objective becoming.

Elsewhere (Faye 1989, pp. 90–91), I have argued that proponents of objective becoming—or as I called them, temporal noncognitivists about the future—can formulate their view in quite a satisfactory manner in terms of tenseless expressions. For instance, they could say:

Any utterance of a tenseless sentence of the form 'e occurs at t' is true or false at t or at any time later than t, but is neither true nor false prior to t.

A similar clause is possible for tensed sentences:

Any utterance spoken at t of a tensed sentence of the form 'e is going to occur tomorrow' is true or false at t^* if, and only if, t^* is at least one day later than t; otherwise, it is neither true nor false.

So what makes such sentences true or false is the fact that events exist tenselessly from the moment they become real (and perhaps stop being real).

Depending on the kind of view a person harbors regarding the unreality or the indeterminateness of future events, he can either insist, as in the noncognitivist case, on the validity of the negation of the principle of bivalence with respect to sentences about the future, or he can merely reject, as in the case of temporal possibilism, the universal validity of the principle, that is, the principle that every declarative sentence p about a future event is determinately true or determinately false. Temporal non-cognitivists maintain their view on bivalence because they consider the future to be nothing at all, whereas temporal possibilists adopt their position because they see the future as a set of tenuous possibilities. Both theories, moreover, come in a weak and a strong form corresponding to the half-full and the empty view. Thus, on the one hand, weak and strong noncognitivism hold (1) $\models \exists p \sim (Tp \vee Fp)$, but only strong non-cognitivism asserts (2) $\models \forall p \sim (Tp \vee Fp)$. On the other hand, weak and strong possibilism support (3) $\not\models \forall p(Tp \vee Fp)$, while strong possibilism also claims (4) $\not\models \exists p(Tp \vee Fp)$.

Thus, nothing prohibits advocates of objective becoming from saying that such a notion about the failure of bivalence implies only a change in the B-series positions. It is merely by tradition, I think, that objective becoming has been identified with a change in the A-series positions because tenses were thought of as necessary for the passage of time. If what I believe is true, it is not sufficient for the detensers, like Oaklander and myself, to debunk the tensers if we want to defend the mind-dependence of becoming. We have to come up with separate arguments against its objectivity, and we have to prove those arguments, considered by objectivists to be positively in favor of their position, to be misleading.

Indeed, in his chapter Tooley holds such a tenseless view by claiming that the world continuously adds new existence to the totality of reality, and the moment a fact comes into being, it exists in a tenseless way. He argues that the idea of being actual-as-of-a-time cannot be cashed out in terms of the tensed concepts of past, present, and future. Rather, it should be expressed in tenseless terms so a state of affairs is said to be actual as of a given time either if the state of affairs exists at that time, together with all earlier states of affairs, or if it only exists at that time.

Oaklander (1999) takes issue with Tooley on these matters, arguing that Tooley cannot reconcile both claims that there is a totality of tense-less states of affairs (including the future) that exists *simpliciter* and that tenseless facts that are not actual as of one time may be actual as of a later time. Oaklander's argument is that if the totality exists *simpliciter*, then there is (tenselessly) nothing that can be added to them. But then nothing can be added to them in a tensed fashion either, since Tooley rejects presentness as part of his tenseless ontology. Hence, Oaklander concludes that Tooley does not successfully combine the tensed and the tenseless view.

Although he himself continues talking about the tensed or dynamic approach, I think it is unfortunate to say that Tooley combines the tensed and the tenseless view. What he does is to combine the tenseless approach with the dynamic or objective becoming approach. But that is something different. Oaklander's and Tooley's opposite views, however, rest on an expression that they seem to interpret differently. If one says that an event occurs tenselessly at time t if, and only if, it is true at any other time that the event occurs at t, then Oaklander has a good point. But if one thinks that an event occurs tenselessly at time t if, and only if, it is true at some other time that the event occurs at t, then Tooley seems to be able to maintain what he says. As long as the discussion need not involve any reference to a past, present, or future time, then it is not so obvious that one reading would be more correct than the other. Here we could talk about tenselessness in a stronger and a weaker sense.

Since the discussion is about metaphysics, is it then possible to give an ontological characterization, contrary to a semantic formulation, that would make the objective becoming approach coherent? I think it is.

First, I take most of the so-called A-theorists as being ontological realists like most B-theorists. Realism does not mean that one necessarily has to ascribe reality to certain kinds of entities, say, future events. One is an ontological realist as long as one thinks that whatever exists, it exists independently of our cognitive capacities.

Second, I believe that the ontological realist can look upon the future (past) in three (five) different ways: (1) as determinate; (2a) as indeterminate or (2b) as partly indeterminate; or (3a) as unreal or (3b) as partly unreal. Both the second and the third view involve the idea of an objective becoming. The difference between those two positions, which is the one between possibilism and noncognitivism, is this. (3a) holds that no state of affairs obtains in the future (later as of a given time); facts become real in the present (in tenseless terms: they come into being at the time at which they are located, not before). (2a) argues, instead, that facts about potential or unactualized events do obtain in the future (later as of a given time), but because some of these events' attributes are not fixed until these attributes become present, facts about those events are not fully determinate until then (in tenseless terms: facts become determinate at the time at which they are located, not before).

As an illustration of my point, consider the sentence 'X is P' about a future state of affairs. If (1) is the case, the sentence is said to be true because the name 'X' refers to X in the future, and X satisfies P; if (2) is the case, the sentence is said to be probably true because 'X' refers to X in the future but X only satisfies P with a certain probability; or if (3) is the case, the sentence is said to be neither true nor false because 'X' doesn't refer to anything at all.

This is also how I read Arsenijević's chapter. He wants to defend the objectivity of becoming; much less does he hold that the A-theory is true. In fact, he seems to favor the detenser's argument that the past, the present, and the future are redundant with respect to defining the truth conditions of indicative tensed sentences. But he still thinks that this argument does not exclude the truth of possibilism. Take $A(e_t)$ to be a sentence about a future event e_t. Arsenijević then objects that it is futile for philosophers like myself, who deny the objectivity of becoming, to say that either $A(e_t)$ or $\neg A(e_t)$ is true *simpliciter* if we cannot answer the question of what makes it true before t. I believe, however, that the problem Arsenijević raises can also be formulated with respect to similar sentences $B(e_t)$ or $\neg B(e_t)$ about a past event. Often we cannot tell after t whether $B(e_t)$ or $\neg B(e_t)$ is the true sentence. Nonetheless, most philosophers would hold that as of the past, one of them is true *simpliciter*. Why? I take the answer to be straightforward. Our cognitive incapacity to ascribe a definite truth value to a certain sentence does not determine whether or not something makes this sentence true. Sometimes we may be unable to attribute any definite truth value to a sentence about the past, not merely by accident, but in principle, because all effects of the past event have disappeared or damped down to the level of noise. Thus, nothing in the world later than t provides the basis on which we can answer the question. Why not call such an event *effect-indetermined*. Similarly, we may sometimes be unable, in principle, to attribute a definite truth value to a sentence about the future because the event in question is *cause-indetermined*. Nothing in the world earlier than t can therefore be used to answer the question. As a consequence, there seems to be no reason for not treating the past and the future equally. Either both are ontologically open or both are ontologically closed.

As I don't think that tenses are necessary for the objectivist regarding becoming, neither do I regard them as sufficient for the objectivist's position. For the full theorist, who denies an ontological asymmetry between the past and the future, could argue that only the present objectively exists but that this fact does not prevent the future from being determinate. I take this position to be the one that Gödel (1949; also Dorato (1995)) argues within the framework of relativity theory, as he distinguishes between reality and existence in the sense that events other than present events have reality but only present events exist. What I do claim is that such a view is logically possible, but I don't say anything about how viable it is.

Also it seems to me that this is a fair way to interpret Smith's view, when he says that "there exist past, present, and future concrete things and events." If I understand him correctly, he argues for a semantic view, according to which tensed sentences have tensed truth conditions, and combines it with the ontological view that nonpresent times are real in the sense that past and future are determinate. He urges that the assertion of a past- or a future-tensed sentence p should be read as p is true or false. He does not maintain that the past and the future are unreal by saying that p's truth conditions consist only of present conditions, nor does he maintain that the past and the future are ontologically indeterminate in the sense that the assertion of a past- or a future-tensed sentence p is equivalent to the assertion that p is probably true and probably false.

In sum, I suggest that, on the one hand, one can deny that the past and/or the future is real (determinate), but one still wants to express this ontological assumption in terms of tenseless truth conditions. On the other hand, one can instead argue that the future is real (determinate), but that we still have objective tenses, and this assumption is expressed by tensed truth conditions. This means, of course, that we should make a clearer terminological distinction between the objectivity of tenses and the objectivity of becoming than we are accustomed to making: A-theories require that tensed sentences have tensed truth conditions, and B-theories take these truth conditions to be tenseless, but these semantic theories of truth conditions can be logically separated from an ontological theory of objective becoming.

References

Andersen, H. B., and J. Faye. 1980. Om Fremtidige Sølag (On Future Sea-battles). In *Studier i Antik og Middelalderlig Filosofi og Idehistorie*, Museum Tusculanum, pp. 40–43. Copenhagen: Museum Tusculanums Forlag.

Dorato, M. 1995. *Time and Reality: Spacetime Physics and the Objectivity of Temporal Becoming*. Bologna: CLUEB.

Dorato, M. 1996. Mental Causation, Tensed Beliefs, and the Reality of Tenses. Ms.

Dyke, H. 2002. Tokens, Dates and Tenseless Truth Conditions. *Synthese* 131, pp. 329–51.

Faye, J. 1981. *Et Naturfilosofisk Essay om Tid og Kausalitet* (An Essay in Natural Philosophy on Time and Causation). Copenhagen: Jørgen Paludans Forlag.

Faye, J. 1989. *The Reality of the Future*. Odense: Odense University Press.

Fitzgerald, P. 1968. Is the Future Partly Unreal? *Review of Metaphysics* 21, pp. 421–46.

Gödel, K. 1949. A Remark about the Relationship between Relativity Theory and Idealistic Philosophy. In P. Schilpp, ed., *Albert Einstein: Philosopher-Scientist*, pp. 555–63. Evanston, Ill.: The Library of Living Philosophers.

Kaplan, D. 1978. On the Logic of Demonstratives. *Journal of Philosophical Logic* 8, pp. 81–98.

Ludlow, P. 1999. *Semantics, Tense, and Time*. Cambridge, Mass.: MIT Press.

Mellor, D. H. 1981. *Real Time*. Cambridge: Cambridge University Press.

Mellor, D. H. 1986. Tense's Tenseless Truth Conditions. *Analysis* 46, pp. 167–72.

Oaklander, L. N. 1999. Review of Michael Tooley's *Time, Tense and Causation*. *Mind* 108, pp. 407–13.

Perry, J. 1977. Frege on Demonstratives. *Philosophical Review* 86, pp. 494–97.

Perry, J. 1979. The Problem of the Essential Indexical. *Noûs*, 13, pp. 3–21.

Priest, G. 1986a. Tense and Truth Conditions. *Analysis* 46, pp. 162–66.

Priest, G. 1986b. Tense, *Tense* and TENSE. *Analysis* 47, pp. 184–86.

Shimony, A. 1993. The Transient Now. In *Search for a Naturalistic World View I–II*. Cambridge: Cambridge University Press.

Zeilicovici, D. 1986. A (Dis)solution of McTaggart's Paradox. *Ratio* 28, pp. 175–95.

Zeilicovici, D. 1989. Temporal Becoming Minus the Moving-Now. *Noûs* 23, pp. 505–23.

Section A

Tenseless Theories of Time

8

Two Versions of the New B-Theory of Language

L. Nathan Oaklander

8.1 Introduction

The most fundamental debate in the philosophy of time concerns the status of temporal becoming. Do events really pass from the future to the present and into the past as A-theorists such as C. D. Broad (1923, 1938), George Schlesinger (1980), Quentin Smith (1993), Storrs McCall (1994), Michael Tooley (1997), William Lane Craig (2000), and others have maintained, or is the passage of time a myth and an illusion as B-theorists such as Bertrand Russell (1915), Donald C. Williams (1951), Adolf Grünbaum (1967), J. J. C. Smart (1980), L. Nathan Oaklander (1984), Robin Le Poidevin (1991), Hugh Mellor (1998), Heather Dyke (2002a), and others have maintained? That is one issue. Another closely connected issue concerns the proper "analysis" of tense in ordinary language and thought. We express the passage of time (or the myth of passage) by means of tensed discourse and tensed beliefs. For example, we ordinarily say, at different times, that an event *will* occur, *is* occurring, and *did* occur, and it is commonplace to believe that, for example, *today* is Monday, *tomorrow* will be Tuesday, and *yesterday* was Sunday. Two questions of analysis concerning these ordinary tensed sentences and beliefs immediately arise: (1) What is the meaning of tensed discourse? and (2) What are the truth conditions or truth makers of tensed sentences? A third issue, intimately related to the other two, concerns the reference of temporal indexicals (such as 'now', 'yesterday', and 'tomorrow'). Do temporal indexicals refer directly to some items (such as times or sentence tokens); or do they refer indirectly to items via a mediating sense (such as the property of *presentness*); or do they, perhaps, perform both functions, or neither?

In recent articles and books on time, defenders of the A-theory have attacked the date analysis, the token-reflexive analysis, and the sentence-type analysis of the meaning and truth conditions of tensed sentences as well as the B-theory account of temporal indexicals. In his most recent publications on the topic, William Lane Craig claims that "if Quentin Smith (1993) delivered the mortal blow to the New B-Theory of Language, then Laurie Paul (1997) has written its obituary" (Craig 1999, p. 265; cf. Craig 2000, passim). Smith is more circumspect. Although he "agree[s] with Craig that 'the B-theory of tense and time, though still widely held, is a theory in retreat'" (1999, p. 249), he thoughtfully acknowledges that "some criticisms of the tensed theory, such as Graham Nerlich's penetrating essay 'Time as Spacetime' (1998) and Oaklander's equally forceful 'McTaggart's Paradox and Smith's Tensed Theory of Time' (1996) require responses before the A-theorist can say the tensed theory of time is fully justified as it stands" (1999, pp. 247–48). Smith's last point is very important since if, as Nerlich and Oaklander argue, there are no tensed propositions, nonrelational tensed properties, or tensed facts, then it is impossible that there are tensed truth conditions in any ontologically significant way. Thus, either all tensed judgments are false, or the B-theory account of their truth conditions must be correct after all. Or is there some third alternative? I shall return to this question later.

What, then, of the plethora of arguments given by Smith, Craig, and others? Do they really sound the death knell for the B-theory of time? I don't think so, although the primary concern of this chapter will not be with them, but with the (truth-conditional) method that protagonists in the debate have more or less taken for granted in their discussions. According to this method, if the truth conditions of one sentence can be given by means of another sentence, then the sentence stating the truth conditions either *has* or *gives* (or states) the meaning of the other sentence and, if those truth conditions obtain, then the sentence expressing them represents the correct ontology of time. The purpose of this chapter is to cast doubt on the method of truth conditions by arguing that tenseless truth conditions sentences cannot have, give, or state the (complete) meaning of tensed sentences *and* also depict the metaphysical truth about time.[1] As a result, the new B-theory of *language* will have to be modified; but when it is, the new theory of *time* will remain intact.

In the course of my discussion, I shall explicate two different versions of the new B-theory of language. What should be emphasized, however, is that on all versions of the B-theory the only temporal facts are B-facts, and the only intrinsically temporal constituents of B-facts are B-relations. All versions of the B-theory, whether old or new, reject A-facts and A-properties (such as *pastness*, *presentness*, and *futurity*). Thus, though there are methodological disagreements among, for example, Mellor (1998), Butterfield (1985), Beer (1994, 2001), Le Poidevin (1991, 1998), Oaklander (1994b,c), Dyke (2002b, 2003), and Smart (1980), there are no significant ontological disagreements among them.[2] Whether we are talking about the old or the new B-theory, temporal reality does not contain an ontological reflection of verbal or conceptual tense. In order to clarify the two versions of the new theory, it will be necessary to say something about the old B-theory of time and the related notions of meaning and truth conditions. To those topics I shall turn next.

8.2   Truth Conditions and Meaning

Although the notion of "truth conditions" is well entrenched in the philosophical lexicon, philosophers have meant different things by it. In the standard semantic use, a truth conditions sentence states necessary and sufficient conditions for a sentence's being true (or false). Ludlow expresses this sense as follows:

> If the semantics of natural language takes the form of a T-theory, and hence the semantics of a sentence is given by theorems like (3), then the right-hand side of the theorem—the portion following "if and only if"—states the literal truth conditions of the sentence of the left-hand side.
>
> (3)   "Snow is white" is true if and only if snow is white.
>
> In this case, the truth conditions are that snow is white. (1999, p. 7)

I have detected three other notions of truth conditions in the literature. Robin Le Poidevin distinguishes truth conditions from truth makers as follows:

The *truth-conditions* of some proposition p are whatever must obtain for p to be true. The *truth-makers* of a token belief that p, in contrast, are the facts which make the truth-conditions of p obtain on a particular occasion. (1999, p. 149)

For Le Poidevin, truth conditions are not necessary and sufficient for truth, but only *necessary* (whatever *must* obtain) for the truth of some proposition p.[3] For Smith, on the other hand, truth conditions are *sufficient* conditions for truth. He says that "'the truth conditions of [sentence] S_1 and [sentence] S_2' does not refer to a relation between S_1 and S_2 but to *the states of affairs that make S_1 and S_2 true*" (1993, p. 5; emphasis added). According to Smith, "A state of affairs is whatever corresponds to a true proposition" (1993, p. 151). Contrary to Smith, Craig wants to separate the truth conditions of tensed sentences entirely from the grounds of truth of tensed sentences. He says:

The giving of truth conditions is a semantic exercise; specifying grounds for a statement's truth concerns ontology. One can lay out semantic conditions which will permit one to determine for any sentence whether that sentence is true or false without saying anything at all about the ontological facts which make that sentence true. (1996b, p. 22)

Given the ambiguity in the notion of "truth conditions," it is not always easy to see what those who reject the B-theory on the grounds that no B-sentence can state all the "truth conditions" of an A-sentence mean. The matter is further complicated by the fact that the B-sentences stating the truth conditions of A-sentences are supposed to have the same meaning (on the old B-theory) or give the meaning (on the new B-theory) as the A-sentences under analysis. It is then argued that since no B-sentence has the same meaning or can give the meaning of an A-sentence, it follows that no B-sentence can state all the truth conditions of an A-sentence and therefore, both the new and the old B-theory of time are false. But as in the case of "truth conditions," the notion of "meaning" is ambiguous.

In one sense of 'meaning', the meaning₁ of a sentence or thought is whatever is (intended to be) asserted by a sentence or represented by a thought. Thus, for example, if I say, 'The cat is on the mat or the dog is on the mat', then what this sentence states and what the corresponding thought intends is that the cat is on the mat or the dog is on the mat. Suppose we call this sense of meaning *intentional meaning₁*. I should note, however, that the ontological status of the intentional meaning₁ of a sentence or thought is ambiguous and open to debate. On the one hand, the intentional meaning$_1$ could be identified with a mind-independent proposition or content represented by a thought or stated by a sentence. On the other hand, since language, viewed as physical marks on paper or sounds in the air, is not intrinsically meaningful$_1$, and it is not by its own nature about anything, one may, for that reason, identify the meaning$_1$ of a sentence with what it is an expression of: a thought, an intrinsically intentional content, or a mind-dependent proposition that each exists in a conscious mental state. I shall return to this distinction later when we discuss the move from the new to the newer version of the B-theory of language.

There is another notion of "meaning," and it involves not what is *asserted* or *thought* to be the case, but what *is* the case. If what is asserted by a sentence is true, then we can say that the meaning$_2$ of a sentence or thought is the fact that makes it true, its *truth maker*. Given this usage, meanings$_2$ are nonlinguistic items, or facts, that make sentence or belief tokens (or the propositions they express) true. They are one of the relata of the correspondence relation. The existence of meanings in this sense does not depend on the existence of true sentence tokens or on language at all. If the B-theory is true and one accepts a date analysis of tense, then the meaning$_2$ of a true August 1, 2001, sentence token of 'It is now raining' is the B-fact that *rain occurs on August 1, 2001*. If the tensed theory is true, then the meaning$_2$ of what is stated anytime by a true sentence token of 'It is now raining' is (or includes) the tensed fact that *it is now raining*. Thus, in the second sense, the meaning$_2$ or, as I shall also call it, the *reference* or *ontological meaning$_2$* of a sentence, word, or phrase is given by its truth maker, its ontological ground, or that to which it refers.

In a still different sense, the *meaning$_3$* of what is asserted by a sentence token is identical to its truth conditions. (Of course, this definition of 'meaning' is inherently ambiguous owing to the lack of clarity in the notion of "truth conditions.") On the token-reflexive version of the B-theory, the meaning$_3$ and hence the truth conditions of what is asserted by an A-sentence token are token-reflexive. That is, the appropriate temporal relation between an A-sentence or belief token and what it is about are the necessary and sufficient conditions for what is asserted by the token to be true. For example, on the token-reflexive account, what is stated by a sentence token N of 'It is now 1980' is true if and only if N is simultaneous with or occurs at or during 1980. Or again, to comprehend the token-reflexive truth-conditional meaning$_3$ of what is asserted by the A-sentence token Z of 'It *was* raining' is to know that what Z asserts is true if and only if Z exists later than it's raining.

B-theorists typically accept either a token-reflexive or date-analysis account of the truth conditions of tensed sentences; but if McTaggart is right, then A-sentences and A-beliefs are logically false because they imply self-contradictions and so cannot have truth makers. Thus, what is expressed by A-sentences cannot strictly speaking have truth conditions, for the B-sentences that state token-reflexive or date-analysis truth conditions are sometimes true and therefore cannot state truth conditions for A-sentences that are never true and cannot possibly be true. Thus, if I (following McTaggart) am right in maintaining that A-sentences and A-beliefs are necessarily false, then neither token-reflexive nor date-analysis sentences (nor tensed sentences for that matter) can state necessary or sufficient conditions for A-sentences' being true.[4] Since, however, some of the arguments against the new theory appeal to token-reflexive and date-analysis truth conditions of A-sentences, I will employ the notion of truth conditions in discussing those arguments. In the end, however, I will reject the claim that the token-reflexive or the date-analysis sentences state truth conditions of A-sentences. At most, token-reflexive and date-analysis sentences state "pragmatic conditions" since their obtaining is what makes A-sentences and beliefs useful even though they are false. I will discuss these points further in section 8.6.

To return to the topic of meaning, in a fourth sense, the meaning$_4$ of sentence or belief types or tokens is the linguistic rules that govern their correct usage. Thus, different tokens of the same tensed sentence type can have the same meaning$_4$ (or, following Kaplan, "character") even though their reference meaning$_2$ and token-reflexive truth-conditional meaning$_3$ differ. For example, all tokens of the sentence type 'It is now raining' (call it 'S^*') have the same meaning$_4$, or what I shall call *linguistic meaning$_4$*, and are, in some sense, saying the same thing; but non-simultaneous utterances of S^* have different token-reflexive meanings$_3$ and are made true by different ontological facts. What, then, is the meaning$_4$ of tensed and tenseless sentences?

Clearly, part of the meaning$_4$ of tensed sentences, such as S^*, is that they are *context sensitive* since the truth value of their tokens varies depending on when they are uttered. Part of the meaning$_4$ of tenseless sentence types, such as 'It is raining on July 8, 2001' (call it 'R'), is that they are *context insensitive*; all tokens of a tenseless sentence have a common truth value regardless of when (or where) they are uttered. Since a token of S^* could be true and a token of R false, tokens of S^* and R can have different truth conditions. Given that sameness of meaning of sentence types implies sameness of truth conditions of all the tokens of those types, it follows that S^* and R have different meanings$_4$ and so cannot translate each other. Nevertheless, there is an important connection between meaning$_4$ and truth conditions (or meaning$_2$): the meaning$_4$ of a tensed sentence is a semantic function or rule whose argument is the context of utterance and whose value is that sentence's truth conditions or truth maker in that context. In other words, the linguistic meaning$_4$ or character of a tensed sentence tells us how the context determines the sentence's truth condition or, to use Kaplan's terminology, "content." (See Mellor 1998, p. 59.) But what is the ontological status of the *context* of utterance; is it an A- or a B-time? And what are the truth conditions of a tensed sentence in a given context of use; are they A- or B-facts? Of those questions, more later.

8.3   A Critique of the Old B-Theory of Language

One can already begin to see that the old B-theory goal of providing a tenseless truth conditions sentence that captures the meaning in the sense that it *has* the same meaning as a tensed sentence, in all these various senses of meaning, is going to be a daunting task. In fact, the enterprise of translation that requires B-sentences to have the same meaning as tensed ones breaks down in at least two main ways. To see why, consider the question, Is what is stated by a tensed sentence or intended by a tensed thought—its intentional meaning$_1$—the same as the ontological fact that makes that sentence or thought true, and is the reference meaning$_2$ of the tenseless truth conditions sentence? The old B-theory said that they were the same, but clearly they are not. When I think, 'It is now raining,' or 'The exam is past', what is stated or thought is the intentional meaning$_1$ *it is now raining* or *the exam is past*, but the meaning$_1$ of tensed language and thought in that sense is not what makes the sentences or thoughts true. What makes them true are B-facts such as *it is raining at t_1* and *the exam is earlier than t_1*. For that reason, the tenseless truth conditions sentence does not state both the intentional meaning$_1$ and the reference or ontological meaning$_2$ of tensed sentences, and therefore cannot translate them.

Another reason why the old B-theory failed is that no tenseless truth conditions sentence has the same linguistic meaning$_4$ as the tensed sentence it is supposed to translate, since they obey different rules of use. All tokens of a tenseless sentence-type have the same truth value, whereas the truth values of tokens of the same tensed sentence-type vary from time to time. Hence, no B-sentence-type has tokens whose truth conditions are always the same as the tokens of the tensed sentence-type they were alleged to translate. Since for one sentence to translate another sentence without loss of meaning the one must be substitutable by the other in all contexts without change of truth value, it follows that tenseless translation of tensed discourse is impossible and that, therefore, the old B-theory of language is unacceptable.

Early defenders of the B-theory, such as Russell (1915), Broad (1921), Goodman (1951), and Smart (1963), were guilty of confusing different senses of the term 'meaning'. Since to give the "meaning" of tensed sentences is to specify the "conditions" under which they are true, they believed that the tenseless sentence that stated the truth conditions that would obtain if a tensed sentence is true—the ontological fact—also captured its "meaning" and could translate it. Unfortunately, we have just seen that there is no single truth conditions B-sentence that can carry the weight it is forced to bear. Early B-theorists may be right, as new B-theorists believe they are, in maintaining that the ontological or reference meaning$_2$ of A-sentence tokens is captured by B-sentences that merely describe temporal relationships between and among terms in the B-series. It does not follow, however, that the linguistic meaning$_4$ or the intentional meaning$_1$ of an A-sentence can be expressed by means of the B-sentence that has the same ontological meaning$_2$ as the A-sentence. Indeed, no tenseless sentence has the same meaning$_1$ or meaning$_4$ as any tensed sentence, and for that reason no tenseless sentence can translate a tensed sentence even if it has the same ontological meaning. Thus, the old B-theory conception of analysis that hoped to capture the (complete) meaning of a tensed sentence and represent the metaphysical nature of time with a single B-sentence had to be abandoned.

To analyze ordinary language so as to render transparent how it enables us to communicate information, engage in timely action, express our thoughts, and depict the correct ontology of time requires recognizing different kinds of meaning and correspondingly different notions of "truth conditions." Thus, to believe that the tenseless truth conditions sentence on the right side of the biconditional, which states the truth conditions of what is asserted by the tensed sentence on the left, can capture *all* the various notions of meaning is a mistake. It is, however, a pervasive mistake that is committed by A-theorists and old and new B-theorists alike. In order to see how it is to be avoided, we need to clarify the new B-theory of language and update it with a newer version.

8.4   The New B-Theory of Language

The new B-theory of language advocated by Smart, Mellor, and Oaklander, among others, rejects the old B-view that the tenseless sentences that state the truth conditions of tensed sentences have the same meaning and so can translate them. However, these philosophers do not go far enough in repudiating the old tenseless theory. For example, Smart held that the A-theory of time is false since the meaning and truth conditions of ordinary A-sentences and their tokens can be stated in a tenseless metalanguage. Recall, Smart's truth conditions sentence says that

When P says at t 'time t is now' his assertion is true if and only if t is at t, so that if P says at t 't is now,' his assertion is thereby true. (1980, p. 5)

Smart thus maintains that since "the *semantics* of indexical expressions can be expressed in a tenseless metalanguage" (1980, p. 11; my emphasis), it follows that tokens containing temporal indexicals convey no information about events or times not conveyed by date-analysis sentences. Smith states this aspect of Smart's theory nicely when he says:

Smart is here saying that the tenseless metalanguage adequately expresses the meaning of (in the sense of "gives truth conditions of") ordinary indexical expressions such as "E is present," and Smart infers from this the thesis of "metaphysical significance," that the tenseless theory of time is true. (1994d, p. 84)

Mellor's token-reflexive account of A-sentences that he gave up for a date-analysis account is also intended to capture the meaning of tensed sentences. For Mellor, tensed sentences "may not *have* the same meaning as tenseless sentences that give their truth conditions [and for that reason cannot *translate* them], but those truth conditions surely *give* their meanings" (1981, p. 25; cf. Mellor 1998, pp. 62–63).

It seems to me, however, that the new B-theorists' view that one can analyze ordinary language by constructing tenseless truth conditions sentences that state the meanings of sentences in a natural language does not sufficiently break away from the old B-theory. Admittedly, new B-theorists abandon the criterion of translatability as the mark of ontological commitment. Nevertheless, they seem to accept the same basic idea as the early detensers, namely, that a single tenseless truth conditions sentence can capture the (complete) meaning of A-sentences and represent what exists in the world that makes A-sentences true. Before I attempt to explain again why I think the method of truth conditions as defined in section 8.1 is a mistake, and indicate how another version of the new B-theory of language can avoid it, I want to explain how, by making the distinctions between the various senses of meaning and truth conditions, we can avoid some of the objections to the new theory posed by Smith and Craig.

The first argument against the B-theory is Smith's entailment argument against the token-reflexive account of the truth conditions of tensed sentences or the propositions they express.[5] We can begin to see what is wrong with this argument by noting that even if token-reflexive "truth conditions" can only capture the meaning$_2$ of tensed sentences in the sense of specifying a fact that is sufficient to make what is stated by an A-sentence token true, it does not follow that token-reflexive reference meaning$_2$ is the only meaning tensed sentences have, nor does it follow that token-reflexive "truth conditions" are necessary and sufficient to account for all the entailment relations between and among tensed sentences in ordinary language. Other truth conditions, for example, the date-analysis truth conditions, are sufficient to do that.

Thus, it seems to me that Smith's (1994b) entailment argument against the token-reflexive theory of tenseless time is irrelevant to a critique of the B-theory. His argument is as follows: If what is stated by a token S of

(1)   It is now 1980

has the same truth conditions (i.e., the same meaning) as what is stated by any token U of 'S occurs in 1980', then, since (1) entails

(2)   1980 is present

(and indeed has the same meaning), the truth conditions of (i.e., the fact statable by) (2) must be among the truth conditions of both S and U. But this is not the case, since V occurs at (or in) 1980 is a truth condition of any token V of (2), but not of U. Therefore, Smith concludes, "since a fact statable by V is a truth condition of S but not of U, it follows that S and U have different truth conditions and fail to translate each other" (1994b, p. 45). And this contradicts the assumption that S and U have the same truth conditions and do translate (have the same meaning as) each other. To put the argument otherwise, the tenseless sentence tokens ('S occurs in 1980' and 'V occurs in 1980') that state the truth conditions that allegedly capture the meaning (or translate) the tensed sentences (1) and (2) do not really do so, since the tenseless truth conditions stated by those tenseless sentences cannot account for the entailment of (2) by (1).

This argument assumes that the tenseless sentences and their tenseless truth conditions that represent the token-reflexive meaning$_2$ of tensed sentences must be the same as the tenseless sentences and truth conditions that account for the entailment between tensed sentences. Perhaps the version of the new tenseless theory initially put forth by Mellor (1981) made that assumption, but I do not think it is integral to the tenseless theory of time and I think we can avoid Smith's entailment argument if we deny it.

Clearly, the truth conditions specified by the date analysis can explain the inference from (1) to (2) since the meaning$_2$ (i.e., the real truth or fact that underlies the vague truths 'It is now 1980' and '1980 is present') is the same for both, namely, the trivial fact that *1980 is at 1980*. To suggest that date-analysis truth conditions can explain the inference from (1) to (2) does not imply that the tenseless sentences that state those truth conditions (or the tenseless truth conditions themselves) can capture the intentional meaning₁ or translate tensed sentences. Nor does it suggest that tensed descriptions of events are unnecessary in ordinary life. Rather, the date analysis suggests that since misunderstanding the tenses can lead to the unacceptable metaphysics of temporal passage, in depicting temporal reality tenseless descriptions are preferable.

By not keeping these different notions of meaning and truth conditions separate, Smith (1994c) offers a fallacious objection to my explanation of the entailment of (2) ('1980 is present') by (1) ('It is now 1980'). Following Kaplan, I have argued that the meaning₄ of (1) and (2) is a semantic function from the context of utterance, namely, the time at which their tokens are produced, to their tenseless truth conditions. Since the context of utterance varies, so do the truth conditions of their tokens, but in each case the truth conditions are tenseless. Thus, in an earlier paper (1994b), I argued that any token of (1) is true with respect to the context in which it is produced (namely, the time at which it is uttered), if and only if the year of that context is 1980, and the same may be said of any token of (2). Consequently, since the truth conditions of (tokens of) (1) and (2) are the same, the difficulty of getting (1) and (2) to be logically equivalent vanishes (Oaklander 1994b). Smith's objection runs as follows:

The tenseless truth conditions of tokens of (1) and (2) are not the same, and Oaklander can create the appearance of sameness only by equivocating on "it." ... But once we replace the occurrences of "it" by names of the relevant tokens, this appearance of similar truth conditions vanishes. The tenseless truth conditions are these:

(3)   Any token of (1) is true with respect to the context of *S*'s utterance if and only if the year of *S*'s context of utterance is 1980.

(4)   Any token of (1) is true with respect to the context of *V*'s utterance if and only if the year of *V*'s context of utterance is 1980.

... These two tenseless facts mentioned after the biconditionals in these truth-condition sentences are *S occurs in 1980* and *V occurs in 1980*. We are now back in the situation I described in Essay (2) [Smith 1994b]. These two tenseless facts do not entail each other. *S* could occur in 1980 even if *V* does not occur at all, and vice versa. Consequently, these facts are insufficient to explain the logical equivalence of *S* and *V*. (1994c, pp. 72–73)

I am not convinced by this argument. Admittedly, if 'It is now 1980' and '1980 is present' are true, then there will be the (token-reflexive) truth conditions *S occurs in 1980* and *V occurs in 1980*, but they are not the only truth conditions, nor are they the relevant ones. If the context in which I utter S is 1980, then its (i.e., S's) truth condition is *1980 is at 1980*. And if the context in which I utter V is 1980, then its (i.e., V's) truth condition is also *1980 is at 1980*. Thus, given the linguistic meaning$_4$ of the tensed sentence tokens S and V, they have the same truth conditions and the inference from S to V is accounted for, although neither the tenseless sentences that state their truth conditions, nor the tenseless truth conditions themselves, capture their meaning$_1$ or meaning$_4$.

Of course, Smith has argued that while the appeal to date-analysis truth conditions may account for the inference from S to V, the date theory of the truth conditions of A-sentences (or what they express) is inadequate and is therefore to be rejected. Indeed, Smith (1993, 1994c), Craig (2000), and Paul (1997) have offered a myriad of objections to the date analysis that deserve attention. Although I shall not attend to all of them here, I do want to consider two of Smith's arguments since I think they can be refuted if we keep the different notions of meaning and truth conditions distinct.

Smith characterizes the date analysis as follows:

The thesis of the date theory is that each successive token of some A-sentence-type corresponds to a distinct date-sentence-type, such that corresponding to the token of "Henry is ill" that occurs on July 28, 1940 is the date-sentence-type "Henry (is) ill on July 28, 1940" and corresponding to the token of this A-sentence that occurs on July 29 there is "Henry (is) ill on July 29, 1940." Thus, if the date theory of A-sentences is to be refuted, it must be shown that the *relevant semantic features* of a given token of an A-sentence-type are different from those of the corresponding date-sentence-type. In this section I shall show that *the truth conditions* of a given A-sentence-token are different from those of its corresponding date-sentence-type and that this refutes both the old and new versions of the tenseless date-sentence theory. (1993, p. 33; emphasis added)

Clearly, Smith is assuming that the relevant semantic features of A-sentences are given in terms of their truth conditions. Therefore, he believes that to show that the truth conditions of A-sentences are not adequately represented on the date analysis is to demonstrate that the semantics for A-sentences is not what the date theory claims it to be, and vice versa. However, I think that if we keep the *metaphysics* (or meaning$_2$) of the date analysis of B-time distinct from the *semantics* (or meaning₄) of the date analysis of tensed language, then Smith's objection can be answered.

According to the date analysis, the A-sentence 'Henry is ill' as spoken by John on July 28, 1940, and the B-sentence 'Henry (is) ill on July 28, 1940' have the same (tenseless) truth conditions. That is, they are each true if and only if Henry (is) ill on July 28, 1940. Smith asserts that

> defenders of the new tenseless theory (such as Smart) will take [these claims] as showing that the date-sentences *suffice to give the truth conditions and thereby the meaning* of the A-sentence-tokens, from which it follows that these tokens convey no information about time not conveyed by the date-sentences. (1993, p. 35)

Smith then argues that the date analysis does not give the correct truth conditions of A-sentence tokens since, for example, 'The Battle of Waterloo is present' (call this '*U*'), uttered in 1814, does not have as a necessary (truth) condition that the Battle of Waterloo (call it '*E*') occurs in 1814. Suppose that '1814' refers to a date and we accept a relational view of time according to which a moment is a set of events simultaneous with a given event. Smith reasons that an 1814 utterance of *U* could be true (in the actual world), but that in some possible world its truth conditions sentence 'The Battle of Waterloo occurs in 1814' could be false. For, if a moment is defined as a set of events simultaneous with some given event, then there is some possible world (w_3) in which *U* and the Battle of Waterloo exist simultaneously (and thus a world where *U* is true), but in which *E* does not occur in 1814. For that reason, and contrary to what the date analysis asserts, *E*'s occurrence in 1814 is not a necessary condition of *U*'s truth.[6]

In a previous reply to this argument, I suggested that we could avoid Smith's criticism by world-indexing truth conditions (Oaklander 1994b). Thus, even if there is a possible world (w_3) where '1814*' denotes a time that contains both *U* and *E*, then the date-analysis truth condition that *the Battle of Waterloo occurs at 1814* in (w_3)* is necessary for the truth of *U* (in w_3). According to Smith, this way out fails since

> world-indexed truth conditions are insufficient to *give the meaning (semantic content) of tensed sentence-tokens. . . .* A truth condition sentence that gives . . . semantic content, or at least gives it up to logical equivalence, must state conditions that obtain in all and only the worlds in which this utterance is true, and

this can be done only in terms of truth conditions that are not world-indexed. (1994c, pp. 74, 75)

More recently, Smith has made the same point as follows:

Once truth conditions are world-indexed, they have no bearing or an accidental bearing on the meaning of the tensed-utterance. (1999, p. 237)

I think we can save the date analysis from *this* objection (recognizing that Smith has others) by distinguishing between linguistic meaning and reference meaning. Let us suppose that the meaning$_4$ of a tensed sentence type and all of its tokens must have a character that is the same in every possible world. That is, let us suppose that there is a common meaning$_4$ to all occurrences of a given A-sentence type regardless of when and where and in what world they occur. Admittedly, the common meaning of all tokens of an A-sentence type cannot be given by the ontological meaning$_2$ (or the date-analysis truth conditions), since the truth makers of A-sentence tokens (or what they state) are not constant, but vary depending on the time and world in which they occur. Thus, even if the linguistic meaning$_4$ of 'The Battle of Waterloo is present' is not world indexed, it does not follow that the truth conditions or truth makers of its tokens are not world indexed. To give the relevant semantic features of U (its meaning$_4$) is not to give its meaning$_2$. If these two notions of meaning are kept distinct, then Smith cannot infer that the *ontological* ground of A-sentences' being true cannot be represented by world-indexed B-sentences merely because the linguistic meaning$_4$ of A-sentences cannot be given in terms of them.

We can see where Smith's argument against the date-analysis account of truth conditions goes wrong in yet another, related way. Smith argues that world-indexing truth conditions do not give truth conditions in the proper semantic sense of 'truth conditions', for if it did,

then the utterance of 'Beth is waking up' at t in w states a truth in world w if and only if *it rains in Paris on June 1, 1914 in w*. Since the clause after the biconditional has no bearing on the meaning of the utterance of "Beth is waking up" at t in w, despite the logical equivalence stated in the biconditional, world-indexing the truth conditions prevents sentences stating truth conditions from explaining or having a relevant bearing on the statement whose truth conditions are given. These are not 'truth conditions' in the intended and proper semantic sense of 'truth conditions'. (1999, p. 237)

Again, there seem to be different senses of 'meaning' and 'truth conditions' at play here. Smith's claim that *it rains in Paris on June 1, 1914 in w* (call it 'P^*') does not state the truth conditions of 'Beth is waking up' at *t* in *w* (call it '*B*') is certainly correct if by 'truth conditions' he means truth makers or reference meanings$_2$. Clearly, the ground of the truth of 'Beth is waking up' at *t* in *w* is not *it rains in Paris on June 1, 1914 in w*. On the other hand, if by 'truth conditions' he means what Craig seems to mean by it, namely, necessary and sufficient conditions for truth, but not what makes a sentence true, then his claim that P^* does not state truth conditions for *B* is not true. Finally, if by 'truth conditions' he means the intentional meaning$_1$ of a sentence, then what he says is true since P^* does not capture the meaning$_1$ of B. All of these points are, however, compatible with the date-analysis claim that an utterance at *t* in *w* of 'Beth is waking up' has *Beth is waking up in t in w* as its meaning$_2$ or truth condition. I conclude, therefore, that if we distinguish the different senses of 'meaning', Smith's arguments against world-indexing date-analysis truth conditions can be refuted.

To sum up, if we distinguish the old B-theory of time from the old B-theory of language, we arrive at the new B-theory of time, or more simply, the *new theory*. According to the new theory, the need for tensed sentences and beliefs, while necessary in ordinary language and thought, does not imply the existence of tensed facts in the world. The new theory thus distinguishes two languages, one necessary for communication and timely action, and the other necessary for a correct description of temporal reality. The former requires tensed sentences; the latter eliminates them since in an ontologically perspicuous language where paradox is to be avoided, the sentences or propositions that represent temporal reality are B-sentences or B-propositions.

Of course, even if tensed sentences or sentences that contain temporal indexicals are eliminated from a language that reflects the metaphysical truth about time, they are ineliminable from the ordinary language that we use to talk about it. Thus, a detenser, no less than a tenser, must give an account of the meaning and reference of indexicals, and the relation of those topics to the metaphysical dispute between A- and B-theories of time. I shall turn to those tasks next.

8.5 The Meaning and Reference of Temporal Indexicals

In the debate over the meaning of temporal indexicals, we must distinguish the reference meaning$_2$ and the linguistic meaning$_4$ of an indexical, and consider the connection between them. The linguistic meaning of a word or phrase is a semantic function or rule of language that, as Kaplan puts it, "determines the content of an occurrence of a word or phrase in a given context" (1994, p. 129). According to Kaplan, one of the rules of use of an indexical is that it is, in each of its occurrences, directly referential. He believes that since 'now' refers to the date at which it is used, the content of a sentence containing an indexical varies with its context, and so does its truth value.

But why does the truth value of different tokens of 'It is raining now' vary with its context? Indeed, what is the ontological status of the context of utterance, and what is the truth condition determined by the context? These questions are closely related to each other and to the tenser-detenser debate. For, if the context of utterance of a sentence containing an indexical is a tensed time, for example, a time that exemplifies *presentness*, then the reason why the truth value of tokens of sentences containing indexicals changes is that the events they are about undergo temporal becoming. And if the meaning$_4$ or rule of use of temporal indexicals is not simply to directly refer to a time, but also to characterize that time as being present, then the truth condition determined by the tensed context will be an A-fact. On the other hand, if the context of utterance is a tenseless date, then the meaning$_4$ of a temporal indexical is directly referential and the truth condition$_3$ of the sentence containing it is a B-fact.

How then do we determine whether the context is tensed or tenseless, and hence whether or not the meaning$_4$ of sentences containing indexicals entails tensed or tenseless truth conditions? It does not seem to me that one can arrive at the correct account of the meaning$_2$ of tensed sentences via the philosophy of language alone since if the metaphysics of a particular linguistic analysis is irremediably flawed, then the analysis is mistaken, and that is not what we mean. Thus, if it turns out, as I believe it does, that the tensed theory is false because it leads to contradictions or other problematic results, then the ascription of tensed properties to dates is not part of the meaning$_2$ of temporal indexicals. Still, I think it is worthwhile to consider one argument for the claim that temporal indexicals are used both to refer to a time and also to attribute *presentness* to that time. To do so will lend support to the new theory date analysis of the meaning$_2$ of tensed sentences and reveal once again how the failure to keep different notions of meaning separate can lead to trouble.

Smith has argued that "the direct reference theory of indexicals according to which indexicals do not refer to items indirectly via a sense, . . . [but] are supposed to refer directly to times, is based on some genuine insights" (1994e, p. 136), but needs to be revised. The revision consists in introducing a sense into the content of temporal indexicals— specifically, the sense of 'is present' or 'has presentness'. Smith's argument for that claim is that unless we introduce the sense of 'is present' into the content of a temporal indexical, we cannot account for entailment relations between sentences containing a temporal indexical and sentences not containing one.

Smith claims that a case in point is the entailment of

(5) The meeting is starting

by

(6) The meeting starts now.

Smith says that (5) contains a present-tensed copula, but no temporal indexical (1994e, p. 141). Thus, the proposition expressed by (5) has "a constant semantic content the same on each occasion of its use" (1994e, p. 141), whereas the proposition expressed by (6) has a variable semantic content (1994e, p. 142). What, then, is the proposition expressed by (5)? On Smith's view, (5) expresses the proposition "that the meeting has the property of starting and that its having of this property *has presentness*. Whenever (5) is uttered it expresses this semantic content" (1994e, p. 142). Given this account of the semantic content of (5), Smith argues that in order to account for the inference of (5) by (6), we must attribute the sense of 'has presentness' to the time denoted by 'now' in (6). It seems to me, however, that we do not need to introduce presentness into the content of temporal indexicals to account for the entailment of (5) by (6) since contrary to what he says, and in accordance with his own analysis elsewhere, present-tensed sentences *do* involve temporal indexicals.

Smith argues that (5) ('The meeting is starting') "contains a present-tensed copula, but no temporal indexical" (1994e, p. 141). Prima facie this is an implausible view. If the copula is present tensed, as opposed to past or future tensed, or tenseless, then it can also be expressed as 'is now'. In that case, however, 'The meeting is now starting' and 'The meeting starts now' would certainly have the same meaning, and the same truth conditions and the entailment would hold without having to postulate an additional sense to the referent of 'now'.

Suppose, however, that Smith is correct and the present-tensed sentence 'The meeting is starting' is indexical free. Let us suppose further that, as Smith says, the semantic content of (5) is "that the meeting has the property of starting and that its *having* of this property *has presentness*" (1994e, p. 142). The problem with introducing presentness into the inherence of presentness is that such a move reintroduces an indexical element into the proposition expressed by any token of 'The meeting is starting'. In discussing the infinite regress of temporal attributions (in the context of McTaggart's paradox), Smith says, "[T]he complete *analysans* of the present-tensed sentence '*E* is present' ... conveys the information that *E* is *now* present rather than *was* or *will be* present" (1994f, p. 185). If, however, the present-tensed sentence '*E* is present' conveys the same information that '*E* is now present' conveys, then mustn't the present-tensed sentence 'The meeting is starting' convey the same information that 'The meeting is now starting' conveys? But then, of course, (5) does contain an indexical and Smith's argument that (5) is not entailed by (6) collapses. For clearly, 'The meeting is now starting' and 'The meeting starts now' have the same date-analysis truth conditions and thus (5) is entailed by (6) without the assumption that 'now' in (6) refers to a date and also ascribes presentness to that date.

Finally, Smith's claim that (5) has a constant semantic content whereas (6) has a variable semantic content does not give credence to the thesis that temporal indexicals express senses that characterize moments as present either, since that claim equivocates on the notion of "semantic content." It is true that (5) has a constant semantic content, in that its linguistic meaning$_4$ is always the same; and it is true that (6) has a variable semantic content, in that its reference meaning$_2$ always varies over time. It does not follow, however, that (5) and (6) differ with respect to either their meaning$_4$ or their meaning$_2$, or that the inference from (6) to (5) requires the ascription of presentness to the referent of 'now'.

Undoubtedly, work in the philosophy of language and particularly in the areas of tensed discourse and temporal indexicals is necessary to complete an analysis of B-time. For even if tensed discourse does not accurately reflect the nature of temporal reality, it is meaningful and the detenser must be able to explicate what it means. But we cannot arrive at the philosophical truth concerning time by an analysis of the meaning$_4$ (or the meaning$_1$) of ordinary temporal language. As Smith has correctly noted, whether the direct reference theory is true "depends on whether the tenseless theory is true" and "if the tensed theory of time is true and uses of 'now' ascribe the property of presentness, then the New Theory of Reference is false" (1994a, p. 12). We are thus led back to the question with which this chapter began: namely, do events really pass through time as the A-theory maintains, or does ordinary temporal language systematically mislead us into believing in the myth of passage, as the B-theory asserts? Although I am a critic of the tensed theory and a staunch advocate of the tenseless theory, a full account of my reasons for rejecting the former and adhering to the latter is clearly a project that lies outside the scope of this chapter. What does not lie outside its scope is another objection to the B-theory that will lead to a newer version of the B-theory of language.

8.6   A Newer Version of the B-Theory of Language

Murray MacBeath (1994, p. 309) claims that the feeling of gladness expressed by a father who says to his daughter, 'Thank goodness I'm never going to sit another examination', exhibits intentionality; it is about something. According to MacBeath, the father is glad about the "intentional fact" that he is never going to sit another examination again, or more simply that a certain event is (forever) past. The new B-theorist maintains that the "intentional fact" is not a tensed fact and does not actually exist at all, for though the situation implies that the *belief* about the intentional fact is irreducibly tensed, the fact that makes the belief true is tenseless.

My concern is with the ontological status, if any, of the "intentional fact" or the intentional object that a tensed belief is about as well as with the tensed belief itself. Clearly, the intentional object of the tensed belief 'X is past' is different from the intentional object of the tenseless belief 'X occurs at t_1' or 'X occurs earlier than t_3'. How is this difference in intentional meaning$_1$ accounted for?

Suppose one maintains, as I believe Mellor does, that the intentional object of a tensed belief is not an A-fact, but an A-proposition. Thus, when I believe (or think) that X is past, what my thought or belief is about, what it means, its intentional object is the A-proposition, X is past. The proposition, the sentence that expresses it, and the belief about it are all made true by the existence of a B-fact. For that reason, we can explain how it *seems* that we are relieved about an A-fact when all that exists are B-facts. As Mellor puts it:

> Being glad has a propositional content, in this case the A-proposition that my pain is past, which differs from the proposition that I believe my pain is past. And it is the former proposition, not the latter, which must be true at t for my gladness at t to be well founded. But the A-proposition can still be made true at t, and hence my gladness well founded, by the B-fact that my pain is earlier than t. (1998, p. 41)

What follows is a difficulty I see with this account.

The meaning of a tensed sentence is an A-proposition, so to know what a tensed sentence or tensed belief means is to intend an A-proposition. The meaning of A-sentences (and A-beliefs) is a function (what Mellor calls a 'tc-function') from the time of their occurrence to their truth conditions at that time. To know what an A-sentence means is to be able to understand and be able to use an A-sentence properly. We can do that if we know that "for any B-place s and B-time t, 's is here' is true at and only at s, and 'It is now t' is true at and only at t" (Mellor 1998, p. 60).

That is all well and good. The difference in meaning$_4$ between A- and B-sentences is accounted for without positing A-facts, for A- and B-sentences have different meanings in virtue of having different rules of use, but not in virtue of having different truth conditions or corresponding to different kinds of facts. But if an A-proposition were the meaning of an A-sentence or A-belief, then it would follow that an A-proposition is the meaning given by the tc-function for an A-sentence. There is, however, something amiss here. What we believe when we believe that X is past is not the linguistic meaning$_4$ or rule of use for an A-sentence. Thus, there seems to be some aspect of meaning$_1$ (cognitive significance?) that is not captured by distinguishing tensed and tenseless sentences and beliefs by means of a difference in their (Kaplan-type) character.

In other words, there is a difference in cognitive or intentional meaning$_1$ between believing that X is now and believing that X occurs at t (even if the thought that X is now occurs at t); they seem to have different contents or intentional objects. However, that difference is not the same as the difference in linguistic meaning reflected in the different tc-functions of the tensed and tenseless sentences or the beliefs that they express. Since, on the B-theory, the content, in Kaplan's sense, is a tenseless content, so that the tensed belief's meaning$_2$ is a B-fact, there seems to be nothing on the side of the subject that accounts for the A-belief's being about or intending the tensed content, namely, that X is past. The fact that the linguistic meaning$_4$ of the A-belief is different from that of a B-belief is not sufficient to account for the difference in intentional meaning between the two kinds of beliefs. What more is needed to account for the intentional meaning of an A-belief is something on the side of the *subject* that is irreducibly tensed. Without such an account, the new B-theory explanation of the meaning$_1$ of irreducibly tensed beliefs seems to leave something out.

Thus, the following questions arise: What does capture the differences in the intentional meaning of A- and B-beliefs? What makes an A-belief intrinsically or irreducibly tensed? In virtue of what does an A-belief mean or intend what seems to be an A-fact, but is not a fact at all? Does the irreducibly tensed belief imply some irreducibly tensed constituent *in* the belief that accounts for the belief's intending what seems to be an A-fact? If not, how is one to account for irreducible A-beliefs' being about or intending what appear to be irreducible A-facts? If there is a tensed element in the A-belief, then is the B-theorist forced to hold that tense is subjective in a way that compromises the commitment to an ontology of time that countenances only temporal relations?

These questions do pose a challenge to B-theorists, and in this chapter I shall attempt to do no more than suggest the outlines of a possible response to them. One possible way of answering these questions begins by distinguishing the intentional "relation" (and intentional meaning$_1$) from the correspondence relation (and reference meaning$_2$). The intentional meaning of an A-sentence or belief is the subjective tensed content that (together with a property such as being a perceiving or being a remembering) is contained in a conscious mental state or "mental act." A belief is irreducibly tensed not only because it does not have the same meaning$_4$ as a B-sentence, but also because it has a certain *content*. A content is a *natural sign* of its object.[7] That is, a content, in virtue of being the kind of entity that it is, stands in the intentional relation to just this certain object. Thus, contents are intrinsically intentional meanings$_1$ of A-sentences. To say that contents are "intrinsically intentional" is to say that they are natural signs of some thing or fact other than themselves. Since, however, there are no A-facts, when I am thinking that *A* is present, what I am thinking about does not exist. Thus, intentionality is an abnormal relation that, in this case, connects what does exist—the subjective tensed content—with what does not exist, an A-fact that has no ontological status whatsoever.[8] The reference meaning$_2$ of a sentence is, on the other hand, the fact or state of affairs that obtains if the content expressed by the sentence is true, that is, if what the content represents, intends, or is about, exists.

Recall that the problem for the new theory is to explain how what is asserted by the A-belief that, say, *X* is past can be genuinely (irreducibly) tensed and so be about an A-fact that does not exist, while claiming that the irreducible A-belief is *true* in virtue of corresponding to a B-fact that does exist. The newer version of the B-theory attempts to answer that question (or rather, avoid it), while remaining consistent with a B-theoretic ontology. However, to do so requires taking the radical step of denying that A-sentences and A-beliefs are true. Let me explain.

According to the newer B-theory of language, A-sentences express subjective contents that are their intentional meaning$_1$ and are what accounts for the representative character (i.e., the aboutness) of thought. Furthermore, contents are the primary bearer of truth and falsity, whereas sentence tokens understood as physical objects are only derivatively so. Since, however, there are no tensed facts that would make A-contents true, they are, literally and metaphysically, false. Thus, A-sentences have an intentional meaning$_1$, but they do not have a reference meaning$_2$ since, given considerations resulting from McTaggart's paradox, there are no A-facts, nor could there be any A-facts, that contents would correspond to so as to make them true.[9] Nevertheless, our having A-beliefs with tensed contents is pragmatically useful in enabling us to get along in the world. They are useful even though they do not correspond to any tensed facts because they are typically caused by B-facts and when they are so caused, tensed thoughts are the basis for timely action and appropriate emotions. I think we can best clarify this newer version of the B-theory of language by seeing how it would deal with some of the objections to the new B-theory that have not yet been considered.

In his most recent book on the tensed theory of time, Craig (2000, p. 91) discusses what he calls 'Mellor's Indexed B-Theory of Language'. His main objection against Mellor's indexed theory, which is nothing other than the date analysis, is that it does not supply truth conditions or truth makers for tensed sentence types or tokens *simpliciter*, such as 'Jim races tomorrow', but only for A-sentences at a time, such as 'Jim races tomorrow' said at t_1. Craig states his objection as follows:

> We want to know, not what makes *Jim races tomorrow* true at June 1, but what makes it true that *Jim races tomorrow* or that *Jim is racing*. If tensed sentence types need truth makers, then we need tensed facts as the truth makers of such tensed sentence types. For if there are no tensed truth makers then it is inexplicable why *P* is true—not true at *t*, mind you, but simply true. (2000, pp. 95–96)

The response to this argument is that it begs the question against the view I am putting forth since it assumes that the A-belief 'Jim is racing' (call it '*P*') is true.[10] On the newer B-theory of language, however, *P* is false since there are no tensed truth makers. Since the content *C* expressed by *P* (its intentional meaning$_1$) is part of a conscious state that occurs at a time *t*, what is true is that the conscious state including *C* occurs at *t*, but what makes that true is a B-fact. And if 'Jim is (tense-lessly) racing' is true, then what makes the content expressed by that sentence true is a B-fact. And if 'Jim is (tenselessly) racing later than the time at which I have a tensed belief' is true, then what is stated—the subjective content—also means$_2$ a B-fact. However, none of those B-facts are the truth makers of 'Jim is (now) racing' or 'Jim is racing tomorrow' since these A-beliefs and the mind-dependent tensed contents they express are necessarily false because they are about tensed facts and there are none and there logically couldn't be any, or so B-theorists typically maintain.[11] For that reason, it is no objection to the B-theory that it is inexplicable why 'Jim is racing' is true, because it is not true and so there is nothing to explicate.[12]

An analogous response would follow if Craig criticized the B-theory of language along the lines of his criticism of Butterfield 1985. To avoid the problem that the token-reflexive account faces in explaining the meaning$_2$ of the proposition *There are no tokens now*, Butterfield countenances tensed propositions that he believes can be given tenseless truth conditions. Craig argues, however, that "if the tense of a sentence is part of its propositional content, then does not a view of truth as correspondence imply that reality is tensed?" (2000, p. 85). My answer to Craig's rhetorical question is no. Since the intentional meaning of a tensed sentence is not a *true* proposition expressed by the sentence, but rather, on the version of the new theory suggested here, a false mind-dependent tensed proposition or subjective content, there is no need or possibility that it corresponds to a reality that is tensed because there are no tensed facts.

It is frequently argued, on the basis of Prior's "thank goodness argument," that the B-theory cannot account for what we are believing when we believe that a given event is past, or analogously when we know that a given event is present, or happening now. The traditional new theory claims that there are no tensed facts, but there are irreducibly tensed beliefs such as 'It is now raining' or 'It was a painful experience' that are true in virtue of B-facts. The view I am proposing agrees with the traditional new theory that there are just B-facts, but disagrees that the meaning$_1$ of a tensed belief, which accounts for its cognitive significance, is adequately explained by appealing to the difference in linguistic meaning$_4$ between an A-belief and a B-belief. What makes a belief irreducibly tensed is the intentional content contained within it. And there is nothing that makes it true, but something that causes it, namely, a certain set of B-facts. Thus, arguments from cognitive significance can be accommodated on the newer B-theory since our beliefs about past and present experiences and events are based on irreducibly tensed beliefs, with tensed contents. Since, however, those beliefs are false, the B-theoretic ontology remains intact.

Finally, it may be objected that if the existence of mind-dependent tensed propositions or subjective contents is indispensable to explain timely actions and our experience of the present, then those propositions or contents must be true and so they must correspond to something tensed that exists in reality. After all, if tensed beliefs are one and all false, why then do we act as if they are true? If they are false, why are they also indispensable? The implication is that if tensed beliefs are in-dispensable, it must be because there are tensed facts to which they cor-respond, and that if we ignore these facts, then we are incapable of navigating our way around in the world. I think that there are two ways of responding to this objection. First, one may grab the bull by the horns and argue that tensed beliefs are indispensable, but the causal connection between tensed beliefs and B-events (including tenseless thoughts) is sufficient to explain our timely actions. Second, one may question the assumption that tensed thoughts and beliefs are indispensable.[13] Of course, to say that tensed beliefs are dispensable does not mean that we can translate A-beliefs by means of B-sentences. We cannot do that for reasons we have already discussed. Nevertheless, the existence of token-reflexive meanings$_2$ may be sufficient for timely action even if there are no tensed contents or facts. Thus, a sufficient condition for my getting to a 1 p.m. meeting on time could be the B-facts that I am (tenselessly) conscious that "this perception" (which is included in my total mental state) of the clock striking 1 p.m. is occurring at roughly the same time as the striking of the clock and that is sufficient for me to get up and go to a 1 p.m. meeting. Or, if I am conscious that "this memory" is later than my very last examination, then I will be relieved that I will never have to take another examination again. Thus, while A-beliefs are useful in helping us keep our appointments and generating certain useful psycho-logical attitudes, since they have a causal connection to B-events in the world, they are not necessary, since our consciousness of certain B-facts is sufficient to explain our different psychological attitudes and our timely behavior.

Of course, a critic may object that the introduction of the indexical 'this' into the intentional meaning₁ reintroduces tense into the content and that would undermine any attempt to render tensed beliefs dispensable. Ludlow expresses this point in the following passage:

Still more perplexing for the B-theorist, the indexical element in 'this utterance' looks an awful lot like a temporal indexical predicate.... It looks for all the world as if the extra indexical element just means *now*, and as if the expression 'this utterance' means something akin to 'the utterance happening now'! (1999, p. 90)

I don't agree that 'this perception' means₁ 'the perception that I am having now'. 'This' simply refers to the perception directly without attributing any property of *presentness* to it. Thus, token-reflexive conditions are needed to know when it is time to act, but once they are introduced, not as truth conditions, but as pragmatic conditions, they enable us to dispense with the need for mind-dependent tensed propositions or contents, or at least to dispense with the need for tensed facts to explain why we have tensed beliefs.

8.7   Conclusion

It should be clear how and why the new theory of B-time that I am suggesting differs from that propounded by other new theorists. Smith explains the thesis of the original version of the new theory of time as follows:

The new tenseless theory of time ... as espoused by Smart, Mellor, MacBeath, and others, is based on the thesis that the tensed theory of time is false *on the grounds that the truth conditions of ordinary A-sentences and their tokens can be stated in a tenseless metalanguage*; that is, it is the theory that tenseless truth condition sentences provide a "logically adequate representation of ordinary temporal language" and therefore that the tenseless theory of time is true. (1993, p. 13)

The version of the new theory put forth here differs from its predecessors in that my grounds for believing that the tensed theory is false is that the A-sentences that allegedly represent or have a tensed ontological meaning are false because of the logical paradoxes that can be generated from tensed ascriptions of properties. Furthermore, I do not agree that the B-theory is true because B-sentences can give the complete meaning of A-sentences. On the new theory as I conceive it, no tenseless sentence can state all the truth conditions, that is, give the complete "meaning" of a tensed sentence. A-theorists such as Smith conclude that the B-theory is false. However, just because no B-sentence type or token gives *all* the truth conditions (read 'meanings') of an A-sentence type or token, it does not follow that no B-sentence truth conditions sentence can state *one* of the conditions of an A-sentence. Indeed, a tenseless sentence can state the most important condition of a tensed sentence, namely, its pragmatic condition that accounts for why A-sentences and -beliefs are useful. A-beliefs, although they are false, are generally useful in getting us to act in an appropriate manner when the event believed to be past, present, or future exemplifies the B-relation of earlier than, simultaneous with, or later than to the time at which it is remembered, perceived, or anticipated. Perhaps A-beliefs are even dispensable, for if we are conscious that certain token-reflexive conditions obtain, then that would be sufficient to cause us to engage in timely actions. Thus, as I said at the outset, the difference between the versions of the new B-theory of language that I have discussed is methodological and not ontological. Concerning matters that matter, there is no difference between the new theory of B-language and my newer theory.

Notes

Earlier versions of this chapter were read at the Philosophy of Time Society meetings in Boston, on December 27, 1994, and December 27, 1999. I have benefited greatly from the comments of, and discussions with, Laird Addis, Heather Dyke, Ronald C. Hoy, Robin Le Poidevin, Joshua Mosersky, and Quentin Smith. I also wish to thank the University of Michigan-Flint for funding in support of the research for this chapter.

1. This method takes different forms and yields different results depending on whether by 'sentence' is meant a sentence token (Mellor 1981; Oaklander 1994c; Smart 1980; Smith 1993), a sentence type (Paul 1997), or what is asserted or the proposition expressed by a sentence token (Beer 1994, 2001; Craig 1996b, 2000; Smith 1999). Dyke (2002b, 2003) and Le Poidevin (1998 and chapter 9 of this book) draw a distinction between meaning (of tensed sentence types) and truth conditions (of tensed sentence tokens), but are still firmly within the camp of the new B-theory of language. Craig argues (2000, pp. 91–96) that for Mellor (1998), sentence types are the bearers of truth value and have truth conditions. It is, however, not clear to me that this is so since Mellor claims that A-propositions

(and not sentence types) are true and false and that true A-propositions have B-facts as their truth makers. B-theorists such as Smart (1980, p. 15) and Le Poidevin (1998, p. 29) claim that their method is consistent with Davidson's (1967) project. Peter Ludlow (1999) explains and pursues an "absolute truth-conditional semantics" derived from Davidson. For a critique of Ludlow's presentist semantics, see Oaklander 2002b.

2. This is somewhat of an overstatement since there are disagreements among B-theorists concerning whether or not temporal relations are definable in terms of causal relations, and over whether temporal relational facts such as *A is earlier than B* are in time or nontemporal. My overall point does, however, hold.

3. In correspondence, Le Poidevin has indicated that what he meant is that truth conditions are necessary and sufficient and not only necessary conditions. I include this quotation from him merely to indicate how easy it is to slide into different interpretations of this term of art.

4. This point does not bar token-reflexive or date-analysis truth conditions from being necessary and sufficient conditions for certain B-sentences' (or what they express) being true.

5. For discussion of this argument, see Smith 1993, 1994a,c, 1999. Smith's arguments against the token-reflexive analysis are criticized in Paul 1997; Dyke 2002b, 2003; Le Poidevin 1998 and chapter 9 of this book; and Mosersky 2000. For responses to Paul 1997, see Smith 1999 and Craig 1999.

6. For a criticism of Smith's argument, see Tooley 2001, pp. 49–54.

7. For an extensive defense of the theory of contents as natural signs, see Addis 1989, 2000.

8. For a discussion and defense of the existence of "abnormal relations" like intentionality, see Reinhardt Grossmann 1984, 1992.

9. For arguments, based on McTaggart's paradox, against the existence of A-facts, see my essays in Oaklander and Smith 1994, pt. II, and see Oaklander 1994a, 1996, 1999, 2002a,b. See also Mellor 1998, Dyke 2002a, Le Poidevin 1991, and Smart 1980.

10. Mellor may object to Craig's argument by asking, On what basis can Craig say that 'Jim races tomorrow' is true? Either he means a *token* of this sentence, in which case the truth conditions *are* for 'Jim races tomorrow' said at *t*, or he means the *type*, in which case it is neither true nor false and so strictly speaking has no truth conditions. Joshua Mosersky pointed out this objection to me.

11. I say "typically" because there are dissenters. Josh Parsons (2002) is a "card-carrying B-theorist" who maintains that McTaggart's paradox does not render A-properties and tensed facts incoherent, and other B-theorists reject A-properties on the grounds that they have no idea (because they don't experience) what A-properties could be (Addis 1975).

12. One may argue that there is something to explicate, namely, the "semantic content" of mind-dependent tensed propositions or contents. I confess that I am

not sure what to say here. The most recent and elaborate A-theory of the content of A-beliefs or the thoughts they express is contained in Ludlow 1999. Another, equally sophisticated account is found in Smith 1993. According to Smith, the A-belief 'Jim is racing' expresses the proposition that the event of Jim's racing exemplifies *presentness*. There is also Tooley's (1997) account of "tensed" propositions, among many others. Perhaps if tensed contents are not dispensable (although I argue below that they are), then some account of what makes them "tensed" (over and above the fact that they represent (falsely) tensed facts) is needed. Since, however, it seems to me that all accounts of tensed reality are logically false, the particular analysis of the precise content of A-thoughts or -beliefs does not, after all, seem to be that important a question for a B-theorist to answer.

13. This assumption has also been questioned in Hoy 1989.

References

Addis, L. 1975. Time and Method. Ms., University of Iowa.

Addis, L. 1989. *Natural Signs: A Theory of Intentionality*. Philadelphia: Temple University Press.

Addis, L. 2000. The Simplicity of Content. *Metaphysica, International Journal for Ontology and Metaphysics* 1, pp. 23–43.

Beer, M. 1994. Temporal Indexicals and the Passage of Time. In L. N. Oaklander and Q. Smith, eds., *The New Theory of Time*, pp. 87–93. New Haven, Conn.: Yale University Press.

Beer, M. 2001. Tenseless Date-Sentences and the Truth Conditions of Tensed Propositions. Paper presented at the Central Division Meetings of the Philosophy of Time Society, Minneapolis, Minn.

Broad, C. D. 1921. Time. In J. Hastings, ed., *Encyclopedia of Religion and Ethics*, pp. 334–45. New York: Scribner.

Broad, C. D. 1923. *Scientific Thought*. London: Routledge and Kegan Paul. Reprinted New York: Humanities Press, 1969.

Broad, C. D. 1938. *An Examination of McTaggart's Philosophy*. 2 vol. Cambridge: Cambridge University Press. Reprinted New York: Octagon Books, 1976.

Butterfield, J. 1985. Indexicals and Tense. In I. Hacking, ed., *Exercises in Analysis*, pp. 69–87. Cambridge: Cambridge University Press.

Craig, W. L. 1996a. The New B-Theory's *Tu Quoque* Argument. *Synthese* 107, pp. 249–69.

Craig, W. L. 1996b. Tense and the New B-Theory of Language. *Philosophy* 71, pp. 5–26.

Craig, W. L. 1999. On Truth Conditions of Tensed Sentence Types. *Synthese* 120, pp. 265–70.

Craig, W. L. 2000. *The Tensed Theory of Time: A Critical Examination*. Dordrecht: Kluwer.

Davidson, D. 1967. Truth and Meaning. *Synthese* 17, pp. 304–23.

Dyke, H. 2002a. McTaggart's Paradox and the Truth about Time. In C. Callender, ed., *Time, Experience and Reality*, pp. 137–52. Cambridge: Cambridge University Press.

Dyke, H. 2002b. Tokens, Dates and Tenseless Truth Conditions. *Synthese* 131, pp. 329–51.

Dyke, H. 2003. Tensed Meaning: A Tenseless Account. *Journal of Philosophical Research* 27, pp. 67–83.

Goodman, N. 1951. *The Structure of Appearance*. Indianapolis, Ind.: Bobbs Merrill.

Grossmann, R. 1984. Nonexistent Objects versus Definite Descriptions. *Australasian Journal of Philosophy* 62, pp. 363–77.

Grossmann, R. 1992. *The Existence of the World: An Introduction to Ontology*. London: Routledge.

Grünbaum, A. 1967. The Status of Temporal Becoming. In *Modern Science and Zeno's Paradoxes*, pp. 7–36. Middleton, Conn.: Wesleyan University Press.

Hoy, R. C. 1989. How to Dispense with Tense. Ms., California University of Pennsylvania.

Kaplan, D. 1994. Demonstratives. In L. N. Oaklander and Q. Smith, eds., *The New Theory of Time*, pp. 115–35. New Haven, Conn.: Yale University Press.

Le Poidevin, R. 1991. *Change, Cause and Contradiction: A Defense of the Tenseless Theory of Time*. New York: St. Martin's Press.

Le Poidevin, R. 1998. The Past, Present, and Future of the Debate about Tense. In R. Le Poidevin, ed., *Questions of Time and Tense*, pp. 13–42. Oxford: Clarendon Press.

Le Poidevin, R. 1999. Can Beliefs Be Caused by Their Truth-Makers? *Analysis* 59, pp. 148–56.

Ludlow, P. 1999. *Semantics, Tense, and Time: An Essay in the Metaphysics of Natural Language*. Cambridge, Mass.: MIT Press.

MacBeath, M. 1994. Mellor's Emeritus Headache. In L. N. Oaklander and Q. Smith, eds., *The New Theory of Time*, pp. 305–11. New Haven, Conn.: Yale University Press.

McCall, S. 1994. *A Model of the Universe*. Oxford: Clarendon Press.

Mellor, D. H. 1981. *Real Time*. Cambridge: Cambridge University Press.

Mellor, D. H. 1998. *Real Time II*. London: Routledge.

Mosersky, J. M. 2000. Tense and Temporal Semantics. *Synthese* 124, pp. 257–79.

Nerlich, G. 1998. Time as Spacetime. In R. Le Poidevin, ed., *Questions of Time and Tense*, pp. 119–34. Oxford: Clarendon Press.

Oaklander, L. N. 1984. *Temporal Relations and Temporal Becoming: A Defense of a Russellian Theory of Time*. Lanham, Md.: University Press of America.

Oaklander, L. N. 1994a. Bigelow, Possible Worlds and the Passage of Time. *Analysis* 54, pp. 244–48.

Oaklander, L. N. 1994b. A Defense of the New Tenseless Theory of Time. In L. N. Oaklander and Q. Smith, eds., *The New Theory of Time*, pp. 57–68. New Haven, Conn.: Yale University Press.

Oaklander, L. N. 1994c. The New Tenseless Theory of Time: A Reply to Smith. In L. N. Oaklander and Q. Smith, eds., *The New Theory of Time*, pp. 77–82. New Haven, Conn.: Yale University Press.

Oaklander, L. N. 1996. McTaggart's Paradox and Smith's Tensed Theory of Time. *Synthese* 107, pp. 205–21.

Oaklander, L. N. 1999. Craig on McTaggart's Paradox and the Problem of Temporary Intrinsics. *Analysis* 59, pp. 314–18.

Oaklander, L. N. 2002. Presentism, Ontology and Experience. In C. Callender ed., *Time, Reality and Experience*, pp. 73–90. Cambridge: Cambridge University Press.

Oaklander, L. N. 2003. Presentism: A Critique. In H. Lillehammer and G. R. Pereyra, eds., *Real Metaphysics: Essays in Honour of D. H. Mellor, with His Replies*, pp. 196–211. London: Routledge.

Oaklander, L. N., and Q. Smith, eds. 1994. *The New Theory of Time*. New Haven, Conn.: Yale University Press.

Parsons, J. 2002, A-Theory for B-Theorists. *The Philosophical Quarterly* 52, 206, pp. 1–20.

Paul, L. A. 1997. Truth Conditions of Tensed Sentence Types. *Synthese* 111, pp. 53–71.

Russell, B. 1915. On the Experience of Time. *Monist* 25, pp. 212–33.

Schlesinger, G. 1980. *Aspects of Time*. Indianapolis, Ind.: Hackett.

Smart, J. J. C. 1963. *Philosophy and Scientific Realism*. London: Routledge and Kegan Paul.

Smart, J. J. C. 1980. Time and Becoming. In P. van Inwagen, ed., *Time and Cause: Essays in Honor of Richard Taylor*, pp. 3–15. Boston: Reidel.

Smith, Q. 1993. *Language and Time*. New York: Oxford University Press.

Smith, Q. 1994a. General Introduction: The Implications of the Tensed and Tenseless Theories of Time. In L. N. Oaklander and Q. Smith, eds., *The New Theory of Time*, pp. 1–14. New Haven, Conn.: Yale University Press.

Smith, Q. 1994b. Problems with the New Tenseless Theory of Time. In L. N. Oaklander and Q. Smith, eds., *The New Theory of Time*, pp. 38–56. New Haven, Conn.: Yale University Press.

Smith, Q. 1994c. The Truth Conditions of Tensed Sentences. In L. N. Oaklander and Q. Smith, eds., *The New Theory of Time*, pp. 69–76. New Haven, Conn.: Yale University Press.

Smith, Q. 1994d. Smart and Mellor's New Tenseless Theory of Time: A Reply to Oaklander. In L. N. Oaklander and Q. Smith, eds., *The New Theory of Time*, pp. 83–86. New Haven, Conn.: Yale University Press.

Smith, Q. 1994e. Temporal Indexicals. In L. N. Oaklander and Q. Smith, eds., *The New Theory of Time*, pp. 136–53. New Haven, Conn.: Yale University Press.

Smith, Q. 1994f. The Infinite Regress of Temporal Attributions. In L. N. Oaklander and Q. Smith, eds., *The New Theory of Time*, pp. 180–94. New Haven, Conn.: Yale University Press.

Smith, Q. 1999. The 'Sentence-Type Version' of the Tenseless Theory of Time. *Synthese* 119, pp. 233–51.

Tooley, M. 1997. *Time, Tense, and Causation*. Oxford: Clarendon Press.

Tooley, M. 2001. Response to the Comments on *Time, Tense and Causation* by Storrs McCall, Nathan Oaklander and Quentin Smith. In L. N. Oaklander, ed., *The Importance of Time: Proceedings of the Philosophy of Time Society, 1995–2000*, pp. 31–58. Dordrecht: Kluwer.

Williams, D. C. 1951. The Myth of Passage. *Journal of Philosophy* 48, pp. 457–72.

9

Why Tenses Need Real Times

Robin Le Poidevin

9.1 Four Theories concerning the Truth Conditions of Tensed Statements

What do I mean when I say that tenses need real times? I mean, in part, that times must feature in the truth conditions for tensed token sentences and cannot be replaced for this purpose by temporal relations. So, I shall argue, the truth value of 'The score is now 15/30' is partly determined by the time at which it is tokened.

But what kind of times are involved here? There are two possibilities. According to the first, times are *tensed*: they are, in some nonrelational sense, past, present, or future. According to the second, they are *tenseless*: they are ordered by the later-than relation, and a time is, say, past only in relation to other, later times. The difference is that an event that occupies a tenseless time occupies it permanently, so that, for example, if it is now true that a comet passed near the earth in 1997, then it is an unchanging feature of that event that it occurred, or rather occurs,[1] in 1997. In contrast, this same event occupies a tensed time only transiently. As I write, the event in question occupies the present, but it will come to occupy the past. At least, that is how (at least some) tensed theorists would put it. One of the conclusions of the chapter is that the times needed by tenses are tenseless times, and my argument for this involves considerations concerning causation.

These causal considerations have a bearing on another issue: the reductionist/realist debate over whether times are constructions from their contents (events, states of affairs, facts, or whatever) or are logically independent of those contents. What times are not, I shall argue, are sets of simultaneous events.

This chapter, then, is concerned with three questions: Do times enter into the truth conditions of tensed token sentences? If so, are these tenseless times? If so, do we need to be realists about them? My answer to all three questions is yes. Thus, (statements involving) tenses need (as a component of their truth conditions) real (and tenseless) times.

My first task is to engage in a piece of conceptual geography. I must apologize for this, since it requires the reader to make the effort of orchestrating a variety of ideas without getting any sense of argumentative progress, and the effect of this can be somewhat frustrating. But, by introducing the main players at an early stage, I hope to make subsequent discussion a little less convoluted. What follows are four theories concerning the truth conditions of tensed tokens.

9.1.1   The Basic Tensed Theory

According to the tensed theory of time, tensed token sentences (hereafter 'tensed tokens', or sometimes simply 'tokens') are made true by tensed facts. The simplest schema, which characterizes what I shall call the *basic* tensed theory, is this:

Any token of '*e* is occurring now' is true if and only if *e* is present.

There is a substantial metaphysical issue over whether presentness should be seen as a monadic property of events. Tensed theorists, following Arthur Prior (1968), have tended to be wary of treating presentness in this way, so I shall not present the basic view as committed to it. For present purposes, the basic theory has these implications: that the truth value of a given token is independent of that token's location in time, that its truth conditions do not involve the token itself, that its truth conditions may obtain at some times and not others, and that, in consequence, its truth value may vary over time.[2]

Nothing in this formulation suggests that we need to quantify over times, tensed or otherwise. We are not obliged, for example, to construe 'is present' as 'is in the present moment'. Those who espouse the theory, however, owe an account of what sorts of things we do need to quantify over.

9.1.2 The Token-Reflexive Theory

This is the first of two versions of the tenseless theory of time. According to the token-reflexive theory,[3] the truth conditions of tensed token sentences do not involve tensed facts, but may rather be stated in terms of the tenseless temporal relations between the token and the state of affairs it describes:

Any token *u* of '*e* is occurring now' is true if and only if *u* is simultaneous with *e*.

The implications of this account, in contrast with those of the basic tensed theory, are these: that the truth value of a given token is dependent on that token's location in time vis-à-vis the event(s) of which it speaks, that its truth conditions involve the token itself, that the truth conditions obtain either at all times or at no times, and that, in consequence, its truth value is invariant over time. It would appear also to imply that the role of 'now' is *not* to refer to a time, a consequence I derive on the, I hope reasonable, assumption that if 'now' did have a referential role in the tensed token in which it occurred, this would be reflected in the truth conditions of that token.

As with the previous theory, this account does not force us to quantify over times. Indeed, the introduction of temporal relations looks like an explicit move to avoid such quantification.

9.1.3 The Date Theory

This is the second version of the tenseless theory I shall discuss, involving the following truth-conditional schema:[4]

Any token of '*e* is occurring now', tokened at *t*, is true if and only if *e* occurs at *t*.

Like the token-reflexive theory, the date theory has these consequences: that the truth value of a given token is dependent on that token's location in time (though possibly in a different sense of 'location'), that the truth conditions obtain either at all times or at no times, and that, in consequence, its truth value is invariant over time. However, unlike the token-reflexive theory, it has the consequence that the truth conditions of the token do *not* involve the token itself.

The differences between the date and token-reflexive theories, I suggest, have tended to be overlooked, or underestimated. One writer (Lowe (1998)) treats them as logically equivalent. But, on appearances alone, it would seem that the token-reflexive theory would be more congenial to a reductionist treatment of time as a construction from events and their relations. For whereas the token-reflexive theory offers us a way of avoiding quantification over times, the date theory explicitly introduces such quantification. This is not yet a commitment to realism, but it is a first step toward such a position.

9.1.4   The Complex Tensed Theory

The schema employed by the date theory can be given a tensed, as well as a tenseless, gloss as follows:[5]

Any token of '*e* is occurring now', tokened at tensed time *t*, is now true if and only if *e* occurred/is occurring/will occur at *t*.

One might wonder whether this complex tensed theory is not, after all, logically equivalent to the basic tensed theory. I shall suggest that it is not. In particular, it gives us a different account of how we should assess the truth value of tensed statements made in the past, and this result is important, as I shall argue in the next section.

9.2   How Tensed Assertions Should Be Assessed

Yesterday, at noon, when the heavens opened, Yvonne remarked, with characteristic understatement, 'It's raining'. Today, at noon, there is not a cloud in sight. How, from our present perspective, do we assess Yvonne's assertion? Do we see how things stand now, or how they stood when Yvonne made her (typically undramatic) announcement? Surely the latter. In these rather elementary considerations can be found an argument against the basic tensed theory, for this, it seems, delivers the counterintuitive result that the truth of Yvonne's statement depends on what is *now* the case, not on what was *then* the case. According to the basic theory, recall, the truth conditions of a tensed token do not depend on the time of tokening. Moreover, the truth conditions will obtain at some times but not others. The consequence is that Yvonne's remark, or, if you prefer, the proposition expressed by that remark, is now false.[6]

The basic tensed theorist could reply that there is no inconsistency in saying that, although Yvonne's statement is now false (since its truth conditions no longer obtain), we naturally assess its truth value with respect to the time at which it was uttered. But the difficulty is then to explain why this is an appropriate procedure. If the truth value does not depend on time of utterance, why is that the time we are interested in? We could say, because Yvonne intended to make a statement just about that time, but if this is so, then it should be reflected in the truth conditions.

The date theorist, of course, has no difficulty in accounting for our practices here. Yvonne's intention is reflected in the content, as given by the truth conditions, of her statement. The content of her utterance, on that account, is that it rains at noon (at such and such a date). If her statement was true when uttered, it is true for always. We obtain a similar result with the token-reflexive theory. However, this is not an immediate victory for the tenseless theory, because there is a tensed theory that is structurally similar to the date theory, namely, the complex tensed theory:

Any token of 'e is occurring now', tokened at tensed time t, is true if and only if e occurred/is occurring/will occur at t.

This has the rather surprising result that the *content* of a tensed token changes over time. Thus, when Yvonne uttered it, her token had the content 'It is raining now', for

Yvonne's utterance of 'It's raining', uttered now, is true if and only if it is raining now.

But now that the utterance has receded 24 hours into the past, it has the content 'It was raining 24 hours ago', for

Yvonne's utterance of 'It's raining', uttered 24 hours ago, is true if and only if it was raining 24 hours ago.

The changing content keeps track of the same time, so to speak, and because of this the utterance has a constant truth value. The following table summarizes the differences and similarities between the four theories:

		Changing content?	
		Yes	No
Changing truth value?	Yes		Basic tensed theory
	No	Complex tensed theory	Date theory
			Token-reflexive theory

The Yes, Yes box has no theory to fill it, which is not surprising, since it is hard to see what could motivate such a peculiar position. It would lack the simplicity of the basic account, while having that account's implausible consequences.

So, of the two versions of the tensed theory, there is reason to prefer the complex over the basic account. But what of the two tenseless theories?

9.3   Defending the Token-Reflexive Theory Against Two Objections

The weakness of the token-reflexive theory lies in its making the tensed token itself a part of the truth conditions. From this follow some unwelcome consequences. Or so, at any rate, it has been argued. I shall briefly consider two objections that Quentin Smith (1993) has raised for the theory and that for convenience I shall name the *prehistoric era objection* and the *logical equivalence objection*. The first concerns a conflict with intuition. The second involves the derivation of a consequence that is certainly false. Of the first I shall contend that there are no non-question-begging reasons to accept the "intuition" with which the token-reflexive theory comes into conflict. Of the second I shall contend that, though the putative consequence should indeed be rejected, it does not follow from the theory.

9.3.1   The Prehistoric Era Objection
The prehistoric era objection draws our attention to the fact that there were truths prior to the existence of beings capable of making utterances or having thoughts. Let us introduce the term *token with propositional content* to cover utterances, thoughts, inscriptions, and the like. Now consider this token:

u: It was true that the era devoid of tokens with propositional content
is present.

Embedded within the proposition expressed by this token is the following proposition:

v: The era devoid of tokens with propositional content is present.

The present truth of *u* requires the truth of *v* during the era in question.
Clearly, *v* cannot be expressed by any true token, for there are no such
tokens when *v* is true. The truth conditions of *v* therefore cannot be
token-reflexive. The token-reflexive theory is therefore false.[7]

9.3.2 Reply to the Prehistoric Era Objection

An initial response to the problem above might be to point out that the
token-reflexive theory is only a theory about the truth conditions of
tensed *tokens*: nothing is said about the truth conditions of propositions
or other truth vehicles that do not count as concrete tokens. But this response obscures the central insight of the tenseless theory, of which the
token-reflexive theory is one expression, namely, that tense belongs only
to representations of reality, not to reality itself. So if a proposition
counts as a representation of reality, even when it is not being entertained by anyone, then either the token-reflexive theory ought to apply
to it, or there should be some simple modification of the theory that does
so apply.

One's next thought might be to wonder whether *v* does not itself count
as a token with propositional content. For if it does, then any time at
which it exists cannot be an era devoid of tokens with propositional
content. So *v* is bound to be false, whether or not one adopts the token-
reflexive theory. However, the sense of 'token' relevant to the token-
reflexive theory is that of an item that has a specific location in space and
time (as opposed to a timeless abstract object such as one might imagine
a proposition to be), for the truth of a tensed token, according to that
theory, depends crucially on its temporal location. *v* is not such an item,
or so we must assume if the objection is to work.

The appropriate response for the token-reflexive theorist to make, I
suggest, is simply to deny that there can be tensed propositions, or tensed
truth vehicles other than those that have a specific temporal location.

The proposition expressed by u is not a tensed proposition of which v is a component, but is rather a tenseless one, as follows:

u is later than the era devoid of tokens with propositional content.

To assume that there are tensed propositions is therefore to beg the question against the token-reflexive theory. It may be part of our intuitions that there were truths during the prehistoric period, but the precise nature of those truths is not, I suggest, intuitively obvious.[8]

9.3.3   The Logical Equivalence Objection

As presented by Smith, the logical equivalence objection goes as follows:

[C]onsider that a token S_1 of 'It is now 1980' is uttered by John simultaneously with a token S_2 of 'It is now 1980' that is uttered by Alice. It is an unimpeachable linguistic datum that the fact stated by S_1 is logically equivalent to the fact stated by S_2. But [the token-reflexive theory] fails to explain or be consistent with their logical equivalence, for [the] theory implies that the fact stated by S_1 is

... S_1 occurs in 1980

and that the fact stated by S_2 is

... S_2 occurs in 1980.

These facts are not logically equivalent; for Alice need not utter S_2 in order for John to utter S_1, and John need not utter S_1 in order for Alice to utter S_2. (1993, p. 90)

9.3.4   Reply to the Logical Equivalence Objection

What is unimpeachable is that, if S_1 is true, S_2 is true, and vice versa. Any position one takes on the question of the facts stated by S_1 and S_2 will be dictated, not by intuition, but by the theory of time one espouses. That is, there is no neutral way, in this context, of settling the properties facts stated by tensed tokens must have, independently of settling the question of *what* facts tensed tokens actually state. So the question to be faced is this: can the token-reflexive theory explain why S_1 and S_2 must have the same truth value? Admittedly, it cannot do this by appeal to their truth conditions, for these are clearly quite different. But there is no need to bring in truth conditions. All the token-reflexive theory need appeal to is the fact that S_1 and S_2 are tokens of the same type, and they are tokened at the same time. That is enough to guarantee identity of truth value. However, this means of dealing with the problem will not, it seems, cover the following case: John says, 'It is now 1980', and Alice simultaneously says, 'It is 1980'. Here, the tokens are not of the same type. At least, they belong to different sentence types. And, as already noted, the tokens have different truth conditions if the token-reflexive theory is true. However, according to the token-reflexive theory, the type 'It is now 1980' and the type 'It is 1980' have exactly the same *truth-conditional schema*. So, to explain both cases the token-reflexive theorist need only appeal to the following principle: two simultaneous tokens whose types have the same truth-conditional schema also have the same truth value.

9.4   Defending the Date Theory against Two Objections

We now move from the token-reflexive theory to the date version of the tenseless theory. Here times make an appearance:

A token of 'The maniac is now approaching', tokened at t, is true if and only if the maniac approaches at t.

In this section, I defend the date theory against two objections, the source for which is, again, Smith 1993. They go as follows.

9.4.1   The Contingency Objection

Any token of 'It is now 4 p.m.' has the truth value it does only contingently. Therefore, whether or not its truth conditions obtain should also be contingent. However, according to the date theory, any 4 p.m. token of 'It is now 4 p.m.' will have the following truth conditions:

It is 4 p.m. at 4 p.m., on ...

But these necessarily obtain. So the token is necessarily true. And, by similar reasoning, any non–4 p.m. token of 'It is now 4 p.m.' will be necessarily false. (See Smith 1993, pp. 42–50, where this objection is explored and developed at length.)

9.4.2   The Irrelevance-of-Absolute-Location Objection

Consider a token, u, of 'The eclipse is taking place now'. If its actual time of tokening is t, then it is true if and only if the eclipse takes place at t.

But now consider the following counterfactual situation: u is tokened simultaneously with the eclipse, but at some time *other* than t. Here, according to the date theory, the token's truth conditions do not obtain. Yet it would be absurd to deny that the token was true in such a situation. Conversely, suppose that the eclipse does indeed take place at t, but that the token is located at some other time. Here, according to the date theory, the token's truth conditions do obtain. Yet it would be absurd to deny that the token was false in such a situation. What the date theory represents as the token's truth conditions, then, seems neither necessary nor sufficient for the token's truth. What matters is not the *absolute* temporal location of the event referred to by the token, but location vis-à-vis the token itself. (See Smith 1993, pp. 35–39.)

9.4.3   Reply to the Contingency and Irrelevance-of-Absolute-Location Objections

The contingency and irrelevance-of-absolute-location objections are closely related, and the following response addresses both. According to the date theory, the content of a tensed token (the proposition expressed) is partly determined by the time at which it is tokened. Thus, a 4 p.m. token of 'It is 4 p.m.' will have the content 'It is 4 p.m. at 4 p.m.'. A 3 p.m. token will have the content 'It is 4 p.m. at 3 p.m.'. Thus, insofar as the temporal location of a given tensed token varies from world to world, the content of that token will vary from world to world. It follows that its truth conditions similarly vary. So, in answer to the contingency objection: the truth value of 'It is now 4 p.m.' is contingent, not because its actual truth conditions obtain only contingently, but because it will not have those very truth conditions in every world. And in answer to the irrelevance-of-absolute-location objection: the truth conditions in some other possible world of 'The eclipse is taking place now' will reflect the token's location in that world, not its location in the actual world.

Does it make sense, however, to say that a token's truth conditions vary from world to world? Surely, one might object, the truth conditions of a token can only convey its meaning if they are the same in every world in which the token exists. (This is Smith's objection to J. J. C. Smart's proposal that the truth conditions of tensed tokens are world-indexed. See Smith 1993, pp. 37–38.) It depends, I would say, how you choose to individuate the token: in terms of its actual content, or as a physical event. If in terms of its propositional content, then its truth conditions remain the same in each world, just because its content does. But if in terms of its physical properties, then there is no reason to suppose that content, and therefore truth conditions, remain invariant. There is no one answer to the question of what constrains the trans world identity of a token. But in any case, Smith cannot insist that the truth conditions of a token are essential to it without undermining his own counterexample. Let t be the time at which, in a given world, a token of 'The eclipse is taking place now' is tokened. The date theorist holds that the truth conditions of this token, in that world, are that the eclipse takes place at t, for the temporal location of the token determines the truth conditions. So if, as Smith insists, a token has the same truth conditions in every world in which it exists, it follows that the temporal location of the token (namely, t) will *also* be world-invariant. Now either Smith is right to insist on the world-invariance of truth conditions or he is not. If he is right, it would make no sense, on the date theory, to suppose that very token to be located at some time other than t. Any such counterfactual supposition is, therefore, question-begging. If, however, he is wrong, then the irrelevance-of-absolute-location objection does not go through.

9.5   The Causal Objection

Of the four theories we started with,[9] only one so far has run into serious difficulties. We have yet to come to any definite conclusions on two of the three questions we set ourselves, namely: Do times enter into the truth conditions of tensed tokens? If so, are these tenseless times? And we have not even addressed the third question. We have, perhaps, succeeded in clarifying the various theories, but it is time we made progress of a more tangible kind. I am now going to consider a difficulty, I hope a novel one, that I believe arises both for the token-reflexive theory and for the complex tensed theory. I shall call it the *causal objection*.

Tensed statements may report, among other things, causal relations between states of affairs. Here is one such report:

r: It has been raining, and as a result, the pitch is now waterlogged.

This (to state the obvious) asserts that (1) it has been raining, (2) the pitch is now waterlogged, and (3) there is a causal connection between (1) and (2). But now see what happens when, in place of (1) and (2), we substitute their truth conditions, according to the token-reflexive theory:

Raining occurs earlier than *r*, and as a result, the pitch is waterlogged simultaneously with *r*.

Something surely has gone wrong. The causal relation is simply between earlier raining and the present waterlogged state of the pitch. It is not between the temporal priority of rain over *r* on the one hand, and the simultaneity between *r* and the pitch's being waterlogged on the other. I do not expect this to be accepted without further discussion, however, so I shall now offer an argument for it, using the following key:

$$\left.\begin{matrix} R \\ W \end{matrix}\right\} \text{ is whatever fact makes true the} \atop \text{component of } r \text{ that asserts that} \left\{\begin{matrix} \text{it has been raining} \\ \text{the pitch is now waterlogged} \end{matrix}\right\}$$

$$\left.\begin{matrix} E \\ S \end{matrix}\right\} \text{ is whatever fact makes true} \atop \text{the statement that} \left\{\begin{matrix} R \text{ occurs earlier than } r \\ W \text{ occurs simultaneously with } r \end{matrix}\right\}$$

According to the token-reflexive theory, $R = E$ and $W = S$. I submit, however, that what holds between R and W, by virtue of which we ascribe a causal relation between them, does not hold of E and S. Suppose that R is in the circumstances sufficient for W. Is E sufficient for S? No, because *r* could have been tokened long after the pitch ceased to be waterlogged, in which case E would have obtained, but not S. Suppose instead that R merely makes W highly probable. For the same reasons, the same does not hold of E and S. What, however, if our original statement had been this?

It was raining twenty minutes ago, and as a result, the pitch is now waterlogged.

Let T be the fact that rain occurred twenty minutes earlier than *r*. Now if raining at one time is sufficient for the pitch to be waterlogged twenty minutes later, then T will be sufficient for S. So the above objection will not extend to such a case. Nevertheless, the objection holds whenever the time of the cause is not precisely specified, and this is enough to undermine the token-reflexive analysis.

There is a further problem, which arises whether or not the time of the cause is specified. Causes, like their effects, have particular spatial and temporal locations. If this were not so, there would be no causal explanation of the fact that what states of affairs obtain in one place and time may not obtain at other places and times. Now R and W have specific locations, but E and S do not. It makes no sense to ask, for example, '*When* is raining earlier than r?' Therefore, E and S cannot be causal relata.

The token-reflexive theory is in difficulties. What of the tensed theories? These too face the causal objection. Consider the following statement:

It rained an hour ago, and as a result, the pitch is now waterlogged.

Substituting, as before, the relevant truth conditions, but this time in accordance with either the basic or complex tensed theory, we obtain the superficially indistinguishable

It rained an hour ago, and as a result, the pitch is now waterlogged.

(Note that, in the case of present tokens, the truth conditions are the same whether we adopt the basic tensed theory or the complex theory.) The cause, then, is the fact that it rained an hour ago. But this cannot be right. For the cause is surely something that is located in the past, whereas the fact that it rained an hour ago is something that only obtains *now*. So the tensed theories pick out the wrong cause in this case. We might wonder whether they pick out the wrong cause in the case we began with:

It has been raining, and as a result, the pitch is now waterlogged.

The fact that it *has been* raining only obtains when raining is *past*. But it cannot be the passing of such an event that is the cause, but rather the event itself—or some fact about the event.

So much, then, for the causal objection to both the token-reflexive and tensed theories. One might at this point make a move characteristic of what has come to be called the new tenseless theory of time, and insist that the token-reflexive truth conditions of tensed tokens are just that: the conditions under which they are true; they do not provide a translation of those tokens. So it will come as no surprise that certain tensed sentences can figure in a true causal statement, even though there is no causal connection between the facts that make them true. But this will not do. The causal relation is supposed to be an extensional one.[10] That is, the truth of causal ascriptions is not sensitive to the way in which the relata are described. *r* reports a causal relation between whatever facts are stated by 'It has rained' and 'The pitch is now waterlogged'. It does not ascribe a causal relation between those facts only as described in a certain way.

Of our four theories, only the date theory does not face the causal objection. Consider yet again the causal report:

r: It has been raining, and as a result, the pitch is now waterlogged.

Suppose *r* to have been tokened at t'. Substituting their truth conditions for the propositional components of *r*, we have

$(\exists t)(t$ is earlier than t' and it rains at $t)$ and as a result, the pitch is waterlogged at t'.

This, I submit, is a true causal statement. But let me just pause a moment to consider a possible problem here. According to the date theory, the facts that make tensed tokens true are themselves tenseless; that is, they obtain at all times. But causal relata, as noted in the previous section, have specific temporal locations. Does this mean that tenseless facts cannot be causes? No, we can (following Mellor 1995, pp. 8–9) allow that whatever fact makes true the right-hand side of the above causal statement (e.g., that it rains) obtains at all times, and yet insist that it has a particular location (viz., 3 p.m.).

9.6   The Significance of the Date Theory for the Word 'Now'

The date theory has now emerged as our preferred theory. In the last two sections of this chapter, I want to consider what consequences it has for other issues. The first issue concerns the role 'now' has in tensed token sentences. Is there a significant difference between 'It is the case that *p*' and 'It is *now* the case that *p*'? The position that answers no to this question I shall call the *redundancy theory*. According to this, 'now' adds nothing in terms of content to a significantly tensed sentence (i.e., where the tense of the sentence has temporal implications).

The redundancy theorist could concede that 'now' may have pragmatic force. It may, for example, alert us to the fact that a sentence is significantly tensed when we might have overlooked the fact. A mathematical constructivist might say, 'Fermat's last theorem *now* has a determinate truth value' (since there now exists a proof of the theorem), when his Platonistic counterpart would have eschewed use of the word in such a context. Relatedly, a sentence containing 'now' could have the conversational implication that the state of affairs referred to has not always obtained: 'Is the flat fit to be occupied?' 'It is *now*.'

Intuitively, we would think that the role of 'now' is to pick out the time of utterance (whether we think of that in tensed, or tenseless, terms). But if we give the same truth-conditional account of 'It is the case that *p*' as we do of 'It is now the case that *p*', then it seems that the job of picking out the time of utterance is already done by the present-tensed copula, and there is nothing for 'now', semantically, to contribute.

It may be a consequence of the date theory that 'now' is redundant in certain contexts. It does not follow that it is redundant in all contexts. That 'now' is capable of having a distinctive role is suggested by consideration of cases where tensed sentences are embedded in temporal contexts, as noted by Smith (1990, pp. 142–43). Consider the following tokens:

(1)   It will be true tomorrow at noon that it is now raining.

(2)   It will be true tomorrow at noon that it is raining.

Do these say the same thing? Arguably not. (1) asserts that it is now raining, not that it will be raining tomorrow. According to Smith, however, what (2) asserts is that it will be raining tomorrow, not that it is raining today. In terms of the date theory, one could characterize the difference between the two assertions as follows: Suppose both tokens occur at noon on July 4, 1997. Then (1) asserts that it is raining at noon on July 4, 1997, and (2) that it is raining at noon on July 5, 1997.

I am inclined to agree with Smith that there is a difference between (1) and (2), but I would hesitate before endorsing the suggestion that the role of 'now', in temporal contexts, is typically to refer to the present moment. The awkwardness of (1) should warn us that it will not serve as a guide to the treatment of other, more idiomatic sentences. Suppose one encountered the following sentence in a narrative:

The road now rose steeply in front of us, obliging us to dismount from our bicycles and continue on foot.

As in (1), 'now' occurs here in a temporal context other than a present-tensed one. Yet no one would suggest that 'now' referred to the present moment (i.e., the narrator's present). Indeed, the sentence seems to convey no more than the slightly more prosaic

The road rose steeply in front of us, obliging us to dismount from our bicycles.

I will pursue the matter no further here. These considerations, I think, are enough to show that, although the date theory naturally suggests a redundancy theory of 'now', there are ways of resisting the move.

9.7   Drawing a Realist Consequence from the Date Theory

We turn finally to our third question, concerning the realist/reductionist debate. I shall argue that the reasons we encountered in section 9.5 in favor of adopting the date theory should also incline us to reject the reductionist theory of time.

Reductionism identifies time with its actual contents. More precisely, a given moment is a set of simultaneous events: those events (or some preferred alternative, such as facts) that we would ordinarily say occur (or obtain) at that moment. Realism, in contrast, holds that times are logically independent of their contents. Now the fact, emphasized earlier, that the date theory involves quantification over times, might suggest that the date theory is realist. This move would be too fast, however. After all, it may turn out that what t quantifies over in the date-theoretic schema is in fact sets of simultaneous events. But let us see what happens when we try combining the date theory with reductionism. Let S range over sets of simultaneous events. The date theory can be given a reductionist formulation as follows:

A token u of 'e is occurring now', where $u \in S$, is true if and only if $e \in S$.

Consider, then, a particular token of '*e* is occurring now', and call it *v*. *v* is true if and only if *e* is a member of a certain set, namely, the set of all events simultaneous with *v*. A necessary part of the truth conditions of *v*, then, is that *e* and *v* belong to the same set: in other words, that they are simultaneous. The time at which the token occurs is, according to reductionism, a set of events, and among those events is the token itself. So, on the reductionist theory of time, the date theory subsumes or entails the token-reflexive theory. But if we reject the token-reflexive theory, on the grounds that it faces the causal objection, then we must reject a pairing of the date theory with reductionism. Insofar as the causal objection is an argument for the date theory, then, it is also an argument for realism.

Or is it? Obviously, rejecting reductionism entails accepting realism if these positions exhaust the possibilities. But they do not. Apart from the extreme position that denies time any reality, and that would undermine the whole of this chapter, there is a modal approach to the construction of times, a position sometimes referred to as 'relationism'. Relationism, as I shall define it, constructs times from actual *and possible* events and their relations.[11] Times, as we might put it, are possibilities of occurrence. The construction goes roughly as follows. Take some arbitrary event, *e*. A time *n* units after *e* is then the set of actual and possible events that occur *n* units after *e*. It follows from this account, of course, that there is no strict transworld identity of times, for clearly the totality of members of a set of possible events will not exist at any one world, but will rather be distributed over worlds. Insofar as we think of a time as existing in a particular world, it will be a subset of the set of possible events. Relationism, then, will go hand in hand with a counterpart theory about times. Two world-bound times are counterparts of each other by virtue, not of shared contents, but of shared relations with other, earlier events. Supposedly, this preserves the kind of intuition that motivates the move away from reductionism, namely, the thought that a certain event might not have occurred at the time it did. In counterpart-theoretic terms, this becomes (1) *e* occurs at *t* in the actual world, where *t* is a world-bound entity, namely, a set of actual simultaneous events; (2) there is a world that contains a counterpart of *t*, *t**; (3) *e* does not occur at *t**.[12]

Relationism does not collapse the date theory into the token-reflexive theory. For although the combination of date theory with relationism results in the same truth-conditional schema as before, namely,

A token u of 'e is occurring now', where $u \in S$, is true if and only if $e \in S$,

the right-hand side can obtain in a world where u does not exist. The truth conditions of tensed tokens would not, therefore, necessarily be token-reflexive.

But now we come to the final twist in the story: this question of whether the date theory collapses into the token-reflexive theory on any but a realist conception of times is a red herring. The real issue is whether the date theory can avoid the causal objection. I would argue that it can only do so by rejecting both reductionism *and* relationism. Consider for the last time our tensed causal report:

It has been raining, and as a result, the pitch is now waterlogged.

What makes this true on both the reductionist and the relationist theory is the obtaining of a causal relation between two facts: (1) a raining event's being a member of a simultaneity set; and (2) a pitch-waterlogging event's being a member of another simultaneity set. For reasons given earlier, however, (1) and (2) are not facts that can stand in causal relations to another; they have no location.

So our final conclusion is that not only do tenses need times, they need times as the realist conceives of them.

Notes

1. Here, 'occurs' is intended to be read tenselessly.

2. The basic theory and its consequences are clearly set out in Priest 1986.

3. The token-reflexive theory is expounded and defended in Mellor 1981; it is abandoned in favor of the date theory in Mellor 1998.

4. Although the date theory has a long history (versions of it can be found in Russell and Quine), its first presentation as a theory specifically about truth conditions and not as a theory of meaning is Smart 1980.

5. Lowe (1987) provides a semantics for tensed tokens that, although it appears to be the date theory, is intended, as the context makes clear, to be a version of the complex tensed theory.

6. This, essentially, is the objection raised by Gareth Evans, in response to a basic assumption of Prior's tense logic, namely, that tense operators attach to core present-tensed propositions. Pointing out the consequences of this, Evans endorses Frege's remark that an evaluation of a statement as true or false should hold good for all times. (See Evans 1985, pp. 349–50.)

7. This is a compressed and simplified version of the objection set out in Smith 1993, pp. 73–74. Smith's own example is 'It was true that the era devoid of linguistic utterances is present', but the objection is obviously much stronger if we widen it to include other tokens.

8. See Dyke 1996, pp. 61–62, for a similar rebuttal of Smith's argument.

9. Since we are now seriously engaged in the business of trying to decide among the theories, this is perhaps the moment to ask whether the four theories exhaust the possibilities. Let me confess that I am not confident that they do. We could, for example, construct a tensed version of the token-reflexive theory. And Tooley (1997) defends a position midway between the traditional tensed and tenseless theories. However, as far as settling the particular questions of this chapter is concerned, we need only examine the four theories presented in section 9.1. A tensed token-reflexive theory will face the same objection as the one I am about to raise against the other tensed theories, and, as I characterized the difference between tensed and tenseless times, Tooley's position treats times as tenseless.

10. The contrast between the extensionality of causation and the intensionality of causal explanation is made clearly, and famously, in Davidson 1967, pp. 153–54.

11. 'Relationism' is, however, sometimes used to include the nonmodal, reductionist position I outlined earlier.

12. This is an outline of a position developed in much greater detail in Forbes 1993.

References

Davidson, D. 1967. Causal Relations. *Journal of Philosophy* 64, pp. 691–703. Reprinted in *Essays on Actions and Events*, pp. 149–62. Oxford: Clarendon Press, 1980. Page references are to reprint.

Dyke, H. L. M. 1996. A Philosophical Investigation into Time and Tense. Ph.D. dissertation, University of Leeds.

Evans, G. 1985. Does Tense Logic Rest on a Mistake? In *Collected Papers*, pp. 343–63. Oxford: Clarendon Press.

Forbes, G. 1993. Times, Events, and Modality. In R. Le Poidevin and M. MacBeath, eds., *The Philosophy of Time*, pp. 80–95. Oxford: Oxford University Press.

Lowe, E. J. 1987. The Indexical Fallacy in McTaggart's Proof of the Unreality of Time. *Mind* 96, pp. 62–70.

Lowe, E. J. 1998. Tense and Persistence. In R. Le Poidevin, ed., *Questions of Time and Tense*, pp. 43–59. Oxford: Clarendon Press.

Mellor, D. H. 1981. *Real Time*. Cambridge: Cambridge University Press.

Mellor, D. H. 1995. *The Facts of Causation*. London: Routledge.

Mellor, D. H. 1998. *Real Time II*, London: Routledge.

Priest, G. 1986. Tense and Truth Conditions. *Analysis* 46, pp. 162–66.

Prior, A. N. 1968. Changes in Events and Changes in Things. In *Papers on Time and Tense*, pp. 1–14. Oxford: Clarendon Press. Reprinted in R. Le Poidevin and M. MacBeath, eds., *The Philosophy of Time*, pp. 35–46. Oxford: Oxford University Press.

Smart, J. J. C. 1980. Time and Becoming. In P. van Inwagen, ed., *Time and Cause*, pp. 3–15. Dordrecht: Reidel.

Smith, Q. 1990. Temporal Indexicals. *Erkenntnis* 32, pp. 5–25. Reprinted in L. N. Oaklander and Q. Smith, eds., *The New Theory of Time*, pp. 136–53. New Haven, Conn.: Yale University Press, 1994. Page references are to reprint.

Smith, Q. 1993. *Language and Time*. Oxford: Oxford University Press.

Tooley, M. 1997. *Time, Tense, and Causation*. Oxford: Clarendon Press.

10

Real Tenses

Miloš Arsenijević

10.1 Introduction

Viewed historically, the so-called real world, understood as that which could be and should be thought of as it is *in itself*, independently of how it *appears* to us, passed through and is still subjected to numerous "ontologico-philosophical purgatories," which have, in one way or another, eliminated various entities and properties that are normally (i.e., pre-philosophically) believed to be its components. Some of the "purifications" seem unquestionable, some are less convincing, some are problematic or at least disputable, and some seem too radical to be acceptable.

Let us recall a few well-known examples. At present, it is hardly questionable, even among nonphilosophers, that *being beautiful* is neither a property of the physical world nor of its parts as such, since, contrary to, say, being of such and such a size or such and such a shape, something or somebody is beautiful only if and when it, he, or she appears to us as such. It is less certain whether the physical world is really colorless, as it should be after having passed through Democritus' "atomist purgatory." According to the "new materialist purgatory," the world is an even more deserted place: the real world as a whole is void of the mental qua mental after all mental processes have become identified with brain processes. On the other hand, Berkeley's "idealist purgatory" produced a world that is completely nonmaterial. Parmenides' "ontological purgatory" has probably been the most comprehensive of all (*pace* Gorgias' ontological nihilism!): it has left the real world without any heterogeneity, plurality, and change.

Time is one of the entities that has been "burnt" more than once, but still managed to "survive" in one gestalt or other. Contrary to Newton's substantivalist view of time, Leibniz's relationalist conception of time has made time dependent on changes and reducible to certain kinds of relations between events (see Newton 1953, p. 17, and 1972, p. 46; Leibniz 1956, pp. 25–26, 52). But having ceased to be an entity existing per se, Leibniz's time has emerged as a property of the changing world. "Leibniz's world" is not timeless: time is real just to the extent to which a certain order between events—the temporal order—is real. Kant's "transcendental purgatory" has been more substantial: Kant has rejected both Newton's view that time is an entity in its own right (which could exist even if nothing else did) and Leibniz's view of time as just the temporal order between events, so that time has become only a *mode* of our knowledge of objects and ceased to be anything ascribable to things in themselves. (see Kant 1911, I.2, secs. 4–7). McTaggart's "neo-Hegelean purgatory" has been even more merciless: understood in whatever manner, time has turned out to be something *contradictory in itself* (see McTaggart 1908, pp. 457 ff.).

Here, I will reexamine a contemporary, very popular, and somewhat merciful purgatory to which time is subjected, which I will call "*Mellor's purgatory*" in honor of one of its most prominent initiators, Hugh Mellor.[1] "Mellor's world" is *not timeless*, but it is void of some properties that are pre-philosophically believed to be primary temporal properties: its *pastness*, *presentness*, and *futurity*. In brief, "Mellor's world" is *tenseless*. Of course, tenses are claimed to be unreal not as features of verbs and sentences, but as features of what sentences (and thoughts expressed by them) are about.

In what follows, I shall take time in "Mellor's world" to be Newtonian or Leibnizian at will, since I do not think that the difference between the two could affect the main argument. But I'll cite in an endnote the variants of deterministic and indeterministic axioms that the Leibnizian conception would require. As for the difference between Newtonian and Einstein-Minkowskian time (see Minkowski 1923), it will not influence the arguments, because we can choose to deal with contested properties in relation to one particular place in the world.

10.2   McTaggart's Proof

As previously mentioned, McTaggart believed that reality must be time-less, because the concept of time, after his analysis, turned out to be contradictory in itself. McTaggart's analysis tacitly assumes that reality should be considered timeless if it is tenseless, and that, at the same time, the world history can be represented by simply placing particular events onto the one-dimensional time axis. The explicit assumption is that *being past*, *being present*, and *being future* are mutually incompatible properties.

Let us consider a segment of what McTaggart calls the B-series, where four events, e_1, e_2, e_3, and e_4, occur successively at some given place and are brought into one-to-one correspondence with four abutting time intervals on the one-dimensional time axis, t_1, t_2, t_3, and t_4, respectively. Then, if the four events are future events that should once become present and then past—and that is what situates them in what McTaggart calls the A-series—each of them must in turn possess mutually incompatible properties of *being future*, *being present*, and *being past* with no change in their fixed position on the one-dimensional time axis, which is absurd.

As it stands, McTaggart's proof is a valid argument, so that, in order to avoid the implication that reality is timeless, one should question at least one of the premises.

Mellor, and all those who are popularly called 'detensers', rejects the assumption that if reality is tenseless, it is *eo ipso* timeless. They rather state the objectivity of the B-series (or various B-series), denying at the same time the objectivity of any A-series.

Some detensers, though not all of them, hold that McTaggart's proof is sufficient to vindicate their move toward the tenseless theory of time.[2] I do not share such an opinion. Why shouldn't we have our cake and eat it too by rejecting the second assumption? Why wouldn't the world history between t_1 and t_4 be represented by the two-dimensional matrix in figure 10.1 (see Schlesinger 1994a,b)? The empty, half-empty, and full circles represent future, present, and past events, respectively. The first row depicts the world history at t_1, when e_1 is present; the second row depicts

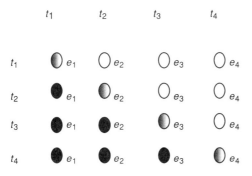

Figure 10.1

the change in the world history resulting from the fact that, at t_2, e_2 is present; the third and fourth rows depict the two consecutive changes in the world history resulting from the facts that, at t_3 and t_4, e_3 and e_4 are present, respectively. The four events $e_1, \ldots, e_4$ are always ordered in the same way, but they are not brought into correspondence with $t_1, \ldots, t_4$ independently of the fact that the world history differs from time to time in view of which event is the present event. Owing to the two-dimensional representation, an event occurring at a particular time *can* be future, present, and past, because it is one thing to say that an event occurs at that time and another thing to say that it is future before that time, present at that time, and past after that time.

10.3   A System of Events Containing Dates and Tenses

Nothing more has been established so far than that the possibility of a two-dimensional representation of the world history prevents detensers' vindication of the alleged necessity to choose between B-series and A-series, that is, between dates and tenses. This doesn't mean that detensers don't have, or couldn't have, other reasons for rejecting the A-series, that is, for rejecting the reality of tenses. The same holds, mutatis mutandis, for those who want to endorse just the A-series and reject the B-series altogether. In this section, I will sketch a *tense logic system* whose interpretation includes both B-series relations and tenses without implying any contradiction or a vicious regress under the two-dimensional representation and the flow-of-time assumption. However, before doing this, I want to be explicit about the main purpose of this chapter as a whole in order to avoid unnecessary commitments concerning the system to be constructed.

Given that McTaggart's proof is not conclusive, it turns out that detensers have two types of opponents, because the anti-detensing program can be shaped as one that is either more or less ambitious. The more ambitious program is that of Prior, developed and comprehensively elaborated from both the semantic and metaphysical point of view in Ludlow 1999. According to Ludlow, the standard B-theory relations 'before' and 'after' can be composed out of more basic A-series relations (p. 126), since every tensed sentence in natural language has either an explicit or an implicit 'when'-clause that serves to do the work of temporal anaphora (pp. 12, 134). So, for instance, by speaking about some past event, stating explicitly the date of its occurrence or not, one doesn't *refer* to a time in the past but simply connects the given event with some other events via a series of 'when'-clauses implicitly given by the context of the utterance. What makes it possible for any such series to be anchored is the fact that indexicals represent an essential part of our tensed language: it is always something *present* that we start or end up with, at least implicitly, when we speak of past and future events. As for the cases in which *reference* to different times seems to be unavoidable, as when we want to say for an event that it happened *more times*, the notion of *times* is simply to be decomposed into *different* sets of 'when'-clauses (p. 128).

Now, the program underlying the tense logic system to be outlined in this section is *less* ambitious, partly because the main purpose of the chapter is to show that the detensing analysis fails at an important (some may claim crucial) point, even if we sympathize with detensers' motives and give credit to their reinterpretation of our tensed language. Namely, though I believe that the tense logic system to be offered is of interest in itself, I will use it, in section 10.4, as a basis for the detensers' reinterpretation of a tensed language, since the system does make use of both dates and tenses. And then, in section 10.5, I will formulate a temporal modal logic of events in a tenseless language in order to show that, in spite of all our sympathies for detensers' motives, the concept of the in-the-world-inherent modalities requires the flow-of-time assumption.

Let us start with an axiomatic temporal system of *intervals* as time's basic stuffs. I find it natural to use such a system, instead of an instant-based one, since the system to be built up on it is a logic of events, and any event lasts for a certain period of time. Individual variables $t_1, t_2, \ldots, t_n, \ldots$ are to be directly interpreted as ranging over the basic set of intervals (as in Hamblin 1971; Needham 1981; Burgess 1982; Bochman 1990), so that intervals are not confined to a metalanguage, as in propositional time logic. However, the time topology will be standard (as I proved in Arsenijević 2003, secs. 2 and 3, one and the same topology can be alternatively defined by an instant-based system and by an interval-based system of axioms). Particular intervals will be denoted by $t_1, t_2, \ldots, t_n, \ldots$, whereas the relation symbols $=, \prec, \{, \cap, \subset$ are to be interpreted as the identity, precedence, abutment, overlapping, and inclusion relations, respectively. The informal reader is asked to understand these relations intuitively, while the formal reader can consult the axioms in appendix A,[3] which define implicitly the relational structure under consideration. The relational structure for which the cited axioms are satisfied is endless, linear, and continuous. The elementary well-formed formulas are $t_1 = t_2$, $t_1 \prec t_2$, $t_1 \{ t_2$, $t_1 \cap t_2$, and $t_1 \subset t_2$, as well as any formulas obtainable by the substitution of t_1 and/or t_2 through some other variable(s) and/or constant(s).

Now, for the sake of argument, we take it that, in our logic of events, $e, e', e'', \ldots$ denote qualitatively and spatially well specified events whose complete individuation is obtained by "pairing" them with particular time intervals that they (completely) occupy. So, for instance, $e(\mathsf{t}_1)$ denotes a qualitatively and spatially well specified event e occurring on interval t_1, while $e(t_1)$ denotes the same qualitatively and spatially well specified event occurring on the interval that t_1 takes as a value by ranging over the set of all intervals.[4]

In order to avoid inessential complications, we shall also take it that events we are dealing with $(e, e', e'', \ldots)$ are qualitatively homogeneous and continuous in themselves, like a position change by the uniform motion. The concept of such events—let us call them *elementary* events—can be easily adjusted to cover various everyday events, such as *uninterrupted raining* or *uninterrupted snowing* (see Arsenijević 2002, sec. 3). As I showed elsewhere, for such elementary events it is reasonable to stipulate that if *e* occurs on t_1, it occurs on any subinterval of t_1. In appendix A, this stipulation is expressed through axiom A_{10}.

We have now reached the crucial point. How are tenses to be introduced?

Let *A* be a sentence-forming operator, so that, for instance, $Ae(t_1)$ is the sentence claiming that *e* occurs on t_1. Now, though the given event is supposedly well individuated, not only spatially but also temporally, the information conveyed by $Ae(t_1)$ is still incomplete, according to the tensers' view presented above, owing to the lack of temporal characterization concerning tenses.

In view of how the system is sketched so far, we cannot use the Priorian strategy (see Ludlow 1999, p. 108) of swapping talk of propositions for talk of events by putting tense operators in front of $Ae(t_1)$. Namely, if $Ae(t_1)$ is true, it is true on any time interval, and if it is false, it is false on any time interval, so that an operator in front of $Ae(t_1)$ would be superfluous. We must treat tenses as *monadic properties of events* and introduce them into our system through *predicate letters* that are to be put *after A*.

Let *N* be a predicate letter that is to be read as 'is present'. How is $ANe(t_1)$ to be understood? First, in our system of intervals there can be no such thing as *absolute presentness*, since the system does not contain either instants or time-minima. Second, the presentness, *N*, of a qualitatively, spatially, and temporally individuated event, $e(t_1)$, is *relative* to time intervals on which $ANe(t_1)$ is supposed to hold.

Before I state the truth conditions for $ANe(t_1)$, let me introduce the rest of the tense predicate letters. Since any two intervals are in just one of the basic relations (identity, precedence, abutment, overlapping, inclusion), there are more tenses than just the past, present, and future. In particular, there can be eight elementary tenses, which will be denoted by the *tense predicate letters* F, F_N, $F\text{-}N$, N, $N\text{-}P$, $F\text{-}N\text{-}P$, N_P, and P, to be read as 'future', 'partly-future-partly-present', 'partly-future-and-present', 'present', 'present-and-partly-past', 'partly-future-present-and-partly-past', 'partly-present-partly-past', and 'past', respectively.

Now, in addition to the elementary well-formed formulas defined above, the atomic sentences are also $Ae(t_1)$, $AFe(t_1)$, $AF_Ne(t_1)$, $AF\text{-}Ne(t_1)$, $ANe(t_1)$, $AN\text{-}Pe(t_1)$, $AF\text{-}N\text{-}Pe(t_1)$, $AN_Pe(t_1)$, and $APe(t_1)$, as

well as all the formulas obtained by substituting for *e* some other letter
denoting an event and/or by substituting for t_1 some other constant or a
time variable letter. Complex formulas are to be built up by the use of
the propositional calculus connectives. Any open sentence, be it atomic
or complex, can be closed in the way to be specified below.

Let us now turn to the truth conditions for atomic sentences.

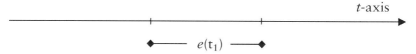

$Ae(t_1)$ is true if and only if the event denoted by *e* occurs on the interval
denoted by t_1.

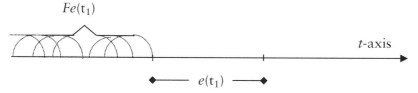

$AFe(t_1)$ is true on, and only on, all the intervals that precede t_1, given
that, in addition, $Ae(t_1)$ is true.

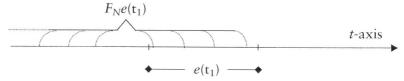

$AF_Ne(t_1)$ is true on, and only on, all the intervals that overlap with t_1,
given that, in addition, $Ae(t_1)$ is true (where 'overlap with t_1' means that
they overlap with t_1 on its left side).

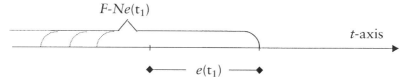

$AF\text{-}Ne(t_1)$ is true on, and only on, all the intervals in which t_1 is included
but which do not have any subinterval that is later than t_1, given that, in
addition, $Ae(t_1)$ is true.

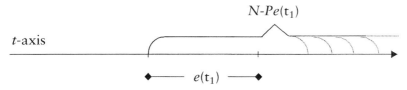

$AN\text{-}Pe(t_1)$ is true on, and only on, all the intervals in which t_1 is included but which do not have any subinterval that is earlier than t_1, given that, in addition, $Ae(t_1)$ is true.

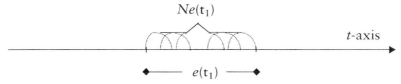

$ANe(t_1)$ is true on, and only on, t_1 as well as all the intervals that are included in t_1, given that, in addition, $Ae(t_1)$ is true.

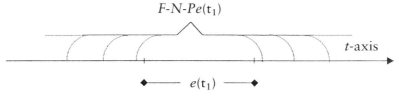

$AF\text{-}N\text{-}Pe(t_1)$ is true on, and only on, all the intervals in which t_1 is included but which have both subintervals that are earlier than t_1 and subintervals that are later than t_1, given that, in addition, $Ae(t_1)$ is true.

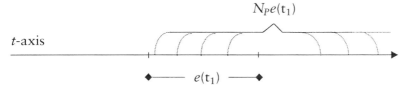

$ANpe(t_1)$ is true on, and only on, all the intervals with which t_1 overlaps, given that, in addition, $Ae(t_1)$ is true (where 'overlaps with t_1' means that they overlap with t on its right side).

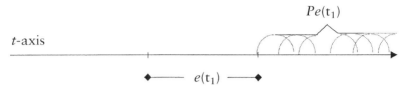

$APe(t_1)$ is true on, and only on, all the intervals that are later than t_1, given that, in addition, $Ae(t_1)$ is true.

It is easy to see how the above truth conditions are to be used in the case in which a variable letter stands in place of t_1. It should be remembered, however, that none of the atomic sentences (whose truth conditions are given above) is closed, since it is not said, for any of them, on which time intervals it is supposed to hold. So, given that T stands for a tense predicate letter, we stipulate that $[t_2]ATe(t_1)$ says that $ATe(t_1)$ holds on t_2, whereas $(t_n)ATe(t_1)$ and $(\exists t_n)ATe(t_1)$ say that $ATe(t_1)$ holds on all intervals and on some intervals, respectively, where the quantified variable must remain seemingly blind, not occurring explicitly in the rest of the sentence (i.e., in place of t_1).

Let us now consider the closures of $Ae(t_n)$ and $Ae(t_n)$.

$(\exists t_n)Ae(t_n)$ is true if and only if there is a value of t_n for which $Ae(t_n)$ is true. Given the above stipulation—expressed through A_{10}: $(t_n)(Ae(t_n) \Rightarrow (t_m)(t_m \subset t_n \Rightarrow Ae(t_m)))$—which restricts all the events we are dealing with to those that we have called elementary, there is never just one interval on which e occurs, if there is any such interval at all. But e can also reoccur after a certain period of time, and there is also no reason for not allowing e to occur throughout time. Thus, $(t_m)Ae(t_m)$ can be contingently true. The crucial question is then, What about the truth of $(\exists t_n)(t_m)ATe(t_m)$ and $(t_n)(t_m)ATe(t_m)$ in such a case?

Given that $(t_m)Ae(t_m)$ is true, $(\exists t_n)(t_m)ATe(t_m)$ is not true, since the order in which the quantifiers are introduced requires that a value for t_n be fixed first, and then it is always possible to find such a value for t_m that the formula under consideration is false. For instance, if t_k is the fixed value for t_n, then $AFe(t_m)$ is false for some t_l (as a value of t_m) such that $\neg t_l \prec t_k$.

Given that $(t_m)Ae(t_m)$ is true, $(t_n)(t_m)ATe(t_m)$ is also not true, since the truth of $(t_n)(t_m)ATe(t_m)$ would imply the truth of $(\exists t_n)(t_m)ATe(t_m)$.

Given that $(t_m)Ae(t_m)$ is true, $(t_m)(t_n)ATe(t_m)$ is not true as well, which is again easy to realize by consulting the truth conditions for any sentence obtainable by substituting a tense predicate for T.

However, given that $(t_m)Ae(t_m)$ is true, $(t_m)(\exists t_n)ATe(t_m)$ is true, since for any t_k as the value of t_m, it is easy to find some t_l as the value of t_n such that $AFe(t_k)$ is true according to the truth conditions for $AFe(t_k)$, and so also, mutatis mutandis, for any other tense predicate standing for T.

Now, since $(\exists t_n)(t_m)ATe(t_m)$, $(t_n)(t_m)ATe(t_m)$, and $(t_m)(t_n)ATe(t_m)$ are all false if $(t_m)Ae(t_m)$ is true, these formulas are also false if $(\exists t_m)Ae(t_m)$ is true, and, a fortiori, if $(\exists t_m)Ae(t_m)$ is false. So, they are never true. At the same time, $(t_m)(\exists t_n)ATe(t_m)$ is true not only if $(t_m)Ae(t_m)$ is true, but if and only if $(t_m)Ae(t_m)$ is true. For if $(\exists t_m)Ae(t_m)$ is true but $(t_m)Ae(t_m)$ false, then the only true closed sentences containing tense predicates are those of the form $(\exists t_m)(\exists t_n)ATe(t_m)$.

However, either in the case in which $(t_m)Ae(t_m)$ is true, or in the case in which only $(\exists t_m)Ae(t_m)$ is true and $(t_m)Ae(t_m)$ false, there is no value of t_n for which any two different formulas obtained from $(t_m)(\exists t_n)ATe(t_m)$ or $(\exists t_m)(\exists t_n)ATe(t_m)$ by substituting different tense predicates for T could be true, as is easy to see by comparing all the truth conditions for tensed sentences. Thus, whether an event is present throughout time or not, it is always (meaning 'on any time interval') *either* future *or* partly-past-partly-present *or* partly-past-and-present *or* present *or* present-and-partly-future *or* partly-past-present-and-partly-future *or* partly-present-partly-future *or* future, where the disjunction is exclusive.

Now, since there are no further relations—in addition to those already envisaged in the above truth conditions for the tensed sentences—that could hold between t_1, occurring in $Ae(t_1)$, and some other time interval, there is no room for the introduction of a new elementary tense: the above exclusive disjunction holding between different tenses is also exhaustive. So, in view of the elementary tenses, there is no way to reveal a contradiction by using a McTaggart-style proof. But what about iterated tenses? Does an iteration of tense predicate letters lead to a vicious regress?

In appendix B, the formal reader can find the recursive definition of the truth conditions for the atomic sentences containing iterated tense predicates, which simply represents a generalization of the definition of the truth conditions for the sentences containing only one tense predicate. The same appendix contains four lemmas, whose philosophical significance I will now summarize for the informal reader.

Lemma 1 shows that by iterating tenses we never obtain a sentence that is true on all time intervals, which means that no elementary sentence, however many tense predicates it contains, is tenselessly true. That's why our logic system is a *tense* logic system in which we are dealing with *tensed truths*: there is always something else to be said about an event of which it is said that it occurs on an interval, and this additional information can be obtained only through a *tensed* truth.

Lemma 2 says that, given that it is true at all that an event occurs on an interval, any tensed sentence about that event is true on some time interval; that is, no tensed sentence is tenselessly false just because it is tensed. If it is tenselessly false, it is so only because the event said to occur on the given interval does not occur on it.

Lemma 3 implies the exclusiveness of any tense in relation to different tenses of the same complexity: if a tensed sentence about some event's occurrence on an interval is true, no other tensed sentence (about the same event's occurrence) that contains the same number of tense predicates is true at the same time.

Lemma 4 shows that no iteration is trivial—in other words, that any new tense predicate transforms the sentence true on an interval into a sentence false on that interval, except when the new predicate is an N-predicate (which is completely in accordance with our intuition that if one says that an event is present (past, future, etc.), one adds nothing nontrivial by saying that its presentness (pastness, futurity, etc.) is present).

Now, all the consequences of the four lemmas are easily and consistently interpretable with the use of the two-dimensional representation and under the flow-of-time assumption. While time has been flowing toward t_1 (or, better, while it has been "producing" intervals that precede t_1), the supposedly true but incomplete information contained in $Ae(t_1)$ is to be completed through $AFe(t_1)$, which is true on all the intervals that precede t_1. Once time has started to "produce" t_1,[5] but still hasn't "produced" it in full, $AFe(t_1)$ ceases to be true, the incomplete information contained in $Ae(t_1)$ being then truly completable through $AF_Ne(t_1)$ or $ANe(t_1)$, depending on the intervals on which the complete information is supposed to be conveyed, where there is no interval on which $AF_Ne(t_1)$ and $ANe(t_1)$ are both true. (Notice that in the two-dimensional representation, there is no time for which any two of $Fe(t_1)$, $F_Ne(t_1)$, and $Ne(t_1)$ would be members of one and the same row!) The flow of time having "produced" t_1 in full, but nothing more than that, $Ae(t_1)$ is completable through $AF\text{-}Ne(t_1)$ or $ANe(t_1)$, depending again on the intervals on which the complete information is supposed to be conveyed, and where there is again no interval on which $AF\text{-}Ne(t_1)$ and $ANe(t_1)$ are both true. And so on, and so forth. It is easy to see at which point $Ae(t_1)$ becomes completable only through $AF\text{-}N\text{-}Pe(t_1)$, $AN\text{-}Pe(t_1)$, $ANpe(t_1)$, or $APe(t_1)$, depending again on the intervals on which the complete information is supposed to be conveyed. It is also easy to see what the explanation would look like if we turned to sentences containing iterated tense predicates.

10.4   *Entia praeter Necessitatem Non Sunt Multiplicanda!*

The above tense logic system together with its interpretation shows that the tensers' view cannot be discredited on the basis of its inconsistency or some other formal insufficiency. But detensers can try to do something much more promising. They can try to reinterpret the meaning of all the tense predicates so that they cease to be interpreted as *monadic properties of events*, being interpreted instead in terms of *basic relations* holding between the times of events' occurrences and the times of the respective sentences' (actual or possible) utterances. If they succeed in doing that, detensers can simply quote Occam's razor and proclaim their view favorable on the basis of this methodologico-ontological principle. For the B-series relations are something already presupposed in the tense logic system outlined above, so that tensed properties of events are entities that, *praeter necessitatem*, ought to be avoided.

There are two points that make such a strategy particularly appealing. First, considering the truth conditions for tensed sentences cited above, we could see that they are tenseless. Second, according to the sketched tense logic system, at least, tensed sentences are something placed in time; so detensers do not change the starting point by trying to reinterpret tenses in terms of relations between the times of events' occurrences and the respective sentences' (actual or possible) utterances. The only difference should turn out to consist in the fact that *being placed in time* does not mean, according to detensers, to be *tensed in an irreducible manner*.

To regard sentences as entities placed in time is something quite natural. Any sentence (about some event's occurrence) is formulated, uttered, thought of, considered, reconsidered, discussed, taken into account, and so on, at some time, that is, in some time interval. But, of course, a sentence can be utterable (though not actually uttered), entertainable (though not actually considered), formulable (though not actually formulated), and so on. Even then, however, it is utterable (entertainable, formulable, etc.) *on an interval* (or *on any interval*, but, in any case, *in time*). The information content of a sentence may be supposed to depend or not to depend on the time of an (actual or possible) utterance, but the utterance time is, in any case, a *particular time interval*.

The last triviality is of great importance, since the detensers' idea (at least as I am presenting it here) is to take what tensers view as an essential part of the information conveyed and reinterpret it as inessential (and rather global) information—not about any event's property but about the time at which the information about the event's occurrence is conveyed (or would be conveyed if the sentence were uttered).[6] So, for instance, if the information about some event's occurrence is to be conveyed via a future tense sentence, then, according to tensers, an essential part of the information is information about something real, that is, about the futurity of the event (or of the event's occurrence). According to detensers, however, there is no such real thing as futurity, the future tense of the sentence indicating only that the time at which the information is conveyed precedes the time of the event's occurrence.

Similarly, the past tense of a sentence indicates, according to detensers, that the time at which the information is conveyed is later than the time of the respective event's occurrence. The present perfect tense indicates that the time of the respective event's occurrence is included in the time at which the information is conveyed (e.g., the present perfect tense in 'It has been raining today' indicates, in contrast to the simple past tense in 'It was raining yesterday', that the time of the event's occurrence—the "rainy time"—is included in 'today' as time explicitly said to be the time at which the information is conveyed). And so on, and so forth. Remembering all the tense predicates—F, F_N, F-N, N, N-P, F-N-P, N_P, P—which mirror exhaustively standard relations holding between intervals, we may say that English needs more tenses, but it is often so when we compare different natural languages or natural and artificial languages: one of the languages compared turns out to be either poor or unnecessarily rich (the tense logic system of German, for instance, is even poorer than that of English: it does not differentiate between the simple past tense and the present perfect tense).

Let us see how the detensers' reinterpretation functions when applied directly to the tense logic system outlined in section 10.3. According to the original interpretation, $Ae(t_1)$ conveys *essential* but still *incomplete* information about the otherwise well-specified event e: it says exactly when e occurs, but the lack of a tense predicate leaves one of e's essential properties unspecified. According to the detensers' reinterpretation, $Ae(t_1)$ conveys *essential* and *full* information about e, since the addition of a tense predicate would not give us information about e's property but only (very globally!) about the time at which the sentence is used in a particular case.

It does not follow, of course, that detensers mean that the information conveyed by the use of tense predicates is unimportant. For various reasons, such information can be extremely important. If I do not have a watch and want to cross a bridge announced to be bombed, it is much more important for me to know whether the bridge *was* already bombed or *will be* bombed soon than to know the exact time of bombing. But the *importance of tenses* does not mean simply their *objectivity* or *irreducibility*. Objectively, the bombing is an event taking place either earlier than or later than the time I am asking about it, and it is only my ignorance about the exact time that makes tenses in the given example more important than dates.

Turning to *iterated* tenses, we can generalize the detensers' interpretation in an obvious manner. For instance, $AF_N N_P e(t_1)$ is true if and only if (1) event e occurs on interval t_1, (2) the relation between the interval on which sentence $AN_P e(t_1)$, conveying that information, is uttered and interval t_1, as the occurrence time of e, is an overlapping relation (on the right side of t_1), and (3) the relation between the interval on which

$ANpe(t_1)$ is uttered and the interval on which $AF_NNpe(t_1)$, conveying this last information, is uttered is also an overlapping relation (on the left side of the utterance time of the former sentence). Now, detensers take the equivalence between $AF_NNpe(t_1)$ and the conjunction of (1), (2), and (3) to be a reductionist reinterpretation of $AF_NNpe(t_1)$. Notice that (1), (2), and (3) are all *tenselessly true or tenselessly false!*

Now, an obvious objection is that there must be something wrong with the very idea of identifying the meaning of $AF_NNpe(t_1)$ with the meaning of the conjunction consisting of (1), (2), and (3), since $AF_NNpe(t_1)$, if true, is true only on some—not all—time intervals, whereas the conjunction of (1), (2), and (3), if true, is true tenselessly, that is, on all time intervals. But then, even worse, how can the equivalence between $AF_NNpe(t_1)$ and (1), and (2), and (3) be true, given that its left side cannot be true tenselessly, while its right side, if true, is true tenselessly? The answer to the last question is, of course, that $AF_NNpe(t_1)$, on the one hand, and (1), (2), and (3), on the other, relate as object language to metalanguage. In such a case, the question concerning conditions under which the equivalence holds is simply wrongly put. The equivalence does not mean that its left side and its right side must be true on the same intervals. It means, instead, that its left side is true on certain intervals (and only on them) if and only if its right side is true at all (and if at all, it is true on all the intervals).

But, no matter whether the question concerning the equivalence between $AF_NNpe(t_1)$ and the conjunction of (1), (2), and (3) can easily be answered, the objection concerning the meaning identification is serious. It must be admitted that the conjunction of (1), (2), and (3) is not a translation of $AF_NNpe(t_1)$. Then what is the equivalence for?

It is often said that, regardless of the fact that tensed sentences are not translatable into tenseless ones, the very fact that tensed sentences have tenseless truth conditions suffices to claim that tenses are not real. As already suggested, I think that the question is more complex. The (material) equivalence between $AF_NNpe(t_1)$ and the conjunction of (1), (2), and (3) only qualifies the right side of the equivalence to be a possible explanans of the fact that $AF_NNpe(t_1)$, if true, is a tensed truth. However, not only is there another possible explanation of the same fact—the one based on the two-dimensional representation and the flow of time—but it is only the comparison between the two possible explanations that clarifies the sense in which tenses are to be said to be real according to one of them and unreal according to the other. Namely, neither of the two explanations can reasonably deny the fact that there are tensed truths, and both can leave the tense logic system standing as it is. The difference between the two explanations lies only in the fact that one of them presupposes the flow of time and the other does not, so that tenses may be said to be unreal according to the latter in the sense in which they are real according to the former.

Let us remember an analogous example mentioned in the introduction. When I say that something (or somebody) is beautiful, I mean that that something (or somebody) has the property of *being beautiful*. Advanced psychology (or perhaps neurophysiology) can reinterpret my statement in terms of my reaction (or my brain's reaction) to that something (or somebody). Now, even though the original meaning is not the same as the meaning of the psychological (or neurophysiological) reinterpretation, psychologists (or neurophysiologists) may still deny that what I assert to be beautiful actually has such a property, that is, the property of being beautiful per se. But they would certainly not say that I am *wrong* when I say of something (or somebody) that it (he or she) is beautiful. They may only make a contrast between two interpretations and claim that the property of *being beautiful* is, according to their interpretation, not real in the sense in which it is real according to the naive understanding.

Ceteris paribus, Occam's razor favors the detensers' reinterpretation, but this reinterpretation can still seem unnatural because of our familiarity with tenses. The following analogy may help us get rid of such a feeling. It seems obvious that by saying of something that it is *here*, I am not ascribing to it a monadic property of *being here*. Instead, I am only saying that that something is there where I am. However, in the Hopi language, which is different from the standard average European language in a way that is important for our purposes, different "tenses" are used for saying that something is occurring *here* and for saying that something is occurring at some distant place (see Whorf 1956, p. 53). A speaker of such a language could be prone to believe that there is, in reality, a difference between *here* and *there* that corresponds to the difference between *presentness* and *futurity* according to our naive tensers' understanding of the difference between tenses. Curiously enough, such a speaker could easily be charged by naive tensers in view of time to be a naive tenser in view of space!

Generally speaking, the so-called naturalistic fallacy consists in one's wrong belief that something is a property of reality in itself (see Frankena 1939). After their detensing analysis, detensers may charge tensers with committing such a fallacy.

10.5   Time and Modalities

Giving credit to the detensers' reinterpretation, I shall now try to differentiate modalities by introducing modal operators into a temporal system that contains neither tense operators nor tense predicates. This means that the system contains initially only tenseless sentences like $Ae(t_1)$. The axioms will be those cited in appendix A.

To differentiate modalities means, in this context, to express formally the difference between *deterministic* and *indeterministic* events.

Contrary to what we had to do in sketching the system of events in section 10.3, where the presence of both dates and tenses required that tense letters be placed *after* the sentence-forming operator A, here we can treat the symbols $\square$ and $\lozenge$ as standard modal operators and place them *in front of A*. Namely, the fact that an otherwise well-specified event e occurs on t_1 according to a deterministic pattern (of any kind whatsoever) can be expressed by saying that the sentence $Ae(t_1)$, though logically contingent, is still necessarily true, which is formally to be written as $\square Ae(t_1)$. Similarly, the fact that the occurrence of e on t_1 is precluded is to be put as $\square\neg Ae(t_1)$. Generally, if a universe is deterministic in view of whatever happens on t_1, it should hold that $\square AE(t_1) \vee \square\neg AE(t_1)$, where E is a schematic letter substitutable by $e, e', e'', \ldots$. Generalizing the last condition so as to cover all intervals, that is, so as to become the axiom holding in a completely deterministic universe, we obtain $(t_n)(\square AE(t_n) \vee \square\neg AE(t_n))$.[7]

Now, in order to get the intended interpretation, we can use the possible-worlds semantics and take the set of possible worlds to be the set of all the worlds that are noncontradictorily describable by atomic sentences claiming various couplings between events and time intervals. Then, if the world for which $\square Ae(t_1) \vee \square\neg Ae(t_1)$ holds is a world accessible from some other world w, it is the only world on t_1 that is

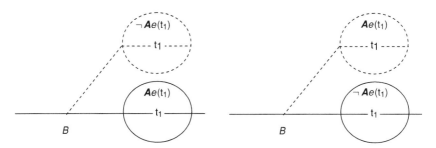

Figure 10.2

accessible from *w*. This means that if we take it that a real world consists of its time segments, the accessibility relation is an equivalence relation definable on the set of those possible worlds that are time segments of that real world (for more about this, see Arsenijević 2002, sec. 4). Consequently, within any completely deterministic real world the allegedly different modalities de facto collapse into just one of them—reality.[8]

In a noncompletely deterministic universe, there must be a sentence—at least one—such that, for some value of t_n, $\Box AE(t_n) \vee \Box \neg AE(t_n)$ does not hold. Let $Ae(t_1)$ be such a sentence. In view of this sentence, $\Diamond Ae(t_1) \wedge \Diamond \neg Ae(t_1)$ should hold. Let us consider how $\Diamond Ae(t_1) \wedge \Diamond \neg Ae(t_1)$ is to be interpreted according to the standard possible-worlds semantics.

$\Diamond Ae(t_1) \wedge \Diamond \neg Ae(t_1)$ means that there are at least two different accessible possible worlds, one in which $Ae(t_1)$ is true and $\neg Ae(t_1)$ false, and the other in which $\neg Ae(t_1)$ is true and $Ae(t_1)$ false. To meet such a condition, both accessible possible worlds must be of the same modal status. This is not the case if one of the two worlds is supposed to be *actual* and the other *merely possible* (see figure 10.2, where, after the branching point, *B*, the solid line depicts the actual world, and the dotted line the relation to a merely possible world). So, the required condition would be met either in the case in which both possible worlds were supposed to be actual or in the case in which both were supposed to be *merely possible* and *not yet actual* (see figure 10.3). The first option requires Lewis's plurality-of-real-worlds assumption (see Lewis 1986). However, I do not want to endorse such an assumption, not only for ontological but also for methodological reasons. Namely, I want to offer

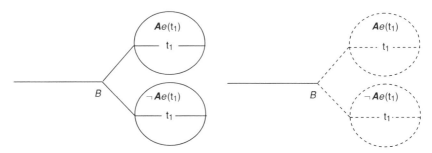

Figure 10.3

a *weaker* explanation for the case that there is just one real world, without precluding the possibility that there are more real worlds. How to fulfill the second option requirement?

The resolution is at hand. Since we are dealing with a *temporal* modal system, the two sentences $\Diamond Ae(t_1)$ and $\Diamond\neg Ae(t_1)$ are reasonably to be considered true on all the intervals that precede t_1. For the assumption that event $e(t_1)$ is indeterministic may be understood as implying that there is nothing in reality that would make either $\Diamond Ae(t_1)$ or $\Diamond\neg Ae(t_1)$ true *simpliciter* on any interval that precedes t_1. In addition, both $\Diamond Ae(t_1)$ and $\Diamond\neg Ae(t_1)$ remain true on all the intervals included in t_1 but not ending together with t_1, given that nothing has happened on them that makes $Ae(t_1)$ false. But on all the intervals that end together with t_1 or are later than t_1, either $Ae(t_1)$ is true *simpliciter* and $\neg Ae(t_1)$ no longer accessible, or $\neg Ae(t_1)$ is true *simpliciter* and $Ae(t_1)$ no longer accessible, so that on all those intervals either $\Diamond Ae(t_1)$ or $\Diamond\neg Ae(t_1)$ is true, and never both. In view of all these facts, the fact that a universe is completely indeterministic should be expressed through

$$(t_n)((\Diamond AE(t_m) \wedge \Diamond\neg AE(t_m) \Leftrightarrow$$
$$\Leftrightarrow t_n \prec t_m \vee (\exists t_k)(t_n \{ t_k \wedge t_k \subset t_m \wedge (AE(t_k) \Rightarrow AE(t_m))))).^{[9]}$$

Note that, by interpreting the sentences about indeterministic events, I did not reject the principle of bivalence (as Łukasiewicz (1920) did). $Ae(t_1)$ and $\neg Ae(t_1)$ are always considered true or false, but on certain intervals *in a qualified sense* (in relation to accessible possible worlds) and on certain other intervals *simpliciter*. (Compare the diagrams in figure 10.4, where $Ae(t_1)$ and $\neg Ae(t_1)$ are, in the first, both true and false

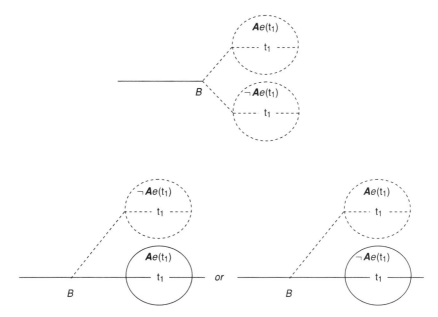

Figure 10.4

—but in different possible worlds—and where, in the second and in the third, $Ae(t_1)$ is true *simpliciter* and $\neg Ae(t_1)$ inaccessible *per accidens*, and $\neg Ae(t_1)$ is true *simpliciter* and $Ae(t_1)$ inaccessible *per accidens*, respectively.)[10]

Now, in a highly interesting contrast to the fact that the tense logic system sketched above could have been reinterpreted without the flow-of-time assumption, the tenselessly formalized system concerning in-deterministic events cannot be consistently interpreted without such an assumption! For there is no other way to reconcile the fact that on some intervals $Ae(t_1)$ and $\neg Ae(t_1)$ are both possible (each true in view of an accessible possible world) with the fact that on some other intervals one of the two is true *simpliciter* and the other false *simpliciter* (i.e., true in an inaccessible possible world only). Namely, it is only the flow of time that can change the modal status of the possible worlds, in which $Ae(t_1)$ and $\neg Ae(t_1)$ are true in a qualified sense, in such a way that one of them ceases to be accessible. Notice that in order to represent such a change we need two different diagrams: one in which the actual world is connected by dotted lines with the possible worlds in which $Ae(t_1)$ and

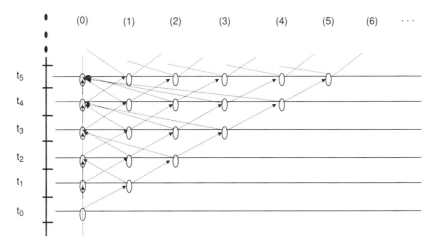

Figure 10.5

$\neg Ae(t_1)$ are true, respectively, and the other in which either $Ae(t_1)$ or $\neg Ae(t_1)$ belongs to the actual world, while the other, which doesn't, can no longer be connected with the actual world at all (see figure 10.4). In other words, the one-dimensional representation does not suffice.

If the existence of indeterministic events is not precluded, we can imagine a device—let us call it the *ontological wheel of fortune*—that would enable God to know which time is the present time by simply being informed about the number of possibilities at any time at which this number is greater than 1 (see figure 10.5). Let $t_0, t_1, t_2, \ldots$ be time intervals such that each of them abuts the one whose subscript is by one less than its own subscript, t_0 being the starting one. The wheel starts working at t_0 and functions by showing the numeral 0 at t_0 and then the numerals $0, 1, 2, 3, \ldots$ at any time so that if it shows k at t_n, it can show only 0 or $k + 1$ at t_{n+1}, where the outcome is not predetermined in any other way. It is clear that at t_0 the number of possible outcomes at t_n is $n + 1$, whereas at t_1, the number of possible outcomes at t_n is n (if $n > 0$), at t_2 it is $n - 1$ (if $n > 1$), and so on, decreasing and sooner or later becoming equal to 1.

The branching possibilities are represented in terms of a B-series. But let us raise the following, only B-series-dependent question: what is the number of possibilities at, say, t_7? There is no answer that can be given independently of referring to t_0, or t_1, or t_2, or..., or t_7. The number of possibilities is 8 at t_0, 7 at t_1, 6 at t_2, ..., 2 at t_6, 1 at t_7 (as well as for any subscript greater than 7). This means that if the number of possibilities *really changes* i.e., really decreases from 8 to 1), then there is a *real flow of time* from t_0 to t_7. What holds for t_7 holds mutatis mutandis for any subscript n ($n > 0$). This means, in effect, that the endless functioning of our *ontological wheel* starting at t_0 implies the endless flow of time starting at t_0.

The passage of time has nothing to do with a metrics of time: t_0 can be a day, t_1 a second, t_3 a minute, and so on ad libitum. So, sitting outside the world, as it were, God could infer, using an appropriate ontological wheel, that t_n is the present day (minute, second, or whatever), by being informed that the number of possible outcomes at t_{n+k}, for $k > 0$, is $k + 1$, just as we can infer that the number of possible outcomes at t_{n+k} is $k + 1$, by perceiving the event $e(t_n)$ as an event occurring now (be this *now* a day, a minute, a second, or whatever).

Moreover, sitting outside a set of worlds, God could infer, using more ontological wheels installed in each of them, which time (day, minute, second, etc.) is the present time in each of them.[11] In particular, He could say for two otherwise indistinguishable worlds that they differ just in view of which time is the present time in each of them.[12] Such a distinction would mean that tenses are real. In effect, such a distinction would mean that by referring to an event as a *present* event, we do refer, inter alia, to an *objective monadic property* of it.

Accepting that the number of outcome possibilities related to an ontological wheel really changes in view of some given time, we must also accept that there is a real flow of time, that is, that the detensers' Occam's razor is no longer applicable because the *praeter necessitatem* clause no longer holds. The temporal-modal logic incorporating indeterministic events cannot tell us which time is present, but its interpretation requires the reality of tenses.

10.6   Conclusion

Not only is "Mellor's world" void of *tenses*, it is also void of *real possibilities*.[13] Detensers cannot speak of real possibilities, that is, of in-the-world-inherent possibilities,[14] for if $Ae(t_1)$ is tenselessly true, it is true *simpliciter* on all the intervals, so that $\neg Ae(t_1)$ never belongs to an accessible possible world. In other words, all events are viewed *as if* they had already happened. However, it begs the question to argue that on all intervals either $Ae(t_1)$ is true *simpliciter* or $\neg Ae(t_1)$ is true *simpliciter* and give no other reason for this except that *on* t_1 either $Ae(t_1)$ is true *simpliciter* or $\neg Ae(t_1)$ is true *simpliciter*.

Given that $Ae(t_1)$ is tenselessly true, detensers can say that $\neg Ae(t_1)$ *could have been* true, for $Ae(t_1)$ is not a truth of logic. But they cannot distinguish between 'it can be otherwise' and 'it could have been otherwise',[15] for it is only the flow of time that changes an accessible possible world into a possible but inaccessible world. That's why detensers can speak of "indeterminism" only in a deviant sense that is not in accordance with the "core meaning" of the term.[16]

The tenseless theory of time is a consistent theory. But it precludes too much, or at least too much for those who as physicists believe in really indeterministic events, who as libertarians believe that our actions are really free, who as theologians believe in God's real intervention in history, or who simply as philosophers believe that all those things in which physicists, libertarians, and theologians believe are, even if not real, then at least possible.

Neither the tensed theory nor the tenseless theory can be simply refuted. But it is good to be aware of their assets and liabilities. Once the *praeter necessitatem* clause in Occam's *methodologico-ontological principle* has ceased to be fulfilled, tensers seem to gain the upper hand.

Appendix A

The axioms of the standard but interval-based time topology

A_1: $(t_n)\neg(t_n \prec t_n)$

A_2: $(t_k)(t_l)(t_m)(t_n)(t_k \prec t_m \wedge t_l \prec t_n \Rightarrow t_k \prec t_n \vee t_l \prec t_m)$

A_3: $(t_m)(t_n)(t_m \prec t_n \Rightarrow t_m \left\{ t_n \vee (\exists t_l)(t_m \left\{ t_l \wedge t_l \left\{ t_n) \right)$

A_4: $(t_k)(t_l)(t_m)(t_n)(t_k \left\{ t_m \wedge t_k \left\{ t_n \wedge t_l \left\{ t_m \Rightarrow t_l \left\{ t_n)$

A_5: $(t_k)(t_l)(t_m)(t_n)(t_k \left\{ t_l \wedge t_l \left\{ t_n \wedge t_k \left\{ t_m \wedge t_m \left\{ t_n \Rightarrow t_l = t_m)$

A_6: $(t_m)(\exists t_n)t_m \prec t_n$

A_7: $(t_m)(\exists t_n)t_n \prec t_m$

A_8: $(t_m)(\exists t_n)t_n \subset t_m$

A_9': For any infinite sequence of intervals $t_1 t_2 \ldots t_i \ldots$ ordered by $\prec$, it holds that $(\exists u)(\bigwedge_{i<\omega} t_i \prec u) \Rightarrow (\exists v)(\bigwedge_{i<\omega} t_i \prec v \wedge (w)(\bigwedge_{i<\omega} t_i \prec w \Rightarrow \neg(\exists x)(x \prec w \wedge \neg x \prec v)))$

A_9'': For any infinite sequence of intervals $t_1 t_2 \ldots t_i \ldots$ ordered by $\succ$, it holds that $(\exists u)(\bigwedge_{i<\omega} t_i \succ u) \Rightarrow (\exists v)(\bigwedge_{i<\omega} t_i \succ v \wedge (w)(\bigwedge_{i<\omega} t_i \succ w \Rightarrow \neg(\exists x)(x \succ w \wedge \neg x \succ v)))$

(The last two axioms are formulated in the language $L_{\omega_1\omega}$.)

Prior's axiom holding for the so-called elementary events

A_{10}: $(t_n)(Ae(t_n) \Rightarrow (t_m)(t_m \subset t_n \Rightarrow Ae(t_m)))$

Appendix B

The recursive definition of the truth conditions for the atomic sentences containing iterated tense predicates

$AT_k T_{k-1} \ldots T_2 T_1 e(t_n)$, for $k > 1$—where $T_1, T_2, \ldots, T_{k-1}, T_k$ stand for tense operators and $t_1, t_2, \ldots, t_{k-1}, t_k$ are variables implicitly present in the application of $T_1, T_2, \ldots, T_{k-1}, T_k$, respectively—is

1. false for any value of t_k (i.e., on all the intervals) *if* $AT_{k-1} \ldots T_2 T_1 e(t_n)$ is false (i.e., $AT_k T_{k-1} \ldots T_2 T_1 e(t_n)$ is false for any valuation for which $AT_{k-1} \ldots T_2 T_1 e(t_n)$ is false);

2. true, for any given valuation for which $AT_{k-1} \ldots T_2 T_1 e(t_n)$ is true,

    a. for all values of t_k such that t_k precedes t_{k-1}—if T_k stands for *F*;

    b. for all values of t_k such that t_k overlaps with t_{k-1}—if T_k stands for *F_N*;

    c. for all values of t_k such that t_{k-1} is included in t_k but where no subinterval of t_k is later than t_{k-1}—if T_k stands for *F-N*;

    d. for all values of t_k such that t_k is either identical with or included in t_{k-1}—if T_k stands for *N*;

    e. for all values of t_k such that t_{k-1} is included in t_k but where there are both subintervals of t_k that are later than t_{k-1} and those that are earlier than t_{k-1}—if T_k stands for *F-N-P*;

    f. for all values of t_k such that t_{k-1} is included in t_k but where no subinterval of t_k is earlier than t_{k-1}—if T_k stands for *N-P*;

g. for all values of t_k such that t_{k-1} overlaps with t_k—if T_k stands for N_P;

h. for all values of t_k such that t_{k-1} precedes t_k—if T_k stands for P.

Four lemmas provable by the use of mathematical induction

Lemma 1: Any closure of the open sentence $AT_kT_{k-1}\ldots T_2T_1e(t_n)$ through at least one universal quantifier related to one of the variables $t_1, t_2, \ldots, t_{k-1}, t_k$ gives a sentence that is false.

Proof. According to the truth conditions for the elementary tenses, $AT_1e(t_n)$ is *not* true for all values of t_1. But then, according to the truth conditions for the iterated tenses, $AT_2T_1e(t_n), \ldots, AT_{k-1}\ldots T_2T_1e(t_n)$, $AT_kT_{k-1}\ldots T_2T_1e(t_n)$ cannot be true for all values of t_1 either. This represents the inductive basis. For the inductive step, let us suppose that $AT_i\ldots e(t_n)$, where $1 \leq i < k$, is true for some valuation. Then, according to the truth conditions for iterated tenses, $AT_{i+1}T_i\ldots e(t_n)$ is true for some but not for all values of t_{i+1}, and so, for values for which $AT_{i+1}T_i\ldots e(t_n)$ is false, $AT_kT_{k-1}\ldots T_2T_1e(t_n)$ is false also. This means that any occurrence of the universal quantifier related to one of the variables $t_1, t_2, \ldots, t_{k-1}, t_k$ gives a sentence that is false.

Lemma 2: If $(\exists t_n)Ae(t_n)$ is true, then $(\exists t_k)(\exists t_{k-1})\ldots(\exists t_2)$ $(\exists t_1)(\exists t_n)AT_kT_{k-1}\ldots T_2T_1e(t_n)$ is true, for whatever tense predicates $T_1, T_2, \ldots, T_{k-1}, T_k$ stand for, and for any k.

Proof omitted

Lemma 3: If the sequences of tense predicates $T_kT_{k-1}\ldots T_2T_1$ and $T'_kT'_{k-1}\ldots T'_2T'_1$ differ at one place at least, there is no valuation for which both $AT_kT_{k-1}\ldots T_2T_1e(t_n)$ and $AT'_kT'_{k-1}\ldots T'_2T'_1e(t_n)$ are true.

Proof. Inductive basis: For any valuation for which $Ae(t_n)$ is false, both $AT_1e(t_n)$ and $AT'_1e(t_n)$ are false, and so are $AT_kT_{k-1}\ldots T_2T_1e(t_n)$ and $AT'_kT'_{k-1}\ldots T'_2T'_1e(t_n)$; while for any valuation for which $Ae(t_n)$ is true, but T_1 and T'_1 do not stand for the same tense predicate, $AT_1e(t_n)$ and

$AT_1'e(t_n)$ cannot both be true, so that either both $AT_k T_{k-1} \ldots T_2 T_1 e(t_n)$ and $AT_k' T_{k-1}' \ldots T_2' T_1' e(t_n)$ are false or, if $AT_k T_{k-1} \ldots T_2 T_1 e(t_n)$ is true, $AT_k' T_{k-1}' \ldots T_2' T_1' e(t_n)$ is false, and vice versa. Inductive step: For any valuation for which both $AT_i \ldots e(t_n)$ and $AT_i' \ldots e(t_n)$ are true $(1 \le i < k)$, but T_{i+1} and T_{i+1}' do not stand for the same tense predicate, $AT_{i+1} T_i \ldots e(t_n)$ and $AT_{i+1}' T_i' \ldots e(t_n)$ cannot both be true, so that either both $AT_k T_{k-1} \ldots T_2 T_1 e(t_n)$ and $AT_k' T_{k-1}' \ldots T_2' T_1' e(t_n)$ are false or, if $AT_k T_{k-1} \ldots T_2 T_1 e(t_n)$ is true, $AT_k' T_{k-1}' \ldots T_2' T_1' e(t_n)$ is false, and vice versa.

Lemma 4:   There is no common value for t_{k-1} and t_k $(k > 1)$ that could render both $AT_k T_{k-1} \ldots T_2 T_1 e(t_n)$ and $AT_{k-1} \ldots T_2 T_1 e(t_n)$ true, except when T_k stands for N.

Proof.   Let us suppose that $AT_{k-1} \ldots T_2 T_1 e(t_n)$ is true for some valuation in which t_{k-1} is substituted for t_{k-1}. It immediately follows from the truth conditions concerning iterated tense predicates that any further application of a tense predicate that is not N moves us left or right along the time axis so that $AT_k T_{k-1} \ldots T_2 T_1 e(t_n)$ must be false under the same valuation when t_{k-1} is substituted for t_k.

Notes

1. See Mellor 1981, chap. 4. Mellor's book was followed by a great number of articles, monographs, and collections directly or closely related to the debate between the tensed and tenseless theories of time (see Faye 1989; Farmer 1990; Le Poidevin 1991; Smith 1993; Oaklander and Smith 1994).

2. For various assessments of McTaggart's proof, see Oaklander and Smith 1994, pt. II, and Ludlow 1999, secs. 7.4, 8.5.

3. For comments and explanations of the meaning of these axioms, see the appendix of Arsenijević 2002.

4. My reason for using the phrase 'on an interval' in the case of an event occurring on (rather than in) an interval is that it has a connotation analogous to that in mathematics—namely, I want to say that the event occupies the whole interval (and not just a part of it).

5. If we represent the flow of time producing an interval as the motion of a point, we can reconcile this representation with the fact that, in our system, there is no such thing as *absolute presentness* by reinterpreting appropriately Whitehead's famous formula, "There is no continuity of becoming, though there is the

becoming of continuity" (for its original meaning, see Whitehead 1971, chaps. 3–4). Namely, however the flow of time is imagined to "produce" time's basic stuffs, they themselves are never extensionless.

6. This is the common feature of various detensing analyses: via token-reflexive truth conditions of tensed sentences (see Mellor 1998, sec. 3.2), via their utterance dates (see Smart 1980), via a co-reporting nature of tensed and tenseless sentences (see Beer 1994, pp. 91–93), via a contextualization of tensed sentence types (see Paul 1997, pp. 62ff.).

7. Since the last formula would be true not only when interpreted in an existing deterministic world but also in the case that no real world existed or nothing happened in the existing world, we can choose, in order to satisfy the Leibnizian requirement, an event—say, e—that supposedly really occurs on some interval—say, t_2—in the world assumed to exist, and add $Ae(t_2)$ as an antecedent of the above conjunction, so that the deterministic axiom becomes

Given that $Ae(t_2)$ is true, $Ae(t_2) \Rightarrow (t_n)(\Box AE(t_n) \land \Box AE(t_n))$.

Though the Leibnizian requirement is not yet fulfilled in the strong sense, since the truth of the second disjunct does not imply that something happens on t_n, the so-called modal version of the requirement *is* met (see Newton-Smith 1980, p. 47). Via $e(t_2)$, we are connected with a particular real world, and all other time intervals, regardless of whether they are "full" or "empty," are at least topologically determined via t_2.

8. Lewis (1973, p. 8) calls the "necessity in respect of all facts ... fatalistic necessity." However, at the most general level, at which we take into account just the core meaning of the term, other kinds of determinism are not distinguishable from fatalism.

9. In order to fulfill the Leibnizian requirement, we may again suppose that, for some e and some t_5, $Ae(t_5)$ is true *simpliciter* (which only means that we are speaking from within a world in which $e(t_5)$ is supposed to be actualized, and not that $e(t_5)$ is actualized according to a deterministic pattern), and we may formulate the indeterministic axiom as follows:

Given that $Ae(t_5)$ is true *simpliciter*, $Ae(t_5) \Rightarrow ((t_n)(\Diamond AE(t_m) \land \Diamond \neg AE(t_m) \Leftrightarrow t_n \{ t_m \lor (\exists t_k)(t_n \{ t_k \land t_k \subset t_m \land (AE(t_k) \Rightarrow AE(t_m))))))$.

10. The medieval logicians used the expression 'necessity *per accidens*' to denote something that is not logically necessary, but yet necessary in the sense that some real fact precludes it. However, in order to avoid ambiguity, I do not say that $Ae(t_1)$ (or $\neg Ae(t_1)$) is *impossible per accidens*, but only that the world in which it is true is *inaccessible per accidens*. An additional advantage is that by saying that $Ae(t_1)$ (or $\neg Ae(t_1)$) is inaccessible *per accidens*, we do not preclude the possibility that the world in which $Ae(t_1)$ (or $\neg Ae(t_1)$) holds is a *real* world. We say only that this world is no longer accessible *from within the world* in which it happened that something de facto precludes the truth of $Ae(t_1)$ (or $\neg Ae(t_1)$).

11. By contrast, consider Oaklander's (1994, p. 326) example, where God, assumed to be outside time, is looking at all facts in the world without being able to take into account in-the-world-inherent modalities.

12. See Mellor 1998, pp. 19ff., where, owing to the absence of in-the-world-inherent modalities, the same example is used to show that there is no real difference between the two worlds.

13. For the concept of *real possibility*, see Deutsch 1990.

14. For the conception of a *real world full of different modalities*, see Stalnaker 1976.

15. Le Poidevin (1991, p. 130) admits that "the future cannot be *ontologically indeterminate*," but only "*epistemologically indeterminate*." By contrast, see Rescher 1968.

16. See Mellor 1998, secs. 10.2 and 11, where determinism is understood as presupposing the existence of a causal chain between events. But then, the difference between deterministic and indeterministic events is still not a difference in view of the fact that, on the tenseless view, particular events and particular time intervals are either "coupled" once and for all or "noncoupled" once and for all.

References

Arsenijević, M. 2002. Determinism, Indeterminism and the Flow of Time. *Erkenntnis* 56(2), pp. 123–50.

Arsenijević, M. 2003. Generalized Concepts of Syntactically and Semantically Trivial Differences and Instand-Based and Period-Based Time Ontologies. *Journal of Applied Logic* 1.

Beer, M. 1994. Temporal Indexicals and the Passage of Time. In L. N. Oaklander and Q. Smith, eds., *The New Theory of Time*, pp. 87–93. New Haven, Conn.: Yale University Press.

Bochman, A. 1990. Concerted Instant-Interval Semantics I–II. *Notre Dame Journal of Formal Logic* 31, pp. 413–14 and 580–601.

Burgess, J. P. 1982. Axioms for Tense Logic II: Time Periods. *Notre Dame Journal of Formal Logic* 23, pp. 375–83.

Deutsch, H. 1990. Real Possibility. *Noûs* 24, pp. 751–55.

Farmer, D. 1990. *Being in Time*. Lanham, Md.: University Press of America.

Faye, J. 1989. *The Reality of the Future*. Odense: Odense University Press.

Frankena, W. K. 1939. The Naturalistic Fallacy. *Mind* 48, pp. 464–77.

Hamblin, C. L. 1971. Instants and Intervals. *Studium generale* 24, pp. 127–34.

Kant, I. 1911. *Kritik der reinen Vernunft*. 2. Auflage. In *Werke*. Berlin: Georg Reimer.

Leibniz, G. W. 1956. *Leibniz-Clarke Correspondence*. Trans. and ed. H. G. Alexander. Manchester, UK: Manchester University Press.

Le Poidevin, R. 1991. *Chance, Cause and Contradiction: A Defense of the Tenseless Theory of Time*. New York: St. Martin's Press.

Lewis, D. K. 1973. *Counterfactuals*. Cambridge, Mass.: Harvard University Press.

Lewis, D. K. 1986. *On the Plurality of Worlds*. Oxford: Blackwell.

Ludlow, P. 1999. *Semantics, Tense, and Time*. Cambridge, Mass.: MIT Press.

Łukasiewicz, J. 1920. *O determinizmie, Z zogadnien logiki i filozofii*. Warsaw.

McTaggart, J. M. E. 1908. The Unreality of Time. *Mind* 17, pp. 457–74.

Mellor, D. H. 1981. *Real Time*. Cambridge: Cambridge University Press.

Mellor, D. H. 1998. *Real Time II*. London: Routledge.

Minkowski, H. 1923. Space and Time. In H. A. Lorentz, A. Einstein, H. Minkowski, and H. Weyl, *The Principle of Relativity*, pp. 75–91. London: Methuen.

Needham, P. 1981. Temporal Intervals and Temporal Order. *Logique et Analyse* 24, pp. 49–64.

Newton, I. 1953. *Newton's Philosophy of Nature*. Ed. H. S. Thayer. New York: Hafner.

Newton, I. 1972. *Philosophiae Naturalis Principia Mathematica* I–II. Cambridge, Mass.: Harvard University Press.

Newton-Smith, W. H. 1980. *The Structure of Time*. London: Routledge and Kegan Paul.

Oaklander, L. N. 1994. Thank Goodness It's Over. In L. N. Oaklander and Q. Smith, eds., *The New Theory of Time*, pp. 325–27. New Haven, Conn.: Yale University Press.

Oaklander, L. N., and Q. Smith, eds. 1994. *The New Theory of Time*. New Haven, Conn.: Yale University Press.

Paul, L. 1997. Truth Conditions of Tensed Sentence Types. *Synthese* 111, pp. 53–71.

Rescher, N. 1968. Truth and Necessity in Temporal Perspective. In R. Gale, ed., *The Philosophy of Time*. London: Macmillan.

Schlesinger, G. 1994a. Temporal Becoming. In L. N. Oaklander and Q. Smith, eds., *The New Theory of Time*, pp. 214–20. New Haven, Conn.: Yale University Press.

Schlesinger, G. 1994b. The Stream of Time. In L. N. Oaklander and Q. Smith, eds., *The New Theory of Time*, pp. 257–85. New Haven, Conn.: Yale University Press.

Smart, J. J. C. 1980. Time and Becoming. In P. van Inwagen, ed., *Time and Cause*, pp. 3–15. Dordrecht: Reidel.

Smith, Q. 1993. *Language and Time*. Oxford: Oxford University Press.

Stalnaker, R. 1976. Possible Worlds. *Noûs* 10, pp. 65–75.

Whitehead, A. N. 1971. *Concept of Nature*. Cambridge: Cambridge University Press.

Whorf, B. L. 1956. *Language, Thought, and Reality*. Ed. J. B. Carroll. Cambridge, Mass.: MIT Press.

Section B

Tensed Theories of Time

11

Reference to the Past and Future

Quentin Smith

11.1   The Presentist and the Maximal Tensed Theories of Time

There is a certain version of the tensed theory of time, sometimes called the 'presentist theory', that claims that only the present exists (in any sense of 'exists') and that there are no exemplified properties of being future or being past. (This is a different sense of 'presentist' than I used in *Language and Time* (Smith 1993).) A. N. Prior is often identified as the founder of contemporary presentism, but most of his work aimed to develop a tense logic that could be used to express presentist ideas. The two most developed ontologies for a presentist theory are Peter Ludlow's in *Semantics, Tense, and Time* (1999) and William Lane Craig's in *The Tensed Theory of Time* (2000). Their ontologies differ greatly, however, and (before I discuss their particular ontologies) I shall concentrate at the outset on some general themes of presentism.

The presentist theory implies that there are no past or future particulars, and thus no things or events that have properties of pastness or futurity. What exists are the things, with their properties and relations, that can be mentioned in certain present-tensed sentences. If the sentence token 'Jane is walking' is true, there is a thing, Jane, that possesses the property of walking. The sentence token 'Socrates was discoursing', even if true, does not contain a name that refers to a past thing, Socrates, since there are no past things. The ontological commitments of past- and future-tensed sentence tokens are merely to presently existing *truth vehicles*, that is, either the sentence tokens themselves or the propositions they express (whether only one or both of these are truth vehicles can be left open at this point). According to the presentist theory, there is no such thing as reference to the past or future since there exist no past or future items that could serve as referents (of names, definite descriptions, individual variables, etc.).

Another version of the tensed theory of time is the maximalist tensed theory of time (sometimes called the 'mixed A-B theory'). This theory implies that there are past, present, and future things and events, and that past items possess the property of pastness, present items possess the property of presentness, and future items possess the property of being future. 'Socrates was discoursing' involves a reference to a past thing, Socrates, and implies that the event of Socrates discoursing has the property of being past. According to the maximalist tensed theory of time, there is reference to the past or future since there are past and future items that can serve as referents of singular terms.

I shall argue in this chapter that if the correspondence theory of truth (as distinct from the eliminativist, coherentist, etc., theory) is true, there is no logically viable form of the presentist theory, and that the maximalist tensed theory of time is viable and thereby preferable to the presentist theory. In the entirety of this chapter I adopt the correspondence theory of truth.

11.2   Explaining the *De Dicto* Presentist Theory

The *de dicto* presentist theories imply that there are true past-tensed sentences (and some versions allow true future-tensed sentences), but that the only ontological commitments of these truths are to certain *dicta*, namely, propositions, sentence types, or sentence tokens. Past and future tenses, it is said, convey information about or pertain only to *dicta*, not to any *res* (thing) or event that is past or future.

Most philosophers who hold a tensed theory of time hold a *de dicto* presentist theory. But (up until Ludlow 1999 and Craig 2000, which I shall discuss later) very little has been said to explain the meaning of this theory. Philosophers such as Christensen, Lloyd, Plumer, Zimmerman, Chisholm, Levison, Wolterstorff, C. J. F. Williams, Bigelow, Markosian, and many others hold this view, but typically they do not explain exactly what it means, apart from the general slogan that "only present objects exist and possess properties." (Perhaps Bigelow and Markosian have said more than the others mentioned.) Most of them refer to Prior, and they convey the impression that Prior has somewhere explained the theory. Prior has, in fact, not explained the theory; his focus is on the syntactics of tense logic and he has little to say about the semantic content of tensed sentences or the ontology implied by a presentist theory. Nonetheless, the tidbits of information from Prior are the largest fare that most presentist have offered, and most presentist theories are not in any significant sense original theories but are mere "footnotes to Prior." (Recall that I discuss Craig's and Ludlow's substantive theories in later sections.) But the tidbits of information offered by Prior are not enough for presentists to rely upon, and so I shall begin by formulating some of the basic ideas of a general presentist theory in order to have some general presentist ideas to discuss.

Since Prior concentrated almost exclusively on logic rather than ontology, it is best to begin with his basic tense logic notions. The first significant presentation appears in Prior 1957. Sentential tense logic, in its simplest form, adds to classical sentential logic two tense operators, P ('It was true that') and F ('It will be true that'). The sentential variables p and q take present-tensed sentences (e.g., 'Plato is thinking') as their values. The sentence 'Plato was thinking' has the symbolic form Pp, which translates as 'It was true that Plato is thinking'. The basic idea of sentential tense logic is to analyze past and future tenses ('was', 'will be') in terms of sentential operators ('it was true that', 'it will be true that') that are attached to present-tensed sentences. Present-tensed sentences do not need present tense operators, since 'It is true that Jane is walking' is equivalent to 'Jane is walking'.

A semantics for tense logic is the interpretation of the meaning of the syntactic symbols, such as Pp or Fp. Translating the symbols into English is merely a preliminary to a semantics for tense logic; we may translate 'P' as 'it was true that' or equivalently 'it was the case that', but we still have the question of the meaning of 'it was true that'. Unfortunately, this translation is virtually all that has been done in the attempts by most presentists to provide a semantics.

The Prior-type version of the presentist theory may be aided and abetted by interpreting sentences in terms of a *de dicto/de re* contrast. If a tense occurs *de dicto*, it follows (we shall say) that the tensed expression ascribes a temporal property to *a dictum*, a proposition. (Of course, literally *dicta* are speech items, but I am here using the term more broadly to include propositions expressible by sentence tokens.) The sentence 'It will be true that the sun is exploding' involves a *de dicto* occurrence of 'will be' since 'It will be true' ascribes a temporal property to a proposition. The property, *having future truth*, is ascribed to the proposition expressed by 'The sun is exploding'.

If a tense occurs *de re*, it follows that the tensed expression ascribes a property to a thing (the *res*) or event. The sentence 'The sun will explode' involves a *de re* use of 'will' since the tensed expression 'will explode' ascribes the temporal property, *exploding in the future*, to the sun.

The semantics for tense logic favored by *de dicto* presentists is based on the idea that all occurrences of past and future tenses are *de dicto* (even though some occurrences might appear to be *de re*) and thereby can be represented by sentential operators, such as 'it was true that'. According to this theory, the sentence 'The sun will explode' might appear to ascribe a temporal property to the sun, but in reality it does not; it ascribes a temporal property to a proposition. 'The sun will explode' means the same as 'It will be true that the sun is exploding'.

The *de re/de dicto* distinction also appears in the presentist approach to quantified tense logic, which is about valid reasoning patterns involving tensed sentences that include the quantifiers 'some' or 'any'.

Quantified tense logic may be formulated in at least two ways. A presentist way is based on the idea that quantifiers ('any', 'some') occur only within the scope of tense operators. In the sentence 'Some thing will fly to Mars', the quantifier 'some' does not occur within the scope of a tense operator. But it does occur in this way in 'It will be true that some thing flies to Mars'.

The *de dicto* presentist holds that quantification over past or future particulars should occur only in the scope of tense operators. Consider the sentence 'Some person did exist who authored *The Republic*'. The presentist will take this to express the same proposition as 'It was true that some person authors *The Republic*', which has the symbolic form $P(\exists x)Gx$. The quantified expression 'some person' occurs within the scope of 'it was true that'; this implies that 'some person' does not now refer to anything (there are no past people for it to refer to), but used to refer to something, to a person who existed at the time the proposition was true.

The assumption of the *de dicto* presentist that temporal properties should be ascribed only to propositions also appears in the treatment of quantification over present particulars. The sentence 'Some person is presently writing a book' is not interpreted as ascribing the temporal property, *presently writing a book*, to a person. Rather, it is taken to mean the same as 'It is true that some person is writing a book', which has a present tense operator. This sentence ascribes the property of being presently true to the proposition *some person is writing a book*. This *de dicto* interpretation of quantification is exemplified in Prior's remark that "a quantifier preceding any such operator [i.e., any tense operator] is naturally taken to be governed by the 'It is the case that-', which is prefixable to anything we say, and therefore to range over what *now* exists" (1967, p. 144). Thus, Prior takes 'Somebody, about whom it is true that she is a musician, is now composing a song' to mean the same as 'It is true that somebody, about whom it is true that she is a musician, is now composing a song'.

The maximalist tensed theory of time, by contrast, allows quantification over past, present, or future particulars to occur outside the scope of tense operators. The expression 'some person' in the sentence 'Some person existed who authored *The Republic*' quantifies over all past, present, and future persons. This reflects the assumption that some people exemplify pastness, some exemplify presentness, and some exemplify futurity.

The maximalist theory implies a *de re* use of the symbols P and F. Traditional tense logic (following Prior) uses P and F only in a *de dicto* manner, to mean 'it was true that' or 'it will be true that'. ('N' is often used for the present tense operator, 'it is true that' or 'it is now true that'.) But in an expression of the symbolic form $(\exists x)Px$, 'P' does not mean 'it was true that' but stands for a property of x, the property of pastness. The expression translates as 'Something is past'. Since 'P' is used here not as a sentential operator but as a predicate, this should be marked in our symbolic notation. We may put an asterisk after P

to mark the use of this symbol as a predicate. Thus, we should say $(\exists x)P^*x$.

The symbol P is also used in a *de re* manner in $(\exists x)[PG]x$. Here, the symbol P operates on the predicate G to form a more complex predicate, PG. This translates as 'Something exemplifies past G-ness' or, equivalently, 'Something's *exemplification* of G has pastness'. In PG, P is used as a predicate operator. To mark this distinctive use of P, we can boldface P, so that we say $(\exists x)[\boldsymbol{P}G]x$.

According to the maximalist tensed theory of time, an adequate quantified tense logic must use P (a sentential operator), P^* (a predicate), and $\boldsymbol{P}$ (a predicate operator). Given these symbolic distinctions, the maximalist can allow that P is used only *de dicto*, since the maximalist has P^* and $\boldsymbol{P}$ to express *de re* occurrences of the past tense.

The distinction between *de dicto* and *de re* occurrences of tense logic symbols is partly analogous to the distinction between *de dicto* and *de re* uses of □ in modal logic. The box is used *de dicto* in □A, where it means 'It is necessarily true that A', where A is some proposition. The box is used *de re* in $(\exists x)$□Fx, which means something is necessarily F.

Prior's rejection of the maximalist tensed theory of time is analogous to Quine's position regarding quantified modal logic. Much as Quine found problematic *de re* occurrences of 'must be', so Prior finds problematic *de re* occurrences of 'was' and 'will be'. Quine objected to the realism about essential properties associated with constructions of the form $(\exists x)$□Fx (something exemplifies *being necessarily F*), and Prior objects to the realism about properties of pastness, futurity, and presentness associated with constructions of the form $(\exists x)P^*x$ (something exemplifies *being past*).

In Prior's case, the rejection of the realist position is in part due to his categorization of pastness, presentness, and futurity as *activities*. Prior suggests that these temporal properties of events (if there are such properties) belong in the same ontological category as activities done by things. Prior denies that there are events "momentarily doing something called 'being present' and then doing something else called 'being past' for much longer" (1967, p. 18). Prior may be interpreted as suggesting that it is a mistake to categorize presentness and pastness along with such activities as running or talking, and then say that presentness and pastness (if there are such properties) are activities performed, not by things, but by events.

The maximalist may grant this point to Prior, but argue that present-ness and pastness need not be categorized as activities performed by events. The maximalist may argue that 'Events possess temporal prop-erties of being present or being past or being future' does not entail 'Presentness, pastness, and futurity are activities done by events'. These temporal properties, like such properties as existence or self-identity, are unusual kinds of properties and should be placed in an ontological cate-gory by themselves.

11.3   "Circumstances of Evaluation" in the *De Dicto* Presentist Theory

11.3.1   A Paradox for the *De Dicto* Presentist

The *de dicto* presentist theory of time is false if there are some true sen-tences whose *de dicto* interpretation turns them into logical contra-dictions. It appears there are such sentences. It is logically possible that 10 billion years ago, before any intelligent organisms evolved, there were no languages or propositions and thus no truths or falsehoods. Consider the sentence 'It is logically possible that there was a time *t* at which there were no truths'. If 'there was' and 'there were' are *de dicto* occurrences of tenses, then this sentence says the same as 'It is logically possible that it was true at time *t* that there are no truths', which is a logical contra-diction. According to the maximalist, the sentence must instead be taken to mean that it is logically possible that some time *t* exemplifies pastness and having contained no truths. It may be objected by the presentist that Platonic realism is true and thus that it is necessary that there be truths at all times. The maximalist may respond that the truth of Platonic realism and the falsity of nominalism are determined by metaphysics, not by logic. 'Platonic realism is true' is not a logical theorem and 'There were no truths 10 billion years ago' is not a logical contradiction. Thus, a purportedly valid system of logic that implies these sentences are logical truths or falsehoods is not in fact valid.

The presentist may have a second response, namely, that the sentence 'It is logically possible that it was true at time *t* that there are no truths' does not imply that there are truths at time *t*. The proposition *there are no truths* exists at present, and the tense operator 'it was true at time *t* that' does not imply that this proposition existed at time *t*. Rather, it implies merely that the time at which the presently existing proposition should be evaluated for truth or falsity is the past time *t* and that the proposition possesses truth at this time. The past time is the circumstance of evaluation (in respect of which the proposition possesses truth or falsity), but the proposition exists in the context of its utterance, the present time.

The maximalist will say that this response depends on the intelligibility of the thesis that the proposition *there are no truths* possesses at time *t* the property of *being true* and yet does not exist (in any sense of 'exist') at this time. How can a nonexistent (at time *t*) possess a property (at time *t*)? Can the familiar notion of a "circumstance of evaluation" resolve these problems? For an argument that all abstract objects, including propositions, exist in time, see Smith 1998.

11.3.2   Possible Interpretations of "Circumstances of Evaluation"

What does it mean (semantically and ontologically) to say that the proposition *there are no truths* is evaluated as being true at time *t*? Does it mean that this proposition now corresponds to the situation that existed at time *t*? Or does it mean that this proposition does not now correspond to the situation at time *t*, but corresponded at time *t* to the situation that existed at time *t*? Or does it mean something else altogether?

It cannot mean that it now corresponds to time *t*. For the proposition *there are no truths* (which is expressed by a present-tensed sentence) is about the present situation, and time *t* is past. The proposition states that the situation of there being no truths is present, and the situation at time *t* is not present.

Does it mean that it does not now correspond to time *t*, but used to correspond to time *t*, that is, corresponded to time *t* at time *t*? This would mean that it exemplified the relational property, corresponding to time *t*, at time *t*. Thus, the proposition's *exemplification of this correspondence relation* is itself part of the total situation that existed at time *t*. But if the proposition is true, the proposition is not a part of this situation; the proposition did not exist at time *t*. When time *t* was present, no truth and thus no true proposition existed. Consequently, when time *t* was present, the proposition did not exemplify the relation of corresponding to the situation at time *t*, since there was then no proposition to exemplify such a relation (*n*-adic propers).

It appears, then, that the presentist is committed to saying that the proposition's having corresponded to time *t* first came into existence after time *t* was past. But this amounts to the coming into existence of a past event, an event that never was present. (We may use 'event' or 'state' in a broad sense to encompass abstract objects' exemplification of properties as well as concrete objects' exemplification of properties.) Thus, we have an event *e*, such that *e* is past but never was present. But that is an implicit logical contradiction, since 'is past' is synonymous with, and expresses the same concept as, 'was present'.

Furthermore, we are committed to past events on this analysis, which is precisely what the presentist wants to avoid. The proposition's standing in the relation of correspondence to time *t* is a past, abstract event. According to Jaegwon Kim (1993), an event is an object exemplifying a certain monadic or relational property at a time. Kim has in mind concrete objects, but there can be abstract events if there are abstract objects that change their properties or relations at different times. Accordingly, we do not have a presentist theory.

It may be said that we still have a *concrete* presentist theory, namely, that the only concrete items that exist are present, and that this may be sufficient to satisfy the presentist. But even this is not true, since correspondence is a relation between a relevant proposition and the concrete state of affairs it is about. If the state of affairs the proposition is about is time *t* and if the correspondence relation obtains at time *t*, then the relatum, *t*, also exists. Since *t* is past, we have a concrete state of affairs that exemplifies pastness.

11.3.3 Indexed Propositions

So far, I have argued that *de dicto* presentism is unable to deal with an unusual sort of case, namely, the logical possibility that there was a time *t* at which there were no truths. But if presentism is false, surely it can be refuted without having to resort to esoteric paradoxes of this sort.

Presentism should break down for any normal proposition. Let us pursue this new line of criticism.

The line of criticism can be developed if we give a precise analysis of the phrase 'evaluating a proposition at a circumstance'. Let us first consider the analyses that ought to be given to the phrases 'circumstance of evaluation' and 'context of utterance' in the semantic interpretations of *modal* logic. If David Kaplan utters the sentence 'I am here now' in a certain context, he expresses the proposition (ignoring the tense), *David Kaplan is in California in 2003*. This is a singular proposition; if we accept Kaplan's account of singular propositions, we may say that this proposition includes California, 2003, and David Kaplan as constituents. But suppose we evaluate it in a possible circumstance in which Kaplan does not exist. According to Kaplan-type theories, this should not mean that the proposition exists in that circumstance and is false. If the proposition exists in that circumstance, Kaplan exists in that circumstance, since he is a part of the proposition. But that contradicts the supposition that Kaplan does not exist in that circumstance. But if the proposition does not exist in that circumstance, *what does it mean to say that the proposition is evaluated as false in or at that circumstance?*

I believe the modal logician is instead tacitly considering a modally indexed proposition, namely, *Kaplan exists in California in 2003 in a merely possible world w*. This proposition exists in the actual world and is false, since (we are supposing) Kaplan does not exist in the world *w*. Further, it is necessarily false, since world-indexed propositions have their truth values necessarily.

We need a concept of an *indexing evaluation*, which is a relation between a nonindexed proposition and an indexed proposition. If we take *Socrates is talking*, we can index it temporally and evaluate the resulting indexed proposition, *Socrates is talking at time t*. And if we evaluate the modally nonindexed proposition *Kaplan exists in California in 2003*, we consider the different proposition that contains the modal index in which we are interested, for example, the world *w*, and we consider *Kaplan exists in California in 2003 in w*.

This enables us to explain the metaphorical statement that the proposition is true "in" or "at" the circumstance of evaluation, even though the proposition does not exist in the circumstance. Kaplan writes:

[(1)]   I do not exist.

Under what circumstances would what I said [the singular proposition expressed by the sentence-utterance] be true? It would be true in circumstances in which I did not exist. (1989a, p. 495)

Likewise, Joseph Almog says:

[O]nly after the proposition gets off the ground can we go on to evaluate it, find its truth value, in various loci of evaluation. (1986, p. 220)

How can the proposition be true *in* the circumstances of evaluation if it does not exist in these circumstances? If a proposition does not exist in the world w, but nonetheless is true in w, then in w a nonexistent (the proposition) possesses a property (being true). But how can a non-existent possess a property? It can't. So it may then appear that Kaplan, Almog, and others are committed to holding that the proposition exists in the circumstances. In fact, however, that is not their view (contra my mistaken interpretation of Kaplan in Smith 1997, where I argued that Kaplan's theory implied that propositions exist in the circumstances of evaluation). Kaplan holds that the proposition does not exist in the circumstance of evaluation, or at least need not exist in the circumstance (David Kaplan, personal communication). Kaplan's view on this matter is most clearly expressed in the following passage, where he writes that there is a distinction

between what exists at a given point and what can be 'carried in' to be evaluated at that point, though it may exist only elsewhere. My "Circumstances of Evaluation" evaluate contents that may have no native existence at the circumstance but which can be expressed elsewhere and carried in for evaluation. (1989b, p. 613)

I suggest that Kaplan's spatially metaphorical talk of a content's being "carried in for evaluation" at a circumstance should be literally analyzed as meaning that the content p is "carried in" to the circumstance C in the literal sense that we turn our attention from that content p to a different content p^* that is p as indexed in terms of C. In other words, we turn our attention from p to p-at-C (where the content p^* is p-at-C) and evaluate the truth value of p-at-C. If C is a possible world, then p is modally indexed and p-at-C is in every case a necessary truth. Each world-indexed proposition, such as *Hume dies in childbirth in the world w_2*, is necessarily true. This is not the familiar theory of context of use/

circumstance of evaluation that is widely employed, and I am not suggesting that this is what Kaplan had in mind. Rather, I am suggesting that it is the most plausible way of literally explaining 'evaluating a proposition at a circumstance'. Given this, the standard symbolism needs to be different. Where F is the true value of false and V the evaluation function, we have, instead of $V(p, w) = F$, the symbolic formula $V(p^*) = \Box F$, where p^* is the proposition formulated by world-indexing the proposition p.

The context-of-use/circumstance-of-evaluation distinction must be analyzed in cases of temporal evaluations in ways that are different from my analysis of modal evaluations. Consider the singular proposition *Kaplan has not yet written "Demonstratives,"* which is transiently false. Suppose we want to evaluate this proposition at the year 1864. It comes out as true. But this means that a different proposition, a tenseless proposition, *Kaplan had not yet written "Demonstratives" in 1864*, is intransiently true. This is the same proposition as *Kaplan's writing "Demonstratives" is (tenselessly) neither simultaneous with nor earlier than 1864*. Just as modally indexing a contingently truth-valued proposition turns it into a different, necessarily truth-valued proposition, so temporally indexing a tensed, transiently truth-valued proposition turns it into a different, tenseless, and intransiently truth-valued proposition.

But there is an important difference between modal and temporal indexing evaluations, since a tensed proposition can be indexed in a tensed way, so that it is turned into a different but tensed and transiently truth-valued proposition. The tensed proposition *Kaplan has not yet written "Demonstratives"* can be indexed in a tensed way when it is evaluated for truth or falsity in 1864. There is an evaluation of a temporally indexed proposition, namely, *It was 1864, 133 years ago, and at this time Kaplan had not yet written "Demonstratives."* This proposition is now true.

Once we analyze the phrase 'circumstance of evaluation' in terms of an "indexing evaluation," we can see clearly how the presentist theory collapses. We now evaluate the temporally indexed proposition *It was 1864, 133 years ago, and at this time Kaplan had not yet written "Demonstratives"* and find it is now true. It corresponds to a concrete state of affairs one of whose parts is the past year 1864. On a relational theory of time, this year is a set of events; the concrete events included in this set are concrete parts of the temporally indexed proposition. On a substantival theory of time, this year is a substance or concrete particular that is contingently occupied by the events in this set.

If 1864 is both past and a part of a concrete state of affairs to which the temporally indexed proposition now corresponds, then 1864 exists in some sense; it now belongs to the past. It exists at least in the sense that it presently has the property of being past by 133 years; this year did not formerly have the property of being 133 years past, and it will not have this property in the future; rather, it now has this property. Further, this year presently has the property of standing in part of a correspondence relation to the true proposition. It follows that the *de dicto* presentist theory is false.

The same applies for general propositions, which do not include concrete things as constituents. Suppose '1864' expresses a sense (*the year that is 1,863 years after Jesus' birth*) and that 'Kaplan' expresses the sense *the author of "Demonstratives."* In this case, the phrase 'It was 1864, 133 years ago' means that the descriptive sense, *the year that is 1,863 years after Jesus' birth*, was satisfied 133 years ago. But this affects nothing essential in my critique of the presentist approach, since it is still the case that this proposition (which exists now) corresponds now to a concrete state of affairs that existed 133 years ago and that includes the year 1864 as one of its parts. The point is that the temporally indexed proposition corresponds to a past concrete state of affairs. It is logically irrelevant if there are singular propositions that include past or future concrete existents as parts. All that is relevant is what stands in a correspondence relation to a proposition, be the proposition singular or general. Even if we assume nominalism and hold that there are no propositions but merely sentence tokens and the truth makers of these sentence tokens, the critique remains unchanged. Let us consider only the true, tensed sentence token 'It was 1864, 133 years ago, and at this time Kaplan had not yet written "Demonstratives"'. This sentence token corresponds to a state of affairs that includes past concreta as parts. Thus, the criticism of the presentist theory is logically independent of the theory of singular propositions and even of the theory of propositions of any sort, since it suffices to state the case in terms of a present sentence token corresponding to a concrete state of affairs that includes past concreta.

11.3.4   A Presentist Theory Based on Plantingian "States of Affairs"

Note that I am using 'state of affairs' in the sense explained in Smith 1993, where I distinguished it from Plantinga's (1974) use of 'state of affairs'. For Plantinga, a state of affairs is a permanently existing abstract object that is similar to a proposition in its structure and parts. It contains no concrete objects among its parts. A Plantingian state of affairs exists and obtains or else it exists and does not obtain (e.g., *Spiro Agnew's being president* exists but does not obtain). This is analogous to a proposition, which exists and is false or exists and is true. A tensed state of affairs permanently exists, but obtains transiently. Plantinga's theory of tensed states of affairs is developed in Craig's ontology for presentism in Craig 2000.

By contrast, I use 'state of affairs' to mean something that (in the relevant cases) consists of a concrete particular or particulars as exemplifying some *n*-adic property. Perhaps 'situation' or 'complex event' could be substituted for my usage of 'state of affairs'. In Smith 1993, pp. 156–58, I argued that Plantinga's "states of affairs" are indiscernible from his "propositions" and are identical with them.

Craig accepts and develops Plantinga's theory of abstract states of affairs and their (alleged) distinction from propositions. I have argued that the Plantinga-Craig theory of abstract states of affairs is false (see Smith 1997, pt. II). But if we suppose, counterlegally, that there is a proposition/state-of-affairs distinction of the Plantinga-Craig sort, would that allow for a logically coherent presentist theory?

If we adopt the Plantinga-Craig theory, we may say that the sentence token 'Hegel used to be alive' expresses the true proposition *Hegel used to be alive* and relates in a relevant way to the obtaining state of affairs *Hegel's having been alive*. This Plantinga-Craig state of affairs is an abstract object and consists only of abstract objects, namely, Hegel's individual essence, the property of being biologically alive, and perhaps something else. But what else? There's the rub. If it consists of nothing else, this state of affairs is a tenseless state of affairs, namely, *Hegel's* [*tenselessly*] *being alive*, and its obtaining is not sufficient for the past-tensed sentence token 'Hegel used to be alive' or the proposition it expresses, *Hegel used to be alive*, to be true. If the tenseless state of affairs obtains, it obtains intransiently and thus at times when the past-tensed proposition is false (e.g., before Hegel was born or while he is still alive).

The Plantinga-Craig state of affairs thus must include some temporal component that makes it a past-tensed state of affairs. What could this be? The only candidate that comes to mind is the property of being past, such that the state of affairs is *Hegel's being alive having the property of pastness*. But if this past-tensed state of affairs now obtains, what concreta suffice to make it obtain? If there is nothing sufficient to make it obtain, and it obtains nonetheless, we have a contradiction; if nothing suffices to make it obtain, that fact suffices to make obtain the negation of this state of affairs. Analogously, if there are no concreta that are the truth makers of the proposition *Hegel used to be alive*, then this proposition is true with nothing sufficing to make it true; this is an implicit contradiction, since the absence of a truth maker suffices to make true *it is not true that Hegel used to be alive*.

It may be said that the concreta consisting of Hegel's bones suffice to make presently obtain the state of affairs of *Hegel's being alive having the property of pastness*. These bones would presumably also be the truth maker of the proposition *Hegel used to be alive*. But this cannot be the case, since the state of affairs and proposition would still obtain or be true if the bones ceased to exist. Furthermore, the issue of truth as correspondence remains unsolved, since *Hegel used to be alive* does not correspond to a present situation consisting of a few bones. Such a proposition is *there presently are bones that used to belong to Hegel*. The proposition is about Hegel, not his bones. If truth is correspondence, then truth makers are correspondents of propositions.

If it is said that only what presently exists makes this state of affairs obtain or the proposition true, then it is false that the proposition corresponds to something past and it is false that the state of affairs obtains by virtue of something past. Rather, the proposition corresponds to something present. But if it corresponds to something present, it is about something present, and thus is not about something past, namely, the formerly alive person Hegel. Likewise, if the state of affairs obtains by virtue of a present item's possessing some property, then the state of affairs does not bear an obtaining-making relation to anything past and is not a past-tensed state of affairs. It is a present-tensed state of affairs.

Furthermore, the proposition *Hegel used to be alive* cannot be about a present *abstract object*. If it is said that the proposition corresponds to the presently existing and obtaining abstract state of affairs, *Hegel's having been alive*, then the proposition is about this state of affairs and is not about Hegel. That is, it is about an abstract object, a Plantinga-Craig state of affairs, and is not about a concrete object, Hegel, and his being biologically alive. But manifestly 'Hegel used to be alive' is not about an abstract object, but about a person, a concrete object.

The proposition about the presently existing and obtaining abstract object is the proposition *the presently existing abstract state of affairs, Hegel's having been alive, presently obtains*. But this is different from the proposition *Hegel used to be alive*, which is not about a presently existing object.

If the proposition is now true and is about Hegel, and truth is correspondence, then there must be a correspondence relation to a past concretum, namely, Hegel and his past possession of the property of being biologically alive. The same holds for the Plantinga-Craig state of affairs; the abstract state of affairs bears an obtaining-making relation (analogous to the truth-making relation) to whatever it is that makes it obtain, and what makes it obtain is some past concretum, Hegel, having possessed the property of being alive. It follows that the presentist theory is false if the Plantinga-Craig theory of states of affairs is true.

In any case, this discussion in a sense is otiose, given what I have argued elsewhere (Smith 1993, 1997), namely, that there can be no such thing as an abstract state of affairs in the Plantinga-Craig sense and that the concept of such a state of affairs, and of its distinction from a *de dicto* proposition, is logically incoherent.

I conclude that for these several reasons, Craig's version of the presentist theory does not succeed. (Plantinga appears to hold a tensed theory of time, but appears noncommittal about whether he holds a presentist or maximalist version.)

11.4   *De Dicto* Occurrences of Tenses Imply *De Re* Occurrences

A characteristic feature of the *de dicto* presentist theory, espoused by Prior, Craig and others, is that it not only denies the existence of the past and future, but also claims that there is no monadic property of presentness that is exemplified by anything concrete. The *de dicto* presentist may allow that there is a monadic property of presentness, but he will insist it is a second-order property, belonging to presently true propositions.

A demonstration of the falsity of this idea will lead us to another argument for the concrete existence of the past and future.

The idea that all occurrences of tenses are *de dicto* leads to a certain semantic interpretation of such present-tensed sentences as 'The moon is bright'. According to the *de dicto* interpretation, this sentence does not report that an event, the moon's exemplification of brightness, has presentness. There is no first-order property of presentness and no event; there is only the thing, the moon, exemplifying brightness, and the proposition, *the moon is bright*, exemplifying being presently true.

This presentist balloon deflates as soon as we ask, *When* does the moon exemplify brightness? If 'exemplify' is tenseless, then there is no answer, and the analysis is faulty, since the present-tensed sentence 'The moon is bright' implies the moon is *now* exemplifying brightness. The sentence 'The moon is (tenselessly) bright' stands on a par with 'There are (tenselessly) dinosaurs' in terms of its temporal information— namely, there is no temporal information.

But if 'exemplify' is present tensed, then we must ask, What is the semantic content of the present-tensed aspect of this verb? The present tense must have some semantic content or meaning, since the present tense conveys some temporal information and thus is not a meaningless syntactic device like 'it' in 'It is raining'. Further, to what ontological category does this temporal information belong?

According to the *de dicto* theory of tenses, the semantic category of the present tense is "Sentential Operator" (the present tense has the same semantic content as 'it is true that') and the relevant ontological category is "Second-Order Property"; the present tense ascribes the property of *being presently true* to a proposition. Of course, no presentist has actually said this, but this is because presentists are mum when it comes to any details about their ontology. (If one says nothing, one can't be refuted. The only problem is that one then has no theory. I am here motivated by the spirit of charity to try and supply the *de dicto* presentist with the minimum essentials of an ontology.)

This presentist theory implies that if the sentence 'The moon is bright' is true, we are ontologically committed to (1) the proposition *the moon is bright*; (2) the proposition's exemplification of the property *being presently true*; (3) the thing, the moon; and (4) this thing's *exemplifying* a property of brightness.

The maximalist may well object to this theory that 'exemplifying' in (4) is present tensed, reflecting the fact that the thing presently exemplifies a property of brightness. According to the maximalist, the thing's *present* exemplification of brightness (rather than a timeless, past or future exemplification of brightness) is the ground for the proposition's being presently true. It is the concrete state of affairs that makes the proposition true. (Here I am again using 'concrete state of affairs' in my sense, to refer to a concrete object's (e.g., a moon's) exemplification of an *n*-adic property or properties.)

The presentist cannot say that 'exemplifying' in (4) is tenseless, since the moon's (tenselessly) being bright is not a sufficient condition of the moon's *now* being bright. The moon's tenseless brightness implies only that the moon is bright at some time; that time need not be the present time.

But if the presentist admits that 'exemplifying' in (4) is present tensed, her analysis is circular. She is analyzing the ontological commitments of 'The moon is bright' as (the concrete state of affairs consisting of) the moon's *being* bright, where 'being' is present tensed. This does not yet give us a semantic or ontological analysis of the present tense.

Perhaps the presentist will say that the present tense of 'exemplifying' in (4) has the semantic content of 'it is true that'. This could mean that the semantic content of the present tense of 'exemplifying' is the property of *being presently true* possessed by the proposition *the moon is bright*. But this cannot work for two reasons.

First, it would make the first-level existents (the thing and its first-order property) consist of a thing and an exemplification relation to brightness, such that this relation does not contain or possess anything that corresponds to the present tense. This relation is named by a tense-less use of 'exemplification'. But this means we are left, on the level pertinent to first-order properties, with a thing and its tenseless exemplification of brightness, and we have seen that this cannot be the truth maker of 'The moon is bright'.

Thus, the *de dicto* presentist theory appears to be implicitly self-contradictory. It claims that propositions that can only be made true by *present* first-order states of affairs are made true by first-order states of affairs that are *not present*.

The second problem with the *de dicto* analysis of the ontological commitments of 'The moon is bright' is its analysis of the proposition and the second-order property of being presently true. The proposition *the moon is bright* exemplifies the property of being presently true. But what does 'exemplifies' mean? Surely, it is present tensed. If so, it would mean 'it is true that'. Thus, the analysis of 'The moon is bright' ends up with the proposition *it is true that it is true that the moon is bright*. Since this proposition exemplifies being presently true, we have an infinite regress.

But this regress is benign and I see no problem with it. (Even apart from considerations of time, for any proposition *p*, there is a benign regress of the form '... it is true that ... it is true that it is true that *p*'.)

The second problem is instead this: if an abstract entity, a proposition, can exemplify a temporal property, why cannot a concrete item, such as a thing or event, exemplify a temporal property? There is no relevant difference between abstract and concrete items that makes the former alone capable of exemplifying temporal properties. Indeed, the metaphysical tradition since Plato has argued just the opposite: abstract objects do not have temporal properties (they exist timelessly), and only concrete items have temporal properties. The presentist has pointed to no relevant difference between abstract and concrete objects that makes the former alone capable of exemplifying temporal properties. This second problem with the idea that presentness is not a first-order property is in essence one of logical arbitrariness; the first problem with this idea is one of implicit self-contradiction.

At this point, I have argued that there are concrete items in the past or future to which some propositions correspond (which refutes the "presentist" aspect of *de dicto* presentism), and I have argued that temporal properties such as presentness are first-order properties (which refutes the "*de dicto*" aspect of *de dicto* presentism). The next step is to clarify the implications of this criticism of *de dicto* presentism, namely, that there exist past, present, and future concrete things and events.

11.5   Is It a Contradiction That: There Exists What No Longer or Not Yet Exists?

According to the *de dicto* theory, the ontological commitments of the sentence 'Plato had been alive' are merely the proposition *Plato is alive* and the proposition's property of having been true. The maximalist tensed theory of time requires further ontological commitments from the sentence 'Plato had been alive'. This sentence commits us to a past thing, namely, Plato, and a past event or state, namely, Plato's being alive. This maximalist conclusion is based on the correspondence theory of truth.

Correspondence is a symmetrical property. (It is a dyadic property and thus a relation.) If the proposition *Plato is alive* had been true, then this proposition exemplifies past correspondence to Plato's being alive. Since correspondence is a symmetrical relation, this implies that some event, Plato's being alive, exemplifies past correspondence to the proposition *Plato is alive*. The reason this event exemplifies past correspondence is that the event exemplifies pastness. Since Plato is a part of this past event, Plato exemplifies pastness. It follows that some events and things are past.

This maximalist conclusion implies that the temporal property *pastness* is *de re*, since it is a property of a thing, Plato, and of an event, Plato's being alive. There was something, Plato, over which we can now quantify; it is the case that $(\exists x)P^*x$. The same results hold for propositions that *will* correspond to something exemplifying some property.

Presentists seem to find troubling or even abhorrent the idea that past or future things or events *presently* possess properties. Is this due to metaphysical angst or logical insight?

Consider the formula $(\exists x)P^*x$. Does not $(\exists x)$ in this formula convey that there presently exists an x? And does not P^*x mean that this x is not presently existing but is past? If so (the presentist may argue), the symbolic representation of *de re* occurrences of tenses turns true sentences into contradictions.

But the maximalist may respond that $(\exists x)$ has at least three different meanings in an adequate quantified tense logic, corresponding to three different senses of 'exists'.

1. If 'exists' is present tensed, it can have one of two senses. In one sense, it is logically equivalent to 'has the property of presentness', so that 'Mount Everest exists' is logically equivalent to 'Mount Everest has the property of presentness'.

2. If 'exists' is present tensed, it can also be equivalent to 'presently possesses some property'. Something that is past or future exists in this present-tensed sense, since if something is now past, it presently possesses the property of pastness. Likewise, if Jones now has the property of having been born 500 years ago, Jones presently possesses the property of having been born 500 years ago. Jones exists in this second present-tensed sense of 'exists', but he does not exist in the first present-tensed sense of 'exists'.

3. If 'exists' is tenseless, it is in effect disjunctively tensed; that is, it is equivalent to 'has existed, exists, or will exist', where the middle 'exists' is equivalent to 'has the property of presentness'. If we say, 'Socrates exists', we mean that Socrates either has existed, or exists (presently), or will exist. The phrase 'has existed' is logically equivalent to 'was present', and 'will exist' is logically equivalent to 'shall be present'.

The maximalist argues that this threefold distinction shows that there is no logical difficulty in the idea that some past or future item presently possesses a property.

For example, the maximalist may note that 'Some past thing presently has the polyadic property of being remembered' is not a logical contradiction. Nor can it be turned into a logical contradiction by substituting synonyms for synonyms. Indeed, the maximalist continues, an analysis of the concept expressed by 'remembering' implies the presentist theory is false. Remembering is not a relation between a present person and a present image. If it were such a relation, it would follow that what is being remembered is in every case an image that exists simultaneously with the act of remembering. But this is an analytic contradiction, since it is a part of the logic of 'remembers' that what is remembered exists earlier than the act of remembering. Remembering a thing is a three-termed relation: *a person* remembers a past thing by forming a *present image* of that *past thing*. The 'of' expresses a relation in which the present image stands to the past thing. (Note that '*x* remembers *y*' expresses a different concept than '*x* seems to remember *y*'. '*x* seems to remember *y*' is consistent with '*y* never existed and what seems to be the case to *x* is not (or never was) the case'. The verb 'remembers' is a verb of success, and '*x* remembers *y*' is equivalent to '*x* seems to remember *y* and this seeming is true'.)

The maximalist may elaborate that there will appear to be a difficulty about nonpresent items' presently possessing properties if one is mistaken about the sorts of properties a past or future item can possess. Since Plato does not now exist, Plato does not now possess the properties of walking, breathing, writing, thinking, and so on. These properties can only be possessed by Plato when he is present. But Plato now possesses the properties of being past, of being referred to by the name 'Plato', of being thought about, of being located earlier in time than Descartes, and so on. Further, Plato now possesses the properties of having walked, having written *The Republic*, having been alive, having been a human, and so on, all of which can be expressed in a symbolic notation of the form $(\exists x)[PG]x$, where $(\exists x)$ can be taken as tenseless or as present tensed in the second sense distinguished by the maximalist. This answers Zimmerman's (1998) criticism of my maximalist theory.

Wolterstorff, Craig, Zimmerman, Levison, Prior, Markosian, Bigelow, Christensen, and many other presentist theorists have argued that it is plausibly or obviously true that "only what presently exists possesses properties." Each of their attempts to make this slogan seem plausible, however, is based on a multiple equivocation upon 'exists', switching from 'exists' in one of its present-tense senses to 'exists' in the other of its present-tense senses to 'exists' in the tenseless sense. See Smith 1992.

11.6   Oaklander and McTaggart's Paradox

Is there a paradox lurking here for the maximalist version of the tensed theory of time? Both presentists and tenseless theorists think an argument involving McTaggart's paradox suffices to refute the maximalist tensed theory. But they are wrong, since all extant arguments of this sort are based on a premise the maximalist theory rejects, namely, that *events simultaneously or timelessly are past, present, and future.* Not a single proponent of the "McTaggart's paradox argument" against the maximalist theory has ever succeeded—or even attempted—to deduce a contradiction from any thesis that actually belongs to the maximalist theory. (I provided textual evidence for this claim in Smith 1993, pp. 169–78.)

There is an exception to this tradition. L. Nathan Oaklander has endeavored to deduce a contradiction from theses *actually espoused* by tensed theorists. In one of these articles (Oaklander 1996), he endeavors to deduce a contradiction from the theory I espoused in Smith 1993 and in my essays in Oaklander and Smith 1994. I shall examine Oaklander's interesting argument.

Oaklander claims my account is implicitly self-contradictory. He argues as follows: If events are present, past, or future, then (to avoid McTaggart's paradox) the events must have these properties successively. It is the case that

(2)   *e* is present, will be past, and has been future; or *e* is past, and has been future and present; or *e* is future and will be present and past.

Oaklander notes that (regarding the second disjunct) the attribution of futurity and presentness to *e* in the past is a contradiction, unless it is specified that *e* has them successively or at different times in the past. This is correct; the second disjunct should be taken as meaning that '*e* is past and has been future and later was present'. (It is not part of my theory to analyze *later* or other B-relations in terms of tensed properties.) This could be put more complexly by distinguishing different degrees of pastness and futurity. For example, it may be true that (using subscripts to indicate different cases of the *inherence* of a property)

(3)   Being one hour past presently inheres$_0$ in *e*, and being two hours past presently inheres$_1$ in the inherence$_2$ of futurity in *e*, and being one hour past presently inheres$_3$ in the inherence$_4$ of presentness in *e*.

Oaklander (1996, p. 210) says the following: "For if *e* was future earlier than *e* was present, then on Smith's analysis that would imply that, say, being past by two hours presently inheres$_1$ in the inherence$_2$ of futurity . . ." (I have substituted my subscripts).

Oaklander claims this implies that

(4)   The state s_1 (being past by two hours *presently inhering*$_1$ in the inherence$_2$ of futurity of e) is EARLIER THAN the state s_2 (being past by one hour *presently inhering*$_3$ in the inherence$_4$ of presentness in e).

Oaklander says this contradicts my claim that the relation *earlier* can obtain between two events only if at least one of the events is not present. However, (3) does not imply (4), and (4) is no part or implication of the tensed theory of time I defended. (4) is Oaklander's invention. The theory I espoused implies that states s_1 and s_2 are SIMULTANEOUS. When e's futurity is two hours past, e's presentness is one hour past. If e was present one hour ago, then e was future two hours ago; presentness inheres in e's being one hour past, and (simultaneously) presentness inheres in e's being two hours in the future.

Phrased in terms of (4), we substitute 'SIMULTANEOUS WITH' for 'EARLIER THAN'.

Oaklander's argument rests on an invalid inference. The valid inference from (3), about the relation of being earlier than, is instead to conclusions such as this: The relation of being earlier than obtains between s_3 (*being past by one hour* presently inhering$_0$ in e) and s_4 (*being past by two hours* presently inheres$_4$ in e). Equivalently, the presentness of e's being past by two hours is a state that obtains *one hour later than* the state of the presentness of e's being past by one hour.

Oaklander's second objection is that if an inherence of a property f in something (perhaps another inherence relation or tie) exists now, then there must also exist now a term in which the property f inheres. But this principle, accepted by many philosophers, including many defenders of presentist theories, is false. It is based on a fallacy of equivocation of 'exists'. If 'exists' is used tenselessly, it means 'existed, exists, or will exist [or has timeless existence]'. In this tenseless sense, something must exist in order to possess a property, for if it does not exist, there is literally nothing there to possess a property. But if 'exists' means 'is present', the principle is immediately implausible. It is true that the events of the year

1996 are earlier than the events of the present moment; this implies that the 1996 events presently exemplify the relation of being earlier than the events that are now present. But the 1996 events are now past; they no longer exemplify presentness. But it is precisely because these events do not now exemplify presentness (or 'existence' in the present-tensed sense) that they now exemplify being earlier than the events that do now exemplify presentness. Further, it is precisely because events do not 'exist' in the present-tensed sense that they can stand in the relation to me of being remembered by me.

In sum, 'Only what exists can possess properties' is plausible if 'exists' is used in a tenseless sense, but it is implausible if 'exists' is used in a present-tensed sense.

I will conclude that the different notions of existence implied by the maximalist tensed theory of time allow the long-discredited theory of "degrees of existence" (espoused by philosophers from Plato to the British Idealists of the late nineteenth and early twentieth centuries) to be revived, although with a different sense given to the phrase 'degrees of existence'.

Being presently present is the highest degree of existence. Being presently past and being presently future *by a merely infinitesimal amount* is the second highest degree of existence. Being presently past *by one hour* and being presently future *by one hour* are lower degrees of existence, and being presently past *by 5 billion years* and being presently future *by 5 billion years* are still lower degrees of existence. The degree to which an item exists is proportional to its temporal distance from the present; the present, which has zero-temporal distance from the present, has the highest (logically) possible degree of existence. These degrees are quantifiable in terms of their inverses, degrees of nonexistence. The present has a zero degree of nonexistence. What is one second past has a one-second degree of nonexistence, and what is two seconds past has a greater degree of nonexistence, namely, a two-second degree of nonexistence. This theory is coherent unless one misinterprets it by assigning a different meaning to 'degree of nonexistence' than I have assigned it.

That existence is degreed explains our phenomenological experience.

There is a difference of degree and not of kind between the present and what is no longer present or not yet present. This is evinced by the fact that our present mental state includes temporal parts that are past by one millionth of a second, and so on, and this small degree of pastness is such a high degree of existence that we cannot experientially distinguish it from present existence, 100% existence. It is arguable that these *degrees of existence* are immediately given in our phenomenological experience, which is evidence for them apart from the semantic and ontological arguments I have given here and elsewhere (see especially Smith 1992).

11.7   Ludlow's Reductive Theory of Presentism

Ludlow advances a reductive theory of presentism in chapter 10 of Ludlow 1999. This reductive theory eliminates the problems of the *de dicto* theory and other versions of presentism I discussed in earlier sections. However, before I examine Ludlow's reductive theory, I shall first discuss his preliminary theory, the theory of *de dicto* presentism (not Ludlow's term) in chapter 7 of his book, and show how his reductive presentism can resolve the problems with this and other theories of *de dicto* presentism.

Ludlow outlines a certain version of what I have generally called '*de dicto* presentism'. Ludlow writes:

[T]he A-theory can treat PAST as an indexical predicate that holds of a proposition-like object, effectively displaying the indexical sense of the past-tense morpheme on the right side of the T-theory axiom:

[(5)]   Val(x, PAST) iff x was true. (p. 97)

By a "proposition-like object" Ludlow means a proposition that changes or can change its truth value. The x in (5) is a proposition and it has the "indexical predicate" that Ludlow calls 'was true'. So far, this is a version of *de dicto* presentism. Note that 'was true' is considered as a predicate of propositions. This conforms to my earlier statement that Prior's operator 'it was the case that' (which means 'it was true that') are logically equivalent to alethic properties of sentences or propositions. Consider the analogy with the modal case: 'It is necessarily true that four equals two plus two'. Here the modal operator 'it is necessarily true that' is equivalent to a predicate of the proposition expressed by 'Four equals two plus two', the predicate 'is necessarily true'. Thus, 'It is necessarily true that four equals two plus two' is logically equivalent to 'Four equals two plus two is necessarily true'. (Of course, we are here talking about the *de dicto* modalities; it is now a commonplace in modal logic that *de dicto* modalities are not equivalent to *de re modalities*, which I have not been discussing in the above sentences.) Likewise, we can agree with Ludlow, who gives a semantics for Prior's tense logic "that is consistent with Priorian metaphysics" (1999, p. 100), that the predicate 'was true' is equivalent to the operator 'it was true that'. In other words, 'It was true that Alice is sitting' is logically equivalent to 'Alice is sitting was true'. This is how the *de dicto* presentist analyzes 'Alice was sitting'. I agree with Ludlow that 'was true' is a predicate of propositions. Ludlow symbolizes this as follows: "Val(x, PAST) iff x was true" (1999, p. 100) The important point to notice here is that x is the proposition expressed by a token of 'Alice is sitting' and 'was true' is a predicate that applies to this proposition. Ludlow holds that predicates, which are linguistic items, associate tokens of properties with the "semantic values" of the predicates, in this case the proposition x, so that 'was true' associates a property token with the proposition expressed by 'Alice is sitting'. Before I explain Ludlow's theory in more detail, let me pause to make a few general observations.

The *de dicto* presentist theory may be construed as holding that either properties or tokens of properties expressed by 'was true' are exemplified by propositions. What is expressed by 'Alice is sitting' is an operand for the operator 'it was true that' and it is the truth vehicle that has the predicate 'was true'. (Some presentists may wish to say, and sometimes do say, that the *sentence token* 'Alice is sitting' is the operand or truth vehicle, rather than the proposition expressed by a sentence token.) Note that there are no further candidates for operands other than propositions or sentence tokens. For example, it violates the logical law of the indiscernability of identicals to claim that there are "facts" or "states of affairs" (conceived as abstract objects) in addition to propositions, for such abstract states of affairs are indiscernible from propositions, as I argue elsewhere (Smith 1993, pp. 156–58). This is a criticism of Plantinga 1974 and Craig 2000a; Ludlow does not adopt an "abstract state of affairs" versus "proposition" distinction and holds a view that is similar in this respect to my own.

Let us see now why Ludlow's preliminary version of presentism, a *de dicto* presentism, motivates a move to Ludlow's subsequent reductive presentism in chapter 9 of his book. If 'was true' and 'will be true' express or refer to property tokens of propositions, then our discussion of *de dicto* presentism would apply to this theory. This can be seen if we distinguish what Ludlow calls the 'semantic value' of a linguistic predicate from its sense. The semantic value of 'is red' as tokened in a sentence token is not the class of red things but the particular that is attributed the predicate in that sentence token. The sentence token 'This blanket is red' is such that the semantic value of 'is red' is identical with this particular blanket. The use of the phrase 'semantic value' may seem to some that Ludlow is saying that predicates refer to their extensions, such as this blanket. But this is not Ludlow's position. Ludlow distinguishes the sense of a predicate from its referent. Let us consider the predicate (or at least the verb phrase) 'is bald'. Ludlow makes three points about predicates in general that I shall apply to this verb phrase:

1. When I say, 'Shelly is bald', the semantic value of 'is bald' is Shelly.

2. Predicates do not refer to their extensions and thus 'is bald' does not refer to Shelly. (See Ludlow 1999, p. 46.)

3. Predicates have senses and their senses specify rules of classification, such that the predicate applies to the referent of the relevant noun phrase or other expression-type in virtue of some property token that that referent possesses.

It seems we may indeed have here a referential role for predicates such as 'is bald'. Let us grant that the semantic value of 'is bald' is the person Shelly. The sense of this predicate is the rule for classifying particulars that are bald and distinguishing them from particulars that are not bald. Since Ludlow (1999, p. 46) adopts Carruthers's theory that the classification rule is based on a property token (which appears to commit Ludlow to a version of trope theory), we have a property token of baldness that is both possessed or exemplified by Shelly and arguably the referent (but not the extension) of the predicate 'is bald'.

Ludlow does not say that predicates "refer" to property tokens; he says the predicate "applies" to the referent of the relevant noun phrase "in virtue of" some property token that that referent possesses. It seems to me that the phrase 'in virtue of' conveys some sort of semantic relation of the predicate to the property token, and I think Ludlow's theory can best be formulated if we call this semantic relation 'reference' (otherwise, what else would we call it?). Let us now reiterate how these ideas apply to the predicates 'is past' and 'is future'. Let p be a proposition and 'was true' in 'p was true' a predicate of the proposition p. Suppose we deny that the referent of 'was true' is a property token of the property *pastness*. Is it then a more complex property token of the second-order property expressed by 'was true'? I think this can be argued to be the case, in line with our earlier discussions of *de dicto* presentism. The sense of this predicate is a rule of classification that is determined by some property token possessed by the proposition p. This property token will be complex, consisting of a token of the truth value of true and a token of the property pastness. That is, p exemplifies being true and its being true exemplifies a property token of pastness. However, if the being true of the proposition is past, it seems that there is some complex state of affairs that is past, namely, the truth of the proposition. If truth is correspondence, it is a relation, which means its two terms exist (in some sense) if the relation obtains. It would seem to follow from this, as I argued in my discussion of *de dicto* presentism, that we do have existents that lie in the past, namely, the past correspondence of the proposition p to the concrete situation Fx that the proposition is about, for example, Jane's walking. It seems here we have a past concrete event, Jane's walking. But this is a result that Ludlow, being a presentist, wishes to avoid.

It is at this point that we can see how Ludlow's move away from *de dicto* presentism to reductive presentism can avoid the series of problems we found with *de dicto* presentism. The presentist wishes to say that "only the present exists" in any sense of 'exists'. We found that this claim cannot be logically reconciled with true sentence tokens containing past and future tenses and the correspondence theory of truth. Ludlow's innovation is to reduce tenses to nontemporal phenomena.

Regarding the so-called temporal morpheme FUTURE, Ludlow's suggestion is that the apparent future tense morpheme is in fact not a future tense morpheme but a nontemporal MODAL. This is true for English, where we do not have 'won', 'win', *and some future-tensed expression*;

rather, we add the modal 'will' to the present-tensed expression 'win', giving us 'will win'. This is also the case for many other natural languages. Ludlow raises the interesting question, Why should we accept the standard view that we are using modals and aspectual markers to express future tense and past tense (hence, to express things about the future and the past)? Why not suppose that we are using modals to express possibility, uncertainty, potentiality, probability, or necessity? For example, 'It must be around eight o'clock' uses the modal 'must' to express necessity.

What do these modals refer to, if not to the future? Modals do not specify an epistemic notion similar to predictability. Ludlow notes that if this is an epistemic notion, we understand it as a prediction of our future, in which case we do not escape reference to the future.

The preference is to use an ontological notion and to say that modals refer to real properties (rather, property tokens) of the world, dispositions. The present world has certain dispositions or potentialities, and these dispositions or potentialities are what we talk about when we say such things as 'I will leave' (Ludlow 1999, p. 160).

Of course, we cannot in this case define dispositions in terms of saying that something *will* come about in certain circumstances. Rather, dispositions are present properties of present things, such as the present position of a car on a cliff-edge.

If this analysis can be carried out successfully, it will dissolve the "problem of the future." The problem may be formulated as the question, There are no future events, so how can future-tensed statements be true? The answer is that there are no irreducible future-tensed statements. Rather, there are sentences containing modals that refer to present dispositions of the present world.

Ludlow suggests that there is no irreducible past tense and that what we call 'past tense' is an evidential, a semantic category discussed in the linguistics literature. The so-called past tense in fact serves to tell us about the kind of evidence we currently have for our claims. For example, one morpheme might indicate that we have first-hand evidence, another morpheme that we have second-hand evidence (e.g., testimony of others), and the like. The root evidentials indicate whether the source of evidence is experience or testimony, and there are more abstract evidentials that include aspectual markers (the so-called progressive, culminative, etc., aspectual markers). Thus, the Norwegian sentence 'Jeg har kommet' has the English meaning 'I apparently/evidently arrived'.

Since the evidence presently exists, there is no longer a problem for the presentist about the past tense having something past as its referent, extension, or semantic value. This also answers the objection that past-tensed sentences are about the past, not about the present, since the objection is mooted by noting that past-tensed sentences are reducible to evidential clauses. What we call past-tensed sentences in fact contain evidential morphemes and serve to indicate the kind of present evidence that we have for our claims.

If there are property tokens as referents of linguistic expressions such as 'was', 'is past', 'will be', and 'is future', these are property tokens of presently existing items of evidence or presently existing dispositions. Thus, Ludlow is able to solve the major problem confronting presentism, namely, not only (1) ensuring that he has an ontology, but also (2) ensuring that his ontology does not imply that there are past or future items.

Now we can address the issue of presentness. Is this a property token? I think Ludlow's theory implies there is no property token of presentness. He argues there is no genuine present tense (1999, p. 123). There is no morpheme PRESENT. What, then, is the referent or semantic correlate of what we normally call 'present tense', such as 'is' 'is present', and the like? It is not evidence or dispositions. I think the best way to understand Ludlow's theory is that (1) the present tense has no referent or semantic correlate and (2) its sense serves merely to indicate that the relevant expression is not an evidential marker or a modal and thereby does not have evidence or dispositions as its semantic correlate. 'Jane is approaching' has a present-tensed 'is', and this serves to indicate that the sentence token is not about evidence for the sentence and is not about a disposition or potentiality. The sentence is about Jane's approach, and the semantic value of both the noun phrase and the verb phrase is Jane, although a property token of the property *approaching* is the referent of the verb phrase (not to be confused with its semantic value). The present tense serves to indicate that Jane's approaching is not an item of evidence or a disposition.

We can see from these remarks that Ludlow's reductive presentism avoids problems that beset *de dicto* presentism. But does reductive presentism have problems of its own?

Ludlow sketches his theory of reductive presentism at the end of his book and is careful to emphasize that this theory needs further development. It seems to me that one area of development is to attempt to deal with objections such as the following ones. It is not a logical contradiction that it is the case both that x will exist and that nothing now possesses the disposition for x to exist. And yet on the reductionist version of presentism, this would be a contradiction, namely, that it is the case both that something now has the disposition for x to exist and that nothing now possesses the disposition for x to exist. Analogously, it is not a logical contradiction that x existed, without there being any present evidence for x's existence. And yet on the reductionist theory, this would be a contradiction, namely, that there is present evidence for x's existence, without there being any present evidence for x's existence.

Furthermore, are the tenses really reduced? If 'roamed' in 'Dinosaurs roamed the earth' refers to present evidence, what is the present evidence *evidence for*? It is not evidence for the existence of the present evidence. Present fossils are not evidence for themselves; rather, present fossils are identical with themselves and are evidence for something else. And what could this "something else" be but the existence of past roamings of dinosaurs? It could be said that the fossils are evidence for the present truth of the sentence "Dinosaurs roamed the earth', but if this sentence is true and is about neither fossils nor an abstract object, what could it be about but the past concrete events of dinosaurs roaming the earth? It cannot be about present concrete objects and contain a reference to their (alleged) property tokens of *being such that dinosaurs roamed the earth*, for this fanciful linguistic construction, even if it does refer to property tokens of this strange sort, does not give a reductive explanation of the past tense since the past-tensed 'roamed' remains in the explanans.

Of course, Ludlow is well aware that his outline of a reductive theory of presentism is open to criticism and further exploration. Ludlow's aim is to suggest a new avenue of thought for the presentist, rather than to embrace definitively a certain theory. He writes:

All of this is extremely sketchy, of course. My point is not that any of this is an inevitable consequence of the A-theory, but rather that this is a possible avenue of investigation that has been opened up. Whether this particular avenue will prove successful is far from clear, and I for one would be hesitant to speculate. (1999, p. 162)

However, I would say that this new avenue, reductive presentism, seems to be the only hope that the presentist has of developing a theory that is consistent with the theory of truth as correspondence. Until and unless the problems with it are resolved, I would suggest the maximalist tensed theory of time is the only tensed theory of time that tensers have available to themselves.

References

Almog, J. 1986. Naming without Necessity. *Journal of Philosophy* 83, pp. 230–48.

Craig, W. L. 2000. *The Tensed Theory of Time*. Dordrecht: Kluwer.

Kaplan, D. 1989a. Demonstratives. In J. Almog, J. Perry, and H. Wettstein, eds., *Themes from Kaplan*, pp. 481–563. Oxford: Oxford University Press.

Kaplan, D. 1989b. Afterthoughts. In J. Almog, J. Perry, and H. Wettstein, eds., *Themes from Kaplan*, pp. 565–614. Oxford: Oxford University Press.

Kim, J.1993. *Supervenience and Mind*. Cambridge: Cambridge University Press.

Ludlow, P. 1999. *Semantics, Tense, and Time*. Cambridge, Mass.: MIT Press.

Oaklander, L. N. 1996. McTaggart's Paradox and Smith's Tensed Theory of Time. *Synthese* 107, pp. 205–21.

Oaklander, L. N., and Q. Smith, eds. 1994. *The New Theory of Time*. New Haven, Conn.: Yale University Press.

Plantinga, A. 1974. *The Nature of Necessity*. Oxford: Oxford University Press.

Prior, A. N. 1957. *Time and Modality*. Oxford: Oxford University Press.

Prior, A. N. 1967. *Past, Present, and Future*. Oxford: Clarendon Press.

Smith, Q. 1992. Time and Degrees of Existence: A Theory of "Degree Presentism." In C. Callender, ed., *Time, Reality and Experience*, pp. 119–36. Cambridge: Cambridge University Press.

Smith, Q. 1993. *Language and Time*. Oxford: Oxford University Press.

Smith, Q. 1997. *Ethical and Religious Thought in Analytic Philosophy of Language*. New Haven, Conn.: Yale University Press.

Smith, Q. 1998. Absolute Simultaneity and the Infinity of the Past. In R. Le Poidevin, ed., *Questions of Time and Tense*, pp. 135–83. Oxford: Oxford University Press. Also see http://www.QSmithWMU.com.

Smith, Q. 2001. Time Was Created by a Timeless Point: An Atheistic Explanation of Space Time. In G. Gegansall and D. Woodruff, eds., *God and Time*, pp. 260–332. New York: Oxford University Press.

Zimmerman, D. 1998. Temporary Intrinsics and Presentism. In P. van Inwagen and D. Zimmerman, ed., *Metaphysics: The Big Questions*, pp. 206–19. Oxford: Oxford University Press.

12

In Defense of Presentism

William Lane Craig

12.1 Introduction

Having emptied his barrels on the partisans of the tenseless or B-theory of time in his *Language and Time*, Quentin Smith now turns his guns upon his A-theoretical comrades-in-arms, taking aim at "another entity that is endangering the truth, namely, the presentist."[1] As a presentist I thus find myself coming under Smith's fire; but as this experience is one to which I have grown accustomed,[2] I cheerfully take up the banner of presentism, confident that his attack can be repulsed.

It is important to be clear about the alternative positions vying for the field. The pure A-theorist, or presentist, holds that the only temporal items that exist are those that exist presently. One of the most recent versions of presentism, Peter Ludlow's theory in *Semantics, Tense, and Time*,[3] which Smith calls a reductive theory of presentism, is based on the idea that past and future tenses are reducible to "evidentials" and "modals," which are semantic categories different from the temporal semantic categories of the past, present, and future tense. Since I defend a nonreductive version of presentism and Smith's main criticism is of nonreductive versions of presentism, I shall concentrate on a nonreductive version of presentism in this chapter.

The B-theorist holds that all temporal items are equally existent. Smith defends a sort of A-B theory, which accepts a B-theoretical ontology but attempts to wed to it objective, changing A-determinations. In other contexts the golden mean between two extremes might seem the course of wisdom; but in this case I am convinced, like McTaggart and countless others, that such a hybrid A-B theory is incoherent, so that we must choose either a pure A-theory or a pure B-theory of time.

I say that correct characterization of the alternatives is important because Smith's attack is launched against a construction of presentism that could not, I think, be recognizably associated with any known presentist thinker. What presentist, for example, affirms the thesis that bears the brunt of Smith's critique, namely, that "there is no such thing as reference to the past or future since there exist no past or future items that could serve as referents (of names, definite descriptions, individual variables, etc.)"?[4] While one sympathizes with Smith's complaint about the paltry "tidbits of information" offered by presentists in explanation of their views, that really cannot justify imputing to them a position that none of them, to my knowledge, would affirm.

In particular, Smith's fundamental distinction between *de dicto* and *de re* tense theories strikes me as misconceived and apt to result only in confusion and distortion of tense logic. Insofar as we do attempt to draw such a distinction, following the model of modality *de dicto* and *de re*, it seems that tense taken *de dicto* would be tense as a feature of one's truth bearers, either the propositional content expressed by tensed sentences or the sentences themselves. Tense taken *de re* would hold that tense is an objective feature of concrete reality. These are not mutually exclusive views of tense; presentists typically hold that there are tensed truth bearers and tensed facts corresponding to them. But Smith associates tense *de dicto* with presentism and tense *de re* with his maximalist A-B theory, interpreting the former to be the view that tense operators ascribe past/present/future truth to certain truth bearers, these being the only "ontological commitments" of the theory, and the latter to be the view that tensed sentences ascribe tensed properties to objects. This is surely a misrepresentation of presentist thinking. I am not sure what Smith means by "ontological commitments" of a theory—this is far from obvious when one thinks about it—but no presentist holds, as Smith alleges, that tense is just a second-order property of one's truth bearers. As Smith styles it, presentism treats tense logical operators as though they were predicate symbols. For he interprets such operators as ascribing, for example, the property *having future truth* to a proposition. But this is just wrong: A. N. Prior's central insight in developing tense logic was that tenses operate adverbially on sentences, and his operators are meant to capture this insight. They do not ascribe predicates to the operand; they qualify when what is said in the operand is the case. Moreover, Smith's own maximalist theory proposes to introduce into tense logic tense predicates and predicate operators in addition to the traditional tense operators and will thus, I fear, only serve to mar the face of tense logic, especially since the distinction between what counts as a predicate or an operator depends on Smith's claim (to be mooted below) that *de dicto* tensed expressions do not refer to past or future individuals whereas *de re* tensed expressions do. What Smith calls *de dicto* presentism is thus purely a product of his own creative imagination.

12.2   In Defense of a Pure A-Theory

Now as his summary sentence at the end of section 11.4 indicates, Smith attempts in his critique of presentism to show that (1) there are concrete items in the past or future to which some propositions correspond and (2) temporal properties such as *presentness* are first-order properties. Section 11.3 is devoted to the task of demonstrating (1); section 11.4 to demonstrating (2).

Smith opens his critique in section 11.3.1 by presenting a paradox for the presentist that he believes does not beset the maximalist, namely, that presentism turns the true sentence 'It is logically possible that there was a time t at which there were no truths' into a logical contradiction. On the basis of Smith's (mis)characterization of presentism, we may presume that this situation results from the presentist's ascribing the property *having past truth* to the proposition expressed by 'There are no truths'. Since the presentist does not in fact do this, one might think the presentist to have eluded Smith's argument. But even if we take the past-tense operator 'P' adverbially, one could argue that the presentist must interpret the sentence at issue to assert that, possibly, it once was the case or was true that 'There are no truths', that is,

(1) Pt (All p : $\sim p$),

which is incoherent. Smith's argument is thus really an attack upon the coherence of Prior's tense logic, rather than on presentism per se. For

Smith's maximalist view would entail that t once exemplified the properties of *presentness* and *containing no truths* without its then being true that 'There are no truths', and I see no reason why presentists could not say the same thing.[5] The fact that presentists believe that t along with its properties has ceased to exist does not imply that they are more committed than maximalists to saying that, possibly, it was once true that 'There are no truths'. Rather, the question is whether Prior's tense logical notation can coherently handle sentences like Smith's example.

Prior dealt with similar cases in discussing what is the case at the beginning or end of time, before or after which there would be no truths.[6] He argued plausibly that the surface grammar of sentences like Smith's example is misleading in just the way Smith indicates. The proper symbolization of Smith's sentence would not be (1), but

(2)   All $p : \sim Pt(p)$.

The sentence symbolized by (2) would become true at the first moment that truths exist. Therefore, it seems to me that, *pace* Smith, Prior's tense logic has the resources to handle properly the situation envisioned by Smith. More importantly, there is no reason to think that the presentist faces any greater difficulty here than the maximalist. Thus, Smith's opening salvo against the presentist falls short of its target.

In sections 11.3.3–11.3.4, Smith seeks to advance his case for the concrete reality of past and future individuals, first by a critique of Kaplan's views on contexts of evaluation and then by a critique of Plantinga's views on states of affairs. It seems to me that these sections of Smith's chapter are permeated by a fundamental confusion of *reference* and *correspondence*. Here a word of clarification may be helpful. Smith's final version of his chapter is the product of a considerable evolution from the ancestral paper delivered at the Santa Barbara conference, and the inconcinnities in the final version are vestiges of that development. Smith originally argued that reference to past and future individuals requires the concrete reality of such individuals, and the notion of correspondence surfaced only intermittently. The chapter's title and the opening characterization of presentism as the view that "there is no such thing as reference to the past or future since there exist no past or future items that could serve as referents (of names, definite descriptions, individual variables, etc.)" reflect the central thrust of the original. In response, I challenged the inference made in this characterization on the grounds that Smith seemed to assume that presentism entails the direct reference theory, according to which propositions have concrete objects among their constituents. But I saw no reason why the presentist should be committed to such a theory. I suggested that one may adopt, for example, Plantinga's view that proper names express individual essences, where an individual essence is a property that is essential to an object and essentially unique to that object.[7] On such a neo-Fregean view, the proper name 'Socrates' expresses an individual essence of Socrates rather than denotes nonconnotatively the actual object Socrates and so does not require Socrates to exist in order for the name to refer. Indeed, Plantinga champions his view in opposition to the direct reference theory precisely because of the latter's failure to deal plausibly with empty proper names and proper names in true, negative existential propositions.[8] On a presentist theory, Plantinga's objections would also be relevant to proper names of no longer existent or not yet existent individuals. Thus, successful reference to past or future individuals does not require the concrete reality of such individuals.

In the final version of Smith's paper, the notion of reference recedes and in its place the issue of correspondence rises to prominence. Now Smith contends regarding Kaplan:

The point is that the temporally indexed proposition corresponds to a past concrete state of affairs. It is logically irrelevant if there are singular propositions that include past or future concrete existents as parts. All that is relevant is what stands in a correspondence relation to a proposition, be the proposition singular or general.[9]

Smith then proceeds to criticize, not Plantinga's theory of proper names, but his understanding of states of affairs, arguing that "the issue of truth as correspondence remains unsolved."[10]

I take it for granted that the notions of reference and correspondence are distinct, the former having to do with how terms serve to pick out individuals and the latter having to do with the relation between reality as it is described by a proposition and that proposition, in virtue of which that proposition can be said to bear the value *true*. Now until some criticism is forthcoming to show that Plantinga's theory of proper

names is defective, Smith has not demonstrated any difficulty with *refer-*
ence to past or future individuals. The question that remains is whether
one who holds to a view of truth as correspondence cannot be a presentist.

Well, why not? This issue has been much discussed, usually in the
context of what I think is a misguided attempt on the part of certain A-
theorists to avoid fatalism by denying the principle of bivalence with respect to future contingent propositions.[11] If they attempt to justify their
denial of bivalence with respect to such propositions on the basis of a
view of truth as correspondence, it is usually enough to point out that
such reasoning cannot be correct, for it would force us to deny bivalence
not only for future contingent propositions, but for all future-tense
propositions and all past-tense propositions as well, which is absurd.
Smith, in effect, agrees that this is precisely what the presentist who is
committed to a view of truth as correspondence is obligated to accept.
Rather than reject the mistaken understanding of correspondence that
underlies such a denial of bivalence for future contingent propositions,
Smith accepts that understanding and instead rejects presentism in order
to avoid the absurd consequence of denying the bivalent status of all
past- and future-tense propositions.

But Smith's rejection of presentism on these grounds is an extreme
measure, since the understanding of correspondence underlying it does
seem so clearly wrong. Smith seems to suppose that in order for a tensed
proposition to possess the value *true* at some time, the entities referred to
in the proposition must actually exist, that all things/events in time are
on an ontological par. This is not to say that the relevant things/events
exist at the time of the proposition's truth; rather, it is to say that they
exist at those times indicated by the proposition. Of course, in one sense
the presentist also affirms this, in that the things/events referred to in a
true proposition did, do, or will exist. But for Smith, even though past
and future things/events do not exist now, they are now as equally real
as the things/events that do, and with that the presentist begs to disagree.
The presentist may plausibly claim that a view of truth as correspondence requires only that the entities referred to in a true past- or future-
tense proposition either did or will exist at the indicated times. As
Charles Bayliss pointed out in his trenchant critique of Łukasiewicz:

For the truth of propositions to the effect that certain events did occur in the past it is necessary only that the occurrence of these events was at the time specified a fact, and, similarly, for the truth of propositions to the effect that certain events will occur at a given time in the future it is necessary only that the occurrence of these events at that time will be a fact.[12]

Whether a future-tense proposition is now true is thus determined by how things will turn out, and the present truth of a past-tense proposition is determined by how things went.

What such an account of the truth of past- and future-tense propositions requires is that there are tensed facts corresponding to tensed propositions, and the A-theorist is only too eager to affirm this conclusion. Thus, the proposition *Plato wrote The Republic* is true, on a view of truth as correspondence, because this event did occur; that is, a man named Plato did exist and wrote the work entitled *The Republic*. These are tensed facts that (depending on what one takes a fact to be) exist or obtain or are true now, but were not so in, say, 5,000 B.C. So a view of truth as correspondence requires the objective reality of tensed facts, facts about what was or will be the case.

Now one way of construing a fact is as a state of affairs that obtains, as Plantinga employs these terms. Accordingly, the A-theorist holds that there are tensed states of affairs that obtain at various times. Exploiting the parallel between presentism and actualism with respect to possible worlds,[13] we may explicate this notion as follows:

Following Plantinga, we may conceive of a possible world as a maximal possible state of affairs, where a state of affairs *s* is maximal if for every state of affairs *s'*, *s* includes *s'* or *s* precludes *s'*. So conceived, possible worlds and the states of affairs that constitute them are normally understood to be tenseless states of affairs; otherwise, we could never speak of events' occurring at different times in a possible world, since, as McTaggart's paradox discloses, there is no maximal or complete description of a temporal world over time owing to tensed facts. Hence, the worlds described in possible-worlds semantics are tenseless possible worlds. In order to handle tensed facts, we need to allow tensed states of affairs as well, like *the Battle of Waterloo's having occurred* and *Clinton's being president*, to be constituents of possible worlds. A tensed possible world is a maximal possible state of affairs at some time *t* of arbitrarily stipulated duration, whether an instant, an arbitrarily brief moment, an hour, a day, and so forth. Tensed possible worlds that did, do, or will obtain are tensed actual worlds. The tensed actual world at *t* will be the tensed actual world that obtains when *t's being present* obtains, or more simply, when *t* is present. The world that presently obtains is simply the tensed actual world. Tensed actual worlds constitute the tensed history of the actual world α, for they are respectively constituted by all states of affairs entailed by α and each successive *t's* being present. This may be generalized to any possible world *w*: the tensed history of *w* will be all the tensed possible worlds constituted by the states of affairs entailed by *w* and each successive *t's* being present in *w*.

To say that a temporal entity *x* exists in a tenseless possible world *w* is to say that if *w* were actual, *x* would exist (tenselessly) at some time *t*; or again, *x* exists in *w* if it is impossible that *w* obtain and *x* fail to exist (tenselessly) at some time *t*. Analogously, to say that *x* exists in a tensed possible world w^t is to say that if w^t were actual, then *x* would exist (present-tense). To say that *x* exists in a tensed actual world $α^t$ is to say that when $α^t$ becomes actual, then *x* exists (present-tense); it is impossible when $α^t$ obtains that *x* not exist (present-tense).

With respect to tenseless possible worlds, to say that Socrates has in *w* the property of being snub-nosed is to say that Socrates would have (tenselessly) the property of being snub-nosed, were *w* to be actual; the state of affairs *w's being actual and Socrates' not being* (tenselessly) *snub-nosed* is impossible. Analogously, to say that Socrates has in a tensed possible world w^t the property of being snub-nosed is to say that Socrates would have (present-tense) the property of being snub-nosed, were w^t to be actual; the state of affairs w^t's *being actual and Socrates' not being* (present-tense) *snub-nosed* is impossible. To say that Socrates has in a tensed actual world $α^t$ the property of being snub-nosed is to say that when $α^t$ becomes actual, then Socrates has (present-tense) the property of being snub-nosed; it is impossible when $α^t$ obtains that Socrates is (present-tense) not snub-nosed.

Each tenseless possible world exists in each world. The actual world α is the maximal state of affairs that obtains (tenselessly). Were some other world actual, α would not obtain, but would still exist as a possible state of affairs. Since only α is in fact actual, none of the other tenseless possible worlds is actual, but each one is actual in or at itself. Each world *w* has the property of actuality in *w* and in *w* alone. That also goes for α. But α is not merely actual in α; in fact, it is actual *simpliciter*. Thus, α is uniquely distinguished as *the* actual world, the one tenseless possible world that obtains. Analogously, each tensed possible world exists in each such world. The tensed actual world *v* is the maximal state of affairs that obtains (present-tense). Were some other tensed possible world actual, then *v* would not obtain, but it would still exist as a tensed possible state of affairs. By the same token, when some other tensed actual world obtains (present-tense), then *v* either does not yet or no longer obtains, but *v* nonetheless exists as a tensed actual state of affairs. Since *v* alone is (present-tense) actual, none of the other tensed actual worlds (not to speak of tensed merely possible worlds) is (present-tense) actual, though they either were or will be actual. Still, each tensed world, including *v*, is actual in itself. But *v* is not merely actual in *v*, but also actual *simpliciter*. Thus, *v* is uniquely distinguished as *the* tensed actual world, the one tensed possible world that obtains (present-tense).

Now Smith argues that such an account of tensed facts is unsuccessful. Here is where Smith's conflation of reference and correspondence emerges. He construes Plantinga's states of affairs as being composed of abstract objects such as Hegel's individual essence, the property of *being alive*, and something else sufficient for tense. But this is a mistake. Hegel's individual essence is relevant only for problems of reference and proper names, not for correspondence of a proposition to a tensed state of affairs. Smith is unconsciously transferring over to Plantinga his own conception of states of affairs as composed of concrete objects and their properties, but just substituting abstract for concrete objects. But on Plantinga's analysis, a state of affairs is just a way things might be, and any sense of composition other than being composed of less maximal states of affairs is inappropriate. Thus, tensed states of affairs like *the Battle of Waterloo's having occurred* are holistically conceived and just obtain at different times. Really, there is no more difficulty in conceiving of a tensed state of affairs than of a tensed proposition, which Smith freely accepts.

But, Smith demands, if a tensed state of affairs like *Hegel's having been alive* now obtains, what concrete objects suffice to make it obtain? Presumably, Smith is not asking why Hegel's life is past rather than present or future, a conundrum that any tense theorist must face.[14] Rather, his complaint is that "if there are no concreta that are the truth makers of the proposition *Hegel used to be alive*, then this proposition is true with nothing sufficing to make it true...."[15] But this complaint presupposes the wooden view of correspondence that we have already rejected. What suffices for the truth of the proposition in question is that the concrete object named Hegel did exist and then died. What more could be needed? Any further inquiry as to why the corresponding tensed state of affairs obtains must either be answered in terms of Hegel's parents and health or else plunge us down the route of explaining why presentness occupies a moment later than Hegel's death rather than earlier, a question the maximalist is in no better position to answer than the presentist.

Smith goes on to object that if it is only what presently exists that makes the relevant state of affairs obtain or the corresponding proposition true, then the proposition is not about something past, the man Hegel, but about something present, namely, the abstract state of affairs *Hegel's having been alive*, which is manifestly incorrect. Moreover, the state of affairs does not in that case bear an "obtaining-making" relation to anything past and so is really a present-tense state of affairs. Smith's argument here is a mare's nest badly in need of untangling. Notions of reference, correspondence, makers of truth, makers of obtaining, and aboutness all get indiscriminately run together. A view of truth as correspondence requires that corresponding to the presently true proposition *Hegel used to be alive* is a tensed fact, which I have taken to be the tensed state of affairs *Hegel's having been alive* that presently obtains. The proper name 'Hegel' expresses an individual essence of the concrete particular named Hegel and so refers to the person so named. What makes the tensed proposition true? One could say that the fact that Hegel used to be alive makes the proposition true, in the sense that the tensed fact is expressed as the truth conditions of the relevant proposition on a view of truth as correspondence. But one could also say that the past-tense proposition is true because the relevant present-tense proposition once was true, a view that Freddoso has called "the primacy of the pure present."[16] What made the present-tense proposition true was the living, breathing, concrete object Hegel. So ultimately the truth of the past-tense proposition derives from the things/events referred to plus the lapse of time. What makes the tensed state of affairs *Hegel's having been alive* obtain? Again, the answer seems to be a combination of Hegel's being alive plus temporal becoming. Thus, the fact that a past-tense state of affairs presently obtains in no way implies that it really is, *per impossible*, a present-tense state of affairs. Nor does the correspondence of a past-tense proposition to a presently obtaining tensed fact imply that the proposition is about the fact. Intuitively, what the proposition is about is the things or events referred to in the proposition, not the fact expressed as its truth conditions. But the proposition *Hegel used to be alive* involves reference to the man Hegel and so is about Hegel, not about the tensed fact *Hegel's having been alive*. Thus, Smith's objections are just misconceived.

Therefore, I do not think that Smith has managed to establish either on the basis of successful reference to past/future individuals or on the basis of a view of truth as correspondence that there actually exist concrete items in the past or future to which tensed propositions correspond.[17]

What about Smith's point (2) that temporal properties such as presentness are first-order properties? In section 11.4, Smith argues that *de dicto* tenses imply *de re* tenses. The fundamental problem with this section of the chapter is that it is misdirected. The presentist denies that temporal items possess properties of pastness and futurity because properties can only be possessed by items that exist and only present temporal items exist. But Smith avers that it is characteristic of the theory not only to deny "the existence of the past and future," but also to claim that "there is no monadic property of presentness that is exemplified by anything concrete."[18] He argues that if an abstract object like a proposition can exemplify a temporal property like *being presently true*, then there is no reason why a concrete object, like a thing or event, cannot exemplify a temporal property. I agree. But it is neither an implication nor an entailment of presentism that presentness is not a property possessed by things, events, or times. It may be characteristic of presentists to subscribe to what Smith has called the 'no property' view of presentism; but the property status of presentness is a subject of in-house debate among presentists. The presentist can happily embrace the view that presentness is the one A-determination that is a genuine property.

But has Smith proved that presentness is a property? I think not, since his argument is based on the erroneous assumption that presentism ascribes to propositions the temporal property *being presently true*. But I should say that even in the case of propositions that change their truth value, those that are true do not exemplify the property *being presently true*; rather, they presently exemplify the property *being true* or *truth*. Smith asks, But to what ontological category does presentness belong, if it is not a property? I have elsewhere tried to get at this metaphysical question by examining the property status of existence, which a great many thinkers, including Smith, have found analogous to presentness.[19] I argue that there are plausible grounds for denying that existence is a property: (1) Kant's objection that adding *existence* to the concept of an object fails to increase the content of that concept, (2) Broad and Moore's several examples of the anomalies that result when existence is taken to be a property, and (3) Alston's argument that the existence of an entity is explanatorily prior to the inherence of properties in it. On the positive side, existence can be taken to be an act, the act of instantiation of an essence. Now presentness is not just existence (though many presentists tend to equate these), for timeless existence is at least possible (imagine a world comprising only abstract objects). Therefore, we may say that presentness is a mode of existence, a temporal way of existing. I find such a construal preferable to Smith's view that presentness and existence "are unusual kinds of properties and should be placed in an ontological category by themselves."[20] If they are really that unusual, if they require a special ontological category especially for them, then this may sound a bit like saying that they are properties that are not properties. But if one wishes to construe them as properties, this will in no way be incompatible with a metaphysic of presentism.

12.3   Critique of Smith's A-B Theory

If presentism, properly understood, thus represents a defensible position, what about Smith's own hybrid A-B theory of time? Is it coherent? Like the Meinongian who asserts that there are things (merely possible objects) that do not exist, Smith seems ensnared by the contradiction that there are things (past and future entities) that do not exist. For on his view there must be something, say, Plato, that has the property *pastness*. But if Plato has this property, that is, presently has it, as Smith avers, then Plato must now exist. But if Plato exists now, then he has both presentness and pastness, which is absurd. In section 11.5, Smith struggles valiantly to avoid this contradiction—but, in my mind, to no avail.

Smith agrees that "... Plato does not now exist ...," but he insists that "... Plato now possesses the properties of being past,..., and so on."[21] Smith must therefore deny that

(3)   In order to possess a property now, a substance must exist now

is true. But (3) seems to be a conceptual truth, since the very concept of a property is of an entity that does not have independent existence but is some sort of modification of a substance. Thus, necessarily, if a substance now has a property, that property cannot exist alone now nor can that property's inherence in its subject occur alone now, but the substance in which the property inheres must now exist along with its property.[22] Remarkably, Smith himself hurls the following challenge at his opponent early in the chapter: "How can a nonexistent (at time *t*) possess a property (at time *t*)?"[23] This question must return to haunt Smith in section 11.5, since he himself claims that Plato does not exist now and yet possesses properties now. Any plausibility that might accrue to a denial of (3) comes only from radically reconstruing (3) as, say,

(3*)   In order for it to be true now that a substance possesses a
        property, the substance must exist now,

which is useless to Smith, since 'possesses' is tenseless in (3*). Smith wants to assert more than that it is now (and at every time) true that Plato tenselessly possesses such properties as *being the teacher of Aristotle, being alive in the fourth century* B.C., and so forth. For Smith holds that Plato's properties change over time, that he now possesses properties he once lacked. How Plato can accomplish the feat of acquiring a new property in 1998 without existing in 1998 remains mysterious.

Smith alleges that presentists who have argued that "only what presently exists possesses properties" make this slogan plausible only by a multiple equivocation of the word 'exists'. Smith distinguishes three meanings of 'exists': (1) 'has the property of presentness', (2) 'presently possesses some property', and (3) 'has existed, exists, or will exist'.[24] Smith agrees that past and future things/events do not exist in sense (1); but he insists that they do exist in senses (2) and (3) and therefore can possess properties.

This explanation solves nothing. Obviously, Plato does not exist in sense (1). He does exist in sense (3), since he has existed; but even the presentist affirms that, and the question still remains, How can a substance that existed, but no longer exists, now possess properties? Smith asserts that past and future things exist in sense (2). But as an account of how Plato can possess properties now without existing now, this explanation is vacuous. Plato can possess properties now, we are informed, because Plato does, after all, presently possess properties. I conclude that Smith has failed to define a coherent and informative sense in which Plato exists so as to presently possess properties.

But now a deeper incoherence in Smith's view emerges. For he not only thinks that Plato now possesses properties, but also believes that Plato now possesses *different* properties than he did before. Consider Plato (or the temporal part of Plato) existing in 389 B.C. In 389 B.C., Plato possessed the property *being alive*. But now Plato—that very same Plato—possesses the property *being dead*. But then Smith runs smack into the problem of temporary intrinsics,[25] to wit: the principle of the indiscernibility of identicals requires that if an object o and an object o^* are identical, then they must possess all the same properties. But on Smith's view, Plato changes in his properties and therefore cannot remain self-identical. Thus, it is false that Plato once possessed the property *being alive* and now possesses the property *being dead*.

In response to the problem of temporary intrinsics, David Lewis offered his temporal parts ontology as an account of intrinsic change that holds that o and o^*, which differ in their properties, are actually different parts of a temporally extended entity that do *not* change in their respective properties. But while that metaphysic works nicely on a pure B-theory of time, it cannot give a coherent account of intrinsic change on a hybrid A-B theory of time. For the temporal part of Plato that has the property *being dead* is not the part that is his corpse or other remains;

rather, it is the *very same* temporal part in 389 B.C. which at that time had the property *being alive*. But how did this change occur? How is it that the same 389 B.C. slice of Plato once had the property of being alive and now has the property of being dead? By introducing change in the temporal parts themselves, Smith raises the problem of temporary intrinsics all over again and threatens to introduce a hypertime in which temporal parts change.

Smith would avoid recourse to a hypertime by maintaining that not only does the property of presentness inhere in a temporal part, but also the property of presentness inheres in its own inherence in that part. On Smith's A-B theory, although all temporal parts are equally real, only one is uniquely present at present; all the rest are past or future at present. Although a benign infinite regress of present inherences is thus generated, this is, he claims, unproblematic because one never leaves the single time dimension. While every temporal part has the property of being present at its time, only one temporal part of a thing can be presently present, which is equivalent to being absolutely present.

But the problem with this solution, it seems to me, is that the absolute property of presentness becomes unintelligible or vacuous on such an account. Since every temporal part exists and is present at its respective time, it is wholly mysterious what more is added to it when it becomes absolutely present. If to become present is not, as the presentist maintains, to become real, then what is it? I must confess that the notion of presentness on Smith's theory is utterly opaque to me. Unless one means that temporal parts become successively present in a hypertime (which Smith denies), then there just is no content left in asserting that each temporal part, all of which are equally real and each of which is present at its respective time, becomes successively present.

12.4   Conclusion

In conclusion, then, I think that not only can Smith's attacks on a pure A-theory of presentism be repulsed, but his own position of the A-B theory has been shown to be untenable. We have not seen any good reason to think that either reference to past/future individuals or a view of truth as correspondence is incompatible with presentism, when this view is correctly characterized. On the other hand, Smith has not been able to tender a coherent account of how on his view past or future individuals can presently possess properties or of how intrinsic change can occur in such entities. The A-B theory of time is thus a teratological hybrid, which occasions only curiosity and offers no viable synthesis of our genuine alternatives, the A- and B-theories of time.

Notes

1. Q. Smith, "Reference to the Past and Future" (this volume). The ominous characterization of presentism cited in the text is found in the version of Smith's chapter read at the 1997 Santa Barbara City College conference "Time, Tense, and Reference." Actually, Smith already adumbrates his disagreement with presentists in *Language and Time* (New York: Oxford University Press, 1993), pp. 166–69, where he calls his own view 'presentism' and opposes it to the 'no property' tensed theory of time.

2. See our debate *Theism, Atheism, and Big Bang Cosmology* (Oxford: Clarendon Press, 1993) and subsequent exchanges.

3. P. Ludlow, *Semantics, Tense, and Time* (Cambridge, Mass.: MIT Press, 1999).

4. Smith, "Reference to Past and Future," sec. 11.1.

5. I have in mind Thomas Aquinas's conceptualist view of propositions (*enuntiabilia*). On Thomas's view, the Platonic realm of abstract objects is not a domain existing externally to God; rather, it is the realm of divine ideas. But in view of the simplicity of God's nature, the divine ideas are not to be understood literally as a plurality in the contents of divine consciousness. God has a simple, undifferentiated grasp of reality that we represent to ourselves in our finite minds as a multiplicity of items, such as individual propositions or truths. It follows that at a time prior to the creation of finite creatures, there were no truths. Since Thomas was also a presentist, he would be an example of someone who actually held to the position imagined by Smith.

6. See, for example, Prior's "The Logic of Ending Time," in *Papers on Time and Tense* (Oxford: Clarendon Press, 1968), pp. 98–115. I am indebted to Peter Øhrstrøm for this reference as well as suggestions about how Prior would quantify over propositions.

7. See A. Plantinga, "The Boethian Compromise," *American Philosophical Quarterly* 15 (1978), pp. 129–38; idem, *The Nature of Necessity* (Oxford: Clarendon Press, 1974), pp. 71–81; idem, "Self-Profile," in J. E. Tomberlin and P. van Inwagen, eds., *Alvin Plantinga* (Dordrecht: Reidel, 1985), pp. 76–87; idem, "Reply to Diana Ackerman," in *Plantinga*, pp. 349–65.

8. Plantinga, *Nature of Necessity*, pp. 137–44, 149–63.

9. Smith, "Reference to Past and Future," sec. 11.3.3.

10. Smith, "Reference to Past and Future," sec. 11.3.4.

11. See discussion in W. L. Craig, *Divine Foreknowledge and Human Freedom* (Leiden: E. J. Brill, 1991), pp. 43–63.

12. C. A. Bayliss, "Are Some Propositions Neither True Nor False?" *Philosophy of Science* 3 (1936), p. 162. See also R. D. Bradley, "Must the Future Be What It Is Going to Be?" *Mind* 68 (1959), p. 204; N. Rescher and A. Urquhart, *Temporal Logic* (New York: Springer-Verlag, 1971), p. 211.

13. See N. Wolterstorff, "Can Ontology Do without Events?" *Grazer Philosophischer Studien* 7/8 (1979), pp. 188–89; Plantinga, *Nature of Necessity*, pp. 44–49. See further J. Bigelow, "Worlds Enough for Time," *Noûs* 25 (1991), pp. 1–19; P. Percival, "Indices of Truth and Temporal Propositions," *Philosophical Quarterly* 39 (1989), pp. 190–99; R. M. Gale, "Lewis' Indexical Argument for World-Relative Actuality," *Dialogue* 28 (1989), pp. 289–304; P. Yourgrau, "On Time and Actuality: The Dilemma of Privileged Position," *British Journal for the Philosophy of Science* 37 (1986), pp. 405–17; G. Forbes, "Actuality and Context Dependence. I," *Analysis* 43 (1983), pp. 123–29.

14. The question "Why is it 'now'?" is raised by J. J. C. Smart and pressed by Adolf Grünbaum as an objection to any theory that postulates an objective, mind-independent present (J. J. C. Smart, *Philosophy and Scientific Realism* (London: Routledge & Kegan Paul, 1963), p. 135; A. Grünbaum, "The Status of Temporal Becoming," in *Modern Science and Zeno's Paradoxes* (Middleton, Conn.: Wesleyan University Press, 1967), pp. 26–27). One may especially wonder on Smith's hybrid A-B theory why the property of presentness should find itself at 1998 rather than earlier or later. Indeed, one wonders whether, having made the rounds of all the moments of time, presentness will not eventually swing back for a second pass (or maybe reverse directions). Obviously, these are the issues raised by McTaggart's paradox.

15. Smith, "Reference to Past and Future," sec. 11.3.4.

16. A. Freddoso, "Accidental Necessity and Power over the Past," *Pacific Philosophical Quarterly* 63 (1982), pp. 54–68; cf. idem, "Accidental Necessity and Logical Determinism," *Journal of Philosophy* 80 (1983), 257–78; also P. Horwich, *Asymmetries in Time* (Cambridge, Mass.: MIT Press, 1987), p. 30.

17. Smith also argues that presentism is incompatible with remembering. Remembering, he explains, is a triadic relation among a person, a mental image, and a past thing. Thus, past things can have the polyadic property *being remembered*. This argument also fails to convince. Smith confuses 'standing in a relation' with 'possessing a property'. Smith presupposes that for something to stand in a relation with something that exists now, both *relata* must presently stand in that relation, and furthermore, that if both *relata* presently stand in a relation, then both *relata* exist in more than a tenseless sense of 'exists', assumptions that are less than obvious. We also are given too superficial an account of remembering. Smith's account fails to make sense, for example, of false memories. We have all had experiences of distinctly remembering something that later turned out to be other than we recalled. It would be phenomenologically incorrect to say that

in such cases we only seemed to remember a thing; for upon further introspection we might well reply, 'No, I really do remember it that way'. In this sense, memory is parallel to anticipation, which Smith himself recognizes to be indeterminate with respect to reference to future objects. Just as I can dread the dental appointment that in fact does not occur, so I can remember putting my keys in the drawer when in fact I left them in my coat pocket. Perhaps it would be helpful to distinguish between the intentional being and the substantial being of the objects of memory and anticipation. All such objects have intentional being as the objects of attitudes; their substantial being is what renders my beliefs true or false. We have seen no reason to think that correspondence requires the substantial being of things in a present-tense sense. If Smith says that the intentional images I form of substantial objects require the present-tense existence of those objects, then we may say that they no more do so than a painting of the Last Supper requires the present-tense existence of the persons and things depicted.

18. Smith, "Reference to Past and Future," sec. 11.3.4.

19. W. L. Craig, "Is Presentness a Property?" *American Philosophical Quarterly* 34 (1997), pp. 27–40.

20. Smith, "Reference to Past and Future."

21. Smith, "Reference to Past and Future," sec. 11.5.

22. One may compare here with profit the debate among medieval thinkers concerning divine conservation and concurrence. Those who held only to conservation maintained that although God sustains a substance in being moment by moment, He is only a cause of its existence, not of its specific properties. Concurrentists argued that the actual existence of a substance involves its existing in all its particularity, with specific properties, so that if God causes a substance to exist at some time, He must concur with secondary causes in causing it to have the properties it does (see excellent discussion in A. J. Freddoso, "God's General Concurrence with Secondary Causes: Why Conservation Is Not Enough," in J. E. Tomberlin, ed., *Philosophical Perspectives*. Vol. 5, *Philosophy of Religion* (Atascadero, Calif.: Ridgeview Press, 1991), pp. 553–85). Smith's position is the mirror image of the simple conservationist's: he maintains that a substance's properties may all exist and be possessed by a substance at a time without that substance's existing at that time.

23. Smith, "Reference to Past and Future," sec. 11.3.1.

24. Smith, "Reference to Past and Future," sec. 11.5.

25. See D. Lewis, *On the Plurality of Worlds* (Oxford: Basil Blackwell, 1986), pp. 203–4. For its application to tense changes, see W. L. Craig, "McTaggart's Paradox and the Problem of Temporary Intrinsics," *Analysis* 58 (1998), pp. 122–27.

13

Basic Tensed Sentences and Their Analysis

Michael Tooley

In *Time, Tense, and Causation,*[1] I set out and defended a dynamic conception of the nature of time that involved some features not normally associated with tensed approaches to time. Of these, one of the most important was the thesis that ordinary tensed sentences are not the most basic tensed sentences—a claim that is universally rejected by those who accept a static conception of time, and almost universally rejected by those who defend tensed approaches to the nature of time.

In spite of the importance of that thesis for my approach, the direct support that I offered for it was not especially extensive, and I was content, on the whole, to argue for it in an indirect fashion by showing that the overall account of the nature of time and tense of which that thesis is an integral part makes it possible to answer, in a very straightforward fashion, objections that many philosophers feel have considerable force against tensed approaches—objections such as McTaggart's famous argument for the conclusion that the postulation of tensed properties gives rise to a contradiction, and related arguments advanced by Hugh Mellor.

While that indirect support seems to me very strong, it is also possible to set out a direct argument—which I believe is, in fact, decisive—in support of the thesis that ordinary tensed sentences, rather than being basic, can be analyzed in terms of other, more basic tensed sentences. My goal in this chapter, accordingly, will be to develop such an argument, and, thereby, to provide additional support for my overall account of the nature of time.

The structure of the discussion is as follows. In section 13.1, I shall briefly outline the views I am defending, first, with regard to the logical form of basic tensed statements, and second, on the question of whether those basic tensed sentences are themselves analyzable, or, on the contrary, semantically basic. Then, in section 13.2, I shall begin by setting out, in a detailed way, the first part of the three-part argument that I am offering for the view that ordinary tensed sentences are not basic tensed sentences. The conclusion of that first part is a conditional one—namely, that a dynamic account of the meaning of tensed language cannot possibly be sound unless at least some basic tensed sentences are not ordinary tensed sentences. The argument I shall offer for that claim involves two crucial, and controversial, premises. The first is that if all basic tensed sentences involved indexicals, then no tensed sentences would entail the existence of irreducible tensed facts, and so a static view of the nature of tensed language would be correct; the second is that all ordinary tensed sentences involve indexicals. Sections 13.3 and 13.4 are devoted to a defense of those premises.

The second stage of the three-part argument is then directed to establishing the further conditional claim that there are sentences that, although they are not *ordinary* tensed sentences, can be shown to be tensed sentences *if* a dynamic account of the meaning of tensed language is correct. This stage, in outline, is as follows. First, in sections 13.5 and 13.6, I turn to the question of whether one can plausibly hold that there are any tensed sentences other than ordinary tensed sentences, and, if so, what those other tensed sentences could possibly be. My answer is that there do not appear to be any plausible candidates other than certain nonindexical sentences that involve tensed concepts—sentences such as 'The birth of David Hume lies (tenselessly) in the past in the year 1997'.

But are such sentences really *tensed* sentences? For isn't the sentence 'The birth of David Hume lies (tenselessly) in the past in the year 1997' just analytically equivalent to the sentence 'The birth of David Hume is earlier than the year 1997'? In sections 13.7 and 13.8, I address this question, and there I appeal to the analysis of tensed sentences set out in *Time, Tense, and Causation* to show that such sentences can be analyzed in a way that entails that they can only be true in a dynamic world. The claim that they are tensed sentences can, therefore, be sustained.

The final stage of the three-part argument then involves establishing the fundamental claim that if a dynamic account of the meaning of tensed language is correct, then ordinary tensed sentences cannot be basic tensed sentences. This is a conclusion that follows very quickly from the conclusion of part two of the argument. For once it has been established that nonindexical sentences such as 'The birth of David Hume lies (tenselessly) in the past in the year 1997' are tensed sentences, it is then a straightforward matter to use such sentences to set out truth conditions for ordinary tensed sentences—such as 'The birth of David Hume lies in the past'—since one only needs to apply whatever technique one favors for stating the truth conditions of indexical sentences in general in terms of the corresponding, nonindexical sentences to the specific case of ordinary tensed sentences. The upshot is that if a dynamic account of tensed language is correct, then no ordinary tensed sentences are basic tensed sentences: all of them can be analyzed in terms of nonindexical tensed sentences.

13.1   An Overview: The Position to Be Defended

Traditionally, advocates of both tensed and tenseless approaches to the nature of time have agreed that sentences such as 'Event *e* is now taking place' constitute at least one type of basic tensed sentence—though they have disagreed, of course, with regard to whether such sentences can then be analyzed in terms of other sentences that do not involve tensed concepts. Thus, on the one hand, all advocates of tenseless approaches to time necessarily hold that such analysis is possible—though their conception of the form that such analysis should take has changed over time. So while early advocates of tenseless approaches to time—such as Bertrand Russell, Hans Reichenbach, Nelson Goodman, and others—maintained, for example, that sentences such as 'Event *e* is now taking place' could be analyzed by being *translated* into tenseless sentences, more recent defenders of tenseless approaches—such as Hugh Mellor, and J. J. C. Smart in his later writings—have agreed with advocates of tensed approaches to time that such translation is not possible. But they have then gone on to claim that this does not mean that tensed sentences cannot be analyzed in tenseless terms, since the reason that translation is impossible, they argue, is simply that tensed sentences involve demonstrative, or indexical, terms. Consequently, even though translation is ruled out, the meaning of tensed sentences can still be explained by specifying, in completely tenseless terms, the conditions under which any particular token of a tensed sentence is true. So tensed sentences are analyzable, since the truth conditions of all tokens of such sentences can be specified completely in tenseless terms.

By contrast, almost all philosophers who accept a tensed or dynamic account of the nature of time hold that tensed sentences of the above sort cannot be analyzed in tenseless terms: it is not possible to translate such sentences into tenseless sentences, nor is it possible to specify in tenseless terms the truth conditions of tokens of such sentences. Indeed, not only can they not be analyzed in tenseless terms: they cannot be analyzed at all. For tensed sentences of the above sort are analytically basic.

With regard to the question of which tensed sentences are the basic ones, I shall be arguing that, contrary to the view that is almost universally accepted by advocates of both static and dynamic accounts of the nature of time, sentences such as 'Event e is now taking place' are not basic tensed sentences. What form, then, do, basic tensed sentences take? My answer will be that it is sentences such as 'Event e lies in the present at time t'—sentences many philosophers would hold are not really tensed sentences at all—that are the basic tensed sentences.

If such sentences are the basic tensed sentences, can they be analyzed, or must the tensed concepts in question be taken as primitive? The answer I shall defend is, first, that tensed concepts cannot be analytically basic, and, second, that the correct analysis of such tensed sentences involves either the ontological notion of the totality of facts that are actual as of a time, or, alternatively, the corresponding semantic notion of truth at a time—notions that have application only if the world is dynamic, rather than static.

13.2   Tensed Facts, Ordinary Tensed Sentences, and Indexicality

The central thesis for which I am arguing in this chapter is that if a dynamic account of tensed language is correct, then ordinary tensed sentences are not basic tensed sentences—where by an ordinary tensed sentence I shall mean any sentence in which the temporal location of an event or state of affairs is given by means of some tensed concept, but where the *meaning* of the sentence itself provides no specification of the time at which the tensed concept is true of the event or state of affairs in question. Ordinary tensed sentences will thus include sentences such as 'The beginning of the first great nuclear war is now taking place' and 'It snowed in Boulder yesterday'.

The claim that if a dynamic account of tensed language is correct, then no ordinary tensed sentences are basic tensed sentences will probably strike most readers as rather implausible, especially given that the vast majority of philosophers hold, I believe, that ordinary tensed sentences are all the tensed sentences there are. So let us turn, then, to the argument. That argument, as I noted above, involves three main steps, with the first directed to showing that a dynamic account of the meaning of tensed language cannot possibly be sound unless at least some basic tensed sentences are not ordinary tensed sentences. The route to this first conclusion is via the following argument:

1. If all basic tensed sentences involved indexical, or demonstrative, terms, then no tensed sentences would entail the existence of irreducible tensed facts, and so a static account of the meaning of tensed language would be correct.

2. The correct account of the meaning of tensed language is given by a dynamic account, rather than by a static or tenseless one.

3. Therefore, not all basic tensed sentences involve indexicals.

4. All ordinary tensed sentences involve indexicals.

5. Therefore, there must be at least some basic tensed sentences that are not identical with any ordinary tensed sentences.

This argument obviously involves at least one highly controversial premise: the claim that a static or tenseless account of the meaning of tensed language cannot be correct. Elsewhere, I have offered what I believe is a very strong argument in support of that contention.[2] As that argument is a rather lengthy one, however, I shall not attempt to set it out here. In any case, a defense of premise 2 is not needed here, since the idea is to conditionalize upon that premise, giving one, in place of conclusion 5, the following conclusion:

6. If a dynamic account of the meaning of tensed language is correct, then there must be at least some basic tensed sentences that are not identical with ordinary tensed sentences.

This conditionalization, in turn, will carry through the rest of the argument, so that the overall conclusion of the argument, rather than being that no ordinary tensed sentences are basic tensed sentences, is, instead, as follows:

7. If a dynamic account of the meaning of tensed language is correct, then no ordinary tensed sentences are basic tensed sentences.

It is, of course, not only premise 2 that is controversial. Many philosophers who favor a tensed view of time would reject either premise 1, or premise 4, or both. In section 13.3, however, I shall argue that if all basic tensed sentences involved indexicals, then no tensed sentences would entail the existence of irreducible tensed facts; and in section 13.4, I shall offer arguments in support of the claim that all ordinary tensed sentences involve indexicals.

13.3   Indexicality and Irreducible Tensed Facts

Let us begin, then, with the initial premise in the first stage of my argument—namely, the claim that if all basic tensed sentences involved indexicals, then no tensed sentences would entail the existence of irreducible tensed facts, and so a static view of the nature of tensed language would be correct. What reason is there for accepting this claim?

This first claim can, I believe, be established by means of an argument that turns upon the fact that, given any sentence token that contains one or more indexicals, one can construct related, indexical-free sentences by replacing every indexical term by a name that refers to the same entity as does the indexical term in the sentence token in question. Given this notion of an indexical-free sentence that is thus related to a given sentence token containing one or more indexicals, the argument can be stated as follows:

1. If there are sentences involving indexicals, any tokens of which entail the existence of states of affairs of type K, then there must be related, indexical-free sentences, tokens of which also do so.

2. Irreducible tensed facts are a type of state of affairs.

3. Therefore, if there are sentences involving indexicals, any tokens of which entail the existence of irreducible tensed facts, then there must be related, indexical-free sentences, tokens of which also do so. (From premises 1 and 2.)

4. Therefore, if there are *tensed* sentences involving indexicals, any tokens of which entail the existence of irreducible tensed facts, then there must be related, indexical-free sentences, tokens of which also do so. (From conclusion 3.)

5. Any sentence that entails the existence of irreducible tensed facts is itself a tensed sentence.

6. Therefore, if there are tensed sentences involving indexicals, any tokens of which entail the existence of irreducible tensed facts, then there must be related, indexical-free *tensed* sentences, tokens of which also do so. (From conclusion 4 and premise 5.)

7. Therefore, if it is not the case that there are any indexical-free tensed sentences, tokens of which entail the existence of irreducible tensed facts, then there are no tensed sentences involving indexicals, tokens of which entail the existence of irreducible tensed facts. (From conclusion 6.)

8. Therefore, if it is not the case that there are any indexical-free tensed sentences, tokens of which entail the existence of irreducible tensed facts, then there are no tensed sentences—either involving indexicals or not involving indexicals—tokens of which entail the existence of irreducible tensed facts. (From conclusion 7.)

9. If there are sentences of type T, then there must be *basic* sentences of type T—that is, sentences of type T that cannot be analyzed in terms of other sentences of type T.

10. Tensed sentences are a type of sentence.

11. Therefore, if there are tensed sentences, then there must be basic tensed sentences—that is, tensed sentences that cannot be analyzed in terms of other tensed sentences. (From premises 9 and 10.)

12. If all basic sentences of type T involve indexicals, then all sentences of type T involve indexicals.

13. Therefore, if all basic tensed sentences involve indexicals, then all tensed sentences involve indexicals. (From premises 10 and 12.)

14. If all tensed sentences involve indexicals, then it is not the case that there are any indexical-free tensed sentences, tokens of which entail the existence of irreducible tensed facts.

15. Therefore, if all basic tensed sentences involve indexicals, then it is not the case that there are any indexical-free tensed sentences, tokens of which entail the existence of irreducible tensed facts. (From conclusion 13 and premise 14.)

16. Therefore, if all basic tensed sentences involve indexicals, then there are no tensed sentences—either involving indexicals or not involving indexicals—tokens of which entail the existence of irreducible tensed facts. (From conclusions 8 and 15.)

This argument involves seven premises—namely, the statements at steps 1, 2, 5, 9, 10, 12, and 14—and all of them are, I suggest, very plausible. Thus, the first of these premises can be seen to be plausible by noticing that for any sentence tokens that contain indexical terms, it must be possible to construct related, indexical-free sentences, and then by asking what the relation will be between the content of any given sentence token involving indexicals and the related, indexical-free sentence.

Let us assume, then, that there are indexical sentences that entail the existence of states of affairs of type K. Is there any reason for thinking that the existence of states of affairs of type K can be expressed by sentences that do *not* involve indexicals? Surely there is, since given any token of any sentence containing indexicals, it seems very plausible, first, that a related, indexical-free sentence can always be constructed, since one needs merely to replace every indexical term by a name; and second, that although such replacement will result in a sentence that differs in meaning from that of the original sentence, it will not make a difference with respect to what *sorts* of fundamental facts are expressed. For there has been no change either with respect to the terms that are used to attribute properties or relations to the entities that one is referring to, or with respect to the entities to which one is referring: the only change is that rather than referring to the entities in question by means of indexical terms, one is now referring to them by means of names. But how could this change affect the sorts of fundamental facts that one is asserting to exist?

The first premise, then, seems plausible. What about the second premise —that is, the claim that irreducible tensed facts are a type of state of affairs? This premise seems unproblematic, since the idea is simply that states of affairs are of a given type because of the properties and/or relations that are constituents of them, and that irreducible tensed facts are such in virtue of the properties and/or relations that they involve.

The third premise—introduced at step 5—says merely that any sentence that entails the existence of irreducible tensed facts is a tensed sentence—something that it certainly seems plausible to view as an analytic truth.

The next premise is introduced at step 9, and it says that, given any type of sentence, there must be some sentences of that type that cannot be analyzed in terms of other sentences of the same type. A defense of this premise would require an account of analysis according to which analyses are characterized by a certain asymmetry: if concept B enters into the analysis of concept A, then concept A cannot enter into the analysis of concept B; and so, for example, if the concepts of grueness and bleenness can be analyzed in terms of the concepts of greenness, blueness, and temporal priority, then the syntactically parallel analytical equivalences relating greenness and blueness to grueness, bleenness, and temporal priority cannot be analyses of the concepts of greenness and blueness.

The claim that analyses are necessarily asymmetric in this way is, I think, very plausible. If that is right, and if, as also seems very plausible, analyses involving infinite regresses are either logically impossible or, at least, impossible in the case of beings who possess only finite minds, then the premise set out at step 9 is sound.

The fifth premise—introduced at step 10—asserts that tensed sentences are a type of sentence. This appears to be completely unproblematic, since there are not really any constraints upon the notion of type that is employed in the premise that was set out at step 9. One can construe the notion of type as narrowly or as broadly as one wishes, and the previous premise will remain true. So there is no problem about construing that notion in such a way that the premise set out at step 10 is clearly true.

The next-to-last premise occurs at step 12, and here the idea is simply that if the analysans of any sentence involves indexicals, then so must the analysandum, and therefore if all *basic* sentences of a given type involve indexicals, then so must all sentences of that type.

The final premise—introduced at step 14—is unproblematic, since it is a logical truth, in the narrow sense.

All seven premises appear, then, to be plausible, and so it would seem that we are justified in concluding that if absolutely all basic tensed sentences involved indexicals, then no tensed sentences would entail the existence of irreducible tensed facts, and thus a static view of the nature of tensed language would be correct.

13.4   Indexicality and Ordinary Tensed Sentences

We have just seen that there is a good reason for accepting the first premise of the argument sketched in section 13.2 for the thesis that if a dynamic account of the meaning of tensed language is correct, then there must be some basic tensed sentences that are not identical with ordinary tensed sentences. Let us now turn, then, to the other crucial premise—the claim that all ordinary tensed sentences involve indexicals—and let us consider what reasons there are for accepting this second claim.

If a sentence contains an indexical term, then that term will pick out different things when the sentence is uttered in different contexts, and so different tokens of that sentence will typically express different propositions. Consequently, if ordinary tensed sentences contain indexicals, then different tokens of a given, ordinary tensed sentence will typically express different propositions.

Do ordinary tensed sentences express different propositions depending upon the context in which they are uttered? Many advocates of tensed views of the nature of time have denied that this is so. Thus, Pavel Tichy, for example, says:

To say that Mrs. Brown is not at home always amounts to affirming the same state of affairs: the failure on the part of the same person to display the same property. But since that state of affairs is intermittent, so is the truth of what is affirmed; the proposition that Mrs. Brown is at home is sometimes true and sometimes false.[3]

According to Tichy, then, the proposition that is expressed by any ordinary tensed sentence, such as 'Mrs. Brown is at home', is always the same whenever the sentence is uttered. Such sentences, accordingly, cannot involve any indexical terms.

Can this view be sustained? A quick way of attempting to refute it runs as follows. Consider the sentence 'World War II is now over'. It is surely true that an utterance of that sentence in the year 1997 would have been true, whereas an utterance of that sentence in the year 1942 would have been false. But then two such utterances of that sentence could not possibly express the same proposition, since the one utterance would have been true and the other false.

If a static view of the nature of time were the only coherent possibility, the above argument would certainly be a decisive argument against the view that different tokens of a given tensed sentence always express the same proposition. But this is not so if a dynamic view of time is also a coherent possibility. For if the passage of time involves either the coming into existence of new states of affairs, or the dropping out of existence of previous states of affairs, or both, then what states of affairs are real may very well depend upon what time it is, and this in turn will mean that the concept of truth *simpliciter*—which is the only concept of truth that is relevant given a static view of the world—might need either to be supplemented by, or perhaps replaced by, a temporally indexed concept of truth at a time. But if the latter concept of truth is coherent, then the person who maintains, as Tichy does, that any ordinary tensed sentence always expresses the same proposition, is left with room to maneuver, since he or she can then argue that the claim that the truth value of a token of a tensed sentence depends upon the time of its occurrence, far from being an undeniable fact, is really the conclusion of an unsound argument—an argument involving the mistaken assumption that such tokens have fixed truth values. For, given the coherence of the concept of truth at a time, one can maintain, first, that what is undeniable is not that 1942 tokens and 1997 tokens of 'World War II is now over' have different truth values, but, rather, that a 1942 token has a different truth value in 1942 than a 1997 token has in 1997; second, that this can be explained in two very different ways: either any token of a tensed sentence has a fixed truth value that depends upon the time of occurrence of the token, or, alternatively, all tokens of a given tensed sentence, though their truth values may vary from one time to another, have the same truth value at any particular time; and, third, that the latter is the correct explanation.

The upshot is that, while the quick refutation succeeds if the notion of truth at a time is incoherent, if that concept is not incoherent, then the apparently undeniable fact concerning the truth values of tokens of tensed sentences can be redescribed in a way that does not preclude the view that every token of a given tensed sentence expresses the same proposition. That alternative description may, of course, still be untenable. But to show that it is, some other argument is needed. The quick refutation by itself does not provide any grounds for that conclusion.

There are, however, a number of other arguments that do show that different tokens of an ordinary tensed sentence do not, in general, express the same proposition. In the first place, consider any two ordinary tensed concepts, such as those of lying in the present and of lying in the past, and any event, such as the birth of David Hume. What is one to say about the relation between the event that is the birth of David Hume and the tensed concepts in question? The natural answer is that it depends upon the time. Thus, there was a time, in the year 1711, when the concept of lying in the present did apply to the birth of David Hume, while the concept of lying in the past did not. But at all subsequent times, it is the concept of lying in the past that applies to the birth of David Hume, and not the concept of lying in the present.

If this is right, if a given tensed concept applies to a specific event at some time or times, and not at others, then one cannot express a definite proposition concerning the applicability of a tensed concept to an event unless one specifies, one way or another, the relevant time. Moreover, this *must* be right, since otherwise an advocate of a tensed approach to time would have no answer to McTaggart's famous argument to the effect that since, on the one hand, every event must be past, present, and future, while, on the other, these determinations of past, present, and future are incompatible, the postulation of tensed properties—or, in McTaggart's terminology, of an A-series—necessarily gives rise to a contradiction. For when one is confronted with this argument, the natural response is that while any event is past, present, and future, it is past, present, and future at different times. So the birth of David Hume was once future; then, later, it was present; and now it is past. And, in general, every event is past, present, and future, but it has those properties at different times.

Any definite proposition concerning the applicability of a tensed concept to an event must involve, then, a specification of the relevant time. But how can one do this? There would seem to be only two possibilities. One is that the very meaning of the sentence in question specifies a time. In that case, which time is the relevant one is not a function of the time of any particular token of the sentence: all tokens of the sentence will specify the same time.

The other possibility is that the meaning of the sentence does not itself suffice to specify a time. But how, then, can any time be specified? The only possibility would seem to be that the sentence contains an indexical element that, by virtue of the context in which the sentence is uttered, serves to pick out directly the relevant time.

Consider, then, the sentence 'The birth of David Hume lies in the past'. The meaning of that sentence—in contrast to that of the sentence 'The birth of David Hume lies in the past in the year 1997'—does not itself specify a time at which the concept of lying in the past applies to the event in question. But, since that concept applies to the event at some times, and not at others, a time must be specified if a definite proposition is to be expressed. Consequently, if an utterance of that sentence is to express a proposition, the time at which the concept is supposed to apply to the event must be fixed instead by the time of the utterance in question, and this can occur only if the sentence contains an indexical element. So different tokens of the sentence 'The birth of David Hume lies in the past' will not, in general, express the same proposition, and precisely the same is true, for the same reason, for any ordinary tensed sentence.

A second argument for the claim that ordinary tensed sentences involve indexicals derives from a consideration of propositional-attitude states. This argument will emerge if we consider an argument that also focuses upon propositional attitudes, but that Tichy offers in support of the view that all tokens of an ordinary tensed sentence express the same proposition. For we shall see that, when Tichy's argument is carefully scrutinized, the result is an argument that points in the opposite direction.

Tichy's argument runs as follows:

... suppose that Mrs. Brown is at home and that Mr. Brown wishes she were not. Mr. Brown is thus taking an attitude to a false proposition, namely, the proposition that Mrs. Brown is not at home. It is this proposition which serves as the object of Mr. Brown's wish. Clearly, Mr. Brown may be lucky and his wish may, as we say, *come true*. But if so, the proposition that Mrs. Brown is not at home must be susceptible of changes in truth-value.[4]

Is Tichy right here? Suppose it is true on Monday that Mrs. Brown is at home, but that Mr. Brown wishes that she weren't. What is one to say if it is true on Tuesday that Mrs. Brown is not at home? Is one to say that Mr. Brown's wish has come true? Surely not. But if to wish for something is to stand in a certain relation to a proposition, and if, in addition, the sentence 'Mrs. Brown is at home' always expressed the same proposition, then its being true on Tuesday that Mrs. Brown is not at home would mean that Mr. Brown's Monday wish *had* come true.

A slightly different way of making this point is to ask about the relationship between Mr. Brown's wishing, on Monday, that Mrs. Brown were not at home, and his wishing on Tuesday, that Mrs. Brown were at home. If the sentence 'Mrs. Brown is at home' always expressed the same proposition, then the two wishes just mentioned would be wishes for incompatible states of affairs. But they are not. So different tokens of sentences such as 'Mrs. Brown is at home' do not, in general, express the same proposition.

The point here is a perfectly general one that applies to all propositional attitudes. Thus, for example, if John had a belief in 1942 that he expressed by saying, at that time, 'World War II is not now over', and he then came to have, in 1946, a belief that he expressed by saying, 'World War II is now over', the latter belief did not contradict his former belief—contrary to what would be the case if the sentence 'World War II is now over' always expressed the same proposition. The conclusion, accordingly, is that an ordinary tensed sentence, uttered in different contexts, will not, in general, express the same proposition. But any sentence that is totally free of indexical terms will always express the same proposition. Accordingly, all ordinary tensed sentences must contain indexicals.[5]

13.5   Indexicality and an Argument for a Tenseless View of Time

In the preceding two sections, my goal was to show that there is good reason for thinking that the premises involved at steps 1 and 4 in the following argument are true:

1. If all basic tensed sentences involved indexical, or demonstrative, terms, then no tensed sentences would entail the existence of irreducible tensed facts, and so a static account of the meaning of tensed language would be correct.

2. The correct account of the meaning of tensed language is given by a dynamic account, rather than by a static or tenseless one.

3. Therefore, not all basic tensed sentences involve indexicals.

4. All ordinary tensed sentences involve indexicals.

5. Therefore, there must be at least some basic tensed sentences that do not fall within the class of ordinary tensed sentences.

This does not suffice to establish conclusion 5, of course, in view of the highly controversial nature of the premise advanced at step 2. But, as I noted earlier, the idea in the present argument is to conditionalize upon premise 2, thereby arriving at the following, more modest conclusion:

6. If a dynamic account of the meaning of tensed language is correct, then there must be at least some basic tensed sentences that are not identical with ordinary tensed sentences.

The situation, in short, is that if the discussion in sections 13.3 and 13.4 is sound, conclusion 6 has been established. The point of this present section is then that conclusion 6 provides the basis of an interesting and apparently strong argument in support of a tenseless account of the meaning of tensed sentences—an argument that runs as follows:

6. If a dynamic account of the meaning of tensed language is correct, then there must be at least some basic tensed sentences that are not identical with ordinary tensed sentences.

7. Ordinary tensed sentences are the only tensed sentences that there are.

8. Therefore, a static account of the meaning of tensed sentences is correct.

This argument, in turn, would seem to lend strong support to the view that the world itself is static, rather than dynamic. It is possible, of course, that the world is a dynamic one in which the totality of facts that are actual as of one time differ from the totality that are actual as of any other time, but that this metaphysical fact is not built into the meaning of tensed language. Advocates of a dynamic account of the nature of time usually maintain, however, that the view that the world is dynamic, rather than being a deep and difficult philosophical discovery, is a belief that arises very naturally; and if this is so, then it would seem, at the very least, somewhat surprising if this fact were not reflected in any way in the very meaning of tensed language.

In any case, the argument for conclusion 8 certainly calls for reflection, if one wants to embrace a tensed, or dynamic, account of the nature of time. How, then, should one respond to this argument? If one wishes to reject a tenseless account of the meaning of tensed language, and if I am right in thinking that premise 6—the conclusion of the previous argument—is correct, then there is only one option: one has to reject premise 7 and hold that ordinary tensed sentences do not exhaust the class of tensed sentences.

What is involved in rejecting premise 7? First, recall how the expression 'ordinary tensed sentence' is being used: an ordinary tensed sentence is a sentence in which the temporal location of an event or state of affairs is given by means of some tensed concept, but where the meaning of the sentence itself provides no specification of the time at which the tensed concept is true of the event or state of affairs in question. So, for example, the sentence 'The birth of David Hume lies in the past' is an ordinary tensed sentence, since it refers to a certain event and says that a certain tensed concept applies to the event in question, but the meaning of the sentence does not itself specify the time at which the tensed concept of lying in the past is true of the event that is the birth of David Hume.

A tensed sentence that is not an ordinary tensed sentence will, by contrast, be a sentence in which a tensed concept is applied to some event or state of affairs, and where a specification of the relevant time is part of the very meaning of the sentence in question. A sentence that is a tensed sentence, but not an ordinary one, will therefore presumably be a sentence such as 'The birth of David Hume is (tenselessly) past in the year

1997'. To reject premise 7, therefore, is to hold that sentences of the latter sort are tensed sentences.

If this is the only way of answering the argument for the conclusion that a static account of the meaning of tensed sentences is correct, it might well seem that dynamic accounts of the nature of time are in deep trouble indeed. For advocates of a tenseless account of the nature of time would contend that a sentence such as 'The birth of David Hume is (tenselessly) past in the year 1997' is not a tensed sentence at all—a contention they would support by arguing, first, that no tensed sentence can be analytically equivalent to any tenseless sentence, and, second, that the sentence 'The birth of David Hume is (tenselessly) past in the year 1997' is analytically equivalent to the tenseless sentence 'The birth of David Hume is earlier than 1997', on the grounds that the one sentence is true when and only when the other sentence is true.

But it is not only defenders of tenseless accounts of the nature of time who would claim that sentences such as 'The birth of David Hume is (tenselessly) past in the year 1997' are not tensed sentences. This claim would also be accepted by most advocates of a tensed view of time as well. George Schlesinger, for example, says that "the property of 'being in the future at time t_1' is exactly the same as 'being later than t_1'."[6] Similarly, Richard Gale, in discussing McTaggart's attempt to define temporal priority by means of tensed predicates, says that "the predicates '____ is past at ____' and '____ is future at ____' are synonyms for '____ is earlier than ____' and '____ is later than ____' respectively."[7]

If these claims were correct, and a sentence such as 'The birth of David Hume is (tenselessly) past in the year 1997' was not a tensed sentence, but a tenseless one, then it would be very hard to see how any plausible challenge could be mounted against the claim, advanced at step 7, that ordinary tensed sentences are the only tensed sentences that there are. For what other type of candidate could there be for a sentence that is a tensed sentence, but not an ordinary tensed sentence as defined above?

If premise 7 could not be rejected, how could an advocate of a tensed or dynamic view of time respond to the above argument? One would have to try to fault the argument leading to premise 6, and, prima facie, the most natural point at which to challenge that argument would seem to be the claim that ordinary tensed sentences involve indexicals. So perhaps the present argument captures an underlying reason why the view that ordinary tensed sentences involve indexicals has been so frequently rejected by philosophers who embrace a tensed approach to time. We have already seen, however, that there are very strong arguments for the conclusion that all ordinary tensed sentences involve indexicals. So this response will not do.

13.6   A Reply to the Argument: Tensed Sentences Involving Dates

How, then, is the above argument to be answered? Simply by showing that, contrary to what is maintained by advocates of tenseless accounts of the nature of time, and also insisted upon, as we have seen, by many defenders of tensed approaches, sentences such as 'The birth of David Hume is (tenselessly) past in the year 1997' *are* tensed sentences.

How can this be done? The most fundamental approach involves showing that an account can be given of the meaning of such sentences according to which they cannot be analyzed in tenseless terms, and this is what I shall do in subsequent sections. Before doing that, however, I want to argue in the present section that if one accepts a dynamic or tensed view of the nature of time, then, regardless of precisely what account one offers of tensed sentences, there is good reason to reject the claim that sentences such as 'The birth of David Hume is (tenselessly) past in the year 1997' are not tensed sentences.

Consider, for example, the tensed approach to time according to which there are special, irreducible tensed properties of pastness, presentness, and futurity. Given that view of the ontology of time, what the sentence 'The birth of David Hume is (tenselessly) past in the year 1997' must be saying is that a certain event—the birth of David Hume—has, in the year 1997, a certain special, irreducible, intrinsic property—that of pastness—and, so interpreted, the sentence is certainly not analytically equivalent to any tenseless sentence, since it asserts the existence of a certain special property that, according to tenseless views of time, does not exist at all.

Might not one argue, however, that when the sentence is interpreted in this way, it turns out, in the final analysis, that it is incoherent? So, while it *would* be a tensed sentence *if* it made sense, it is not in fact a genuine tensed sentence, since it is incoherent.

It is certainly possible that the sentence in question, thus interpreted, is ultimately incoherent. Indeed, I have argued elsewhere that the idea that tensed properties are intrinsic properties of events does give rise to a contradiction.[8] The point here, however, is that it is not possible to take that view *if* one holds that there is such an intrinsic property, and that it enters into the states of affairs that are truth makers for ordinary past-tense sentences—such as 'The birth of David Hume is past'. The reason is that, if there is such an intrinsic property, it is one that an event does not always possess: at a certain time in the year 1711, the birth of David Hume had the property of presentness, not the property of pastness. This being so, it can surely not give rise to incoherence if one goes on to specify one of the times at which a given event has the special intrinsic property of pastness, and this is precisely what is being done by a sentence such as 'The birth of David Hume is (tenselessly) past in the year 1997'—or, more explicitly, by a sentence such as 'The birth of David Hume has (tenselessly) the special, irreducible, intrinsic property of pastness in the year 1997'.

This point can be put in a more general way that is neutral with respect to the exact nature of the tensed ontology that one is postulating, by talking simply about the concept of lying in the past. Thus, suppose simply that there is some tensed ontology or other that makes it true to say now that the concept of lying in the past is true of the event that is the birth of David Hume. Once again, it is not the case that the concept of lying in the past was always true of the birth of David Hume, and this being so, how can any incoherence be generated if one specifies explicitly one of the times at which the concept is true of the event in question? But it is precisely this that is done by the sentence 'The birth of David Hume is (tenselessly) past in the year 1997'.

The advocate of a tenseless or static view of time will want, at this point, to press a certain issue—namely, that of the relation between the purportedly tensed sentence 'The birth of David Hume is (tenselessly) past in the year 1997' and the tenseless sentence 'The birth of David Hume is earlier than the year 1997'—and this is certainly a crucial question. What someone who accepts a dynamic view of time will want to say, of course, is that, while the former sentence entails the latter, it cannot be analyzed in terms of it. But can this contention be sustained? To answer that question, we need to turn to the issue of the analyzability of tensed sentences.

13.7   Are Tensed Sentences Analyzable?

Can sentences involving the tensed concepts of past, present, and future be analyzed? Advocates of a tenseless account of the nature of time hold that this is possible, and the general sort of program that they advance rests upon the idea that tensed sentences, such as 'It rained yesterday', are similar, in two crucial respects, to sentences such as 'There is a mountain over there'. First, the term 'yesterday', like the term 'there', is an indexical, and, consequently, just as any token of 'There is a mountain over there' has truth conditions that involve reference either to the token itself, or to its (spatial) location, so any token of 'It rained yesterday' has truth conditions that involve reference either to the token itself, or to its (temporal) location. Second, just as whether any particular utterance of 'There is a mountain over there' is true depends only upon how things are spatially related to the utterance in question, so, it is claimed, a similar thing is true of tokens of tensed sentences, such as 'It rained yesterday': whether a particular utterance of the latter sentence is true depends only upon the tenseless temporal relation in which that utterance stands to the event in question.

If the first of these claims is correct, and tensed sentences do involve indexicals, then it is impossible to translate tensed statements into tenseless ones. But, on the other hand, if the second claim is also correct, then, just as one can specify truth conditions for sentences such as 'There is a mountain over there', even though one cannot offer any translational analysis, so it will also be possible to specify truth conditions for tokens of tensed sentences in tenseless terms.

This program of analysis is rejected by advocates of tensed approaches to time—the latter generally maintaining, on the contrary, not only that the concepts of past, present, and future cannot be analyzed in tenseless terms, but that they cannot be analyzed at all. As regards the second of these claims, however, there are exceptions. C. D. Broad, for example, in the tensed approach that he developed in his book *Scientific Thought*, argued that statements about the past and about the present can be analyzed in terms of statements about the sum total of existence at various times.[9] He also held, however, that statements about the future could not be analyzed along similar lines, nor indeed, in any way at all:

> We cannot then analyse *will* away, as we can *has been* and *is now*. Every judgment that professes to be about the future would seem to involve two peculiar and not further analysable kinds of assertion. One of these is about becoming; it asserts that further events will become. The other is about some characteristic; it asserts that this will characterise some of the events which will become.[10]

With regard to the concept of the future, then, Broad shared the view that is almost universal among those who follow a tensed approach to time—namely, that that concept is unanalyzable.

But is it true that the concept of lying in the future is not analyzable? Contrary to the views of virtually all advocates of a tensed approach to time, it seems to me that there are very strong arguments in support of the claim that the concept of lying in the future must be analyzable. One such argument, for example, is as follows.[11] First, what characterizes the class of analytically basic, descriptive concepts? A very plausible answer, I suggest, is that a descriptive concept cannot be analytically basic for a given person unless that concept picks out a property or relation that, for the individual in question, is, or has been, either an object of direct, noncausal awareness, or an object of immediate perception. For, in the first place, it is not easy to see what account one can give of the class of analytically basic descriptive concepts if one does not appeal either to direct acquaintance or to immediate perception. In the second place, the above account is neutral between internalist accounts and externalist accounts of immediate perception. Finally, the account does not commit one to any form of reductionism—such as phenomenalism—since one can employ, for example, a Ramsey/Lewis approach to theoretical terms in order to assign a realist interpretation to those terms.[12]

Given the above criterion for analytically basic descriptive concepts, the argument proceeds as follows. First, both immediate perception of a property, and direct awareness of a property, seem to imply that one has noninferential knowledge of the fact that something has the property in question. Second, the conclusion that the concept of the future cannot be analytically basic then follows very quickly, since even if, as some have argued, it is logically possible to have noninferential knowledge of the future, humans at present certainly do not possess such knowledge.

Next, let us turn to the concept of the past, and ask whether there are reasons for thinking that this concept must also be analyzable. In particular, can one parallel the argument just offered in support of the analyzability of the concept of lying in the future?

To do so, one needs to show that the property of lying in the past is not an object of direct awareness, or immediate perception. Can this be done? The argument here is admittedly less straightforward than in the case of the concept of lying in the future, for there one could appeal to the uncontroversial thesis that one does not have noninferential knowledge of the future, whereas the corresponding claim—that one does not have noninferential knowledge of the past—would certainly be rejected by some epistemologists. Nevertheless, I believe that the corresponding claim is in fact correct, since it seems to me that memory knowledge of the past is most plausibly viewed, not as involving noninferential knowledge of past events, but as a matter of noninferential knowledge of present beliefs about the past, coupled with an inference to the best explanation of those beliefs.

One can, however, avoid this controversial issue by developing the argument in a different way. The alternative line of argument turns upon a principle—which I suggest is very plausible—to the effect that one cannot be directly aware of, or immediately perceive, a state of affairs without being directly aware of, or immediately perceiving, all of the constituents of the state of affairs in question. Given this principle, one can then argue that if memory knowledge of a past event did involve a direct awareness, or immediate perception, of some event's having the property of pastness, one would also have to have a direct awareness, or an immediate perception, of the event in question, and this in turn would require a direct awareness, or immediate perception, of at least some of the other properties of the event. A comparison, however, of the phenomenological content of memory, on the one hand, and perceptual experience, on the other, seems to make it clear that the remembering of an event does not involve the sort of direct acquaintance with the properties of that event that there is when one is experiencing the event: a memory of having experienced greenness, for example, does not involve the same raw-feel quality that an experience of greenness itself does. If this is right, then, regardless of whether one has, in some sense, noninferential knowledge of past events, it is not the case that any such noninferential knowledge involves either direct acquaintance with, or immediate perception of, the event in question, as it would have to do if one were directly acquainted with, or immediately perceived, the state of affairs that consists of that event's having the property of pastness. Hence, there is no property of pastness with which one is directly acquainted, or which one immediately perceives, and so the concept of lying in the past cannot be analytically basic.

Two of the three most important tensed concepts must, then, be analyzable. But what of the most central tensed concept of all—that of lying in the present? The arguments that I have just offered in the case of the concepts of the past and of the future cannot be paralleled in the case of the concept of the present. Nevertheless, that concept, too, is analyzable, as I shall show in the next section.

13.8   The Analysis of Tensed Sentences

13.8.1   The Concepts to Be Used in the Analysis
If tensed concepts are analyzable, what are the more basic concepts in terms of which they can be analyzed? My answer is that there are two concepts that are more fundamental, and that provide the basis for the correct analysis. These are the concept of the totality of what is actual *as of* a time, and the concept of temporal priority.

The second of these concepts is certainly familiar. But what is meant by the totality of what is actual as of a time? How is this temporally indexed concept of actuality to be understood?

There is a temporally indexed concept of existence, or actuality, that is relatively unproblematic—namely, that of being actual, or of existing, *at* a time—since to say that something is actual at time t can be analyzed in terms of either the idea of being located at time t, or the idea of having a temporal part that is located at time t. But the concept of the totality of what is actual *as of* a time cannot be identified with the concept of the totality of what is actual, or exists, *at* a time. The temporally indexed concept of actuality that is needed in the present context is, instead, a much more controversial and problematic concept, since it is related to the idea that propositions can have different truth values at different times. Consider, for example, the proposition that there are (tenselessly) dinosaurs. Some philosophers have maintained that one can make sense of a temporally indexed concept of truth, and that, for example, while the proposition that there are (tenselessly) dinosaurs was true, for example, in the year 1997, it was not true at any time prior to the first appearance of dinosaurs on earth. The idea is then that if this notion of truth at a time makes sense, and if truth is a matter of correspondence between propositions (or other bearers of truth, such as statements or sentences) and what facts, or states of affairs, there are, then what facts are actual will have to be different at different times. The concept of what is actual as of a time is, accordingly, the ontological counterpart of the semantic notion of truth at a time: what is actual *as of* a given time consists, not of those things that exist *at* that time, but, rather, of everything that enters into the states of affairs that can serve as truth makers for propositions at that time. So, for example, though there are no dinosaurs that exist in the year 1997, the states of affairs that are actual as of the year 1997 include ones that involve dinosaurs, since the proposition that there are (tenselessly) dinosaurs is true in the year 1997.

An advocate of a tensed approach to time should not, I think, find the use of this temporally indexed concept of actuality troubling. For first of all, the most fundamental difference between tenseless or static views of the nature of time and tensed or dynamic views concerns precisely the issue of whether one can speak only of what is actual *simpliciter*, or whether, on the contrary, the temporally indexed concept just set out is legitimate. According to static views, this concept is not acceptable, and it makes no sense to say that there are states of affairs that are actual as of one time, but not as of some other. One can speak of what facts exist, of what facts are actual, *simpliciter*, and one can also refer to the things that exist *at* a given time, in the uncontroversial sense mentioned above; however, one cannot make sense either of the semantic notion of truth at a time or of the corresponding ontological notion of the facts that are actual as of a given time. By contrast, according to a dynamic view of the nature of time, propositions can change their truth values with the passage of time, and so it must be the case that what states of affairs are real or actual is constantly changing. The controversial, temporally indexed notion of the totality of facts that are actual as of a particular time is therefore crucial.

Second, there would seem to be no hope of cashing out the idea of being actual as of a time in terms of the tensed concepts of past, present, and future, since philosophers who do not disagree with regard to the extensions of those tensed concepts may very well disagree about what is actual as of a given time. Thus, for example, according to some philosophers, the states of affairs that are actual as of a given time consist of the states of affairs that exist *at* that time, together with all earlier states of affairs, while according to other philosophers, the only states of affairs that are actual as of a given time are states of affairs that exist at that time. But if the concept of being actual as of a time were analyzable in terms of the concepts of past, present, and future, then the truth values of all propositions about what states of affairs are actual as of a given time would be logically supervenient upon facts about what states of affairs are past, present, and future. It would then be at least somewhat surprising that complete agreement concerning the latter is often accompanied by very sweeping disagreements concerning what states of affairs are actual as of a given time. In short, a temporally indexed concept of what is actual is crucial for a tensed or dynamic view of time, and it does not seem at all likely that that concept can be analyzed in terms of tensed concepts. So the use of that concept in providing an analysis of tensed concepts, within the context of a dynamic approach to the nature of time, would not seem to be in any way objectionable.

But what about the other concept that I shall be employing—the concept of temporal priority? Almost everyone who favors a tensed approach to time would hold that the use of this concept *is* illegitimate, on the grounds that temporal priority is to be analyzed in terms of tensed concepts, and so to use the concept of temporal priority in analyzing tensed concepts would mean that one's analyses of tensed concepts were implicitly circular.

This is certainly a crucial objection to the analyses that I shall be setting out. But I shall argue that this objection is open to a decisive refutation, since it can be shown that the relation of temporal priority cannot be analyzed in terms of tensed concepts.

Elsewhere, I have argued for this claim in a detailed way.[13] Here, I shall confine myself to looking at one, representative attempt to analyze temporal priority in tensed terms, and to briefly outlining the two central problems that doom not only that attempt, but all such attempts to analyze temporal priority in tensed terms.

First, however, I need to motivate the analysis on which I shall focus. This can be done if we begin by asking why the idea that temporal priority can be analyzed in terms of the familiar tensed concepts of past, present, and future might seem initially tempting. One important reason, I think, is the fact that there are certain entailments between statements involving tensed concepts and statements involving the concept of temporal priority: the statement '*A* is past and *B* is present', for example, entails the statement '*A* is earlier than B'. Given such entailments, it may be tempting to suppose, first, that, for any tenseless temporal statement, one can construct tensed statements that say everything the tenseless statement says—and perhaps something more—and, second, that tenseless statements must therefore be analyzable in terms of tensed ones.

How might such an analysis run? Given the entailment just mentioned, along with the related entailments of '*A* is earlier than *B*' by '*A* is past and *B* is future' and by '*A* is present and *B* is future', a natural starting point is the following, disjunctive analysis of temporal priority:

(1)   *X* is earlier than *Y*

means the same as

Either *X* is past and *Y* is present, or *X* is past and *Y* is future, or *X* is present and *Y* is future.

This first attempt, however, is obviously unsatisfactory, since it does not capture the case where *X* is earlier than *Y*, and *X* and *Y* are either both in the past or both in the future. How might one deal with this difficulty? One rather natural idea was suggested by Wilfrid Sellars,[14] who proposed a more sophisticated analysis that, for our purposes here, can be expressed as follows:

(2) X is earlier than Y

means the same as

Either X is present and Y is future, or X was present and Y future at the time of X, or X will be present and Y future at the time of X.

This account avoids the objection to which the initial attempt fell prey, since, whenever X is earlier than Y, Sellars's proposed analysans will be true. But Sellars's account is exposed to two other objections, both of which are, I believe, decisive. First, the analysis involves a concept that, as we saw earlier, cannot be analytically basic—namely, the concept of the future. One therefore needs to ask how that concept is to be analyzed, and it is here that a serious problem arises, since the most natural analysis of the concept of the future involves the earlier-than relation (or its inverse): by definition, something lies in future if and only if it is later than the present. But if this natural analysis of the concept of the future is right, then any analysis of temporal priority that makes use of the concept of the future is implicitly circular, and so unsound. The challenge, then, is either to find a tensed analysis of temporal priority that does *not* employ the concept of the future, or else to set out an analysis of the concept of the future that involves neither the earlier-than relation itself, nor any other relation—such as that of causation—that might provide the basis of a tenseless analysis of temporal priority. The prospects do not seem at all promising for either of these projects.

Second, in addition to the familiar tensed concepts of being present and being future, Sellars's analysis employs an explicitly relational analogue of one of those concepts—namely, the concept of being future *at a time*—in order to be able to handle the cases where the two events in question are either both past or both future. The use of this explicitly relational concept, however, provides another reason for thinking that the analysis is implicitly circular. For if the ordinary tensed concept of lying in the future cannot be analytically basic, it seems very unlikely that the explicitly relational concept of being future at a time is analytically basic. Moreover, the fact that the sentence 'Y is future at the time of X' entails that Y is earlier than X makes it seem very likely indeed that the analysis of the explicitly relational tensed concept will involve the relation of temporal priority. So we have a second reason for concluding that Sellars's analysis is implicitly circular.

Sellars's account, however, does not differ in this respect from other proposed tensed analyses of temporal priority: all such accounts can be shown to suffer, I believe, from implicit circularity.[15] Consequently, the familiar tensed objection to the use of the concept of temporal priority in analyzing tensed concepts—an objection that may at first seem plausible —cannot be sustained.

What account is to be offered, then, of the concept of temporal priority? An advocate of a tensed or dynamic account of the nature of time could adopt the view that is accepted by some advocates of tenseless approaches, and hold that the concept of temporal priority is analytically basic. I believe, however, that there is good reason to reject this view. The argument in question turns upon the ideas, first, that, given a proposition that seems to express a necessary truth, some explanation of that necessity is surely desirable; and, second, that Quinean doubts about the intelligibility of analyticity notwithstanding, the most satisfactory type of explanation is one that shows how the statement in question can be derived from logical truths, in the narrow sense, simply by substitution of definitionally equivalent expressions. If these points are sound, one can then appeal to the fact that the relation of being earlier than appears to have certain necessary properties—in particular, irreflexivity, transitivity, and asymmetry. As a consequence, acceptance of the view that the concept of temporal priority is analytically basic rules out the most satisfactory sort of explanation that might be offered of why it is the case, for example, that no event can be earlier than itself.

I think it is plausible, then, to regard the concept of temporal priority as analyzable. But how is it to be analyzed? The approach that I favor involves giving a causal analysis. Causal accounts of temporal priority are exposed, however, to a number of important objections that need to be answered if such an approach is to be acceptable.[16]

13.8.2   An Analysis of the Concepts of Past, Present, and Future
I have now covered most of the basic ideas that are involved in the analysis of tensed concepts that I shall be briefly setting out in this sec-

tion. Let me now bring all of the relevant ideas together, so that my overall approach is clear.

Five claims are crucial, four of which I have discussed above:

1. All ordinary tensed sentences involve indexicals.

2. There are tensed sentences that do not involve indexicals.

3. A temporally indexed notion of actuality is coherent and can be used in analyzing tensed concepts.

4. The concept of temporal priority can be used in analyzing tensed concepts.

The fifth and final thesis is one that I have not discussed above, as it rests upon a rather complex argument in support of the view that the world is dynamic, rather than static:[17]

5. The present is the point at which events come into existence.

Given these five claims, the basic idea is, first, to begin with tensed sentences that do not involve indexicals, and to give a translational analysis of such sentences using the concept of being actual as of a given time, together with the concept of temporal priority. Then, second, one can set out a nontranslational, truth-conditional analysis of ordinary tensed sentences, using whatever general method seems best for formulating the truth conditions of sentences containing indexicals.

13.8.2.1 Nonindexical Tensed Sentences Let us start, then, with tensed sentences that do not contain indexicals, and that say that a certain tensed concept applies to a certain event at an explicitly specified time—sentences such as 'The birth of David Hume lies (tenselessly) in the past in the year 1997'. How are such sentences to be analyzed?

The first stage involves explaining what it is for an event to be past at a time, or future at a time, in terms of what it is for an event to be present at a time, together with the concept of temporal priority. One very natural way of doing this is as follows:

(3)   Event e lies (tenselessly) in the past at time t

means the same as

Event e is earlier than time t, and t lies in the present at time t.

(4)   Event *e* lies (tenselessly) in the future at time *t*

means the same as

Event *e* is later than time *t*, and *t* lies in the present at time *t*.

Alternatively, one might opt instead for the following, slightly different analyses:

(5)   Event *e* lies in the past at time *t*

means the same as

There exists (tenselessly) a time, t^*, such that t^* is earlier than *t*, and event *e* is present at time t^*.

(6)   Event *e* lies in the future at time *t*

means the same as

There exists (tenselessly) a time, t^*, such that t^* is later than *t*, and event *e* is present at time t^*.

The second stage then involves giving an account of what it is for an event to lie in the present at a given time. The analysis needed here rests upon the claim that the present is the point at which events and states of affairs come into existence, and the basic idea is that, since this view of the present entails that future events and states of affairs are not yet real, an event is present at a given time if and only if the totality of what is actual as of that time does not contain an event or state of affairs that is later than the event in question. One has, accordingly, the following analysis:

(7)   Event *e* lies (tenselessly) in the present at time *t*

means the same as

Event *e* is actual as of time *t*, and no state of affairs that is later than *e* is actual as of time *t*.

13.8.2.2   Indexical Tensed Sentences   Let us now consider the analysis of ordinary tensed sentences. Here there are two main sorts of sentences that we need to consider. First, there are indexical tensed sentences that assign a temporal location to a specific event that is picked out non-indexically—for example, the sentence 'The birth of David Hume is now taking place'. Second, there are tensed sentences—such as 'It is now snowing heavily'—that do not contain terms or expressions that pick out the event or state of affairs in question in a nonindexical fashion.

Given the preceding account of the truth conditions of nonindexical tensed sentences about past, present, and future events, it is easy to give an analysis of both types of indexical tensed sentences. However, because of the indexical element involved in the term 'now', the required analysis cannot, at least in the case of sentences of the first sort, take the form of a translational analysis. The specification of the meaning has to be given, instead, through a description of the conditions under which any given token of such a sentence will be true, false, or indeterminate at a time. (Reference to a third truth value is needed here because the view that the future is not real means that at least some statements about the future are not now either true or false.)

In the case of statements of the first sort about the present, the truth-conditional analysis will run roughly as follows:

(8)   Any utterance, or inscription, at time t^*, of the sentence 'Event e is now occurring' is true (false, indeterminate) at time t

      if and only if

      It is true (false, indeterminate) at time t that event e lies in the present at time t^*.

Similarly, truth conditions for indexical statements about past events and future events can be stated, in a precisely parallel fashion, as follows:

(9)   Any utterance, or inscription, at time t^*, of the sentence 'Event e has occurred' is true (false, indeterminate) at time t

      if and only if

      It is true (false, indeterminate) at time t that event e lies in the past at time t^*.

(10) Any utterance, or inscription, at time t^*, of the sentence 'Event e will occur' is true (false, indeterminate) at time t

      if and only if

      It is true (false, indeterminate) at time t that event e lies in the future at time t^*.

However, this account, even though it is satisfactory as far as it goes, is not quite complete, in view of the fact that there are relevant activities that one can engage in other than saying, or writing, that *e* is now occurring: one can believe that *e* is now occurring, doubt that *e* is now occurring, and so on. The reference to an utterance or inscription needs to be replaced, therefore, by something more inclusive that takes into account the fact that the proposition that *e* is now occurring may be the object of a propositional attitude without there being any nonmental token of the sentence in question.

Sometimes it is suggested that one should deal with this problem by referring not only to utterances and inscriptions, but also to thoughts. However, that is still not sufficiently comprehensive, given that a person can believe that *e* is now happening, without having the thought that it is happening, or can want it to be the case that *e* is now happening, without that desire's being accompanied by any conscious thought.

How best to refine the above account is not, however, a question that we need to pursue here, since the issue is not one that is peculiar to *tensed* sentences containing indexicals. It is, rather, a general issue that arises in connection with any sentence containing an indexical. Whatever appears to be the best answer to the general question will apply, in a perfectly straightforward fashion, to tensed sentences involving indexicals.

The preceding account provides truth conditions for sentences that refer nonindexically to specific events—such as 'The first trip to Mars lies in the future'. But there are also very simple sentences—such as 'It is now snowing heavily' or 'The grass was very green in England'—that do not contain terms or expressions that pick out specific events, or states of affairs, in a nonindexical fashion. How are sentences of the latter sort to be analyzed?

Given an analysis of statements containing expressions that refer nonindexically to events, or states of affairs, and that assign tensed, temporal locations to such entities, it seems to be a straightforward matter to provide an account of indexical tensed statements that do not contain such expressions. One very simple and natural approach, for example, is to view sentences of the latter sort as related, via existential quantification, to indexical tensed sentences of the first sort. Thus, for example, the sentence 'It is now snowing heavily' contains terms that specify a certain *type* of event—namely, an event that consists of its snowing heavily—and one can thus interpret the sentence 'It is now snowing heavily' as saying that there is an event that is of that type and that has the relevant temporal property at the indexically indicated time. So we have the following, translational analysis:

(11)   It is now snowing heavily

means the same as

There is (tenselessly) an event, *e*, of the snowing-heavily variety, and *e* lies in the present.

Similarly, the sentence 'The grass was very green in England' does not contain any expression that picks out a specific event nonindexically, but it does contain terms that specify a certain type of state of affairs. So, once again, an analysis like the following that treats the logical form of the sentence as involving existential quantification seems very natural:

(12)   The grass was very green in England

means the same as

There is (tenselessly) an event, *e*, of the grass's-being-very-green-in-England variety, and *e* lies in the past.

Tensed sentences can, of course, come in more complex forms than those I have considered here. In particular, one can have temporal operators nested inside temporal operators, to any depth that one likes. The extension of the above approach to more complex sentences is, however, a relatively straightforward matter.[18]

I indicated in section 13.2 that I would be offering a three-part argument for the conclusion that no ordinary tensed sentences can be basic tensed sentences. The thrust of the first stage was that a dynamic account of the meaning of tensed language cannot possibly be sound unless there are basic tensed sentences that are not identical with ordinary tensed sentences, and the central argument for that claim was set out in sections 13.3 and 13.4.

The second stage of the three-part argument was then directed to establishing the further conditional claim that there are sentences that are not identical with ordinary tensed sentences and that, moreover, can be shown to be tensed sentences, *if* a dynamic account of the meaning of tensed language is correct. The argument in support of this claim was set out in section 13.6.

The third and final stage of the argument involved the claim that no ordinary tensed sentences are basic tensed sentences, and this thesis has been established by the analyses just offered, since we have seen that ordinary tensed sentences can be analyzed, truth-conditionally, using non-indexical tensed sentences. So ordinary tensed sentences cannot be basic tensed sentences.

The analyses offered in this section also show, however, that *not all* nonindexical tensed sentences are basic tensed sentences, since we have seen that sentences asserting that some event is (tenselessly) past at a time, or future at a time, can be analyzed in terms of the concept of temporal priority together with the concept of being present at a time. The upshot is that the only basic tensed sentences are sentences asserting that an event is (tenselessly) present at a specific time.

Finally, we have also seen that even the concept of being present at a time is not analytically basic, since sentences involving that concept can be analyzed using the concept of temporal priority together with the concept of the totality of states of affairs that are actual as of a specific time. No tensed concepts, therefore, are analytically basic.

13.9   Some Advantages of the Present Account

In this section, I shall briefly indicate some attractive consequences of the above account of the nature and analysis of basic tensed sentences. First, consider McTaggart's famous argument for the unreality of time.[19] McTaggart's argument involves two parts, with the second being relevant here. In that second part, McTaggart argues that the idea that there are objective features of reality corresponding to the concepts of past, present, and future gives rise to a contradiction, and the heart of his argument involves the contentions, first, that if one is to avoid a contradiction, one needs to be able to specify the times at which a given event has the different, and incompatible, tensed properties, but then, second, that the attempt to specify, in tensed terms, when an event has the various tensed properties gives rise to a vicious, infinite regress.

The most common response by those who favor a tensed view of time involves arguing that the regress in question is not vicious. Perhaps this response can be shown to be correct, but I think it is fair to say that the situation is, at least, murky—as is shown both by the fact that different interpretations have been offered of the crucial regress argument and by the fact that Hugh Mellor, who has certainly thought deeply about this argument, is convinced that McTaggart's argument can be shown to be sound.[20]

On the present approach, by contrast, there is a clear and absolutely decisive answer to McTaggart's argument, and one that avoids completely the rather muddy waters associated with the infinite regress that McTaggart claims is vicious. For one can specify the times at which an event has the different tensed properties, not by means of ordinary tensed sentences, but by means of nonindexical tensed sentences containing dates. McTaggart's regress, then, does not even get started.

Second, the above account of tensed sentences also provides a very clear answer to some arguments that Mellor has offered against tensed accounts of the nature of time. Consider, for example, the following argument:

> The sole function of tensed facts is to make tensed sentences and judgments true or false. But that job is already done by the tenseless facts that fix the truth-values of all tensed sentence and judgment tokens. Provided a token of '*e* is past' is later than *e*, it is true. Nothing else about *e* and it matters a jot: in particular, no tensed fact about them matters. It is immaterial, for a start, where *e* and the token are in the A series; and if that is not material, no more *recherché* tensed fact can be. Similarly for tokens of all other tensed types. Their tenseless truth conditions leave tensed facts no scope for determining their truth-values. But these facts by definition determine their truth-values. So in reality there are no such facts.[21]

The thrust of this argument is that for a token of an ordinary tensed sentence—such as 'Event *e* is past'—to be true, it suffices that the token be later than *e*, and that, since this is sufficient, there is no way that tensed facts can be relevant. But according to the analysis offered in the previous section, if the sentence 'Event *e* is past' is uttered at time *t*, the fact that the token is later than *e* will *not* suffice to make the token true: it must also be the case that time *t* is present at time *t*. Mellor, of course, would respond that all that can be meant by the statement 'Time *t* is present at time *t*' is that *t* is simultaneous with itself, and that since this is an analytic truth, an appeal to this condition does not show that anything more is required for a token of 'Event *e* is past' to be true than that the token be later than *e*. But this response presupposes that the analysis offered above of 'Event *e* is (tenselessly) present at time *t*' is incoherent. For if that analysis makes sense, then the statement 'Time *t* is present at time *t*' is not analytically equivalent to 'Time *t* is simultaneous with *t*', since the former sentence entails, while the latter does not, that the world is one where the concept of being actual as of a time has application, and where, in particular, no states of affairs that are later than time *t* are actual as of time *t*. So unless Mellor can go on to show that the temporally indexed notion of being actual as of a time is ultimately incoherent, his argument cannot succeed.

Third, in rejecting the view that temporal priority can be analyzed in terms of tensed concepts, the present approach makes it possible to employ the concept of temporal priority in offering analyses of the concepts of the past and the future: the past is simply what is earlier than the present, and the future is what is later. Traditional tensed approaches, by contrast, cannot offer such analyses, since they hold that temporal priority is to be analyzed in tensed terms. This in turn means that they cannot avoid the very implausible claim—and one that is incompatible with traditional empiricism—that the concepts of the past and the future are analytically basic.

Fourth, by holding that tensed concepts can be analyzed in terms of the concept of temporal priority, together with the concept of what is actual as of a time, one escapes some very serious difficulties associated with alternative ontologies that involve intrinsic, irreducible, tensed properties. In particular, there is a very serious problem concerning how an instantaneous event can have different intrinsic properties at different times, since the type of explanation that can be offered in the case of persisting objects, where the possession of incompatible properties by a persisting object at different times can be analyzed in terms of the possession of those incompatible properties by different temporal parts of the object, cannot be paralleled in the case of anything that exists only for an instant. Nor can one appeal to the idea of an enduring object that is wholly present at different times, in the case of instantaneous events. But if, on the other hand, pastness and presentness are relational properties of events, rather than intrinsic ones, and if, in particular, whether an object lies in the past or in the present at a given time is a matter of whether there are, or are not, later states of affairs that are actual as of the time in question, then there is no difficulty about explaining how an instantaneous event can be present at one time, and past at another.

Finally, the view that some tensed sentences involve indexicals, and others do not, allows one both to avoid the implausible claim that any ordinary tensed sentence expresses the same proposition, regardless of when it is uttered, and to do so without falling prey to the type of argument in favor of a static analysis of tensed language that was set out in section 13.5, and that appears to be inescapable if all tensed sentences contain indexicals.

13.10   Summing Up

The overall picture that has emerged is as follows. First, advocates of tenseless approaches to time are correct in maintaining both that ordinary tensed sentences contain indexicals, and that such sentences can be given truth-conditional analyses. On the other hand, they are mistaken in thinking that the truth conditions of such sentences can be specified in tenseless, or static, terms.

Second, and contrary to views that are generally shared by defenders of both tensed and tenseless approaches to time, ordinary tensed sentences are neither the only tensed sentences there are, nor are they basic tensed sentences. For, in the first place, there are other tensed sentences that, unlike ordinary tensed sentences, involve no indexicals, and in which the time at which an event has a certain tensed property is explicitly specified; in the second place, ordinary tensed sentences can be analyzed in terms of sentences of the latter sort; and, finally, it can be shown that the only basic tensed sentences are indexical-free sentences that say that a certain event has (tenselessly) the property of lying in the present at an explicitly specified time.

Third, the claim that ordinary tensed sentences are the only tensed sentences that exist turns out to be an error that has very serious philosophical consequences, since that thesis, together with the very plausible claim that ordinary tensed sentences involve indexicals, provides the basis of a very strong argument for the conclusion that a tenseless account of the meaning of tensed language must be correct.

Finally, it is not only ordinary tensed sentences that turn out not to be analytically basic, since even a basic tensed sentence such as 'Event *e* lies (tenselessly) in the present at time *t*' can be analyzed. The analysis involves, however, the ontological notion of the totality of states of affairs that are actual as of a time—a notion that has application only if the world is dynamic, rather than static. So tensed sentences are, without exception, analyzable, but in such a way that they can be true only in a dynamic world.

Notes

An earlier version of this chapter was presented as a talk to the Department of Philosophy of Tokyo University, and I am indebted to those who took part in the discussion that followed for helpful questions and incisive comments that led me to make some important changes. I am also indebted to the editors of this book for close critical comments on an earlier draft.

1. M. Tooley, *Time, Tense, and Causation* (Oxford: Oxford University Press, 1997).

2. Tooley, *Time, Tense, and Causation*, chap. 4.

3. P. Tichy, "The Transiency of Truth," *Theoria* 46 (1980), pp. 165–82. See p. 166. Tichy proceeds (pp. 167–69) to offer a number of arguments against the view that different tokens of a given tensed sentence express different propositions.

4. Tichy, "The Transiency of Truth", p. 168.

5. For another argument for this conclusion, see Tooley, *Time, Tense, and Causation*, pp. 219–23.

6. G. N. Schlesinger, *Aspects of Time* (Indianapolis, Ind.: Hackett, 1980), p. 133.

7. R. M. Gale, *The Language of Time* (London: Routledge and Kegan Paul, 1968), p. 90.

8. See Tooley, *Time, Tense, and Causation*, pp. 225–29.

9. C. D. Broad, *Scientific Thought* (London: Routledge and Kegan Paul, 1923), p. 76.

10. Broad, *Scientific Thought*, pp. 76–77.

11. Another argument for this conclusion is set out in Tooley, *Time, Tense, and Causation*, pp. 179–80.

12. D. Lewis, "How to Define Theoretical Terms," *Journal of Philosophy* 67 (1970), pp. 427–46. For a discussion of some objections to a Ramsey/Lewis approach, see M. Tooley, *Causation: A Realist Approach* (Oxford: Oxford University Press, 1987), pp. 13–25.

13. See Tooley, *Time, Tense, and Causation*, pp. 158–72.

14. W. Sellars, "Time and the World Order," in H. Feigl and G. Maxwell, eds., *Scientific Explanation, Space, and Time* (Minneapolis: University of Minnesota Press, 1962), pp. 527–616. See p. 546.

15. Tooley, *Time, Tense, and Causation*, pp. 161–70.

16. For a defense of a causal account of temporal priority, see Tooley, *Time, Tense, and Causation*, chap. 9.

17. See Tooley, *Time, Tense, and Causation*, chap. 4.

18. A detailed account can be found in Tooley, *Time, Tense, and Causation*, pp. 203–9.

19. J. M. E. McTaggart, *The Nature of Existence*, vol. II (Cambridge: Cambridge University Press, 1927). An earlier, but in some ways less satisfactory version of his argument can be found in his article "The Unreality of Time," *Mind* 17 (1908), pp. 457–74.

20. D. H. Mellor, *Real Time* (Cambridge: Cambridge University Press, 1981), pp. 92–98. In *Time, Tense, and Causation*, pp. 329–31, I have argued that Mellor's version of McTaggart's argument is, in fact, unsound.

21. Mellor, *Real Time*, p. 102.

14

Actualism and Presentism

James E. Tomberlin

In the metaphysics of time and tense, *presentism* is the view that there are no objects that do not presently exist.[1] According to the presentist, there are no philosophical problems whose solution calls for or requires an ontological commitment to non–presently existing individuals. In the metaphysics of modality, *actualism* is minimally the view that there are no objects that do not actually exist.[2] By the lights of actualism, there are no philosophical problems whose proper treatment demands an ontological commitment to nonactual objects. Now, I harbor a deep skepticism as regards both of these ontological stances. In what follows, accordingly, I aim to extend and sharpen the skeptical concerns previously voiced in Tomberlin 1993, 1996a,b, forthcoming a, and Tomberlin and McGuinness 1994.

14.1 A Deontic Case

Consider the following case:[3]

Jones, as it happens, has taken up nouvelle cuisine with its laudable emphasis on fresh and unusual ingredients. One weekend, in seclusion, he opts to prepare for himself the remarkable ragoût of wild mushrooms with veal stock and red wine concocted by Alice Waters for her renowned restaurant, Chez Panisse. For the preparation, Jones decides, why not utilize wild mushrooms he gathered from the nearby woods just yesterday? A splendid dish indeed, he observes upon dining. But alas, some time later, Jones, still home alone and miles from the nearest person, is rendered comatose. Several of the wild mushrooms were highly toxic and Jones, alone and physically incapable of conveying his plight, faces certain death.

In this situation, I take it, (1) and (2) are true but (3) is false:

(1)   For any individual *x*, if *x* is a moral agent and *x* is available and able to come to Jones's assistance, *x* ought prima facie to provide Jones with aid.

(2)   No actual moral agent is available and able to come to Jones's assistance.

(3)   For any individual *x*, if *x* is a moral agent who is available and able to come to Jones's assistance, *x* ought not prima facie to provide Jones with aid.

If so, however, the actualist cannot read (1) and (3) as universally quantified material conditionals. For suppose otherwise. Since no actual individual satisfies the open sentence

x is a moral agent who is available and able to come to Jones's assistance,

every actual individual satisfies both (1′) and (3′):

(1′)   (*x* is a moral agent who is available and able to come to Jones's assistance) ⊃ (*x* ought prima facie to provide Jones with aid).

(3′)   (*x* is a moral agent who is available and able to come to Jones's assistance) ⊃ (*x* ought not prima facie to provide Jones with aid).

But then (1) and (3) are both true, after all.

These considerations lead directly to a serious challenge for actualism:

Challenge 1

With objectual quantification,[4] provide an interpretation of (1) and (3) satisfying these conditions: (1) and (2) are true, (3) is false, and the quantifiers range over actual individuals only.

The above deontic case likewise poses a serious threat to presentism. For in the scenario around Jones, it is also the case that whereas (1*) and (2*) are true, (3*) is false:

(1*)   For any individual *x*, if *x* is a moral agent and *x* is available and able to come to Jones's assistance, *x* ought prima facie to provide Jones with aid.

(2*) No presently existing moral agent is available and able to come to Jones's assistance.

(3*) For any individual x, if x is a moral agent who is available and able to come to Jones's assistance, x ought not prima facie to provide Jones with aid.

If so, the presentist must not read (1*) and (3*) as universally quantified material conditionals. For suppose otherwise. Because no presently existing individual satisfies the open sentence 'x is a moral agent who is available and able to come to Jones's assistance', every presently existing individual satisfies both (1′) and (3′):

(1′) (x is a moral agent who is available and able to come to Jones's assistance) ⊃ (x ought prima facie to provide Jones with aid).

(3′) (x is a moral agent who is available and able to come to Jones's assistance) ⊃ (x ought not prima facie to provide Jones with aid).

But then (1*) and (3*) are both true, after all.

As with actualism before, these considerations yield the following challenge for presentism:

Challenge 1

With objectual quantification, provide an interpretation of (1*) and (3*) satisfying these conditions: (1*) and (2*) are true, (3*) is false, and the quantifiers range over presently existing individuals only.

14.2   How Not to Meet Challenge 1

The above trouble with treating (1*) and (3*) as universally quantified material conditionals naturally suggests that the presentist construe the notion of conditionality at work in (1*) and (3*) in such a way that a conditional of the sort in question does not come out true just because its antecedent is (merely) in fact not satisfied. This in turn suggests that the presentist entertain one of the following proposals.

Strict conditionals. By this alternative, (1*) and (3*) are to be construed as universally quantified strict conditionals, where a strict conditional $\Box(A \supset B)$ is true (at a world w) if and only if B is true in every logically and/or metaphysically possible world (relative to w) where A is true. So understood, however, this proposal scarcely meets our challenge:

since it is *logically* possible that some presently existing moral agent who is available and able to come to Jones's assistance does not have a prima facie obligation to provide Jones with aid, (1*) turns out false under this interpretation.

Nomic conditionals. According to this view, (1*) and (3*) are to be taken as universally quantified conditionals of nomic necessity, where a conditional of nomic (= physical) necessity $\boxed{p}\,(A \supset B)$ is true (at a world w) exactly on the condition that B is true in every physically possible world (relative to w) in which A is true. While more modest than the previous interpretation owing to a switch from logical to physical necessity, the present alternative nevertheless clearly fails: insofar as no (actual) law of nature or statement of nomic necessity is violated under the assumption that some presently existing moral agent is not prima facie obligated to provide Jones with aid even though he or she is available and able to come to Jones's assistance, true (1*) won't be true, after all.

Soft (or hedged) laws. Under the present view, (1*) and (3*) are deemed seriously incomplete because each implicitly contains a ceteris paribus clause. Bringing this clause into the open (1*) results in the allegedly true *soft law*: For any individual x, if x is a moral agent who is available and able to come to Jones's assistance, *all things being equal*, x ought prima facie to provide Jones with aid. For soft laws, we are told, the consequent holds in any physically possible situation in which the antecedent and the ceteris paribus condition are jointly satisfied.[5] If so, however, this interpretation likewise fails the challenge: because no law is violated under the condition that some presently existing moral agent is not prima facie obligated to provide Jones with aid, even though this agent is available and able to come to Jones's assistance and all other things are equal, (1*) comes out false under this interpretation. No, statements like (1*) concerning moral obligation just do not express nomological laws, soft or otherwise.

Counterfactuals. With the current alternative, (1*) and (3*) become the universally quantified counterfactuals (1″) and (3″), respectively:

(1″)   For any individual x, if it were the case that x is a moral agent who is available and able to come to Jones's assistance, it would be the case that x ought prima facie to provide Jones with aid.

(3″) For any individual x, if it were the case that x is a moral agent
who is available and able to come to Jones's assistance, it would
be the case that x ought not prima facie to provide Jones with aid.

A tempting view indeed for anyone who demands an account of the
truth conditions for our target sentences while insisting on an ontology
devoid of non–presently existing individuals. Unfortunately, any such
theoretical attraction notwithstanding, this counterfactual interpretation
is fraught with difficulties, including each of the following prominent
ones:

First, as we learned from Stalnaker (1968) and Lewis (1973), transitivity and contraposition both fail for counterfactuals. And yet, (I) and
(II) seem harmlessly valid:

(I) For any individual x, if x is a moral agent who is available and
able to come to Jones's assistance, x ought prima facie to provide
Jones with aid. For any individual x, if x ought prima facie to
provide Jones with aid, x will attempt to help Jones. Thus, for any
individual x, if x is a moral agent who is available and able to
come to Jones's assistance, x will attempt to help Jones.

(II) For any individual x, if x is a moral agent who is available and
able to come to Jones's assistance, x ought prima facie to provide
Jones with aid. Thus, for any individual x, if it is not so that x
ought prima facie to provide Jones with aid, x is not a moral agent
who is available and able to come to Jones's assistance.

Of course, (I) and (II) would not be valid unless the embedded notion of
conditionality in each case obeyed transitivity and contraposition.

Second, while there is room for genuine disagreement over the correct
rule of truth for a counterfactual $A \square \rightarrow B$, to facilitate matters I assume
the one provided by Lewis (1973):

$A \square \rightarrow B$ is true (at world w) if and only if either (1) there are no
possible A-worlds (in which case $A \square \rightarrow B$ is vacuously true) or (2) some
A-world where B holds is closer (to w) than is any A-world where B
does not hold.

Next, suppose with Kripke (1980) *genetic essentialism*: any presently
existing individual necessarily has the origin it in fact has. Return now to

Jones and permit me to expand on his background. Rebounding from a failed and childless marriage, Jones, vowing not to contribute to a world of overpopulation, underwent a successful and irreversible vasectomy three years ago. That is, we have the truth of (4*):

(4*)   No presently existing individual is a biological offspring of Jones.

Now surely any reason for treating (1*) and (3*) as (1″) and (3″), respectively, should likewise dictate that (5*) and (6*) are to be parsed as (7*) and (8*), in turn:

(5*)   For any individual x, if x is a moral agent who is available and able to come to Jones's assistance and x is a biological offspring of Jones, x ought prima facie to provide Jones with aid.

(6*)   For any individual x, if x is a moral agent who is available and able to come to Jones's assistance and x is a biological offspring of Jones, x ought not prima facie to provide Jones with aid.

(7*)   For any individual x, if it were to be the case that x is a moral agent who is available and able to come to Jones's assistance and x is a biological offspring of Jones, it would be the case that x ought prima facie to provide Jones with aid.

(8*)   For any individual x, if it were to be the case that x is a moral agent who is available and able to come to Jones's assistance and x is a biological offspring of Jones, it would be the case that x ought not prima facie to provide Jones with aid.

With all of this, however, presentism comes to grief; owing to the Lewis rule of truth for counterfactuals, genetic essentialism, and the truth of (4*), presentism demands that (7*) and (8*) are both true. But in the scenario involving Jones it seems clear that whereas (5*) is true, (6*) is false. By parity of reasoning, the proposal that (1*) and (3*) are to be construed as (1″) and (3″), in order, should be rejected.

Conditional obligations. At this juncture, the presentist directs our attention to fairly recent developments in deontic logic. After van Fraassen (1972), Lewis (1974), and others, a statement of *unconditional* obligation is represented as OA, where O is the familiar *monadic* deontic operator of standard deontic logic. OA is adjudged true (at a world w) if any only if A is true in all of the deontically ideal worlds (relative to

w). In sharp contrast, a statement of *conditional* obligation is represented as $O(A/B)$, with $O(/)$ a newly introduced *dyadic* deontic operator. $O(A/B)$—the assertion that under conditions satisfying B it is obligatory that A is satisfied—obeys a different (and weaker) rule of truth: some value realized at some B-world where A holds is better than any value realized at any B-world where A does not hold (Lewis 1974, p. 4). To accompany this axiological interpretation of conditional obligation, Lewis supplies the following axioms and rules of inference (Lewis 1974, pp. 11–12), where $P(/)$ reads 'it is permissible that ... given that ...,' T stands for tautology, and $\perp$ is the negation of any tautology.

R1. All truth-functional tautologies are theorems.

R2. If A and $A \supset B$ are theorems, so is B.

R3. If $A \equiv B$ is a theorem, so is $O(A/C) \equiv O(B/C)$.

R4. If $B \equiv C$ is a theorem, so is $O(A/B) \equiv O(A/C)$.

A1. $P(A/C) \equiv \sim O(\sim A/C)$.

A2. $O(A\&B/C) \equiv [O(A/C) \,\&\, O(B/C)]$.

A3. $O(A/C) \supset P(A/C)$.

A4. $O(T/C) \supset O(C/C)$.

A5. $O(T/C) \supset O(T/B \vee C)$.

A6. $[O(A/B) \,\&\, O(A/C)] \supset O(A/B \vee C)$.

A7. $[P(\perp/C) \,\&\, O(A/B \vee C)] \supset O(A/B)$.

A8. $[P(B/B \vee C) \,\&\, O(A/B \vee C)] \supset O(A/B)$.

In the above logic of conditional obligation, this feature is salient for our purposes here: since $A \supset OB$ does *not* imply $O(B/A)$, the latter (unlike the former) is not automatically true when A is false.

Return to (1*) and (3*). The challenge confronting presentism is to provide an account of (1*) and (3*) meeting the constraint that (1*) is true and (3*) is false with quantification over just presently existing individuals. According to the present suggestion, (1*) and (3*) become statements of universally quantified conditional obligation. Thanks to the rule of truth for $O(A/B)$, it is urged, (1*)—so construed—is indeed true whereas (3*)—so interpreted—is surely false; and this remains so even when the quantification involved is presentistic.

Against this intriguing proposal, I offer these objections:

First, in the various systems of conditional obligation articulated by van Fraassen (1972), Lewis (1974), and more recently Åqvist (1987) and Feldman (1986), the detachment principle $O(A/C) \supset [C \supset OA]$ is *not* a theorem. And yet, I submit, (III) is plainly valid:

(III)   For any individual x, if x is a moral agent who is available and able to come to Jones's assistance, x ought prima facie to provide Jones with aid.
Scott is a moral agent who is available and able to come to Jones's assistance.
Thus, Scott ought prima facie to provide Jones with aid.

If so, however, the notion of conditionality embedded in (1) cannot be the one embodied in the above systems of conditional obligation.

Second, as I have argued at length elsewhere,[6] each of the systems of conditional obligation in question succumbs to one or more versions of the notorious paradoxes of deontic logic. Without rehearsing the details of these paradoxes, the following observations are pertinent here.[7] To generate one of the paradoxes against a particular system of deontic logic, a possible situation is described and a set of natural language sentences is produced where the sentences in question all seem true if the possible situation were to occur. Next, it is documented that under the most judicious representations of the natural language sentences within the deontic system at stake, the result is a logically inconsistent set. This is of course powerful evidence that such a deontic system fails to provide a theoretically viable account of the natural language target sentences. Now sentences just like (1*) and (3*) loom large in some of the deontic paradoxes, most notably the knower paradox and the contrary-to-duty imperative paradox.[8] And consequently, if the above systems of conditional obligation fall prey to one or more of these paradoxes, this is ample reason to find that (1) and (3) are not to be treated as statements of universally quantified conditional obligation.

Conclusion as regards the deontic case. With this negative verdict on six alternative presentistic interpretations of (1*) and (3*), I scarcely claim to have exhausted all of the positions in logical space facing the presentist. Still, I do think I have addressed the most promising ones. If so, until and unless some other interpretation is offered that suits presentism, it appears quite appropriate to theorize that non–presently existing individuals are to be invoked for a correct account of deontic sentences like (1*) and (3*). Turning to actualism, in Tomberlin 1996a, forthcoming a, I provide a negative verdict against seven actualistic treatments of (1) and (3). Once again, then, without some other construal of these sentences that fits actualism, it seems proper to quantify over possible but nonactual objects for an account of items like (1) and (3). But let's not end here. For there awaits another but very different problematic case for both actualism and presentism.

14.3   Intentional Verbs

Like Chisholm (1986), assume an actualism that includes these key ingredients: an ontology confined to actual individuals and attributes (some exemplified, others not), a relational account of believing, and a Russellian treatment of definite descriptions. Since a position of this sort requires that no person ever has genuine *de re* beliefs toward nonactual individuals, the question of the proper treatment of items such as (9) becomes acute:

(9)   Ponce de Leon searched for the fountain of youth.

After all, if Ponce de Leon may be said to have really searched for the fountain of youth, to have hoped to find it, and the like, he presumably can be said to have entertained beliefs of or about the object of his search. To deny that Ponce de Leon had any *de re* beliefs toward the fountain of youth, therefore, dictates that one who adopts the aforementioned ontological position embrace one of these alternatives: either deny the truth of (9), or interpret (9) so that its truth does not stand Ponce de Leon in a genuine *de re* relation to the (nonactual) fountain of youth.

Chisholm, quite correctly, rejects the first option. Instead, against the background of his theoretically elegant account of believing as a relation between a believer and an attribute,[9] Chisholm proposes that the intentional verb in (9) be taken as expressing a dyadic *searched for* relation holding between Ponce de Leon and an *attribute*. That is, Chisholm would have us parse (9) as follows (Chisholm 1986, pp. 56–57):

(10)   Ponce de Leon endeavored to find the attribute of being a unique site of a unique fountain of youth.

Because there *is* such an attribute even though it fails to be exemplified, (9)—so construed—does not require that Ponce de Leon bear a genuine *de re* relation to the nonexistent fountain of youth.

A similar actualist view is advanced independently by David Kaplan in his classic essay "How to Russell a Frege-Church" (1975). To begin with, Kaplan rightly observes that Russell's own primary-secondary scope distinction for eliminating descriptions within intensional contexts fails in the case of (9), owing to the fact that the intentional verb there takes no sentential complement. In accord with Chisholm, Kaplan suggests, why not model (9) semantically (and ontologically) as the bearing of a dyadic relation between Ponce de Leon and an attribute where the resulting paraphrase of (9) turns out much like (10) (Kaplan 1975, p. 729).

To my mind, there are ample reasons for rejecting the Chisholm-Kaplan model for items such as (9). And I have so argued at length, where the critique is successively refined in Tomberlin 1988, 1994, 1996a, forthcoming a. This negative verdict on the Chisholm-Kaplan account, if correct, prompts another serious test for actualism:

Challenge 2
Tender a credible treatment of (9) meeting this constraint: (9) is true but its truth does not require Ponce de Leon to stand in a *de re* relation to some nonactual individual.

What now of presentism in the case of intentional verbs? Clearly enough, the presentist faces a parallel difficulty. Take an instance of (α)—call it (β)—

(α) x searched for y

where (in (β)) the singular term replacing 'x' refers to a presently existing individual, the singular term replacing 'y' does not, and yet (β) formulates a truth. Like actualism before, (β) generates the following challenge for presentism:

Challenge 2

Tender a credible account of (β) meeting this constraint: (β) is true but its truth does not require a presently existing individual to bear a *de re* relation to a non–presently existing one.

14.4 How Not to Meet Challenge 2

Fitch (1996) provides a novel and intriguing actualistic treatment of (9), one promising a straightforward response to challenge 2. His proposal roundly deserves close and careful examination.

By Fitch's lights, when confronted with the troublesome (9), the actualist need only "go adverbial." Very roughly, the suggestion is that (9) becomes (9*):

(9*) Ponce de Leon searched-for-a-unique-fountain-of-youthly.

Here 'a-unique-fountain-of-youthly' behaves like an *adverbial modifier of* the now *monadic* predicate 'searched for'. According to this proposal, (9), so construed, does not ascribe a relation between Ponce de Leon and the nonactual fountain of youth. Quite the contrary, parsed as (9*), (9) is seen to ascribe a complex but non-relational property to the single individual Ponce de Leon. As a result, we are told, the truth of (9) does not require an actual individual to stand in a *de re* relation to some nonactual object; and consequently the second challenge is supposedly conquered.

Without worrying over the missing semantics for this adverbial treatment of (9), there appear to be decisive objections to any such account. For consider again (α):

(α) *x* searched for *y*.

If the singular terms replacing '*x*' and '*y*' should both refer to actual concrete individuals, let us assume, then even under Fitch's proposal the resulting instance of (α) ascribes a dyadic relation between those very individuals. (When Bob searched for his missing daughter last night, that is, he really did stand in the *searched for* relation to his daughter.) Suppose, however, that whereas the singular term replacing '*x*' picks out an actual concrete individual, the one replacing '*y*' does not, as in (9):

(9)   Ponce de Leon searched for the fountain of youth.

By Fitch's model, we are to hold in effect that 'the fountain of youth', as it occurs in (9), does not function as a singular term. (After all, (9) is parsed as (9*).) With the present interpretation of Fitch's proposal, therefore, the instances of (α) come in (at least) two sorts. When '*y*' is replaced by a singular term denoting a concrete individual, the instance in question ascribes a dyadic relation between actual concrete objects; and yet, if the term that replaces '*y*' fails to pick out a concrete individual, the instance at issue ascribes a complex but nonrelational property to one actual object.

This alleged shift in semantic behavior of the various instances of (α) seems incredible on two counts: first, outside of a prior commitment to an ontology devoid of possible but non-actual individuals, the semantic shift at stake appears impossible to independently motivate or support; and second, any such view requires intolerably that *logical form* turns on matters of contingent fact—to know what sort of proposition is expressed by an instance of (α), I must already know whether the singular terms involved do or do not refer to concrete but contingent objects.

As formulated so far, my objection to Fitch's model has centered around the pivotal assumption that under this model instances of (α) ascribe a dyadic relation between actual concrete individuals when the singular terms replacing '*x*' and '*y*' both refer to concrete objects. What happens if this assumption is abandoned? Why not, that is, interpret Fitch's model in such a way that every instance of (α) receives the sort of treatment accorded to (9), even when the singular term replacing '*y*' refers to a concrete individual? As I see it, there is a fatal objection to any such view. For even if the *searched for* relation never holds between actual concrete individuals, this surely is not true for the *loves* relation— Bob really does bear the latter relation to his missing daughter, Jane. But then Fitch's model, under the current interpretation, cannot do justice to truths like (11):

(11)   Bob searched for Jane, his missing daughter he deeply loves.

After all, 'his missing daughter he deeply loves' incontestably ascribes the dyadic *loves* relation between Bob and Jane. It follows, therefore, that (11) won't be true unless 'Jane', as it occurs in 'Bob searched for Jane', refers to Bob's missing daughter. And this is precisely what 'Jane' fails to do according to the present interpretation of Fitch's model.

This is no way to preserve actualism (or presentism).[10]

Notes

For rewarding correspondence and/or discussion, I am grateful to David Armstrong, George Bealer, John Biro, Roderick Chisholm, David Cowles, Michael Devitt, Kit Fine, Greg Fitch, Gilbert Harman, Terry Horgan, David Kaplan, Bernard Kobes, Bernie Linsky, Kirk Ludwig, Bill Lycan, Chris Menzel, Al Plantinga, Greg Ray, Nathan Salmon, Bob Stalnaker, Ed Zalta, and my colleagues Frank McGuinness, Jeff Sicha, and Takashi Yagisawa. I do not mean to imply, of course, any agreement on their part with what I have argued here.

1. See Bealer 1993, Bigelow 1996, Chisholm 1990, Hinchliff 1996, and Menzel 1991. For extensive references on presentism, see the bibliography in Bigelow 1996.

2. There are in fact *grades* of actualism. Alvin Plantinga (1985a,b), for example, endorses actualism as the view that there neither are nor could have been objects that do not actually exist. But Nathan Salmon (1987) embraces actualism only by affirming the first half of Plantinga's characterization while explicitly rejecting the second (and modal) half. In addition, there are more technical characterizations of actualism in Menzel 1990 and Fitch 1996. As the reader may verify, the discussion here applies to all of the above. For extensive references on actualism, see the bibliographies of Tomberlin and McGuinness 1994 and Tomberlin 1996a.

3. As set out here, the present case combines features of Case One and Case Two in Tomberlin and McGuinness 1994.

4. As opposed to substitutional quantification. For criticisms of the latter, see Tomberlin 1990a, 1993, forthcoming b.

5. For recent discussions of soft laws, see Antony 1995, Horgan and Tienson 1990, and Schiffer 1991.

6. In Tomberlin 1981, 1986, I evaluate the conditional obligation systems of van Fraassen (1972), Mott (1973), and Al-Hibri (1978) negatively against the contrary-to-duty imperative paradox and the knower paradox, respectively. In Tomberlin 1989b, I document that Lewis (1974) falls prey to the knower paradox. In Tomberlin 1989c, I argue that Feldman (1986) fails against both the knower paradox and the contrary-to-duty imperative paradox. And in Tomberlin 1991b, I establish that Åqvist (1987) succumbs to a version of the contrary-to-duty imperative paradox.

7. For additional discussion, see Feldman 1990 and Tomberlin 1995.

8. See, for example, Tomberlin 1989c, 1991b.

9. There are extended critiques of Chisholm's ingenious version of self-ascription for believing in Tomberlin 1990b, 1991a. The very different formulations of self-

ascription in Brand 1983, 1984, and Lewis 1979, 1986, are critically evaluated in Tomberlin 1987, 1989a, respectively.

10. Should the presentist seek to apply Fitch's model to items like (β), the negative critique here of this model of actualism carries over mutatis mutandis.

Linsky and Zalta (1994) propose an original and important version of actualism. I critically examine their view in Tomberlin 1996a. For their reply, see Linsky and Zalta 1996.

References

Al-Hibri, A. 1978. *Deontic Logic*. Washington, D.C.: University Press of America.

Antony, L. 1995. Law and Order in Psychology. *Philosophical Perspectives* 9, pp. 429–96.

Åqvist, L. 1987. *Introduction to Deontic Logic and the Theory of Normative Systems*. Naples: Bibliopolis.

Bealer, G. 1993. A Solution to Frege's Puzzle. *Philosophical Perspectives* 7, pp. 17–60.

Bigelow, J. 1996. Presentism and Properties. *Philosophical Perspectives* 10, pp. 35–52.

Brand, M. 1983. Intending and Believing. In J. E. Tomberlin, ed., *Agent, Language, and the Structure of the World*, pp. 171–94. Indianapolis, Ind.: Hackett.

Brand, M. 1984. *Intending and Acting*. Cambridge, Mass.: MIT Press.

Castañeda, H.-N. 1983. Reply to Alvin Plantinga. In J. E. Tomberlin, ed., *Agent, Language, and the Structure of the World*, pp. 329–72. Indianapolis, Ind.: Hackett.

Castañeda, H.-N. 1986. Replies. In J. E. Tomberlin, ed., *Hector-Neri Castañeda*, pp. 333–94. Dordrecht: Reidel.

Castañeda, H.-N. 1989. *Thinking, Language, and Experience*. Minneapolis: University of Minnesota Press.

Chisholm, R. M. 1981. *The First Person*. Minneapolis: University of Minnesota Press.

Chisholm, R. M. 1986. Self-Profile. In R. Bogdan, ed., *Roderick M. Chisholm*. Dordrecht: Reidel.

Chisholm, R. M. 1990. Referring to Things That No Longer Exist. *Philosophical Perspectives* 4, pp. 545–56.

Feldman, F. 1986. *Doing the Best We Can*. Dordrecht: Reidel.

Feldman, F. 1990. A Simpler Solution to the Paradoxes of Deontic Logic. *Philosophical Perspectives* 4, pp. 309–42.

Fitch, G. W. 1994. Non-Denoting. *Philosophical Perspectives* 7, pp. 461–86.

Fitch, G. W. 1996. In Defense of Aristotelian Actualism. *Philosophical Perspectives* 10, pp. 53–72.

Hinchliff, M. 1996. The Puzzle of Change. *Philosophical Perspectives* 10, pp. 119–36.

Horgan, T., and J. Tienson. 1990. Soft Laws. *Midwest Studies in Philosophy* 15, pp. 256–79.

Kaplan, D. 1975. How to Russell a Frege-Church. *Journal of Philosophy* 72, pp. 716–29.

Kripke, S. 1963. Semantical Considerations on Modal Logic. *Acta Philosophica Fennica* 16, pp. 83–94.

Kripke, S. 1980. *Naming and Necessity*. Cambridge, Mass.: Harvard University Press.

Lewis, D. 1973. *Counterfactuals*. Cambridge, Mass.: Harvard University Press.

Lewis, D. 1974. Semantic Analyses for Dyadic Deontic Logic. In S. Stenlund, ed., *Logical Theory and Semantic Analysis*, pp. 1–14. Dordrecht: Reidel.

Lewis, D. 1979. Attitudes *De Dicto* and *De Se*. *Philosophical Review* 88, pp. 513–43.

Lewis, D. 1986. *On the Plurality of Worlds*. Oxford: Blackwell.

Linsky, B., and E. N. Zalta. 1994. In Defense of the Simplest Quantified Modal Logic. *Philosophical Perspectives* 8, pp. 431–58.

Linsky, B., and E. N. Zalta. 1996. In Defense of the Contingently Nonconcrete. *Philosophical Studies* 84, pp. 283–94.

Menzel, C. 1990. Actualism and Possible Worlds. *Synthese* 85, pp. 355–89.

Menzel, C. 1991. Temporal Actualism and Singular Foreknowledge. *Philosophical Perspectives* 5, pp. 475–508.

Mott, P. L. 1973. On Chisholm's Paradox. *Journal of Philosophical Logic* 2, pp. 197–211.

Plantinga, A. 1985a. Replies. In J. E. Tomberlin and P. van Inwagen, eds., *Alvin Plantinga*. Dordrecht: Reidel.

Plantinga, A. 1985b. Self-Profile. In J. E. Tomberlin and P. van Inwagen, eds., *Alvin Plantinga*. Dordrecht: Reidel.

Plantinga, A. 1987. Two Conceptions of Modality. *Philosophical Perspectives* 1, pp. 189–232.

Salmon, N. 1987. Existence. *Philosophical Perspectives* 1, pp. 49–108.

Schiffer, S. 1991. Ceteris Paribus Laws. *Mind* 100, pp. 1–17.

Stalnaker, R. 1968. A Theory of Conditionals. In N. Rescher, ed., *Studies in Logical Theory*. Oxford: Blackwell.

Tomberlin, J. E. 1981. Contrary-to-Duty Imperatives and Conditional Obligation. *Noûs* 15, pp. 357–75.

Tomberlin, J. E. 1986. Good Samaritans and Castañeda's System of Deontic Logic. In J. E. Tomberlin, ed., *Hector-Neri Castañeda*, pp. 255–72. Dordrecht: Reidel.

Tomberlin, J. E. 1987. Critical Review of Myles Brand, *Intending and Acting*. *Noûs* 21, pp. 45–63.

Tomberlin, J. E. 1988. Semantics, Psychological Attitudes, and Conceptual Role. *Philosophical Studies* 53, 205–26.

Tomberlin, J. E. 1989a. Critical Review of David Lewis, *On the Plurality of Worlds*. *Noûs* 23, pp. 117–225.

Tomberlin, J. E. 1989b. Deontic Logic and Conditional Obligation. *Philosophy and Phenomenological Research* 50, pp. 107–14.

Tomberlin, J. E. 1989c. Obligation, Conditionals, and Conditional Obligation. *Philosophical Studies* 55, pp. 81–92.

Tomberlin, J. E. 1990a. Belief, Nominalism, and Quantification. *Philosophical Perspectives* 4, pp. 573–79.

Tomberlin, J. E. 1990b. Critical Review of R. Bogdan, ed., *Roderick M. Chisholm*. *Noûs* 24, pp. 332–42.

Tomberlin, J. E. 1991a. Belief, Self-Ascription, and Ontology. *Philosophical Issues* 1, pp. 233–60.

Tomberlin, J. E. 1991b. Critical Review of Lennart Åqvist, *Introduction to Deontic Logic and the Theory of Normative Systems*. *Noûs* 25, pp. 109–16.

Tomberlin, J. E. 1993. Singular Terms, Quantification and Ontology. *Philosophical Issues* 4, pp. 297–309.

Tomberlin, J. E. 1995. The Paradoxes of Deontic Logic. In R. Audi, ed., *Cambridge Dictionary of Philosophy*, pp. 220–21. Cambridge: Cambridge University Press.

Tomberlin, J. E. 1996a. Actualism or Possibilism? *Philosophical Studies* 84, pp. 263–81.

Tomberlin, J. E. 1996b. Perception and Possibilia. *Philosophical Issues* 7, pp. 109–16.

Tomberlin, J. E. Forthcoming a. Naturalism, Actualism, and Ontology. *Philosophical Perspectives*.

Tomberlin, J. E. Forthcoming b. Quantification: Objectual or Substitutional? *Philosophical Issues* 8.

Tomberlin, J. E., and F. McGuinness. 1994. Troubles with Actualism. *Philosophical Perspectives* 8, pp. 459–66.

van Fraassen, Bas C. 1972. The Logic of Conditional Obligation. *Journal of Philosophical Logic* 1, pp. 417–38.

Index